Intelligence in Ape and Man

Intelligence
in Ape and Man

DAVID PREMACK
UNIVERSITY OF PENNSYLVANIA

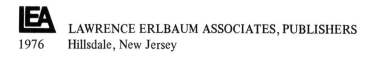

LAWRENCE ERLBAUM ASSOCIATES, PUBLISHERS

1976   Hillsdale, New Jersey

DISTRIBUTED BY THE HALSTED PRESS DIVISION OF

JOHN WILEY & SONS

New York   Toronto   London   Sydney

Lawrence Erlbaum Associates, Inc., Publishers
62 Maria Drive
Hillsdale, New Jersey 07642

Distributed solely by Halsted Press Division
John Wiley & Sons, Inc., New York

Library of Congress Cataloging in Publication Data

Premack, David.
    Intelligence in ape and man.

    Bibliography: p.
    1. Intellect.   2. Animal intelligence.   3. Languages—
Psychology.   4. Animal communication.   5. Chimpanzees—
Psychology.   I. Title.
BF431.P683   156'.3'9   76-26570
ISBN 0-470-98909-2

Printed in the United States of America

Contents

for ANN—
Ben, Lisa, Tim

Preface

Twenty years ago I received a NIMH postdoctoral fellowship to teach visual language to a chimpanzee–but I was diverted from doing so for over a decade. In 1954 I had gone to Yerkes Laboratories in Orange Park, Florida, with my wife and son, on my first job, to learn about chimpanzees. After a few months there I discussed the language project with Henry Nissen, who was acting director during Karl Lashley's illness, and persuaded him to lend me an animal. Together we settled on Sally, an 18 month old female, sufficiently unfavored to be an ideal candidate for loan. Although Professor Nissen was loathe to see any chimpanzee depart, he not only consented but also wrote Paul Meehl, then chairman at Minnesota, underscoring the difference between Sally and King Kong. Images had begun to form at Minnesota, the intended site of the fellowship, of a brute swaggering mutinously through the hall, even perhaps commandeering the faculty washroom. Nissen put these images to rest and the fellowship application was once again untroubled.

However, the fellowship was awarded late and by the time it was, Sally was engaged in another project. Nissen was not able to release her or provide a substitute. It became necessary to buy a chimpanzee, although hardly possible to do so with the $500.00 research budget of the fellowship. I was tempted by an advertisement for a one-armed, subadult male on sale for $450.00, but decided that a one-armed ape was not a propitious beginning for a language to be based on manipulation. Advised by Klüver's (1937) monograph, I bought Cebus monkeys instead–friendly, manipulative, a poor man's chimpanzee. However, with them I ended up studying not language but reinforcement: how a more probable lever press would reinforce a less probable one.

Part of the background for the chimpanzee project and for this book came from a seminar on Philosophy of Psychology, known as the Meegel–Feegel, in honor of its redoubtable teachers, Herbert Feigl and Paul Meehl. Taught during a lively period in the development of psychology, it was a high water mark of a kind: some of us took the seminar not once but annually. The focus of the seminar was not entirely experimental. We scrutinized data to be sure, and encircled many topics, but the discussion always gravitated toward a small set of questions.

Was the difference between man and (other) animals radical, or resolvable within a properly formulated behaviorism? How much of the difference was attributable to language? Did language differ in principle from other behavior, or was this difference, too, resolvable within an enlightened behaviorism? What was language?

In this period I learned with regret that I could not be a philosopher, only a psychologist, for I was able to juggle an issue only so long before dropping it to propose the resolving experiment. I was glad to be able to show philosophers how to do this, although greatly dismayed later when, standing for hours in foul-smelling rooms, I found myself actually running some of the experiments. Much of the pleasure I have found in writing this book has come through resurrecting discussions of that period.

My wife Ann has influenced my thought more than any one else. For 20 years we have begun most mornings with a talk over coffee; I tell her the latest, and she seeks to destroy it—often before I have finished describing it. Sometimes in defending ideas especially dear to me because of their nascent condition, I am driven to extreme positions, some of which have proved to be advisable. She is an extraordinary listener, more active as a listener than many are as a speaker.

Several years ago I had the benefit of discussing linguistics with a former colleague, Arthur Schwartz. He sought to teach me generative grammar, in exchange for which I was to show him how to do an experiment. The only service I provided Art was a negative one, proving to him there were no algorithms for producing experiments. One went about in a normal way, buying groceries and brushing one's teeth, and experiments came to one. As a humanist he understood this well—how else produce poems and novels?—but he was aggrieved, I think, to find that scientists had not gotten hold of something more reliable. In what sense then had science advanced beyond literature? In the beginning he watched closely, to see if I were secretly using formulas, having a joke on a humanist by pretending to do science with humanistic unreliability. He soon saw, however, that I had no formulas. Experiments come to one somewhat as gumballs come from a dispenser. They pop out, although other times nothing comes, and the best one can do then is to shake one's head and hope this will get the gumballs rolling again. He also saw how essential it was to scrutinize what came out. By no means would one want to put into his mouth everything that came out; this too was another kindredness between science and literature. We had excellent discussions, and I regret that they ended before I mastered generative grammar.

Martin Braine made an incisive contribution to this book, reading the entire previous draft, meticulously criticizing each chapter. Braine's readership was of particular benefit to me, for his standards for clear statement and close argument go far beyond my own. Braine has a delicate almost imperceptible way of communicating his disappointment. Lofted by Braine's praise, I nonetheless found myself strangely dizzy. The vertigo was greater than could be explained by praise alone. The praise it turns out was a veneer for a terrible disappointment—brought on by the shabbiness of the manuscript: tenuous distinctions, loose argument, casual sentences. The writer collapsed, seasick, lapsing into a final enfeeblement—his only escape a major purification of the text—which he undertook immediately, as soon as he could catch his breath. In this gentle way Braine led me to see that what I mistook for a final draft was at best next to final.

Walter Kintsch read Chapter 15 and I am indebted to him for lending me his considerable scholarship. I owe a special debt to the principal trainers, Mary Morgan, Amy Samuels, and Debby Barone, upon whose patience and ingenuity the research turned. They were consistently uncanny in translating elliptical instructions into straightforward training procedures. Many other trainers stayed briefly but assisted ably, including Randy Funk, James Olson, Richard Sanders, Debby Petersen, Jon Scott, and Ann J. Premack.

The research was supported by grants from the National Institute of Mental Health and the National Science Foundation. I am indebted to the Center for Advanced Study in the Behavioral Sciences, Stanford, California, where most of this book was written—an ideal place to resurrect discussions from the past. Finally, I must thank Ellen Arntz whose only complaint in typing draft after draft was an occasional hint of disbelief.

1

Introduction

In the first phase of the research dealt with here I sought to operationally analyze language, to decompose it into atomic constituents and to provide training procedures for each constituent.[1] The tedium of interminably designing and applying training programs was relieved by two factors: first, by the operational analysis itself, and second, by the challenge of designing nonverbal procedures for assessing the conceptual structure that underlies language. When a subject learns the words "same" and "different," it is, I assume, because it is capable of carrying out judgments concerning whether items are same or different. Similarly if it learns the quantifiers "all" and "none," it is because it can distinguish between nonverbal conditions that exemplify all and none. Further, a subject that learns the use of "if–then" or a functionally equivalent conditional particle does so, I assume, because it is capable of making a causal analysis of experience. To test the assumption that language maps existing concepts, it was necessary to devise tests that were themselves free of language, that could be applied in advance of language training, and that would serve to determine whether or not the presumptive cognitive element was present. This is the direct way of testing the assumption that the interesting part of language lies offstage, in the concepts and perceptual judgments that antedate language. (Once a subject has acquired some degree of language, it can be taught further language metalinguistically, including labels for distinctions that were generated by language. However, even the language-generated distinctions can be reduced to combinations of predicates that antedated language.)

---

[1] An unanticipated yet deeply gratifying byproduct of this phase has been the growing use of the training programs to teach language to pathologic human populations, both retarded and autistic children, and aphasic adults (Carrier, 1973; Deich & Hodges, 1975; De Villiers & Naughton, 1974; Hughes, 1975; Premack & Premack, 1974; Velettri-Glass, Gazzaniga, & Premack, 1972).

The success of the first phase made it possible to turn to the second phase and to a question more directly related to intelligence. Why were the training programs effective? What is the intellectual equipment of a species such that the training program could be used to teach it language? If the program that taught language to an ape were applied to a rat or pigeon, there is ample reason to believe that the program would fail. These nonprimates are not destined to acquire language in the nontrivial degree that the ape can. Why? Even though the second phase of the research is at a tender stage, it is nonetheless possible to suggest some answers.

Of the several capacities upon which the acquisition of language depends, at least two appear to be lacking in nonprimates. The first is an ability to respond to second-order relations, that is, to a relation between relations. The second is the ability to respond to representations of various items, including one's self—one's body, behavior, or knowledge. I leave it to the text to show in detail how broadly these capacities underlie language.

My objective is to understand human intelligence and its evolution by comparing it with that of other species. The attempt to do so is painfully handicapped in that man has no cognitive neighbors. Human intelligence stands alone, so removed from nonhuman intelligence that comparison does not bring the illumination to be expected from more intimately related alternatives. Perhaps if man did not tower over the planet but shared it with species of more nearly comparable intelligence, each might help the other to understand itself. There would then be several views of each species, e.g., man's view of man but also views of man entertained by intellectually neighboring species. However, on this planet, largely because of an evolutionary accident, we are evidently destined never to have the nonhuman view of human intelligence.

ACQUISITION MODEL

Given the distance between man and his cognitive neighbors, the child–adult comparison may always be our richest resource. The brilliant Piagetian comparison of child with adult helps us to imagine what an intimate interspecies comparison may be like, should we be in a position to make one, even to get the feeling of entrapment by unfathomable puzzles that such comparisons are sure to bring. Yet other comparisons can contribute to the objective of understanding human intelligence. For instance, by comparing different cultures, or even Western man at different historical times, we learn something about the experiential conditions that are necessary for the acquisition of basic human skills. Great emphasis has been laid on the fact that language, the most basic of all human skills, develops without explicit pedagogy, essentially on an observational basis (e.g., Lenneberg, 1967). This kind of acquisition is thought to be unique; to find anything comparable some writers have found it necessary to leave the cognitive domain entirely—only in the motor skills, such as crawling, walking, and the like, do they find anything comparable. Comparisons of this kind suggest that perhaps not even observational learning is necessary, or at least that it is no more so for speech than it is for locomotion. It is as if in both cases we need only guarantee the organism nourishment while awaiting mylenization of the nervous system.

However, one need only make the intercultural comparison to see that the development of language, the form of its acquisition, is in no way unique. In some hunter–gatherer societies, observational learning is the *general* model (Turner, 1965). Every human skill—dietary selection, food preparation, tool making, hunting, elementary horticultural technologies, ritual and myth, not to mention basic socialization and the inevitable moral theories this leads the child to invent—is acquired on an observational basis. Moreover, in this respect a member of the Cayapo tribe is not markedly different from the infrahuman primate, which also imparts its skills, lesser ones to be sure, on an observational basis, that is, without a self-conscious model and without correction for errors and encouragement for success.

When a Cayapo child fashions a tool improperly, as apparently he frequently does in the beginning, the father does not intervene in any fashion; nor does a chimpanzee mother correct the improperly fashioned termite-fishing straws that its child makes in the beginning (Van Lawick-Goodall, 1968); nor does a contemporary human mother correct the improper morphological endings in her child's speech (Brown & Hanlon, 1970). Nevertheless, in all cases the normal young organism acquires the adult skills. Indeed, we define normality in these terms, considering as abnormal that child who does not acquire basic human skills on an observational basis.

Not all hunter–gatherers leave socialization and other skills to observational learning. The Kong bushmen are reported to intervene at many points, including even the motor skills where the infant is held up, its feet grazing the ground, causing it to flex and extend its limbs as though walking (DeVore & Konners, 1974; Konners, 1972). Cultures differ enormously in how they "train" their young, parents varying from passive model to active pedagoge. Yet in all cases the young ultimately acquire the same skills, albeit at slightly different rates, suggesting that the intercultural differences may depend less on what the student needs than on what the teacher needs. Sometimes this is indicated quite openly. In the Japanese culture mothers were reported to awaken their infants more often than the infants awoke themselves, promptly ministering to the "needs" of the awakened infant (Caudill, 1950). It is interesting to note the great differences among cultures in the claim each is likely to make as to how a child must be trained in order to acquire a given skill, and to consider that each of these claims is probably false—false because for each skill it seems possible to find the zero case, that is, a culture where the skill exists and the "training" consists of observational learning.

The present obsession with pedagogy is of quite recent origin. It is only today that, for better or worse, we analyze one skill after another, devise written instructions, and teach each of them with explicit intervention. This may be an efficient way to proceed, but, as a glance at the record shows, it is not a necessary one. In Western society, from the time the historical record justifies reconstruction up until as late as the eighteenth century, many children were apparently left to acquire most if not all basic skills on an essentially observational basis (Aries, 1962; Darnton, 1974, personal communication).

These considerations imply a rather different acquisitional model than the ones urged either by Skinner (1957), on the one hand, or by Chomsky (1965), on the other. I dwell on this point because it is all too clear that the errors which devolve about it are not going to be easy ones to correct. We understand most things in terms of binary contrasts, and in the issue at hand both anchor points are already occupied. Skinner, at one end, holds that everything is learned and language is in no way unique, and Chomsky, at the other, argues that language is unique and syntax is built into the nervous system. In this perfect example of what Herbert Feigl (1953) used to call "nothing but versus something more," the need for what's what is as acute as ever. Unfortunately, I cannot provide the what's what, except to note that any acquisitional model must take into account two key facts: reinforcement plays no direct role in learning (cf. Dulany, 1962; Estes, 1969), and not only language but all basic human skills can be and have been acquired on an observational basis.

CAUSAL INFERENCE

In comparing the intelligence of man to that of other species, we must face such questions as (1) How does the species perceive the world; i.e., how does its ontology compare with ours? (2) What concepts does the species have; e.g., is it capable of same–different judgments? (3) If, like us, it invents theories about the world, what form do these theories take? Even when we have full access to the speech of another individual, we can arrive at confident answers to these questions only with the greatest difficulty. How much greater the difficulty if the species being dealt with had no language and could not answer our questions. In fact, is it possible to characterize the intelligence of another species if it is not possible to talk to that species?

Consider this question not in the abstract but in a specific, yet presumably representative, context. Do any species other than man engage in causal inference? Causal inference is a central facet of human mentation, presupposing human ontology, and all the key relations—agent–object, agent–patient, etc.— that are the underpinnings of grammar. Philosophers since Hume (1952) have admonished against causal inference, but it is not the legitimacy of the inference that concerns us, simply the fact of its occurrence. The philosophers' admonishments serve only to further assure us that the inference does occur. Is man the only creature that engages in causal inferences (or in logically indefensible inferences in general)? If the species can acquire enough language to enable it to be asked "What do you consider to be the relations between those events?" then the question about causal inferences can be answered. There is no more definitive way of answering any of the original questions than by interrogating the species.

NONVERBAL INTERROGATION

Nevertheless, the claim for this inference can be supported in at least some degree with quite simple nonverbal tests. Basically the subject is given two objects, such as an intact apple and a severed one, and asked to choose from alternatives that include a knife, a bowl of water, and a crayon. The subject's choice of knife, which it places between the intact and severed apple, producing the sequence *apple–knife–severed apple,* is considered correct; knife is the appropriate instrument for producing the change in question. Likewise, when shown a dry and wet sponge, the subject's choice of a container of water is considered the appropriate choice. Three of our four chimpanzees passed tests of this kind.

These results are notable in part simply because they occur in the face of the ambiguity to which nonverbal items are inherently subject. Consider the sequence: intact apple–blank space–two halves of apple (see page 253 for pictures of actual test sequences). This sequence can be read as: one–blank–two; round–blank–flat; whole–blank–parts; edible–blank–edible; red–blank–red; and in innumerable other ways. You and I–and apparently the chimpanzee–do not read the sequence in these other ways. We read it as asking, in effect, with what item do you change an intact object into a severed one? And by merit of this reading we answer this question and all others like it in a consistent way. For any species that answers in this consistent way I infer a schema, a structure which assigns an interpretation to an otherwise infinitely ambiguous sequence.

There are three basic ways in which to interrogate a nonverbal organism. In one form, the experimenter lays before the subject a complete instantiation of a schema or paradigm, gives the subject a set of items, and then requires the subject to produce another instantiation of the same schema. For instance, the experimenter might lay out the sequence *apple–knife–severed apple* and require the subject to respond with, say, *orange–knife–severed orange.* This would be a weak test, examining the specific schema of cutting and not the general one of action or causality. To test for the general concept, one would lay out the same exemplar but require the subject to respond with, say, *sponge–water–wet sponge* or *raw egg–fire–cooked egg.*

In the second basic version of nonverbal interrogation, one lays out an incomplete instantiation of a schema and requires the subject to complete it. The incompleteness can be for any of the elements in the sequence; e.g., the subject may be required to supply the missing instrument, as in the examples described so far, or the missing terminal state of the object, as in some of the tests given the chimpanzees (see page 253). However, the incomplete exemplar is only one version of this form of nonverbal interrogation. Other versions are exemplars that differ from the veridical one by having too many elements, duplicates of correct ones, and/or extraneous ones or by having correct elements in incorrect orders. In these cases the subject must use deletion and/or rearrangement to bring the instantiation into conformity with the schema.

The third and last version simply carries the second version to its logical conclusion. The schema is not instantiated at all; instead the subject is given a pile of items along with a frame that discloses, say, three empty slots. Nothing is instantiated except the number of elements in the sequence and their geometric arrangement, and even these features may be eliminated. Nonverbal interrogation of this open variety has already produced some interesting results with the chimpanzees. When given a pile of items along with a three-slot frame, the animals do not always compose causality-exemplifying schema on their own; but on those occasions when they do—which range from about 15 to 25% of the time for different animals—the composition of the schema often bears an interesting relation to the act that has preceded it. The animal may take the knife from the pile of items, poke it into an apple in the animal's style of cutting, and a moment later fill the slots in the frame with an apple, a knife, and a severed apple (as often as not using material different from that it used in the actual act of cutting). The three-item nonverbal sequence appears to be an abstract replay or description of the immediately preceding act and in that sense comparable to verbal self-description, which is also seen in these same animals. For example, after poking the knife into the apple, some of the animals turn to the plastic words and write "Elizabeth apple cut" or "Peony apple insert," descriptions by Elizabeth and Peony of their own immediately preceding behavior (see page 89). When words are present, the animals may use them descriptively but when words are not present, the chimpanzees appear to use abstract nonverbal sequences in the same descriptive way as they use words.

When the apes do not use the pile of items to compose causality-exemplifying sequences, they compose others of a simpler form, such as *apple–apple–apple* or *knife–knife–knife,* which we label the identity schema, as well as many other sequences that regrettably are not so easily interpreted. If the sequences the animals composed were all immediately interpretible, the open form of interrogation would be exceptionally revealing. It would reveal an inventory of the animal's schemas as well as an ordering of their salience. However, this is not the case; to find out what schemas the animal has, we must first decide which ones they may have and then ask relatively structured questions about them. The animal may give evidence of having a particular schema by completing an incomplete version of it, although not giving evidence of the same schema by composing it from scratch. This is not different from verbal interrogation; to obtain specific information it is rarely sufficient simply to listen to what a subject says. Instead, to elicit specific information it is often necessary to ask specific questions. Successful interrogation, in both the verbal and the nonverbal cases, depends on knowing what question to ask.

REPRESENTATIONAL CAPACITY

Nonverbal interrogation can be used with the chimpanzee in the first place because this species can recognize representations of its own behavior and/or behavior it has observed in others (where behavior is given the customary definition—topography or effect on the environment). Probably there are very few species, none below the primates I should guess and perhaps not all of them, that have this capacity. For example, Gallup (1970) has shown that the chimpanzee responds to its mirror image in a manner compatible with the inference that it recognizes itself, whereas even the monkey—let alone the nonprimate—responds to its mirror image as though it is another organism. Although it must be misleading to equate language with any one function—language involves many functions—nonetheless some of the functions are critical and others are secondary. A species that could not acquire, say, tense markers, personal pronouns, or even some of the complex syntactic forms might still be said to have language, some degree of it, even a nontrivial degree. However, consider a species that cannot make judgments about the relation between a nonlanguage condition, for example, Sarah is in heat, red is on green, caramel is sweet, and a sentence describing that condition. There is no sense in which such a species can be said to have language.[2]

The chimpanzee can be interrogated not only in the implicit nonverbal way but also in an explicit verbal way. For instance, the experimenter can arrange a simple state of affairs, such as place a red card on a green one, and then ask the chimpanzee "? red on green" (Is red on green?). The chimpanzee is no less adept at answering questions of this kind (see Chapter 5) than at filling in blanks in nonverbal tests.

This should come as no surprise, however. Once it is known that the species has the capacity to recognize representations of various conditions, it is virtually certain that it can be taught language, or at least the most basic language function: to carry out judgments about the relation between an item and a representation of that item. In the *yes–no* question above, the subject is required

---

[2] It is possible that some species do not have a general representational capacity but have one limited to certain domains. Such species might be taught some degree of language but only for those domains to which their representational capacity applied. "Small"-range capacities, specialized for or linked to specific domains, are foreign to human thinking. The capacities of human intelligence appear to be general, applicable to all domains; chimpanzee capacities appear to resemble human ones in their generalness.

to judge the agreement between specifically a nonlinguistic condition, red on green, and a linguistic representation of that condition, "red on green". In the nonverbal example the subject is required to judge a similar kind of agreement, one between a nonlinguistic condition, e.g., acts of cutting in which it has engaged and/or observed others to do, and a pictorial representation of that condition. The problem is not changed in any basic way by the fact that the representation is verbal in one case and nonverbal in the other. (The pictorial representation apple–knife–severed apple is far from a simple icon. Hardly a motion picture of an act of cutting, it is instead a highly abstract digital representation of an analog sequence (see page 253). Neither is the problem changed in any basic way by the fact that the subject expresses its judgment in one case by answering "yes–no" and in the other case by operating on the representation to make it conform with the referent. In fact, in one sense the present nonverbal example poses more difficulty than the verbal one, for it obliges the subject to reconstruct from memory one of the two conditions about which it is to make a judgment (the actual or observed acts of cutting), whereas in the verbal example both conditions are present—red on green, as well as "red on green."

The difference between verbal and nonverbal interrogation can be further reduced by considering the *wh-* rather than *yes–no* form of the question. In the *wh-* form the subject is required to supply the missing element exactly as it is in the nonverbal tests. Returning to the simple example of a moment ago, we can ask the subject not whether red is on green, but what is on green. In the chimpanzee language this question took the form "? on green" (What is on green?), and the correct answer consisted of replacing the interrogative marker with the word "red."

One can appreciate the capacity of the chimpanzee by contrasting it with the almost certain parallel incapacity of the bee. The bee has a code—a correlation between items inside and outside of its body—but not a language in the sense that a language is a code that can be used in specific ways. The most critical of these ways depend upon the capacity in question, upon being able to recognize representations of one's own self—body, behavior, and knowledge.

Suppose a forager bee were allowed to gather information about the location and quantity of a food source relative to its hive. Although the bee can encode this information in its dance (and a second bee decode the dance), if the first bee was shown a dance, it could not judge whether or not the dance accurately represented the location and quantity of the food source. That is, presumably the bee could not recognize the dance as a representation of its own knowledge.

It is, however, precisely this kind of judgment that the chimpanzee can make and it is the capacity for this judgment, more than any other perhaps, that qualifies the chimpanzee for language. When shown one or another condition, such as an apple in a pail, a red card on a green one, even an act of one kind or another carried out by some trainer, the chimpanzee can be asked to judge the agreement between the condition it has observed and a representation of the condition. The chimpanzee can be interrogated, as the bee cannot, and, as a consequence, it can make truth–false judgments, as the bee cannot.[3]

Filling in blanks in nonverbal sequences and answering *yes–no* or *wh-* questions both depend on the same basic capacity—the ability to recognize the relation between an item and its representation. The recognition can be witnessed not only in the two ways we have seen—*yes–no* judgments and operating on the representation to make it conform with its referent—but in other ways as well. For example, in special cases when the referent is itself available, the subject can operate on it rather than on the representation, making the referent conform to the representation instead of vice versa. Indeed, on occasion one of the subjects adopted this approach in a format essentially combining the verbal and nonverbal response forms. When asked "? red on green" (Is red on green?) at a time when green happened to be on red, for example, Sarah, the most able or inventive subject, sometimes changed the position of the cards, bringing them

---

[3] Ironically, the species that can be most easily taught language and therefore can be interrogated most explicitly is at the same time the species that least needs the explicit form of the question. Given an incomplete configuration of virtually any kind, its "answer," generally speaking, does not consist of reducing the complexity, structure–information level—that is already present. Instead, it will answer so as to increase (or attempt to increase) the amount of information already present.

Proponents of a different view of comparative intelligence will regard this an ethnocentric view of intelligence. A bird, for example, should not be asked to complete puzzles but should be given a task suited to its purposes. We should give the bird an incomplete nest and see if it can choose a piece that completes the nest. Alternatively, we might give it an incomplete fledgling or mate, and see whether the pigeon could choose the eye, beak, wing, etc., that would complete its conspecific. In yet another approach, we can exploit the pain-induced aggression paradigm; after the bird has been shocked, give it an incomplete model, allowing it to add the missing element so that with a complete model it can aggress with maximum relief or fulfillment. However, it is quite possible that the bird cannot do any of these. The problem is not that the bird will give the wrong answer, select an eye rather than a wing, or attempt to complete the nest with a piece too large or small for the lacuna. Instead, the bird will not grasp the question. No matter how canonical the structure the bird may be incapable of recognizing incompleteness, of demonstrating its recognition by selecting the completing alternative. We do not say that species is intelligent which answers questions as we do, but that species is intelligent which discovers in ambiguous configurations the same questions we do.

Any potentially complete structure can be raised to a higher level of information by being completed. Probably there is no more self-evident way of increasing the information level. The case is interesting, however, not only because of its simplicity but also because the verbal question can be formulated in the same terms. That is, the question is a potentially complete structure that at a given moment is incomplete. "How old is Jack?" which can be written as "Jack is X years old," is the incomplete version of, say, "Jack is 12 years old." In answering a question one completes a verbal structure in quite the same way that one can complete a visual structure by supplying the missing element. In both cases, one increases the information level. It is no accident, I think, that chimpanzees can do both—answer questions and supply elements that complete nonverbal structures.

into conformity with the verbal representation, and then answered "Yes" (instead of leaving the cards alone and answering "No").

Thus far we have considered two cases in which a judgment is made on the agreement between two items: one in which both items are nonlinguistic (nonverbal interrogation) and a second and more traditional case in which one item is linguistic and the other is nonlinguistic (verbal interrogation). The major remaining case is that in which both items are linguistic. This is the subject matter of synonymy or paraphrase, where the basic question is "Do these sentences have the same meaning?" In Chapter 14, where synonymy is discussed at length, we see the chimpanzee make same–different judgments on pairs of sentences. Therefore, a progression that has begun with two nonlinguistic items and advanced to one linguistic and one nonlinguistic culminates in synonymy, where both representations are linguistic.

Although synonymy is the most impressive case, it is likely that its realization is all but predictable from the first and most primitive case. One might entertain reservations if nonverbal interrogation disclosed severe limitations on the items that the species could match. For instance, if the species could match an actual act of cutting with a motion picture of cutting but not match when the transformation was—in a sense that remains to be defined—greater than that between three- and two-dimensional representation, then one would have to qualify the predictions, taking into account the perceptual transformations that the species could and could not negotiate. Data of this kind for the chimpanzee are so limited as to make prediction foolish, although so far, at least, they speak to capacity rather than incapacity. Furthermore, the ability to use specifically verbal representations, as opposed to matching different kinds of nonverbal representations, has less to do with perceptual transformations than with memory, with the ability to store adequate representations in the first place and to use arbitrary items to retrieve them in the second. The data on chimpanzee memory (see Chapter 15), moreover, do not suggest that memory specifically limits the language the chimpanzee may be able to acquire. Indeed, if the chimpanzee is as much like man in certain of its perceptual abilities as it appears to be in its mnemonic abilities, then like man it may also find less difficulty in matching, say, a picture of Henry's face with "a picture of Henry's face" than in matching a picture of Henry's face with an inverted picture of Henry's face (Yin, 1969). In general, provided a species has the basic representational capacity, which can be assessed by nonverbal interrogation, there seem to be no essential constraints on the pairs of conditions it can judge or the forms its judgments can take.

Species that can recognize the relation between an item and its representation act automatically to protect the match or agreement between the two. For instance, children do not have to be rewarded for describing their own acts, that is, for producing sentences that constitute a representation of their prior nonverbal behavior. Nor do chimpanzees have to be rewarded for completing nonverbal sequences that, when completed, accord with their previous acts and/or observations. Which is to say, if a species has the capacity to symbolize or form representations, it will have an indigenous disposition to do so (and this must be true of all capacities (see pages 220–211).

Both of these cases—self-description and the nonverbal case—are examples of imitation, although one may not recognize as much from traditional discussions of imitation. In particular, such discussions fail to point out that imitation of one's self, as in the description of one's own behavior, is probably more basic than imitation of another.

THREE GENERAL TRAINING FACTORS

Three factors go into language training—the vehicle, the conceptual content, and the extralinguistic context. Of these the vehicle is the simplest factor. The assets and liabilities of any vehicle can be rather easily summarized, so that one can compare vehicles and then choose one suited to the needs and capacities of the subject. Whenever the population being trained is human—retarded and/or autistic children, or aphasic adults—the objective is the same: a vehicle that permits communication in the real world with the largest possible population. To realize this objective, one would choose speech when possible, otherwise sign, and certainly not a permanent visual language, such as the plastic words. That is, one would make this choice if everything else were equal. However, many severely retarded children did not acquire language when taught with speech or sign but succeeded in varying degree when plastic words were used (Carrier, 1973). Ultimately, moreover, the plastic words preserved the original objective, for although the children failed to acquire speech when it was taught as a first step, they acquired it as a second step. That is, once they had learned the plastic words, they succeeded in mapping speech onto them.

The second factor in language training, the elements into which language should be decomposed and the order in which they should be introduced, is the primary content of this book. Once considered formidable, it is now clear that strict training programs require only a moderate degree of language sentience plus an immoderate degree of perseverance.

The real challenge emerges with the third factor—assuring that the trainer and subject interpret the training situation in the same light. This is not unique to language training but is the basic problem of all pedagogy. The problem has two sources. First, a subject can learn to identify the trainers' concept only if that concept is included among those the subject entertains. Marvin Levine's (1971) work shows this with admirable directness. Although his conclusions are based on simple features, red, square, larger and the like, they apply equally when names are taught for more complex cases such as classes, relations and logical connectives. Here, too, names can be associated with the target concept only if the concept is included among those the subject entertains.

Whereas the first source of the pedagogic problem is in a sense a shortage of concepts (the teacher's concept is not among those the subject entertains), the second source is the opposite, not a shortage but a superfluity of concepts. Assume that nonverbal procedures have already established the presence of the target concept. The problem now lies in arranging that the teacher and student read the situation in the same light, focusing on the same features, so that the potential name becomes associated with the intended concept and not with any of the indeterminately many others that are present.

How difficult this can sometimes be was brought out in our ill-fated attempt to teach one of the subjects the exclusive "or," A or B but not both (see pages 244–249). In hindsight it was clear that our failure came from a nonfelicitous training situation, one that did not point the subject in the right direction. It was also clear how to improve the training situation. Suppose a third party placed between the subject and trainer a small cake cut in two pieces; knowing something about the appetites of both parties, he wrote out the instruction, "Sarah (the subject's name) take this piece X that piece." What is "X" the unknown particle in this instruction likely to mean?

The instruction hopes to call the subject's attention to the fact that it can take one piece or the other but not both, and in that way introduce the exclusive "or." The subject is likely to join the trainer in interpreting the unknown term as "or" provided it shared certain assumptions with the trainer. The social intelligence of the chimpanzee is such that if it has shared similar cakes with the trainer in the past, it should have no trouble reaching these assumptions (cf. Menzel, in press); indeed it could probably reach similar assumptions from evidence that was far more circumstantial.

I should like to be able to propose some heuristic devices that could be used to lead the subject to read training situations in the light of the trainer's intent and thus to associate new words with the target concepts. Devices of this kind could be used to put pedagogy on its feet. The best I can do, unfortunately, is to describe a test that can be run in advance of training and that, in a crude way, can be used to predict whether or not the intended outcome is likely to be realized.

The test asks whether judges given access to the same information as the subject could guess the meaning of the unknown term. I ran this test on two occasions, each time giving the judges a brief account of the training situation which I described as follows "the trainer and chimp face one another; a second trainer places a small cake between them which has been cut in two pieces." Next I wrote on the board in English the sentence that the subject was to receive, giving the judges the meaning of every word except that of the unknown: "Sarah take this piece ? that piece." At this point I asked them to write down what the question mark meant, "what word does the ? stand for?" If they were unable to say, as most were, or guessed incorrectly, I gave them the internal or dispositional information, the only information that should have separated them from the subject and that was left to give them; for they already knew the external information, the sentence and the physical layout. "Both the chimp and the trainer like cake," I told them. "Each knows that the other likes cake—and they have a tradition of sharing." Given all this information, five of six visitors to the lab (two groups of three) correctly guessed that the unknown stood for "or." The errant party was a psychologist like the others but from a different culture. He seemed not to understand my account and needed to be assured that the animal and trainer would not fight.

The problem highlighted by the alien judge, that of putting the judge in the "subject's shoes" (a metaphor troubled by treating the ape as a man) could be ameliorated by using as judges not people but other chimpanzees. Other animals that had already been taught "or" but in a different way and, of course, with a different plastic word, would observe the training situation, be given alternatives that included their word for "or," and be required to complete the training sentence. If these judges reached a quick and accurate consensus we could be sanguine about their colleague's ability to learn the new word, but not so if their guesses were consistently wide of the mark.

BASIC EVIDENCE FOR LANGUAGE

We do not say of one another, "You know, I've been listening to John lately and I don't think he really has language." We reject as a premise the possibility that a normal person may not have language. [In fact, there are hundreds of thousands of human beings who are language deficient in sufficient degree to require therapy. In this country alone, the number of such children is presently estimated at over 600,000 (R. Schiefelbusch, personal communication, 1974).] The most we say along these lines is that someone is not "very verbal," by which we do not intend a serious condition.

Even as we have no tradition of doubting the language competence of our peers, so we have no science that questions what an organism must do or be able to do in order to be judged competent in language. However, we shall have to answer this question at least provisionally before trying to teach language to a species that does not acquire it in the normal course of events. We want to be in a position to judge our accomplishment, to be able to say whether or not the subject has acquired language. I shall not hesitate to accept degrees of language even though there is what seems to be an almost mystical tradition to talk about language in either/or terms; actually this is more ethnocentric than mystical, for it is simply the equating of all possible language with human language. I hope this text to make clear that while language is a system it can be separated into a number of skills. In the normal adult all of the skills are very likely to be present, but that is a fact rather than a logical necessity. Not all of the adult's competences are present in the child at different stages, nor are they in the subnormal human adult or in the infrahuman species given special training by man.

The two most basic language exemplars are reference relations and a sentence generating capacity. In man, reference relations include names of objects, agents, actions, and properties. These are the basic categories of human ontology, the classes of items in terms of which we perceive the world and, not surprisingly, the classes of items which we name. One can conceive of a language-competent species whose reference relations do not include all of our categories (alternatively, we can conceive of the opposite, a species whose reference relations are richer than our own, but the conception is idle or vacuous, for we have no way to describe the distinctions that they can make but we do not). The categories most likely to be omitted are properties and actions; as discussed at length in Chapter 8, these categories impose psychological demands not made by either objects or agents.

Still more important than the range of lexical items is the psychological nature of the reference relation itself. What is a word? What is meant by the classical phrase "power of a word?" Finally, is a chimpanzee word like a human one? Although in Chapter 15 we deal at length with this topic, the answer we come to is simple. The classical phrase "power of the word" celebrates the ability of the human word to substitute vigorously for its referent. In match-to-sample tests, the ability of the word to substitute for its referent is shown in the blunt fact that subjects can match attributes of objects to names of objects as well as to the intact objects themselves. Thus, the first basic evidence for language, reference relations, can be expressed by two factors:

1. Arbitrary items (words) can serve as information retrieval devices, in the limiting case, providing as much information about their associated referent as is contained in the referent itself.

2. The kind of items for which words can serve as information retrieval devices in the human case are agents, objects, actions, and properties.

The second basic property is a sentence-generating capacity. If the species could do no more than commit to memory some fixed inventory of admissable strings of words this would be of little interest and would not be evidence for language. The achievement is interesting only if, in order to explain it, we are forced to infer that the species has induced a theory which enables it to produce in principle indeterminately many sentences. This is the linguistic creativity of which the generative grammarian is fond of talking. It assumes that each individual can produce and comprehend sentences that he or she has not yet heard or said. Notice that there appear to be no ethnographic data showing how many new sentences the child or adult produces in, say, a day; the sense in which the sentences are new; how redundant such sentences are relative to their context compared to old sentences; how the processing time for new sentences compares with that for old sentences; what parameters affect the rate of production; etc. Nevertheless, we accept the view that language is not a fixed inventory of sentences.

When shall a sentence be judged new? In the first of the two major possibilities the structure of the sentence remains the same and the sentence is new merely by merit of lexical substitution. For example, "Mary wash banana for Sarah" could replace nearly all its former words to become "Donna cut apple for Peony" while still retaining its former structure. In the other possibility there is a structural change as when, for example, "Mary gives me fruit" and "I like Mary" combine in a sense to form "I like Mary's giving me fruit," "I like Mary because she gives me fruit," "Mary's giving me fruit is why I like her," etc. Structural innovation depends on factors and capabilities not required by mere lexical innovation. The nature of some of these factors can be specified hypo-thetically in terms of formal models and the models defended on the usual grounds of parsimony, but there is no evidence that steps in the formal models correspond to steps in the psychological process. On the contrary, every attempt so far to produce evidence of this kind has led to failure (see Fodor, Bever, & Garrett, 1974).

There is no evidence in this book that the chimpanzee can produce structural innovation of the kind described. It is capable of lexical substitution and more; it can comprehend five or six sentence forms structurally different from any on which it was trained (page 320). However, evidence that the chimpanzee has pure grammatical classes and can engage in either relativization or nominaliza-tion—the two most interesting and complex recursive forms—is not at hand. I mention it here so that readers concerned with the syntactic limits of the ape need go no further. Such aspirations for the chimpanzee may or may not be absurd—I think they are absurd—but surely they are premature. It is unreason-able to anticipate that apes trained from 1 to 3 years can either relativize or nominalize.

From a psychological point of view, recursive forms are of interest, in part, because the operations needed to produce them take place not in the world but in the head. They therefore presuppose the ability to carry out various kinds of operations on internal representations. Here the data are less likely to disappoint the reader.

The internal representations that the chimpanzee can generate must be reliable and of considerable tangibility for the animal can operate on them with the same accuracy that it operates on external events. For example, it can make same–dif-ferent judgments on two objects (external events) but also on an object and an internal representation, and even on two internal representations (see page 311). Intelligence involves, among other things, the ability to operate on internal events, in the ideal case to be able to carry out in the head all the operations one is capable of carrying out on external items. When the events inside the head are fleeting or vague one cannot perform in this way. However, if the internal event has the tangibility of, say, a block of wood, one should be able to operate on the internal event almost as efficiently as on the external one. This capacity is not irrelevant to structural novelty; the latter depends on the ability to form and operate on various kinds of internal representations.

"CREATIVE WRITING"

About midway through the project, after Sarah had achieved a moderate degree of language competence, virtually every lesson included a period in which the words were passed to Sarah and she was allowed to use them as she chose. No longer required either to comprehend the trainer's instructions or to answer her questions, Sarah produced constructions of her own. We called this section of the lesson "creative writing," and in it Sarah produced constructions of basically two forms—assertions, such as "Cherry is red," and questions, such as "? is fruit" (What is a fruit). By and by large Sarah dealt with the same topics as those dealt with by the trainer in the earlier portion of the lesson; but she also departed from the trainer both lexically and syntactically, using different word combinations in the first case and making assertions as opposed to the trainer's questions, and vice versa, in the second case. Two things are notable about "creative writing."

First, although, as we shall see, production and comprehension begin as separate systems, they become one system, words taught in either mode transferring completely to the other mode (see Chapter 6). In addition, if after the systems are unified the subject's performance is confined to one mode, it may insist on or press for the opportunity to perform in the other mode. At least such was the case with Sarah. Once Sarah's lessons came to rely increasingly on comprehension—for she could be required to comprehend longer and more complex sentences than she was likely to produce—giving Sarah the words became a virtual necessity. It forestalled her seizing them and running off to the middle of the cage where she wrote on the floor, hunching over her constructions, making them difficult to read. When given the words, she wrote on the language board and could be easily read and recorded.

Second, Sarah's accuracy in "creative writing" was close to 100%, 10–20% higher than her accuracy for the same material when dealing with the trainer's assertions or questions. Elizabeth, a less adept subject than Sarah, showed a similar difference in accuracy in describing herself, on the one hand, and describing the trainers, on the other. The acts, words, and sentence form she used in the two cases were all the same, yet Elizabeth was almost 100% correct in describing herself and 10–20% lower in describing the trainer. How can we explain these differences?

A simple factor would seem to account for the difference in both cases. In Sarah's "creative writing" as well as in Elizabeth's self-description, the behavior was self-paced. Sarah did not answer questions at the trainer's discretion but only when she chose to ask herself a question in the first place. Likewise, her comments or assertions were not made in response to specific requests by the trainer but only when she chose to make them and then only in response to aspects of the situation that she selected rather than to those the trainer selected for her. The same distinction applies with probably even greater force to Elizabeth. When required to describe the trainer, Elizabeth was subject to the standard forced-response constraint that is typical of all tests. Each time the trainer acted, Elizabeth was required to describe the act. She could not choose which act to describe, or whether to describe any at all, but was required to describe all of them and was scored incorrect for any failure. Contrast this with self-description, where she was free to describe (or not describe) whichever of her acts she chose, described less than 25% of them, but was virtually 100% correct in doing so.

Self-pacing per se is probably not the critical factor here, but what self-pacing allowed. In the cases in question, both Sarah and Elizabeth not only chose when to respond but also more critically to which events to respond. Presumably you are not likely to describe acts in which you are not interested, which you have not attended to closely in the first place, or for which the words needed to describe the act are less well known to you than others; some or all of these factors may play a role. There may even be a tradeoff between your interest in the act and your willingness to incur the risk of describing it with the difficult or little-known words that the description requires. Similarly, you are presumably not likely to ask yourself questions that are difficult to answer, because you either are not much interested in the subject, know little about the subject, or do not know the words needed either to ask or answer the question as well as you know some other words.

In view of these considerations, it may seem advisable to discount these data. Data that come from self-paced situations do not seem to represent the strict test of language competence that is represented by data drawn from situations in which there is a forced-response constraint. With self-pacing of the present kind, one can choose the easy trials, as it were, and therefore, not surprisingly, perform better than in the forced-response case where there is no choice and one must deal with hard trials as well as easy ones.

This analysis is sound, I think, but the recommendation from it certainly is not. Far from discounting the data, we should instead note the human situation to which these data apply. A recurrent criticism of this work is that the animals have averaged only about 85% correct, unlike people who, the criticism implies, never misuse words and are always a 100% correct. To begin with, it is evident that people are not always 100% correct either in word choice or in word order; this mistaken presumption seems to be based on that remarkable forgetting that comes to the fore whenever a reader finds chimpanzee performance threatening to human uniqueness. However, that is the tail side of the coin, not the interesting side.

Grant that people are 100% correct in language use some of the time, and consider instead the similarity between people's everyday use of language and the use by Sarah and Elizabeth in what we are calling the self-paced situation (although we have already seen that more is at stake than merely pacing). In the everyday use of language, a speaker speaks when he chooses, and a listener listens when he chooses. The agreement is seldom perfect between the two parties; because it is not, the listener may occasionally request repetition or have repetition forced on him (should the speaker observe his flagging attention) or bluff, wearing a facial expression that feigns understanding while actually picking up the speaker's meaning downstream in the conversation at points convenient to him, a tenable strategy provided the speaker does not change horses too often. There is generally enough agreement (between speaker and listener) in successful conversation, so that the listener can limit his replies to those occasions that are functionally equivalent to the easy trial; he has been listening, he is interested, he has understood and therefore is in an excellent position to reply. Moreover, if these optimizing conditions are not met and the listener is obliged nonetheless to respond, there are standard strategems that all but eliminate even the possibility of error. The listener may say "What?" or "I don't think I follow you," or even "I don't know." The reader will find that none of these prerogatives were extended to the chimpanzees. They were never allowed to escape a hard trial by saying "I don't know" and, indeed, one never is in a test situation.

The comparison between the chimpanzee's 85% level of accuracy and the human level has been widely misunderstood. For various writers (e.g., Brown, 1973) the difference confirms their suspicions. Sarah's performance is not really language, not sentences generated by deep and powerful rules, but only a kind of game behavior that resembles but is not really language. In point of fact, many tests are needed to determine whether the processes that underly languagelike behavior in the chimpanzee are like those that underly language in man. However, let us not mislead ourselves in the meantime, misinterpreting the data, prematurely assuring ourselves that the underlying processes have already been shown to be different.

The difference between the ape's 85% level and the customary human level is less likely to be a species difference than simply a difference between test situations, between forced and nonforced response. On the one hand, in a test situation, the human subject does not always use language at the 100% level; indeed he may not reach the 85% level if the test is difficult or if the training on which his performance depends has deliberately been made inadequate. On the other hand, when the chimpanzee uses language in a nonforced response situation, which in that factor at least approximates the human everyday use of language, it does not perform at the 85% level but approaches the customary human 100% level.

EXOBIOLOGY VERSUS EXOLINGUISTICS

An appealing possibility is to define language as a general system and then distinguish the human variant of the general system from other possible ones. Even though none of the other possibilities are realized here—man is evidently the only species with natural language— a treatment in which language is seen as a family of systems with the human case as an instance can escape much of the ethnocentrism that presently pervades the study of language. Then a system that does not exactly duplicate the human one can nonetheless be language and we can escape some of the less profitable forms of argument that go, "Yes but that's not language"—where the intent is "not human language." If we could arrive at a sufficiently general characterization, even though we were agreed that on this planet only one species had language, it would be necessary to speak not of language but of X language or Y language; and then it could be said that the species had X variety but did not have or even could not have Y variety.

One is led to think this may be possible by exobiology—the attempt to characterize life on other planets (Simpson, 1964; Dobzhansky, 1960). Could we not invent an analogous field, exolinguistics—the attempt to characterize languages that might suit different species, or even planets where the evolutionary course led to species of more nearly comparable minds than is the case here? The exobiologist regards life as a family of states, the instance on earth being a product of a particular evolutionary history. Parameter values may have differed elsewhere, giving rise to different forms of life. All forms must share one function, however: they must be self-reproducing and, ideally, provide for enough variability (e.g., sexual reproduction) to survive external changes.

Although we know nothing of how language has evolved—and cannot therefore mimic that part of exobiology—we do know something about the functions that language serves. Therefore we might try to describe a family of systems with the appropriate critical functions. The functions of language cannot be defined nearly as concisely as those of life, yet there are at least three that I think a language system must realize: (1) communication between organisms; (2) information storage, thinking, or problem solving in the individual; and (3) what I cannot do better than call "rerun," borrowing this apt term from Nancy Munn (1974). In rerun the individual recreates or replays a previous experience. Man especially, but all organisms to some extent, can experience any event in a number of ways. For example, he can eat a bit of food, draw or observe a picture of himself eating the food, tell or listen to a story about his eating the food, as well as imagine any one of the previous three, i.e., imagine himself eating, drawing a picture of eating, telling a story about eating. It is inconceivable that a species should have the capacity for this multiple representation of experience without having a deep need for the capacity. However, we need not settle here why rerun may be a vital function; it is sufficient to note that language, in being the most efficient means we have for repeating experience, may serve this function better than any other system.

Unfortunately, however, the parallel between exobiology and a potential exolinguistics is not thoroughgoing; they differ in one critical respect. In seeking to describe versions of life different from the human one, the exobiologist can use all the resources of human language to describe the possible forms that life may take elsewhere. The fact that he himself represents only one of these forms does not itself constrain the possible forms that he can describe. However, the exolinguist does not share this advantage. The possible language forms that he can describe are constrained by the fact that he speaks only one of the forms. In attempting to describe languages different from the human one, he has the problem of using language X to formulate $Y, Z, \ldots$, etc. How different from X (the formulating language) can Y (the language to be formulated) be? All the concepts of Y must be formulated in terms of concepts from X. Every lexical item in Y, every grammatical class, and every rule concerning grammatical operations must be stated in terms of lexical items, grammatical classes, and rules from X. This, so far as I can see, sets a disappointing limit on how far Y can depart from X. It appears to say that the only departures from human language of which we can conceive are reductions on human language, in terms of either lexicon, or syntax, or both. I return to this matter in Chapter 16, where I describe some examples. Although some variants are fairly radical and begin to lose the character of human language, it is disappointing that these variants must always be a reduction and not an amplification on human language.

2
Subjects and General Procedure

In trying to teach language to the ape we have made no attempt to simulate the "natural approach," mainly because the natural approach is far from well defined and it is difficult to simulate an ill-defined condition. Instead, we attempted to devise the most efficient training procedure possible, without regard to whether it did or did not simulate the human one. Of course, the procedure we used may turn out to be, in its one essential feature—step by step mapping of the presumptive cognitive structures—far closer to the experience the child receives than was once supposed.

SUBJECTS

Our subjects were four African-born chimpanzees (*Pan troglodytes*), three females and one male. Most of the data were based on the one subject, Sarah, whom we obtained when she was less than a year old but to whom we did not begin teaching language until she was between 5 and 6 years old. She lived in the laboratory, sharing a large cage with Gussie, another African-born female that we received with her. Despite being housed in the laboratory, both animals were reared in close contact with people. They were bottle fed and diapered for the first 3 years and taken outdoors to play, where the scene was not that of a cage but of Southern California—students, dogs, cars, ocean.

From the time the two infants arrived—in a small shipping crate at the St. Louis airport—Gussie appeared to be backward. When we opened the crate, Sarah emerged, whereas Gussie had to be plucked out, clinging to a tattered cloth. This difference did not diminish over time but expanded into a series of scenes preserving and elaborating the original theme.

One infant stood up in the crib and lunged about on the mattress; the other lay on its back clinging to the blanket that had replaced the worn out cloth. Gussie's position was so often supine that one came to think of her as a pair of brown eyes staring up from below. By the time Sarah was walking about the room and Gussie still mainly lay in the trainer's lap, we asked the attending pediatrician to check Gussie for neurological damage. However, he had already decided that her condition was not organic but caused by the trauma of having been separated from her mother—and he chided us for psychological insensitivity. He had learned how chimpanzee infants are often obtained in Africa—the hunter, after first shooting the mother, carries off the infant—but apparently no one had told him that Sarah also came from Africa. We will never know whether Gussie was retarded—she was sent to Oklahoma and drowned there accidentally—but we do know that she did not learn the language we tried to teach her. Sarah learned her first words slowly, only after months of failure, described in Chapter 3; but Gussie did not follow her on that occasion as she had come to do otherwise in their play and movement about the room. When Sarah's vocabulary progressed from two words to five, and then sufficiently beyond so that the mere addition of words was no longer of interest, Gussie still had not learned any words. We hired a special tutor for her who had some success, but the results were not definitive when both his work–study time and our funds ran out. In quitting we conceded something less than defeat—only that we could not afford to teach language to a possibly retarded ape.

Peony and Elizabeth were added to the project at a later date, and Walnut after them. Peony was also received when less than a year old. Although reported to be in excellent health, in fact she was heavily infected with intestinal parasites. It was possible to control all six of the different species identified except for *Giardia lamblia*. This flagellate is less dangerous than some of the roundworms Peony has had and in man is cured easily. But with Peony none of the many drugs we tried were permanently effective. As a result she was often listless and had to be excused from "school." She sat in the middle of the training materials, head down, whimpering, unwilling to try; on the worst of these occasions she could not even be coaxed to play. Each time microscopy reconfirmed her diagnosis and we gave her yet another round of drugs. Typically, in less than a week she was educable again, but only temporarily; after 6 weeks or so she fell into the same lassitude, and the whole cycle was repeated. Peony was bottle fed and diapered for over a year. She began language training when only about $2\frac{1}{2}$ years old, much earlier than Sarah and Gussie.

Elizabeth did not come to the lab until she was already about 3 years old, as a gift from another campus where she had been received from Africa when less than a year old. I do not know the exact circumstances of her early rearing but infer from her later behavior that it may have included a great deal of solitude. She showed more than one autistic symptom, the most dramatic being a drifting arm, which floated off as though moving on its own until, when it attracted the corner of her vision, she seized it and bit it. She was dangerous not only to herself but to others. She bit one trainer on the face, inflicting a wound requiring 46 stitches. On another occasion, when handed a $2\frac{1}{2}$-year-old ape, she threw it against the wall, in contrast to the careful handling shown the same infant by the other animals. Although the other animals have also bitten trainers, no wound has required even one stitch and all of these swipes and cuffs have been administered with heated emotion. In other words, the latter were communicative acts the messages of which—don't test her before me, don't put me down, etc.—were highly redundant, leading to inferences for which there was immediate consensus. Elizabeth's 46-stitch gash may also have contained a message but if so it was not a redundant one; each trainer interpreted it differently. In the last year Elizabeth has developed new symptoms, forcing us to reconsider the diagnosis of experiential autism. At odd times of day trainers began to find Elizabeth apparently asleep on the cage floor. If she did get up when they entered, she was wobbly and hardly able to accompany them down the hall to the school room. Later, we saw a few actual convulsions; they were bilateral, did not radiate directionally from one spot, and left her comatose although not unconscious for perhaps 15 min. They are undiagnosed at the present time.

Walnut, whose name is the silk purse version of the pig's ear "Peanuts" which he was given by his original owner, was also African born and obtained by the original owner when an infant. However, because his former owner was a commercial animal trainer, Walnut was not reared like the other animals but was struck with a lead pipe whenever he went awry. I do not know whether he was struck often or struck seldom and threatened often—but the effect was not disastrous. After 5 years removal from any semblance of punishment, Walnut was an extraordinarily benign animal. Although he was sexually mature, weighed in excess of 120 lb, and was of formidable strength, trainers still worked inside the cage with him. Sitting across from him on the floor, they adjusted his posture by tugging his feet into the position they wanted him to occupy; during the lesson they pulled his great head one way or the other to direct his gaze at some chosen stimulus. From a slow start he became a steady student. He differed from the other animals in one major respect. He did not play with or manipulate the objects about him as all the other animals did and, at the same time, he was the only animal to fail the causality tests (see Chapter 12). These tests ask the subject to indicate the instrument that can change a familiar object from one state into another, such as a knife can change an intact apple into a severed one, or a pan of water can change a dry sponge into a wet one. Walnut failed all such tests repeatedly, whereas all other subjects did remarkably well on them. Of course, we do not know why he did not manipulate objects or whether this was the source of his difficulty with the causality tests. Even the suppression brought on by severe punishment is reported to extinguish in time (e.g., Azrin & Holz, 1966).

FIG. 2.1 (a)

FIG. 2.1 (b)

TRAINING SITUATION

Sarah's training went through three phases. In all of them, the language vehicle, which is discussed in detail in Chapter 3, has been based on pieces of plastic which are metal backed and ahdere to a magnetized board. Each piece of plastic was wordlike in its function. Sentences were written on the vertical, as shown in Figure 3.1. In the first and most efficacious training phase, Sarah's trainers worked inside the cage with her, they sitting on one side of the table, Sarah squatting on a stool on the adjacent side as shown in Figure 2.1. The writing board was bolted to a wall alongside the table, within easy reach of both Sarah and the trainer. Sarah could pick up the words laid out on the table and place them on the board without even extending her arm. Trainers had only a slightly longer reach. The whole arrangement was intimate. Sarah's hand could be guided when needed and her head turned gently in a desired direction to assure attention. Astute cajoling often served to stretch out the lesson. Trainers held her hand, patting and encouraging her with affectionate tones. Sometimes she reciprocated, gently chucking the trainer under the chin.[1]

In this phase Sarah learned all the basic mechanics of the procedure. For example, to answer the many questions given her, she learned to remove the interrogative marker and to replace it with the word or particle of her choice, which is the form questions and answers took in this system. If she had operated on the question in other ways—rearranging words, deleting some of them, adding words at points other than those marked by the interrogative particle—the training method would not have worked. The resulting constructions might not then have been acceptable sentence as, in fact, all the constructions were, once she had added the proper missing word.

---

[1] If a trainer came with a hand that had suffered a bruise or cut, the lesson could not go forward until Sarah had inspected the wound. She squeezed the cut not by opposing her thumb and forefinger in the human manner, but by opposing her left and right forefingers in the chimpanzee manner. The pressure was exquisitely graded, just right to assure a "short" delay between application of pressure and the first appearance of blood. When blood oozed forth in a thin red line along the cut, Sarah looked intently into my eyes, I looked back with equal intentness, nodding to acknowledge her "success" but could never figure out what it was that she was asking me, if indeed it was anything, and therefore I could not settle on the look to give her in return. Howling loudly when blood appears, as I did on several occasions, did not affect her as it might a child. She looked curious but not dismayed and went on staring into my face, asking a question the nature of which I could not divine. The response captive chimpanzees make to their cuts is not at all like that Western children make to theirs. Chimps do not whimper or show self-sympathy, and therefore perhaps they do not show sympathy for others on the occasion of their cuts.

FIG. 2.1   (a) Sarah's training situation (Phase 1), showing the writing board, the table on which words were placed, and the relation of Sarah and the trainer to the board, table, and each other inside Sarah's home cage. (b) Trainer and Elizabeth in the schoolroom seated at the language board. The sentence reads "Elizabeth give apple Amy."

Erasure was a second mechanic taught her in this early phase. After she had produced a sentence from scratch or completed one by answering a question, she was taught to remove the words from the board and to replace them on the table. The speaker, not the listener, was made responsible for removing his own constructions in these "conversations." Whenever a word was applied clumsily and did not adhere to the board, she dropped to the floor and retrieved it. She did not use words in nonlanguage ways, except for the occasional tantrum brought on by a string of errors longer than she could tolerate. Then she knocked words off the board with a swipe that trainers were careful to avoid. Ordinarily, however, she accorded the language material a deference not shown other objects. Clothes, sunglasses, and painting materials were often mangled, sometimes in a matter of minutes. In contrast, the writing board, which she could easily have torn from the cage, was never mishandled. It has shared the cage with her for 7 years, bolted to its original position.

Noncorrection training was used for the most part. When Sarah produced a sentence from scratch, say, "Mary give Sarah banana" in the presence of banana, or answered a question by completing a string she was told either "correct" or "incorrect" in her own language; that is, the trainer placed the appropriate word on the board, below Sarah's construction. The verbal judgment was accompanied by appropriate paralinguistics, such as (in English) "Good girl" or "No you dummy," as well as patting her hand on the occasion of a correct construction or holding out the hand to hasten the return of words from the board on the occasion of an incorrect one. Sarah often sought to correct her own errors. On being told "incorrect," she reexamined the construction, placed her finger on the word she thought to be the troublemaker, and then looked insistently to the trainer for guidance. The trainers were just as insistent in denying her guidance. Typically, after repeated unsuccessful attempts to obtain information from the trainer, she moved the dubious word to one side—rather than removing it from the board as she did with the interrogative marker—and then sought its replacement from the words on the table. It was on these occasions that a tantrum was most likely. Indeed, if Sarah's second guess was also wrong, the gun-shy trainer often removed the words from the board herself before Sarah could knock them down. Yet on other occasions, Sarah made no attempt to correct her errors. She received the announcement of "incorrect" with placid indifference, handed back the words, and waited patiently for the next trial. It was not easy to predict which occasions would be dangerous and which safe.

In addition to being told "correct" with the word in her language and being given a pat along with a kind tone of voice, after several correct trials she was offered an egg carton filled with goodies and allowed to choose as many items as she had answered correctly. The carton was filled with jelly beans, marachino cherries, nuts, and the like, all things that Sarah liked. Only choice morsels could have attracted Sarah, for neither she nor any of the other subjects were deprived of food or water. They were maintained on *ad libitum* Purina monkey pellets supplemented by vitamins and fruit, along with the fresh and dried fruit they received in the lessons.

Were the contents of the egg carton a reward? To find out would have required trials on which the egg carton was denied, despite the fact that she was correct. If performance fell off, recovering when the egg carton priviledge was restored, we could regard the latter as a reward. (Provided, of course, the effect was a consistent one and not simply pique or surliness brought on by the arbitrary denial of priviledges). But the question was not worth the cost of disrupting her lesson in order to answer it. Social approval, I would guess, would have proved to be a more potent reward than the tidbits. Moreover, reinforcement is a performance variable and in this study we have been concerned with learning.

The first phase of the study, in which Sarah was accustomed to all the basic mechanics, lasted about 16 months, from February 1969 to May 1970, when she had her first menstrual period. When this phase ended Sarah was approximately 8 years old. She had been reared with little discipline. The few times she was struck, to prevent biting or destruction of experimenter's clothing, hurt the trainer's hand far more than Sarah. She does not respond to pain as we do. When she miscalculated in her gymnastics and fell 6–8 ft to a concrete floor, she rose without a whimper, often to come over to investigate the grimacing trainer whose face was wreathed in empathetic pain. One or two trainers still went into the cage to play with her, but her tantrums had not decreased and her swipes were more dangerous than ever. Direct contact was brought to an end, except for occasional play sessions, and the next phase was begun.

A port built on the side of the cage on the wall adjacent to her writing board had not yet been used. Now the port was opened to a distance of about 12 in., a training table was rolled up to the port, and the trainer sat or stood alongside it. Sarah and the trainer again confronted one another across the table but now only Sarah was inside the cage. Nevertheless, Sarah had as good access to the writing board as ever. Although the words were outside the cage and Sarah inside, the words were scarcely farther from her than before, a matter of inches. The loss was to the trainer: the board was not equally accessible to her or him nor, more important, was Sarah. Moreover, the port did not actually provide the security it was thought to. One day Sarah stuck out her head and wiggled through the port. Dropping into the corridor alongside the trainer, she made it plain that she could join the trainer whenever she chose. Despite the realization that Sarah was a voluntary prisoner, the port was not reduced. It was difficult enough for the trainer to reach Sarah as it was. Moreover, merely being outside the cage protected the trainer from Sarah's frantic swipes, which was the point of the separation. The main loss was to the cajoling that could no longer be used to prolong lessons. It was now difficult to pat Sarah and hold her hand, and she rejected far more lessons than she had in the first phase. In all, the second phase lasted about 8 months, from May 1970 to December 1970. Although Sarah was not as readily controlled as in the first phase, much of the more complicated material was taught her in this phase, for instance, all of the material on connectives (Chapter 12) as well as that on the quantifiers (Chapter 13).

In the sixth month of the second phase, when Sarah reached sexual maturity, there was no immediate change in her temperament. By the time of her fourth cycle, however, she twice attacked her previously favored trainer. The actual causes of the attacks are unknown, of course, and cannot simply be attributed to the onset of menses. Several other events coincided with the attacks, notably the arrival of the sexually immature Walnut (about 4 years old), the first male chimp to join the lab. Walnut was brought into Sarah's room and introduced to her in the same way that Peony, a sexually immature female, had been introduced to her 4 or 5 months earlier. Sarah's response to Walnut was not the indifferent one she had given Peony. She drew Walnut fast to the cage. Clutching his scrotum with her other hand, she took his penis into her mouth almost immediately. From the time she had come from Africa when only about 9 months old, Sarah had been caged alone or with another female chimp. Therefore, Walnut was the first male of her species she had seen in perhaps 7 years, presumably one of the relatively few she had ever seen. The alacrity of her response suggests that some forms of sexual behavior in the female chimp are not dependent on elaborate learning. However, we have observed sexually immature females in the context of play respond to the male in the same fashion. A tumescent penis may be salient to the observer, and therefore likely to be investigated. In the choice between investigating with mouth or hand, the chimpanzee appears to favor its mouth over its hand to a greater degree than the child (Carlyle, Jacobson, & Yoshioka, 1932). Whenever a trainer arrived wearing new shoes, the animals inspected with their mouth, only later touching the shoes with their hands as a kind of afterthought. In my observation of children, the inspection order tends to be the reverse, the mouth being added as the afterthought.

Sarah became increasingly disinclined to work. Having previously rejected an average of one of the four lessons offered daily, over a period of about 3 weeks she came to accept no more than a lesson a day. Her attacks on the trainers increased, and although they were confined to grabbing and finger bending, it was no longer safe to offer Sarah a port through which she could emerge into the corridor whenever she chose. We diminished the port and attempted to work with her through a safer opening. This only aggravated the problem. Walnut, not symbolic logic or doing well for her previously cherished trainers, was what interested her.

For a brief period Walnut was used as a contingent event. On a board outside her cage we wrote such things as "Sarah is good ⊃ Mary give Sarah Walnut" (If Sarah is good Mary will give Walnut to Sarah) and the more explicit "Sarah insert cracker red dish ⊃ Mary give Sarah Walnut" (If Sarah inserts the cracker in the red dish then Mary will give Walnut to Sarah). Instructions of this kind restored Sarah's work habits. When Sarah carried out the required actions, Walnut was brought in on a leash and for a moment she was allowed to paw him through the cage. Then the two screaming animals were torn apart and a highly excited Walnut was led from the room. Some of the difficulty was alleviated by putting Walnut on a schedule, bringing him in only after Sarah had carried out some number of instructions. Sarah carried out some of the instructions at a higher level of accuracy than at any previous time. But we abandoned the use of packaged sex, on grounds both of possible injury to Walnut and of its repugnant character. Except for an occasional lesson or two on Sarah's rare good days, the first leg of the experiment came to an end. Plastic words could no longer be used with Sarah, and we began to make plans that culminated in the keyboard.

SOCIAL CUES

Were Sarah and the other subjects merely clever Hanses, or Gretels as the case may be, different only in sex or species? In its response to social cues, the chimpanzee is not remotely like a horse. Clever Han's trainer was apparently totally unaware that he was cueing the horse. When the chimpanzee tried to use facial cues, however, only the most naive trainer failed to observe it. Chimpanzees and children are alike in this regard: when they do not know the answer to a question and decide to use social cues, they peer visibly into the trainer's face. Often on these occasions one can observe the experienced trainer wag his finger in the subject's face with unconcealed disgust and then, taking the subject's head in both hands, turn it down so that the subject faces into the test material, away from the trainer's face. Of the more than 20 trainers we have had occasion to use in the past 10 years, we only once found a beginning trainer so apparently absorbed in setting out the test items, following the data sheet—and doing all of this without being bitten—that he did not sense the brown eyes intently watching his every move. The first suggestion that something was awry came from the subject's abruptly improved performance. Peony suddenly performed well above chance—on words she failed with the experienced trainers. Instead of informing the trainer, we televized the lesson and, as a routine part of his training, showed him his own performance. We did not retain this trainer, although even he caught on to his mistakes after watching the film. There is no question but that both chimpanzees and children try to use social cues on occasion. However, I have never seen either do so with sufficient stealth to go undetected by an experienced trainer, and especially not by a second trainer who observes the first trainer and the subject.

There were numerous informal contraindications of social cues, the most vital of which were the clever innovations made by the subjects themselves. These innovations delighted and surprised the trainers, for they were in no way traceable to the training. Many cases of this kind are sifted throughout the book, so I will cite only two or three here.

One of our most basic test procedures was to ask the subject *yes–no* questions. For example, after the trainer placed, say, a red card on a green one, she asked the subject "? red on green" (Is red on green?). The subject had to examine the placement of the cards, compare it with the conditions described in the sentence, and answer "Yes" or "No," depending on the agreement between the cards and the sentence. Sarah did this quite well. But she also introduced a striking innovation, specifically for occasions on which the conditions did not agree and the appropriate answer was therefore "No." Sometimes, of course, she answered "No" but other times she changed the cards in such a way as to make a "Yes" answer possible. For instance, if the question were "Is yellow on blue?" when, in fact, yellow was on green, she removed the blue card, substituted a green one and answered "Yes." There was more than one suggestion that Sarah had an aversion not only to "no" but to the negative form of predicates in general and this aversion was apparently the motive force for the innovation.

A second general occasion for innovation were sentences requiring that Sarah give something to someone else rather than serve as the recipient for someone else's giving. These occasions gave rise to a family of innovative forms, the most notable of which was the use of her own name in the manner of a possessive pronoun. When told "Sarah give apple Mary," instead of handing over the fruit she took the piece of plastic that meant "Sarah" and applied it vigorously to the apple, which struck me as her version of shouting "Mine! mine!" This response was of interest, too, as a specifically linguistic refusal; she could just as easily have seized the apple and withheld it.

A less dramatic although extremely early form of innovation was her use of words to request items that were preferred but not present. The use had not been taught her, for in her early training she was required always to request the fruit that was set before her. Her early performance on trials of this kind seemed singularly disappointing, until we awoke to the possibility that what we construed as errors—failures to associate the word with its intended referent—were perhaps requests. For example, when she put "banana" on the board in the presence of apple, this was perhaps not an error but a request for banana. We tested for this possibility by giving her paired comparisons over the six fruits she had been trained on at that time and then, independently, paired comparisons over the would-be names of the six fruits. We found a concordance of about 80% between her preference order for the fruit and for the names. Further innovations, some by Peony and Elizabeth as well as others by Sarah, can be found in the text.

Contraindication of social cues can come from the subject's success when such cues are not available, as we have seen, but also from the subject's failure when such cues may be available. A test of Sarah's ability to subitize, or make numerosity judgments for small numbers of items, provided a unique case of the latter kind. The test was made in the context of match-to-sample, the sample consisting of one to 13 items and the two alternatives of sets that did and did not agree in number with the sample. Five was the largest sample Sarah was able to match correctly, and she had difficulty even with that when the incorrect alternative was as large as four. Sarah's failure to match beyond five was of interest because the trainer knew the correct answer on all trials, of course, and more imprtant did not know that there was any limit to the magnitude one could match without being able to count. There was no reason why the trainer should have anticipated a limit, for on all previous matching tests (dealing with features other than numerosity) Sarah had done remarkably well—about as well as the trainer—and the trainer had no basis for supposing that she would not do as well now.

This was brought out poignantly by the trainer's mistaken recollection of Sarah's performance. When asked about Sarah's performance several months after the test, she replied that Sarah had reached 11. On reexamining the data, however, we found that Sarah's limit was about five. This was a case then in which the trainer knew the answers but obviously managed to keep them to herself.

A third kind of evidence that speaks informally against social cues was the difficulty that Sarah had in acquiring certain words. "Is," "if—then," and the quantifiers "all," "none," "one," etc., are good examples. If social cues were the basis of Sarah's learning, she should have had no more difficulty learning complex predicates than simple ones. The ease with which the trainer can cue the animal bears no relation to the complexity of the predicate. It is determined simply by the numer of alternatives from which the animal chooses, and this was routinely the same in all cases. Therefore, if an animal was learning by social cues it should have had no more difficulty acquiring difficult words than easy ones. However, as the text will show, not all words have been learned with equal ease. Beyond this, words that were especially troublesome could always be related to a well-defined impropriety in their training. For instance, Sarah was unable to learn the quantifiers "all—none" until we recognized belatedly that the training lacked the usual positive and negative exemplars. When the missing material was added, Sarah learned not only "all—none," but also "one—several." Similarly, the many errors she made in learning "if—then" can be traced to some basic errors we made in teaching "if—then" (see Chapter 12).

Roger Brown (1973) has expressed reservations about Sarah's performance on the grounds that she does all things well, the hard no less than the easy. However, Brown's account of the data is inaccurate. Sarah did not make the same number of errors in reaching criterion on all words. In general, as the text shows, she made more errors in learning difficult predicates than in learning easy ones. Actually, however, this difference in the rate at which she has acquired words is far less interesting than another one. For if each training program had fully achieved its objectives, Sarah should not have shown any difference of this kind. Each training program should have confronted her with only one un-known. Assuming that each unknown represents an atomic step of roughly equal magnitude, she should then have learned difficult predicates in more steps than easy ones but not have made more errors along the way.

The burden of a difficult predicate should always fall on the trainer, not the subject. It is the trainer's task to decompose the more complex predicate into a greater number of steps. The subject must therefore pass through more preliminary steps in acquiring the complex predicate, but the difficulty of each step should be approximately the same. The fact that Sarah has made more errors in acquiring certain predicates reflects inadequacies of the teacher more than the subject—for example, the difficulties I have had in translating such concepts as the conditional relation and class membership into training programs.

There are other data which relate to difficulties that were more specifically Sarah's. Each time Sarah attained criterion on a new word, she was given further lessons in which the word was embedded in a series of sentences. She was required to read the sentences and carry out their instructions. Her comprehension level varied little, being typically between 80 and 85% correct for both hard and easy words. What did vary, however, was the time it took her to process the sentences. It was not practical to actually time her and we did not acquire television facilities until later, when training Peony and Elizabeth. Therefore we have no quantitative latency data. However, to sustain the distinction at issue none are needed. For material of standard difficulty, she typically processed between 15 and 20 sentences before terminating the lesson by refusing to work further, whereas for sentences that contained a demanding predicate she often processed no more than seven or eight sentences before showing the same reluctance; lessons in both cases took about the same length of time. Sometimes when carrying out a particularly difficult instruction, she appeared to coach herself, pointing to a word in the sentence, then to the object to which it referred, to another word, to the object to which it referred; processing time for such sentences was of the order of minutes. Yet even for the most slowly processed sentences, her level of accuracy remained about the same. Moreover, with repeated practice on complex instructions, such as that given her on the conditional sentences (see Chapter 12) her processing time decreased, until she carried out almost as many of the complex instructions as she had simpler instructions from the beginning. Also, her processing time was slowed down in production, and not only comprehension, when she was required to observe what was for her a demanding word order (see page 128).

DUMB TRAINER

These informal arguments do not settle the issue, however. To make a formal test of Sarah's ability to process the language without extralinguistic cues, we used a dumb trainer, an individual who behaved as though he knew the language but in fact did not. His ability to simulate a speaker depended on a microphone and earphones that connected him to a trainer in the hall. Was the sentence that Sarah wrote correct or not? The dumb trainer could not say. But after first translating each column of words into a sequence of numbers with a code that was given him, he reported the number sequence to the trainer in the hall. She in turn consulted an answer sheet and told the dumb trainer either "right" or "wrong." Depending on the answer he received through his earphones, the dumb trainer either smiled and handed Sarah the item she had correctly requested or withheld his smile and did not hand over the item.

Neither the dumb trainer nor the one in the hall could correctly influence Sarah's choices. The former did not know the meaning of the words, and the latter did not make contact with Sarah's behavior until after the sentence was written. This was a necessary but not a sufficient condition for the test. Equally important was the fact that the dumb trainer had spent at least some time with Sarah, not in language work but in play, for Sarah would not "talk" to strangers. Indeed, she would not accept lessons of any kind from people with whom she was unfamiliar.

The dumb trainer's code was a list of paired associates—pictures of the plastic words, each one associated with a number. On a production trial the instruction sheet told him which words to put out, for example, 4, 12, 3, 9, 16, 8, along with which objects, for example, a piece of apple. Sarah's task on these trials was her usual one: to request the object before her by writing a four-word sentence. After Sarah wrote out her request on the board, the dumb trainer translated the column of words into a sequence of numbers and, depending on the decision relayed to him through his earphones, either did or did not give Sarah the piece of apple along with a bit praise.

On each production test, Sarah was given a set of eight words, five of them relevant and three irrelevant. The items placed before her on each of three such tests were apple, banana, candy; candy, nut, cracker; cookie, banana, candy. A representative set of the words given her was: "give," "Sarah," "candy," "nut," "cookie," "John," "Debby," "eat." She was required to request the item placed before her with a four-word sentence of this form: "John give X Sarah," where X was the name of the object. The trainer's name was made known to her simply by hanging it around his neck like a medallion. Since this is how proper names were taught Sarah in the beginning, we were confident that she could make the necessary inference, and in fact she did. On the first, second, and third test of this kind, she made two errors in 16 trials, six errors in 20 trials, and two in 11 trials, or 87, 70 and 82% correct, respectively.

A second kind of production test consisted of simple questions of the following kind: "Red ? apple" (What is the relation between red and apple?); "Small ? nut" (What is the relation between small and nut?); "Square ? caramel" (What is the relation between square and caramel?); "Orange ? object orange" (What is the relation between orange and the object orange?), etc. Her alternatives consisted of "color of," "size of," "shape of," "name of," and "if–then," the latter being irrelevant in these tests. She made three errors in ten trials, or 70% correct.

On comprehension trials, the dumb trainer first placed a column of words on the board corresponding to the numbers on the instruction sheet and then laid out a set of alternatives, such as a red and a green card along with a pail and a dish. After Sarah chose an alternative, he relayed her choice to the hall and, depending on the information he received, did or did not reward her. On the first such test, a blue, a yellow, and a green card were placed before her and she was given the instruction "Sarah take blue," "Sarah take yellow," or "Sarah take green." On two lessons of this kind, she was correct on 11 of 15 and 12 of 17 trials, respectively, or 73% and 71% correct, respectively. On a second type of comprehension lesson, a yellow and a green card, a plastic cup, a cracker, and a pile of nuts were placed before her on each trial and she was given instructions of the following kind: "John insert yellow ⊃ Sarah take cracker," "John insert green ⊃ Sarah take nut," etc. She was correct on 7 of 10 and 8 of 11 trials, or 70 and 72% correct, respectively.

Fifty-eight different sentences were used in the present tests. That is probably not too many for a chimpanzee to memorize, and indeed Brown (1973) has proposed that that is what Sarah did. According to Brown, Sarah used nonlinguistic cues to learn individual sentences, rather than the rules underlying the language, and then stored the sentences in long-term memory; when any sentence reappeared on the present test, she had only to recognize it in order to respond appropriately.

Of the several things wrong with this proposal, consider two. First, by the time Sarah received the present tests she had experienced something over 2,600 different sentences. It was not possible for Sarah to predict which 58 of these 2,600 sentences would be on the tests. Hence, to pass the tests by the mechanism Brown proposes, Sarah would have had to memorize not 58 sentences but 2,600. Second, not all of the sentences used in the tests were among those Sarah had already experienced; 14 sentences or about 25% of the total were new. On new and old sentences, Sarah performed at approximately the 74 and 76% level correct, respectively (not significant at 5% level).

More surprising than the decrement in her accuracy was a deterioration in the form of her behavior. The most striking aspect of this deterioration was a regression to an earlier form of sentence production that was once her dominant form. Earlier in training she had not produced sentences in their final order but had put correct words on the board in incorrect orders and then rearranged them before settling on a final order (see pages 104–106). Although she had abandoned this mode of sentence production at least 10 months earlier, she reverted to it with the dumb trainer. In addition, the verticality of the sentences suffered. Ordinarily she placed words more or less below one another, but with the dumb trainer she failed to maintain this orderliness. The sprawling sentence was another characteristic of her early behavior.

At the end of the test period, it was necessary to test the dumb trainer, for it was possible that although he began uninformed he had learned the language during the course of testing. During testing he had the opportunity to observe which of Sarah's constructions were correct and which incorrect and to note the nonlinguistic conditions that corresponded with each. He was given a number of tests, of which the following four are both representative and revealing of his overall performance.

The first test, deliberately a weak one, asked merely whether he could distinguish a sentence from a nonsentence. Twenty of Sarah's words were arranged in 50 three-, four-, or five-word strings. Of the 50, 15 were sentences or acceptable strings; the other 35 were not. The dumb trainer had used all 20 words in testing Sarah and had seen all 15 of the legitimate sentences. Each of the 50 strings was presented to him one at a time and he was asked to say whether it was or was not a sentence. He was given no feedback on this test or on any of the others. In the 50 trials he made only eight errors, showing that in the course of testing Sarah he had indeed learned to recognize the sentences she had produced.

In the next test, the same 20 words were arranged into 50 new strings. Twenty-five were nonsense and 25 were sentences. This time, of the 25 sentences 23 were new to the dumb trainer. He made 20 errors in 50 trials, chance, indicating that although he could recognize familiar sentences he had not induced the grammar, i.e., could not distinguish a novel sentence from a novel nonsentence.

The next test given him was an exact duplicate of one he had given Sarah. A blue, a yellow, and a green card were laid out before him and he was given the instruction "John take blue," "John take yellow," or "John take green." He made 20 errors in 20 trials, the result of a consistent misassociation between the names of the colors and the colors. Next, he was given a test on Sarah's class concept words "color of," "size of," "shape of," "name of," which was an exact duplicate of the one he had given Sarah. He made nine errors in ten trials, again the result of a systematic misassociation between the words and their referents. The dumb trainer had learned some things but he had mislearned more.

Virtually all of the dumb trainer's errors were systematic, consistent misassociations between words and referents, whereas none of Sarah's errors were of this kind, suggesting that she did not even try to extract social cues from him, as she should not have for material as simple and presumably known to her as the material used in the dumb-trainer test. Moreover, Sarah performed as well on the first session, before the dumb trainer could have learned anything, as she did on later sessions. Such knowledge as the dumb trainer had acquired, therefore, could not account for Sarah's performance.

In view of the decrement that Sarah showed on the test with the dumb trainer, one could say that about 10% of her accuracy was attributable to nonlinguistic cues. Alternatively, one could attribute the decrement to disruptive features of the test, for example, to the aberrant latency between Sarah's production, on the one hand, and the dumb trainer's approval or disapproval, on the other, since this had to be relayed from the hall. My guess is that young children tested in the same way would show a similar decrement. There are several ways to resolve the issue. One is to do similar tests on young children. Another is to adapt the subject to aberrant latencies with normal trainers before giving the dumb-trainer test.

No matter how we interpret the decrement, however, the fact remains that Sarah's performance on the double-blind test is highly significant. The probability of choosing four words from eight alternatives and putting them in the correct order by chance is extremely small, one in 1,680. Chance expectancy is increased if we consider that, because the trainer's name is essentially told by the medallion, Sarah has only to choose three words from seven alternatives and arrange them in correct order; even then chance probability is still less than 0.5%, compared to her average percentage correct of 75. In contrast to double-blind tests reported for other chimps (Gardner & Gardner, 1971), this was a test for sentence production and comprehension, not merely one for vocabulary. In vocabulary tests, the subject has only to give the correct name for the object the trainer holds up, establishing in that way that it has learned to associate different responses with different objects. In view of the chimpanzee's capacity, however, is there any serious reason to doubt that it can learn to associate different responses with different objects? It seems that to be of interest the double-blind test must show more than lexical mastery.

3
The Physical Basis of Language

Because man is the only creature with a known natural language, we tend to assign a definitional weight to every aspect of human language. Yet it is equally reasonable to suppose that only some properties of human language are definitional and that others are secondary, adaptations to limitations of human information processing. The phoneme is surely such an example. Although it may be unique to man, and therefore one of several ways to distinguish human language from animal communication (Hockett, 1959), it is not a necessary condition for language. No syntactic or semantic distinction depends on whether the primitive level of language is the word or an element below the word. To assign a definitional weight to a property of language solely on the grounds that human language has the property is to adopt an unjustifiably ethnocentric view of language. It is tantamount to assuming that the only possible form of language is the human one.

The principal traits of human phonology, the phoneme and the auditory channel, are both parts of a solution to a common problem. Limitations on man's memory, on the one hand, and ability to generate discriminably different responses, on the other, make it impossible or highly inefficient for him to attempt to map a large world by devising an irreducibly different response for each word. Instead of attempting to generate and store 40,000 or even 5,000 different words, he produces instead only about 50 or so different phonemes. By combining these manageably few responses, he produces the large number of words needed to map his complex world.

The auditory channel also makes its contribution to the same problem: indeed, in an important sense it makes the combinatorial approach possible. Not the auditory channel per se, but the fact that the modality of man's language is different from the primary modality in which he perceives his world. If the modalities were not different, it would be impossible to distinguish at a glance a member of the language system from a member of the system referred to by the language. This simple distinction—telling a word from that to which the word refers—requires an inquiry of a kind that is difficult to appreciate if your experience with language is confined to the human case. Moreover, if the language modality and that of the primary perception of the world did not differ, the language might well end up iconic, not phonemic. Such a development would be in complete opposition to the need for a small set of meaningless elements—meaningless in the sense that they match nothing in the world—the combinations of which are used to produce words. However, the only arrangement that could fully guard against the iconic possibility is a disparity in modality, a difference in the channels in which language is expressed and the world is perceived. Therefore, a primarily visual organism, such as man, would require an auditory or at least a nonvisual language, even as an auditory organism, if there were one, might end up with a visual language.

However, the need to map a "large" world is not a pressure that a system must accommodate in order to qualify as language. Nor is it essential that the system serve an organism limited in such a way that a combinatorial approach to lexicon is necessary. Picture an artificial situation where the territory to be mapped is so slight that the number of words required does not demand a combinatorial approach, or an organism devoid of human limitations, capable of mapping an entire world with irreducible responses. Either augmenting the organism or shrinking the world could overcome the need for a phonemic level.

Do the basic functions of language require a world of human complexity, or can they be carried out in small spaces—arbitrary "corners" of a real world, or a diminished artificial world? Sarah had only about 120 words, although in all likelihood this could have been, say, 400 if the focus were vocabulary. But I have no interest in vocabulary per se, not a large one in any case. The more intriguing question is: What is the smallest lexicon in which it is possible to carry through all the basic functions of language?

ADVANTAGES OF WRITTEN LANGUAGE

Many of the reasons offered as to why animals may be unable to learn language reduce to engineering problems and can be eliminated simply by "building the bridge out of appropriate materials." For example, it has been suggested that the capacity for temporal patterning in animals is insufficient to support the heavy demands of syntax; this fails to observe that word order is dispensible and can be replaced by inflection. In addition, it has been proposed that in language the subject is uniquely dependent on his own behavior, responding not only to the outside world, but also to his own prior verbal behavior. Finally, Geschwind (1965), arguing from neuroanatomical considerations, has suggested that non-human primates are incapable of the high degree of intermodal association that words, auditory—visual associations, require.

Even if these claims are accurate, which I think is doubtful, they can be made wholly irrelevant simply by adjusting the physical basis of the language. One need only make the language written in order to bypass all three problems. A written language (1) utilizes spatial rather than temporal patterning, (2) gives each response a product so that the subject is not required to respond to his own behavior but only to products of his behavior (which products need not differ from any other part of the outside world), and (3) does not require intermodal (auditory–visual) associations. Given how easily these conditions can be bypassed, it is almost regrettable that they are not better founded.

Consider Geschwind's thesis, which is the most interesting of the three. If an animal were given food without being able to see what it was eating, it would be unable later to select on a visual basis the food it had eaten: correct choice would require an intermodal association, gustatory–visual. Moreover, because words in the present language are visual objects, no association should develop between any of the food names, for example, "apple," "banana," "grape," and the taste of the food; for these associations too are intermodal. But none of these implications is correct.

When Sarah was "blindfolded" and bits of concealed fruit were placed into her mouth, she was subsequently able to identify not only the fruit (on a visual basis) but also the names of the fruits. Required to pick the correct fruit from a set of four fruits and the correct name from a set of four names, she was correct about 83% of the time. But can we be certain that she has not stolen a glance at what is being placed into her mouth? We dyed pieces of apple red and green with tasteless vegetable dye and, concealing the food in the same way as before, placed into her mouth either a red or a green piece. She was unable subsequently to pick out the color of the fruit she had eaten. However, when we repeated the test, deliberately showing her the fruit before placing it into her mouth, she was then able to pick out the color fruit she had just eaten about 85% of the time. Other more elaborate tests described in Chapter 15 support the same point. Intermodal associations in apes were also demonstrated by Davenport and Rogers (1970), whose orangutans (*Pogo pygmaus*) and chimpanzees could select haptically presented objects that matched visually presented samples.

Nevertheless, Geschwind's hypothesis may still be defended on the grounds that, although the above cases are intermodal, they are not specifically auditory–visual. Indeed, in one of the few auditory–visual cases that I can find, a case both old and vulnerable to the charge of doubtful methodology, the chimps do fail to learn the associations (Kohts, 1935). In data that we recently collected, in contrast, chimpanzees not only learned auditory–visual associations but learned them on an incidental basis. The tests were suggested by observations made on retarded children. When retarded children are taught plastic words they frequently pick up the spoken English the trainers have used incidentally while teaching the plastic words (Carrier, 1973). The tendency of the human trainer to accompany nonvocal language symbols with speech is apparently strong, for in teaching plastic words to the chimpanzees trainers also have tended to speak the corresponding English words. Of course, the chimpanzees, unlike the retarded children, gave no evidence of having acquired speech along with visual symbols, for they cannot produce human speech sounds. However, when they were tested for comprehension, not production, we found that the chimpanzees had indeed acquired auditory–visual associations.

The tests were done in the context of match-to-sample, the sample consisting of a phrase in which the test word was embedded and emphasized—either "Give me (the) ___" or "Where's (the) ___?"—and the alternatives of some combination of three objects, pictures, or both. For example, on a representative trial the alternatives were a picture of Debby (a trainer), an actual coffee cup, and a ball. The trainer said to the animal either, say, "Give me the ball," or "Where's the ball?" using the word in a phrase because this was mainly how speech was used in training.

The tests were of two kinds, one requiring only a category level and the other an item level association. The categories used were agents (chimps and people), food and food-related items, and nonfood objects. The tests differed only in the composition of the alternatives. In the category form, each alternative came from a different category, as in the representative trial above where Debby, coffee, and ball each come from a different category. In the item form, all three alternatives came from the same category, for example, pictures of three different people or three different foods. Two forms of each test were given in counterbalanced order, involving a total of 36 different items with nine on each test.

The tests were given to only two subjects, Sarah and Peony. On the category form Sarah was correct on 12 out of 18 trials on both tests ($p < .05$, with three alternatives); corresponding scores for Peony were 12 out of 18 and 10 out of 18 ($p < .05$). On the item tests, Sarah was correct on 9 out of 15 ($p < .05$) and 8 out of 15, respectively ($p < .05$); corresponding scores for Peony were 9 out of 15 on both tests. Sarah performed somewhat better on the category (66.7%) than on the item form (57%), although the difference did not reach the 5% level. Differential feedback was given during the test, yet it is highly unlikely that the associations were formed during the test, since the same trial was repeated at most twice and sometimes not at all. Therefore, the associations were formed either on the basis of one explicit feedback, or as is more likely on the basis of incidental learning in the course of training. In either case there is evidence for auditory–visual associations in the chimpanzee.

PLASTIC WORDS ON A MAGNETIZED BOARD

The physical basis of the language used with Sarah and the other three subjects was plastic words arrayed in vertical sentences on a magnetized board. Words varied in shape, size, texture, and color and were metal backed so as to adhere easily to the board (Figure 3.1). A literal translation of the two sentences shown

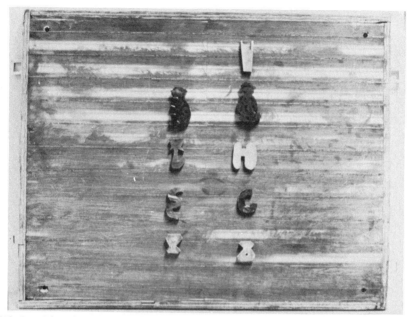

FIG. 3.1 The physical basis of the language. Each word is a piece of plastic varying in shape, color, size, and texture, backed with metal so that it adheres to a magnetized board. Sentences were written on the vertical. Literal translations of the sentences shown from left to right are "Sarah jam–bread take" and "No Sarah honey–cracker take." (From Premack, 1971. Copyright 1971 by the American Association for the Advancement of Science.)

in Figure 3.1 would be: "Sarah honey–bread take" and "no Sarah jam–cracker take." The vertical array is one of many ancient forms of writing (Hewes, 1949), still used by the Chinese, of course, but adopted here for reasons that have turned out to be nonessential. First, the vertical array seemed to be Sarah's preferred style. Second, we were uncertain as to the age at which the chimpanzee could distinguish right from left as opposed to up from down but thought that the latter would precede the former. Third, originally trainers and subjects were to write on different boards, across from each other. With this plan a horizontal sentence could have been a drawback, for if subjects had learned to produce sentences by duplicating the trainer's behavior, their word order would have been the reverse of the correct order. This problem does not apply to a vertical sentence. Actually, we ended up using the same board for all parties; Sarah's apparent preference for the vertical order was short lived; and because Sarah was already 5 years old when training began, it is possible that she was as able to distinguish right from left as up from down. But having started Sarah with the vertical sentence, we continued this format with Peony, Elizabeth, and Walnut for the sake of ultimate communication among them.

   Plastic words, in addition to involving a form of manipulation highly available to the species, offered two major advantages plus some minor ones. First, plastic words are permanent not transient, as they are in both vocal and gestural language, and sentences are displaced in space rather than in time. The permanence of the sentence makes it possible to study language without a memory problem and also to study memory in the context of language by regulating the duration for which the sentence remains on the board before the subject is allowed to respond. Memory could easily becloud the issue of linguistic competence. Tests of syntax and of complex semantic relations often require the use of long sentences or a number of sentences, and failures under these circumstances can be quite ambiguous. Was the subject unable to understand the sentences or simply unable to remember them? It is important to eliminate failures that result from nonlinguistic factors. We do not want to pronounce a species linguistically incompetent because it cannot produce human sounds, it is motivationally disinclined to carry out the instructions, or it cannot remember the instructions.

The second major advantage concerns the simple training program that is made possible by the plastic words. Because the subject merely uses the words, whereas the experimenter makes them, the words available to the chimp at any moment in time can be varied in any way the experimenter chooses. In the limiting case, the subject can be given only one word, thereby providing for errorless training. The word given the subject can be the answer to a question the experimenter poses or, in general, the word that exactly completes an otherwise incomplete sentence. At the other extreme, once there is reason to believe the training has been effective, the limits of a subject's knowledge can be tested by giving it sets of alternatives designed to maximize difficulty. Although comparable to a written system, the plastic words differ from the paper and pencil version in that the "speaker" cannot generate its own words but must obtain them from another organism. The subject forms sentences by combining words and is therefore a sentence generator. However, at the level of the word it is a user and not a generator.

In this system, unlike the human one, production need not lag behind comprehension. The subject is almost immediately proficient in causing the pieces of plastic to adhere to the magnetized slate and need not undergo elaborate motor learning in order to produce words or sentences. Therefore, training can occur in production as early as in comprehension. This can be an advantage in the training of young subjects, whose attention is often better controlled by requiring them to respond rather than merely to observe. More important, because the earliest training can be given in both the production and comprehension mode, the question of transfer from one mode to the other can be raised almost from the beginning (see Chapter 6).

The human infant is apparently innately sensitive to speech sounds (Eimas, in press; Morse, 1972), yet the complex phonological basis of natural language may greatly delay the onset of language. Deaf children of deaf parents are reported to produce their first signs by as early as 5 months (Schlesinger & Meadow, 1972). In addition, the normal child may acquire plastic words earlier than spoken ones. Mary Morgan, Sarah's favorite trainer, used Sarah's plastic words and training procedure to teach her 10-month-old daughter the names of four baby foods at a time when the infant's natural lexicon consisted only of "Mama." The child was taught to "speak" with the use of a large hole in the board attached to its highchair (see Figure 3.2). To obtain a particular food, the child was required to dispatch the appropriate plastic word into the hole in any way it could. At first, words were seized and mouthed. Slightly later they ended up on the kitchen floor. Ultimately, however, the child "shot" the plastic words down the hole accurately and with shouts of delight. The associative and memorial processes necessary for language may be available to the infant in advance of its phonological readiness. Since neither hand signs nor plastic words depend on complex phonological development, they may be acquired earlier than spoken words.

Because words are concrete visual objects rather than ephemeral sounds, processes that may otherwise be internal, subject only to inference, tend to be externalized. One such process is the organization the subject imposes on its lexicon. Although we have not yet tested the matter, if a language-competent subject is given a substantial supply of words, it seems likely that he would store them in a way that enhances their availability for sentence construction, or that he could be taught to adopt such schemes. The trainers have already done so. Instead of keeping their large supply of words mixed together in a one-celled container, such as a pail, they have stored them in a set of cells, each of which holds multiple tokens of any word. Neighboring cells are not a chance matter either but tend to carry out some organizing principle, such as food names or words of like grammatical class.

A second process externalized by the plastic words is the manner in which a sentence is generated. In a spoken or gestured language, the order of the words

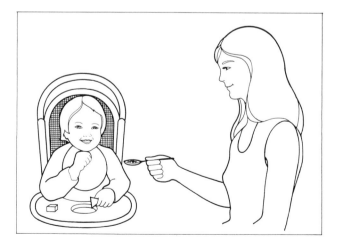

FIG. 3.2 Mary Morgan, principal trainer, teaching plastic words to her 10-month-old daughter. The child obtained a specific food by pushing the appropriate plastic word down the hole in the highchair board.

in the sentence is the same as the order in which the words are produced. That is, when words are distributed in time rather than space, the order of the product and the order of production are necessarily the same. But this need not be the case in a written language and especially not in the present version. Words placed on the board in one order can be rearranged, added to, or deleted before the subject settles on a final order. All the separate acts that go into the construction of a sentence, as well as the sequence of the acts, are externalized by the plastic words. As it turned out, Sarah and the other subjects built their sentences in an orderly way but, in the beginning, in a way different from that of the trainers. Sarah passed through two stages before finally arriving at the economical form of sentence production that the trainers had used from the beginning. All of these stages were made quite visible by the tangibility of the plastic words.

WORDS

A picture of a major part of the lexicon taught Sarah is shown in Figure 3.3. Every word differed from every other word on a multidimensional basis, except for two pairs "same–different" and "good–bad." Restricting these strong opposites to a unidimensional difference was the unintentional consequence of the strong language habits of the experimenter. One other class of words, personal names, was intentionally differentiated from all other words. Names of both chimps and people were made larger than other words so that they could be threaded and worn like a necklace, which is how they were taught in the beginning. (Later on, when certain sentences became too long for the board, personal names were shrunk by a factor of about two and a half, with no impairment in Sarah's ability to use them.) Visual onomatopoeia was almost wholly lacking; the obvious cases were scrupulously avoided. For instance, all color names were achromatic, names of the several shapes were not themselves square, round, etc., and fruit names bore no resemblance to their referents. Although occasional words took the shape of the first letter of their English name, for example, the words for honey, cracker, and jam looked like "H," "C," and "J," respectively, this was a mnemonic aid to the trainers and of no known benefit to the chimpanzee.

The avoidance of visual iconism was intended to show that the chimpanzee could learn totally arbitrary symbols. It was a step beyond natural language, however, for natural language is shot through with iconism or sound symbolism (Bloomfield, 1933; Sapir, 1929). American sign language is also heavily iconic (Schlesinger & Meadow, 1972). In the future, it may make more sense to study iconism rather than to avoid it and even to incorporate it in the language so as to give the chimps benefits comparable to those available to man.

Although all self-evident iconism was eliminated, it is not possible to say that there was no functional iconism in the language. No studies were made of the

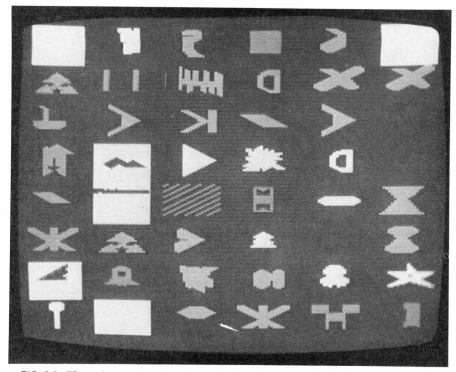

FIG. 3.3 The major portion of a lexicon of 130 words. These are not the plastic words but simulations of them produced by the visual symbol generator, outputed on the television monitor, and photographed from the monitor.

perceptual basis of the language and we cannot say, therefore, how the subjects actually discriminated one word from another. It may be safe to predict that despite the deliberate withholding of gross forms, the language nonetheless contained at least some icons. Because each word is a complex object, there was nothing to prevent the subject from abstracting features of the word that matched features of the referent. Consider a hypothetical piece of plastic that is round, yellow, pitted on the surface, and crenalated along the border. This piece of plastic might be thought to bear only a negligible resemblance to, say, apple, banana, strawberry, or prune and thus to be incapable of serving as an iconic name for any one of them. Yet the subject might attend selectively to the piece of plastic and, depending on which fruit the word was assigned to, abstract shape (round) for apple, color (yellow) for banana, texture (pitted) for strawberry, and border (crenalated) for prune, thus ending up in each case with an iconic relation between word and referent.

If there are any words that we can definitely say are not icons, names of color (or other properties) may be the closest case. Because colors are unidimensional values and the names of colors have been colorless, no similarities can develop between the word and its referent. However, this overlooks the possibility of metaphorical relations between wavelength and brightness, or even wavelength and size. For example, pink may go with a small word, red with a larger one.

Sarah did not place words on the board in a standard orientation (nor did the trainers). Although we have no quantitative data on the actual distribution of word orientations, observation and occasional movies made it clear that Sarah was highly variable in this regard. The word "yes," for instance, a thoroughly asymmetrical word, was used often and in virtually every possible orientation. The unimportance of word size was already mentioned. Personal names were shrunk by a factor of two or more, in order to accommodate long sentences to the board, without disturbing Sarah's understanding.

EARLY PHONEMIC SYSTEM

On an earlier occasion Arthur Schwartz and I described a phonemic system that might be used as a basis for an artificial language with chimpanzees (Premack & Schwartz, 1966). The apparatus is essentially a joystick that can be swiveled in all directions and tilted to a maximum of $40°$. Attached to the side of the stick is a small pressure gauge, registering strength of the grip on the stick.

An auditory circuit is connected to the stick, so that different sounds are produced by different stick positions. Both the stick as a motor system and the associated auditory system are an attempt to instance Jakobson's (Jakobson, Fant, & Halle, 1952) distinctive features model. Any displacement of the stick can be described in terms of five different motor dimensions. These are pressure on the stick, tilt (the angle the stick makes with the horizontal), displacement in the east–west direction, displacement in the north–south direction, and the duration the stick is displaced from resting position. With each of the five motor dimensions is associated an auditory dimension, although how best to correlate the motor and auditory features remains an experimental question.

IMPLICIT GRAPHEMES

Consider a system intermediate between the plastic words and the phonemic one above, a system of words with an implicit graphemic structure that can be made explicit at any time the experimenter chooses. This system would permit separating two demanding tasks, the acquisition of words, on the one hand, and of letters, on the other. The subject would begin by using words. Not until he is proficient in their use is he shown that words—which thus far have appeared to be solid units—can actually be broken apart.

Implicit graphemes can be readily incorporated in a system of plastic words. Each word would be built out of lesser pieces, more or less as a jigsaw puzzle, and then glued together until such time as the experimenter thought it advisable to dissolve the glue and disclose that the words were not solid but could be reduced to more elemental units. A small distinctive features system might be used to generate the elemental units. Using five dimensions, each in two degrees, all the letters or "lesser pieces" could be some combination of either (1) round or square, (2) large or small, (3) black or white, (4) rough or smooth, or (5) solid or with a hole at some point. These visual features can be combined to generate a set of visual objects quite as the previous motor–auditory features were used to generate a set of entities that could be described in either auditory or motor terms (see Figure 3.4).

Because the letters are generated on a systematic basis we may produce words in a similar fashion. Arbitrarily designating every round piece a vowel (V) and all other pieces consonants (C), we might use CVC, or variants thereof, as the word formation rule, for example, CV, VC, CVCC, CCVC. If the chimp's behavior were under the control of the word formation rules, it should be able to sort the plastic forms into three piles: (1) known words; (2) potential words, that is, forms compatible with the word formation rules; and (3) plastic forms that could not be words. The subject would not be burdened with letters until it was reasonably proficient in the use of words, which would be possible because the subject would not make the words but merely use them. Once the subject was proficient at the word level, the trainer could drop a few words into an appropriate solvent, inviting the subject to observe the words dissolve into their constituents. The experimenter could then reveal that all words, and not only the few in the solvent, were built up out of letters. He could discuss the matter with the subject because of the subject's already established proficiency with words. Pointing to the letters on the table, the trainer could inform the subject that "These are letters," "The larger units are words," and "Words are made of letters." Care should be taken to insure that all vocabulary and sentence construction needed for the instructions have been established through prior training. Only then should the words be dissolved and the subject shown that there is another level to the language. In principle, there are two advantages to this approach. First, the burden of learning both words and letters could be separated, with a likely benefit to both. Second, the learning of letters could benefit by the language already known at the word level and could be taught by explicit instruction, probably the most efficient training method of them all.

TYPEWRITER

When Sarah became sexually mature and potentially dangerous to work with directly, we needed a new system that would retain the advantages of the old one while avoiding what had become its dangers. A modified keyboard seemed to answer most of these needs. It also permitted automatic data recording, which had become a virtual necessity in view of Sarah's progress. For a long time we had wanted to give Sarah free rein with the language and simply see what she

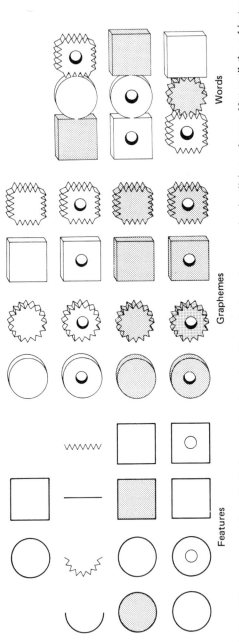

FIG. 3.4 Implicit graphemes. A hypothetical system based on four binary features for generating implicit graphemes. Not until the subject was proficient in the use of both words and sentences would the words be dissolved into their graphemic constituency and the subject taught the graphemes.

Features

Graphemes

Words

would do with it. Would she talk to herself through the day? Would there be presleep monologues such as the late Ruth Weir (1962) found with young children? Even if working in direct contact with Sarah had not become dangerous, we could not easily entertain these questions with the plastic words. Large amounts of data might have been recorded with intermittent pictures of the language board, but that has problems: ultimately someone must read the photographs.

A picture of the keyboard, showing both keyboard and the television monitor on which the words appear, is shown in Figure 3.5. A similar device has been reported by the Yerkes group (Rumbaugh & von Glaserfeld, 1973). The next months should reveal how suitable it may be, not only for Sarah but for language work with the adult chimpanzee in general. There are two keyboards, separate ones for the subject and the trainer—one in the cage and one out of it—but only one large overhead TV monitor on which messages from all parties

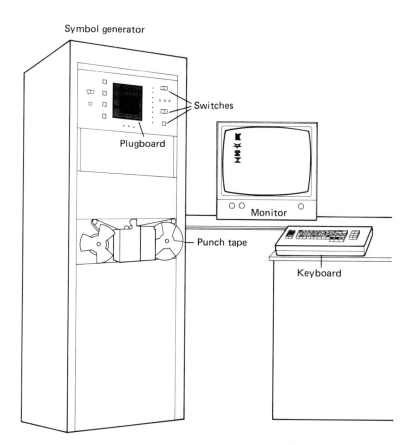

FIG. 3.5 Keyboard system, showing the visual symbol generator, colored television monitor, and a keyboard.

are displayed. The single screen is hoped to retain the advantages of the single writing board, which we found to be markedly superior to two boards. The young animal seems disinclined to look at a board on which it does not itself write.

The keys are marked with pictures of the plastic words, miniaturized to fit into the top surface of the keys. Actually, several keyboards, or one keyboard on which the words can be changed, are needed to accommodate even the present vocabulary of about 130 words. We tentatively considered approximately 60 words as the maximum number that could be effectively presented on one keyboard, and we have made some attempt to arrange them in a semantically sensible manner. For example, we placed verbs, object names, and personal names in separate locations. Although the fact that the subject is given only part of its vocabulary at one time partly defeats the purpose of the keyboard, the proportion of total lexicon that can be given in this way is far greater than any we have so far given Sarah with the plastic words.

The complication of adapting even a 130-word lexicon to a fixed visual representation immediately recalls the advantage of the graphemes we shunned at the beginning of the study. Now, of course, we would like to have them. Probably the basic question is not whether a preword base is desirable but when is the best time to introduce it. To teach an alphabet at the beginning puts the burden on the naive subject, seemingly the least appropriate victim. The implicit grapheme may be the preferred approach; it waits until the subject has mastered the system at the word level before introducing the preword level. Whether introduced early or late, however, graphemes seem to be needed if the system is to keep pace with the apparent ability of the chimpanzee. Notice that it is the success of the chimpanzee that recommends introducing a level more elemental than the word, and not its failure.

Words were "drawn" by inserting wires in the plug board device shown in Figure 3.4, selecting one of eight colors, and then placing the word into memory at a known location in the 1,024-symbol memory drum. The position a word took on the TV monitor was determined by prearranged rules. The first word typed appeared in the top of the leftmost column, the next word immediately below it, and so on until the sentence was complete, thus preserving the vertical format. The monitor consisted of an invisible 8 × 6 grid, providing for a maximum of six eight-word sentences. If the subject wrote a sentence of less than eight words and punctuated it with an end of sentence marker, the next sentence began in the adjacent column. If a sentence exceeded eight words, as relatively few did, it simply continued on into the next column. With the magnetic board, no explicit provisions were needed to separate sentences. Trainers and subjects simply started the new sentence alongside the old one, leaving space between them. But the keyboard could not detect the end of a sentence; the end of sentence marker was needed to enable the subject to signal the end of a sentence, automatically moving the next word to the adjacent column.

The trainer's ability to control the words available to the subject, an advantage of the plastic words, was managed quite directly with the keyboard. The trainer could darken and render inoperable any key he chose; a dark key could be depressed (and be recorded) but it would not have the normal effect of visually displaying the word on the screen. Indeed, this method had an advantage over the plastic words; with the keyboard the trainer could always take words away from the subject, whereas with the other system he was sometimes reduced to coaxing. This was not an unqualified blessing, however. Any loss of a degree of freedom for the subject is at the same time a loss of a possible datum for the experimenter. If the subject can no longer steal words—or cling to those given to it earlier—the experimenter can no longer observe the interesting fact of such thefts or attachments.

Other degrees of freedom were also lost with the keyboard. At an early stage of training all three female subjects, as noted, often formed sentences by rearranging the words they had placed on the board. Sarah abandoned this style of sentence production at an intermediate stage of training but reverted to it whenever stressed. Automated apparatus always loose degrees of freedom, for which the typical justification is the resulting automatic data recording. The justification is a trifle moot, however, for it overlooks the question of how valuable are the data that remain to be recorded. If we had started with the keyboard we should not have seen certain of the subject's capacities, for example, their ability to invent and carry out systematic rearrangements.

There is little relation between the chimpanzee's natural form of communication and writing with the plastic words. In the wild, communicants not only face one another, but at times the "speaker" may funnel his gaze, cries, and manual gestures into the face of his listener. When writing with the plastic words the speaker does not even face his listener, but faces toward the board and directs his words at it. This is a rarified form of language exchange, particularly when compared with the direct and even physically explicit forms communication can take. Just how direct communication can be was shown to me in a compelling fashion by an exchange with a child. The first of the several exchanges I had with the child took place when he was about a year old—able to walk only by concentrating on every step. Sitting in a friend's living room, I was distracted from our conversation by the sight of his child tottering toward me. As soon as the child reached my side, he looked at me earnestly and then pressed into my hand the damp remnant of a teething biscuit. The child and I had several exchanges of this kind, and in the course of them I learned to return the child's gaze unwaveringly, and to keep without reservation the well-chewed toy or biscuit—among the most deliberately bestowed of all gifts I was likely to receive in my lifetime. The child required that I acknowledge the gift unqualifiedly; a donor cannot consummate an act of giving unless the recipient acknowledges the donor's act. Also, to my experience acknowledgment was absolutely all the child wanted.

I tested this assumption on two occasions by reaching into my pocket and offering the child something in exchange, both times puzzling him so that he dropped the coin without fully receiving it the first time, and carried it only a short distance before dropping it the second time. Several years earlier I had made a similar test with my daughter; though made in a different circumstance, it produced basically the same result. As she pointed excitedly at the goldfish swimming in the bowl overhead—the fish being among her favorite objects—and shouted "ff! ff!," I took the bowl down from the shelf, held it at her side, and wordlessly bid her to reach in and take the fish. This invitation appeared to puzzle her in much the same way that the coin puzzled my friend's son. Her cries diminished and she did not fully resume pointing and shouting until I had restored the bowl to its place on the shelf. She too wanted nothing more than acknowledgment. (This incident is of additional interest for it suggests that some of the speech acts in the child's earliest communications are closer to being assertions, for example, "that's a fish!" than to demands, for example, "I want" or "give me the fish.")

In view of the bluntness of early communication, it is noteworthy that the chimpanzee can learn to realize its communicative intentions in a system as indirect as the plastic words. In learning that communication does not take place in the usual space between the speaker and listener, but on the board, the animal must learn both to write on the board and to observe what the trainer writes there. My impression from early pilot work, when Sarah and the trainers wrote on separate boards, is that Sarah often failed to attend to the trainer's board. Her attention became more certain later when we changed to a single board, and she and the trainer wrote in the same place. This impression needs to be confirmed by an actual study.

4
Early Failures

Not only did all four of the apes discussed here ultimately succeed in varying degree—making this account of their initial failure expendable—but our attempts to understand the failure themselves fail. It is success that can be explained, not failure.

The method used to teach words to Sarah and the other subjects evolved out of a number of false starts with Sarah. After trying one approach and then another, we settled finally on a method that was used first as a means of assessment and only belatedly as one of training. At an early point in Sarah's training we tried observational learning. Arthur Schwartz and I devised several scenarios that we thought would hold Sarah's interest. One of them, a homespun sequence that might be found in any nursery, concerned preparation of baby bottles; despite their advanced years, Sarah and her cagemate Gussie were then still receiving bottles. The other two scenarios dealt with feeding a bird and with crushing ice cubes. In all three routines, short "conversations" (between the trainers) were insinuated at would-be critical points—designed to bring the words (pieces of plastic) into effective conjunction with the key objects and actions of the routines.

In the homespun routine, one trainer brought out a bottle of milk; holding it up to assure that Sarah would see it, he was met with the request from the other trainer "Give milk." "Give what?" the first one inquired, as though he had not seen the two plastic words his companion had handed him. "Milk," was the reply, the repetition intended, of course, to give Sarah a second opportunity to observe the association between the milk bottle, on the one hand, and the piece of plastic intended to mean "milk," on the other. The rest of the routine continued the attempts to highlight an object on some occasions and an action on others, and in both cases to do so in conjunction with a particular word or piece of plastic.

The difficulty of establishing the boundaries of an act and of bringing a word into association with the desired portion of the sequence sometimes seemed insuperable. The verb "pour" provides a case in point. "Pour" was used in conjunction with filling the baby bottles, one trainer commanding "Pour milk," and the other carrying out the act. The visual events that came into conjunction with "pour" included: the trainer raising the baby bottle to a given height, centering the milk bottle on the baby bottle, pouring from the former into the latter, the milk rising visibly in the baby bottle, returning the milk bottle to the table, reading the miniscus on the baby bottle, sealing the latter with the nipple. Sarah and Gussie watched all of this quite closely, especially the reading of the miniscus, bringing to bear on the trainer's act an attention comparable to the one the trainer brought to bear on the miniscus.

With what components in this only partially described sequence was the word "pour" associated? More generally, what are the rules according to which a sequence is divided and a word is associated with an event contained in the sequence? One possibility is that a word is associated with all the material that is in view at the time the word is in view. Should the sequence continue, but no subsequent word be brought forth, no part of the sequence would then be associated with any word. Further associations would not form until a new word was presented, but new associations would form the instant the new word was shown, etc. In other words, the sequence would not be divided by properties intrinsic to the sequence, but solely by the arrival and departure of the words. I deliberately put the matter in these terms to suggest that, in fact, exactly the opposite must be the case. The sequence will be divided according to perceptual rules, and the resulting units will be available for association with words; but what constitutes a unit will not be affected by the arrival and departure time of the words.

EXCURSUS: PERCEPTUAL UNITS AND WHAT IS A RESPONSE

The question of how a sequence of action is perceptually divided into units, the components of which become associated with words, is in every respect like the old question concerning what is a response. Various authors have pointed out that although behavior is a continuous stream, it nonetheless has "joints" (Skinner, 1938), natural divisions, and that a response class is a unit in the stream bounded by such "joints." Interestingly, no one has ever described a joint or natural breaking point such that, if a Martian were turned loose on an Earthling's behavior stream, he could partition the stream at its joints. Nevertheless, we find few instances of unnatural responses in the literature, suggesting that we know a response when we see one, even though we have difficulty stating the criteria.

To divide a stream of behavior into its natural units, let us make two assumptions. First, access to a representation of one's own behavior is reinforcing; that is, it is easy to find acts that are less preferred than watching one's own behavior. Second, the reinforcement function will be maximized by a unique portion of the behavior stream, and that portion will correspond to the response unit. For example, consider that we have made a movie of the social play of two chimpanzees. One of them is subsequently given a lever that when operated, produces the previously made film, giving the subject an opportunity to observe itself play. However, lever presses do not produce the intact film, only preselected portions of it. Were Martians to use the above assumptions, they might literally cut the film at random points, trying each of the indeterminately many pieces for its effect as a contingent event. Relying on our intuitive knowledge, we could greatly shorten the test. For example, we are likely to find embedded in the behavior stream a unit we call a hug; two seated chimps face one another, each embracing the other with its arms. When a lever press produces the opportunity to see a hug from beginning to end, the increase in lever pressing is greater than if what can be seen is less than or other than an intact hug.

A nonveridical hug could be produced in several ways. The beginning of the hug could be shown but not the end; the end could be shown without the beginning; or the entire hug could be shown but in a discrepant order, the tape having been cut into pieces and spliced in a nonsentential order. A fourth way in which to produce a nonveridical unit is to synthesize a unit by putting together pieces of other units. For instance, a "monster unit" could be composed of fractions of hugging, eating, and urinating. In brief, we have four basic possibilities. The veridical unit; less than the veridical unit with the deficiency found either at the beginning, the end, or the middle; the intact unit but in a discrepant order; and the monster unit, built up of parts of several different units. The method for finding the natural joints of behavior streams is based on the assumption that these units have different reinforcement effects when used as contingent events.

Any of the nonveridical acts may have an inflated reinforcement value in the beginning, a novelty effect. However, the prediction is that, in the long run, the reinforcement value is greatest for the veridical unit.

After an organism has had ample opportunity to see the veridical unit, it may be interested in seeing distortions of the unit. Yet it may reject the distortions or assign a lower reinforcement value to them if it is not first shown the undistorted version. That such an order effect may obtain is suggested by observing children reconstruct the disassembled elements of a face or other familiar figures

(Premack, 1975a). Some children make a veridical reconstruction and then transform it, sometimes in ways that distort rather than conserve the figure. However, if these nonconserving transformations occur at all, they do so only after the child has first made a veridical reconstruction. Given that these properties occur in the child's production with visual materials, they may also show up in its comprehension of similar materials. These facts may prove useful in the tests made to discover the breaks in the behavior stream.

The hug is only one of the many units that can be used in describing a play episode; wrestle, somersault, jump, and ride on the other one's back are some of the others. Play is not the only behavior that would be so described, moreover. Comparable units would occur in the description of episodes of all kinds. In describing eating, for example, we speak of taking or seizing food, biting, chewing, and swallowing it. However, eating is not only an activity of the mouth. Especially when it occurs in a social setting, as it most often does, it is accompanied by a characteristic body posture, interpolated vocalizations of a given kind (muted cries of pleasure), facial expressions—configurations that often lead observers to laugh and make inferences about the motivational status of the eater, for example, "How smug Elizabeth is with her apple," or "Peony is gobbling it down before Elizabeth gets there." Segments of film that combine all the appropriate concurrent events presumably have greater reinforcement effect than those that leave out some or that introduce improper events, for example, vocalizations or facial expressions that do not normally accompany eating, or that present the events out of sequence. Several times in the past 10 years we have started research based on the present simple assumptions—access to one's own behavior can be used as a reinforcer, and the reinforcement function is maximized by specific portions of the behavior stream—but each time the effort has been aborted by an attempt to answer other questions with a higher priority. So it is still not possible to do more than recommend the assumptions as a possible way of operationalizing our intuitions about perceptual or response units, which, presumably, are the same thing seen from two different viewpoints.

In addition to the bottle preparation routine, we tried two other scenarios. In one, food was given to a caged pigeon, leading to an interesting clatter as the hungry bird pecked vigorously in the metal food dish. However, Sarah turned out to resent the bird's noisy feeding or to misunderstand it, for instead of showing an interest in being the one who fed the bird—the prerogative that was ultimately to be obtained on a verbal basis—she sought to grab or hit the bird, prerogatives we decided not to use as the basis for teaching vocabulary. In the other routine, ice cubes were removed from a tray, thrown back and forth across the room from one trainer to another with good manic side effects, and finally deposited in a plastic bag. One trainer then requested a wire from the other, bound the bag with it, and proceeded to crush the ice by slamming the bag against the side of the sink. Sarah watched closely. On those occasions when the bag did not tear, the ice was poured out into a container. Then it was offered to Sarah, who turned out to be quite fond of ice (as I remember many young children to have been when ice was not a routine item but was delivered on alternate days in a horse-drawn wagon). "Give," "milk," and "pour" were the major words in the nursery routine; "ice," "wire," "bag," and "crush" were the major words in the other routine.

A simple procedure was devised to determine whether, in observing the scenarios, she had learned any of the words that were used in them. Because the easiest words to test were those that named objects, such as "ice," "milk," and "wire," the test was made by putting out one item, such as an ice cube, along with two or more would-be words. The words were placed closer to Sarah than the item, and Sarah was required to give the correct word to the trainer or merely to push it toward her or him. When she did so, she was given the ice, milk, wire, or whatever item was present on the trial.

The early data suggested that the scenarios were not a complete failure; "milk" and "ice" were probably learned on an observational basis, although there was no evidence that any of the other words were. However, it was difficult to rule out conclusively that learning did not take place during the assessment of the observation trials. The two effects could be separated by rewarding either all or none of the responses made during the test; but these procedures were likely to undermine whatever learning there might have been. Moreover, our objective was not primarily to assess observational learning but to teach words. It was therefore not long before we abandoned the observational approach altogether and converted the procedure designed to assess the observational learning into the main training procedure.

EARLY LEARNING

Peony, Elizabeth, and Walnut were all given a series of first errorless and later choice trials on three different pairs of foods. The pairs were: apple–banana, raisin–date, and apricot–orange. Different amounts of training were given on the three pairs to determine whether what a subject learned varied with the amount of training it was given. The number of errorless and choice trials given the several subjects on each pair of foods is shown in Table 4.1. The basic procedure used was the same as that ultimately used with Sarah. All training was in the production mode. On errorless trials, one piece of fruit was put before the subject along with one word. The subject was to place the word on the magnetic board, after which it was given the piece of fruit. Choice trials differed from errorless ones only in that two words were given on each trial, in the presence of one piece of fruit. To receive the piece of fruit, the subject had to place the correct word on the board. If it placed the incorrect word on the board, it was told "No," was not given the fruit, and was either advanced to the next trial or, in the case of an anxious subject, allowed to correct and then advance to the next trial.

In the early stages, when the subject appears to be learning nothing, it must in fact learn a number of things. Procedures that do not work at first succeed later, indicating that something has changed in the subject. What are these changes? The two classical proposals are elimination of inadequate hypotheses (Harlow, 1958), on the one hand, and adoption of an optimizing strategy (Restle, 1962), on the other. Both interpretations are probably correct, but there is yet another aspect to the problem. Does the naive subject learn nothing in the beginning? This is itself a mistaken impression based on too restrictive a definition of learning. The subject is said to have learned nothing when, given a choice between two words in the presence of one fruit, it performs at chance; it gives no evidence of knowing what word goes with what food.

If we broaden our view of learning we will see that in the early stages of apparent total failure the chimp actually learns various things. A first suggestion of early learning came from data on Sarah's consistent disuse of nonsense words, that is, pieces of plastic that had never been paired with a referent. At a time when she did not yet know what word went with what fruit, two words on which she had been trained were presented with either of two potential words, and she was given 240 trials of this kind. Although she continued to respond at chance level on the old words, she never chose the potential words. Novelty could not have been the determining factor. In 240 trials, familiarity of potential words must have approached that of old words, yet her choice of potential words did not increase over the course of the trials but remained at zero. Therefore, Sarah could distinguish a trained from a potential word even though she had not formed any detectable associations between the trained word and its referent. Her ability to make this distinction raised the question of whether there were not other distinctions she could also draw in this period of apparent failure. As it turned out, the hypothesis could not be tested with Sarah, for by the time it was formulated she was no longer a naive subject. We were able to substitute Peony, Elizabeth, and their male colleague Walnut, however, because like Sarah they also appeared to learn nothing in the early stages of training.

We say the subject has learned nothing when, for example, it is given the would-be words "apple" and "banana" in the presence of apple on some trials and banana on others, and responds at chance level. By learning we have in mind an item–item or word–food relation. There are other kinds of information contained in the training situation, however. For instance, we could ask: Could the subject divide the items used in this situation into two classes, words and referents? Could the subject tell a word from a nonword, a referent from a nonreferent? Could it tell a word on which it had been trained from a potential word—an item that met the properties of a class but had not yet been linked to a referent—and could it tell a potential word from a nonword, a familiar referent from a potential referent, and a potential referent from a nonreferent?

These questions concern classification rather than associations between stimuli and responses. A subject who could answer the questions would have a knowledge of what a word was and what a referent was, knowledge which might be a prerequisite for the development of associations between members of the classes. Indeed, it is possible that associations cannot develop between members of the classes until the subject is first able to divide items into two classes and second able to distinguish members from nonmembers in the case of each class (see Underwood & Schultz, 1960, for a similar claim about learning which are the stimuli and which are the responses as the first stage of paired-associate learning).

Moreover, there is at least one association that may take priority over associations between specific words and referents. In our concentration on item—item relations, such as the associations between "apple" and the object apple, we overlook the possibility of a superordinate relation such as that between the class *word* and the class *referent.* Yet the superordinate relation may be a prerequisite for the development of associations between individual members of the two classes.

One way in which to get at the possibility of a superordinate relation is to ask whether or not the subject has formed a relation between the two classes and their respective operators. The knowledgable subject will eat members of the one class (without first trying to stick them on the board) and place members of the other class on the board (without first trying to eat them). This consistent application of the two operators to their respective classes is not, as we shall see, part of the original performance. Instead, it too is part of what must be learned in this situation. Moreover, as at least one example shows, it is learned before the subject learns any of the restrictive item—item relations in the exclusive terms of which we have tended to define learning.

We may also ask whether, during the failure to learn item—item relations, the subject has learned the apparent one-to-one character of the transaction, viz., that it is to place only one of the two words available to it on the board, in return for which it receives only one piece of fruit. In one sense, the one-to-one character of the word—referent mapping is instanced explicitly by the training: there are neither synonyms nor words with multiple meanings in the early training, so that each word always goes with the same piece of fruit, and vice versa. Yet, in another sense the one-to-one character of the word—referent exchange is only weakly exemplified. True, all exchanges are one to one, but there are no exchanges in which two words are traded for two referents, three words for three referents, etc. Why no such cases are included in the training is clear. Language does not, in fact, have this character—sometimes many words are required to get one piece of fruit—and it is strictly an incidental feature of the initial training that suggests it does. The one-to-one rule would nevertheless be instanced by the training and if tests were to show that the subject had induced such a rule, it would be informative but unfortunate, for the subject would have to be divested of the rule. Numerous relations, unintended by the trainer, may "hide" in all training programs and may be learned along with or in place of those which the instructor has in mind.

To test the chimp's ability to distinguish words from nonwords, a number of objects dimensionally similar to the plastic words, e.g., paper clips and erasers, were outfitted with small magnets so they too would adhere to the writing board. It was not necessary but we thought it more interesting to eliminate simple inadhesiveness as a basis for differentiating words from nonwords. Although perhaps not as distinctive as speech sounds, the plastic pieces were nonetheless a unique class, distinguishable from all other object classes in the chimp's environment. An occasional test object, for example, coin or marble, instanced some of the properties that characterized the plastic words, but few items instanced all of the defining properties, no more perhaps than the number of occasional environmental sounds that imitate speech sounds. (A problem that does differentiate this case from natural language is that words and things mapped by words belong to the same modality. See Chapter 3.)

WORDS VERSUS NONWORDS

Consider the tests given Peony, which were representative in all major respects. During training, members of a pair were consistently presented only with each other—for example, "banana" was the only would-be word presented with "apple"—and this arrangement was maintained throughout the present series. Because apple—banana was the pair on which she had received the most training, the first test was made with it. Despite 128 choice trials, plus a total of 90 errorless trials, Peony still had formed no detectable association between the words and fruits. Could she nevertheless distinguish the would-be words "apple" or "banana" from nonwords? Six nonwords were introduced—magnet, ice-cream stick, car, box, eraser, paper clip—all approximately word size and all either metallic or given a metal backing. She was given 20 trials consisting of a nonword paired with a word in the presence of either a piece of apple or a piece of banana; each nonword was presented at least three times with each word. When she responded correctly she received the fruit and otherwise not, as in the original training. Following tests on apple—banana, she received the same kind of test on raisin—date, and then on apricot—orange, pairs on which she had received an intermediate amount and the least amount of training, respectively. She made a total of three errors in 60 trials, with two on the first problem, one on the second, and none on the third. Even the three errors were probably not true errors but simply attempts to see whether or not the new object would stick to the board. In chimpanzees, an error evidencing a mistake in judgment is typically accompanied by visible displeasure. The signs vary from a pout or merely a trembling of a lip to stomping and pounding heralded by piercing screams.

Peony's "errors" were not accompanied by any such signs and therefore were more probably explorations than mistakes. The ability to distinguish words from nonwords—at a time when the subject had not learned a single word—referent association—was not confined to Peony. As Table 4.1 shows the other two chimps gave largely comparable results.

POTENTIAL WORD VERSUS NONWORD

In the next test series, potential words were substituted for words and the subject was required to choose between members of the word class (on which, however, no training had been given) and nonwords. Four new pieces of plastic were assigned as the names of pineapple, cherry, pear, and grape, respectively. (For Elizabeth and Walnut, who were tested somewhat later, "fig" was substituted for "grape" because grapes were out of season.) Peony was given 20 trials, ten pairing "pineapple" with nonwords in the presence of pineapple and ten pairing "cherry" with nonwords in the presence of cherry. She was given comparable tests on "pear" and "grape," the other two new words. She made one error on each test, of a kind indicative more of exploration than of a mistake in judgment. The other subjects performed comparably.

WORD VERSUS POTENTIAL WORD (WITH THE LATTER INCORRECT)

The consistent disuse of the nonwords could be based on recognition of class properties or merely on a difference in familiarity between would-be words and nonwords. In the next test series, potential words were substituted for nonwords and the subjects were required to choose between words (on which training had been given) and potential words. A potential word was physically a full-fledged member of the class "plastic words"; it differed from a trained word only in that it had yet to be introduced in training and therefore had yet to be used as a word. Twenty trials were given on apple—banana: ten in which the potential word "blackberry" was paired with "apple" in the presence of apple, and ten in which it was paired with "banana" in the presence of banana, with the two kind of trials intermixed. Comparable tests were given on raisin—date and on apricot—orange. The old word was always correct, there being no trials on which blackberry or the fruits corresponding to the other new words were presented. Peony made two, eight, and zero errors per 20 trials, respectively, on the first, second, and third test of the series, as shown in Table 4.1. Elizabeth was also correct on two of the three tests, but, more reasonably, failed on words for which she had been given the least training; Peony failed on the pair given intermediate training. Walnut was also correspondingly poorer on this test. It is

TABLE 4.1

Early Learning Results for Peony, Elizabeth, and Walnut[a]

		Production (incorrect/total)		
	Foods	Peony	Elizabeth	Walnut
Base data	Apple (A)/ banana (B)	61/128	36/64	30/70
	Raisin (R)/Date (D)	64/153	10/20	63/137
	Orange (O)/ apricot (A)	20/54	55/131	30/60
Word	A/B	2/20	0/20	2/20
Nonword	R/D	1/20	0/20	0/20
	O/A	0/20	1/20	5/10
New word	Pineapple (P)/ cherry (C)	1/20	2/20	0/20
Nonword	Pear/fig	1/20	1/20	1/20
Word	A/B blackberry	2/20	1/20	4/20
Potential word	R/D peach	8/20	5/20	10/20
	O/A grapefruit	0/20	0/20	5/20
Word	A/B, B	8/20	10/20	9/20
New Word	R/D, P	11/20	9/20	9/16
	O/A, G	8/20	5/12	9/20

		Comprehension (incorrect/total)		
	Foods	Peony	Elizabeth	Walnut
Base data	A/B	16/20	6/12	2/10
	R/D	16/40	10/20	17/40
	O/A	14/31	9/20	29/56
Fruit, nonfruit	A/B	22/80	1/20	4/20
	R/D	5/20	2/20	10/20
	O/A	3/20	1/20	5/20
New fruit, nonfruit	Cantaloupe/grape	0/17	2/20	1/20
	Watermelon/plum	2/20	1/20	
Fruit, potential fruit	A/B prune	3/20	0/20	6/20
	R/D cranberry	1/20	4/20	13/20
	O/A blueberry	2/20	0/20	0/20
Fruit, new fruit	A/B, P	11/20	10/20	4/40
	R/D, C	12/20	8/20	8/20
	O/A, B	11/20	9/20	

[a]From Premack (1973a).

more difficult to distinguish a word from a potential word, both of which fulfill the same physical properties, than to distinguish either from a nonword. This is essentially the same test given Sarah, and on which she never made a mistake, although in her case the potential words were not contrasted with either weakly or intermediately trained words but only with highly trained words.

WORD VERSUS POTENTIAL WORD
(WITH THE LATTER SOMETIMES CORRECT)

An additional test was made with the potential words, of a kind that could not be made with a nonword. Each potential word was advanced to the status of a word by being paired with a new fruit. For example, potential Words 1, 2, and 3 were assigned as the would-be name for blackberry, peach, and grapefruit, respectively. The training was given in the course of 20 trials on which the words "blackberry" and "apple" were offered, half the time in the presence of blackberry and half in the presence of apple; the words "blackberry" and "banana" half the time in the presence of blackberry and half in the presence of banana; and finally the words "apple" and "banana" half the time in the presence of apple and half in the presence of banana. Trials were mixed and approximately equal numbers given on the three pairs of words. Comparable tests were then given on the new word "peach" and the old words "raisin–apricot," and finally on the new word "grapefruit" and the old words "apricot–orange."

Peony performed at chance on all three tests (see Table 4.1). Her error distributions were not the same for the three tests, however. In the first test, "blackberry" paired with either "apple" or "banana," almost all errors came from a consistent disuse of "blackberry." In this performance she held firm to her "rule" from the first test with potential words, viz., never take the new word. Now, however, she held to this even when the fruit present was blackberry. She put either the word "apple" or "banana" on the board despite the presence of a new fruit. This would seem to be compelling evidence of her failure to associate either "apple" or "banana" with their respective referents, except for the fact that when the alternatives were "apple" and "banana" she made only one error in eight trials. The latter suggests that perhaps she was finally learning this most heavily trained pair of words. [Further suggestion to that effect came from a preference test given at the end of the present series. The two fruits Peony chose most often on paired comparison tests involving 8 different fruits were apple and banana (33 out of 62, significant at $p < .01$ with 8 alternatives); the two words she chose most often on independent paired comparison tests of words (with fruits absent, of course) were also "banana" and "apple" (30 out of 62). There was no evidence that any other of the words had been learned. For example, the least preferred fruits, orange and raisin, were chosen only nine out of 62 times, whereas the corresponding words were chosen 22 out of 62 times.]

On the second and third test of the series she no longer desisted from using new words but chose "peach" in the one case and "grapefruit" in the next almost as often as she chose old words. Also, in contrast to the first test in this series, she was no longer more accurate on old than on new words. Elizabeth showed this same tendency to an even greater extent; only on the last test in the series did she use the new word "grapefruit"; on the preceding test she never chose either "peach" or "blackberry" but chose old words exclusively. Walnut, at the other extreme, showed no avoidance of new words; he chose them with the same frequency as old words in all three tests in the series.

Although the results in this series—new versus old words—can be given several interpretations, one of them is of special interest. Clearly we find it convenient both for the sake of thinking about the results and for discussing them to divide the words into the categories "old" and "new." Chimps may engage in a similar classification (as inescapably and unthinkingly as we do). Such a division of the stimulus world would leave the animal with two response dispositions of quite different strengths. Members of the class "old" have been rewarded 50% of the time; members of the class "new" have never been rewarded and should have no response strength except for that derived from either preferences and/or generalization through physical overlap between members of the two classes. If the subject can distinguish members of the two classes, it should be more likely to choose "old" than "new" words. Both females showed this bias, although the male did not.

Once the subject was rewarded for choosing a new word, however, this should increase its disposition to respond to other new words. That is, reward for using a new word should have this effect provided the subject coded words as "new." If, instead, it coded them in terms of salient features, e.g., color, then reward could not increase the subject's choice of new words. Because the female subjects did show an increase of this kind, it seems reasonable to grant them, in this case at least, use of the same "old–new" coding device that we find so convenient to use in discussing the results.

COMPREHENSION: REFERENT KNOWLEDGE

In the next series of tests we shifted to the comprehension mode and raised the same questions concerning referents that we had asked earlier concerning words. For example, could the subject tell a referent from a nonreferent, a potential referent from a nonreferent, a potential referent from a used or familiar referent? In the production mode, to which training had been restricted to this point, the trainer placed two words before the subject along with one piece of fruit; the subject was required to place the correct word on the board. In shifting to comprehension, the trainer for the first time put a word on the board and two pieces of fruit before the subject. What should we require the subject to do, given this change?

The strongest requirement would be a reversal of roles: when the trainer puts a word on the board, the subject should regard it closely and then hand over to the trainer the fruit named by the word. This is an improbable outcome, however, for more reasons than one. The chimp has had no training whatsoever on comprehension; even the training it has had on production has not yet achieved its objective, viz., word–referent associations. Nevertheless, with no more training than it had the chimp might still respond appropriately to the shift in mode, if the present situation were not so thoroughly lacking in the essential factor that underlies role reversal in normal communication. In the wild, chimpanzees routinely engage in what amounts to a reversal of the speaker–listener roles (Teleki, 1974a). When chimp A has no meat, it is likely to extend its cupped palm and beg from chimp B, which does have meat, even as, when the distribution of food is reversed, chimp B will beg from chimp A. Although the trainer has put a word on the board—and so can be said to be extending his palm—there has been no accompanying reversal in the social relations between trainer and chimp. The trainer is still obviously in control of the fruit: why should he now request it of the chimp? In effect, if the chimp is to give fruit to the trainer in this situation, it must realize two conditions: appreciate the reversal in roles entailed by the shift from production to comprehension but also infer that the situation is one of play, such that though the trainer is as much in control of the fruit as ever, he is pretending not to be. In fact, chimpanzees are capable of both independent acts, pretense or duplicity, and reversal of role but are not necessarily capable of combining them in this situation or any other.

We left Peony to her own resources at first, because we did not know what to expect of her. She was brought to the test room and deposited on the table next to the writing board in the usual way. The trainer placed the word "apple" on the board, called Peony's attention to the word, and then placed before her pieces of apple and banana. Peony hesitated for a moment, then picked up the piece of apple, touched it to the board, and ate it. The trainer, laughing nervously, remonstrated Peony sharply, to the extent at least that her laughter would permit. She got out the materials for the next trial, this time placing the word "banana" on the board with an even broader gesture, designed to call Peony's attention to the fact that a word was already on the board. Peony was still more hesitant, whimpered, but carried out the same behavior as before. She smeared the piece of banana on the board as though encouraging it to stick there but then put it into her mouth and ate it.

Because requiring the chimp to hand over fruit was motivationally unreasonable and interfered with the questions we wanted to answer at this time, we reduced the demand. Peony was required only to point to or touch the correct piece of fruit, after which, if she was correct, the trainer gave it to her. She was shaped largely by guidance. The trainer brought Peony's hand to the piece of fruit, but no further, and then gave her the fruit. The eventual gesture was a kind of pointing or throwing of the hand in the direction of one piece of fruit or the other. Peony repeated her original act twice after the shaping on the first lesson and on two other occasions, once on the second comprehension lesson and once again on the third, but thereafter she responded only in the required manner.

Unfortunately, neither Elizabeth nor Walnut, who were tested later, were as bold or inventive as Peony. Although also left to their own resources, at first they did not respond at all. Both looked at the pieces of fruit but did not move toward them. When coaxed by the trainer, Elizabeth gingerly took one of the pieces of fruit and ate it. Walnut took both pieces. After a few trials of this kind, both subjects were shaped in the same way as Peony and comprehension tests were carried out with them using pointing or touching as the index response.

What the production training appeared to have taught Peony to this point was something along these lines: "You can get fruit in this situation by placing something on the board." This was a reasonable conclusion in light of the original training, since Peony had been taught that she could not simply take the fruit but had first to perform a designated act. Peony appears to have assigned a greater weight to the act of placing something on the board than to the outcome of that act, viz., word on the board.

In a sense this conflicts with the methodological decision, following Skinner (1938), to define response classes in terms not of their action or form but of their outcome or product. Experimenter convenience may be served by this decision, but it should be recognized as basically a methodological decision, not to be confused with a substantive claim. Despite the experimenter's decision to ignore action and to code it in terms of its effect, the subject may assign greater weight to the action than to its effect. This may even vary with the case so that action may be salient sometimes, products of the action other times. The point is not to condemn methodological decisions but to caution against confusing them with substantive claims. The classical example of this sort of confusion is the once stoutly defended claim that associations can develop only between stimuli and responses. Given that all evidence in psychology must ultimately make contact with the subject's responses, it would be a great methodological convenience if the claim were true. But there is no substantive reason why it should be true. The construction of an organism does not rule out associations between stimuli and stimuli or responses and responses, and the controversy becomes even more pointless when we recall that associations are never between stimuli or responses but are necessarily between their internal representations.

Peony and the other subjects were given tests on knowledge of the referent class analogous to those given on the word class. Referents were contrasted with nonreferents, all of which were foodstuffs, however, and some of which were fruits. Potential referents (fruits not yet used in training) were contrasted with nonreferents (all foods, but no fruits); and finally, trained or actual referents were contrasted with potential ones. Peony's performance was generally comparable to her earlier performance on the word class, although her error level was higher, as may be seen in Table 4.1. Results for Elizabeth and Walnut were generally comparable.

In this period, all the subjects were at chance on the comprehension of item—item relations no less than on their production. For example, Peony made 145 errors in 325 trials on production, and 46 errors in 71 trials on comprehension—chance on item—item relations in both modes. Nevertheless, she could tell a referent from a nonreferent, a potential referent from a nonreferent, and a potential from an actual referent in all three cases. All the foods used as nonreferents were ones she had experienced, indeed relished, outside the training situation and included cookies, potato chips, Fritos, and several vegetables. Moreover, the overall results could not be attributed to preferences: in tests made outside the language training situation, all three subjects showed a preference for most cookies over most fruits. Also, quite interestingly, in the tests in which lime was pitted against cookie (potential referent vs nonreferent) Peony chose lime on every trial but quit after only 17 trials instead of the usual 20. On the first three trials she ate the small piece of lime, but on the last 14 trials, although she chose lime, she did not even put it to her mouth. She chose lime as the "appropriate kind of thing to take in this situation," despite the fact that she neither ate it nor made any attempt to take it with her after leaving the test situation.

STIMULUS GENERALIZATION

The choice of words over nonwords, potential words over nonwords, and words over potential words might be explained by stimulus generalization. Words had received 50% reward, greater than that for nonwords; moreover, familiar words, coded either as "old" or in terms of physical features, had received more reward than unfamiliar pieces of plastic. What cannot be explained by generalization, however, is the order in which various relations have been learned. The subjects had learned to select certain plastic objects and certain referents, at a time when they had not yet learned any specific associations between the plastic objects and the referents. Perhaps this is just a matter of difficulty. The level of attention required for the formation of specific associations may be greater than that required for learning the class properties, on the one hand, and for distinguishing between actual and potential members of the classes, on the other. Is this appeal to two levels of attention an explanation, however, or merely another way of describing the results?

A further difficulty for stimulus generalization comes from some early, and so related, observations on Sarah, made before she had learned a single word, indeed before the project was funded. One morning Arthur Schwartz and I were standing in the corridor before Sarah's cage, surveying the mottled scene, wondering how it would strike a site visit team that was expected soon. We were sipping coffee, something we had not done previously in Sarah's presence, while staring balefully into the cage, paying less than the usual amount of attention to its occupant. Shortly we noticed Sarah reaching out from the cage, more or less waving her arm at us. She proved to have a monkey pellet in her hand, an object about the size of her plastic words, and the only object of that dimension available to her. Her waving a pellet at us was a novel act, as was our drinking coffee in her presence. To guess what she had in mind required only putting the two novelties together. We accepted the pellet from her and then offered her a sip of coffee. She accepted the sip and returned almost immediately with another pellet. We took this one from her and gave her another sip. After four or five such exchanges, we gave her the rest of the coffee; the hypothesis was not one that could be proved further on this occasion.

Ordinarily the above case would be seen as an impressive example of transfer or stimulus generalization. The generalization would appear to be of more than usual interest because it concerned both items in the relationship, that is, both the wordlike monkey pellet and the referent-like coffee, whereas in most generalization studies only one stimulus is changed, for example, a bird trained on yellow is tested on red.

The monkey pellet could be considered wordlike on three grounds: (1) dimensional properties—they were about the same size and weight as the plastic words; (2) location—the sink top was the site of the language lessons at this stage, and words were spread out there during the lesson even as monkey pellets were poured out there as a food supply during other times of the day; (3) relative value—most important perhaps, coffee was preferred to the monkey pellets even as the food or prerogatives that Sarah received for the plastic words were preferred to the words. Indeed, if they were not, she could not be expected to use the words as she did.

Coffee can be considered food or referent-like because chimpanzees can obviously identify eating or drinking when these acts are instanced by man. When the chimp observes man eat, it shows the same eagerness to have a bite that it does when it observes a conspecific eat. Experiments in the social facilitation of eating would show this conclusively. Indeed, if facilitation were proportional to the status of the model, observing a trainer eat might have a more appetizing effect than observing one's cagemate eat. Chimps are not alone in being able to identify eating on the basis of human exemplars; both monkeys and dogs can also do this.[1]

In the light of the abundant apparent similarities between words and monkey pellets, on the one hand, and coffee and food, on the other, Sarah's apparent

---

[1] Of the species capable of identifying eating on the basis of human exemplars, how many can make the same identification for one another? For example, can the chimp or dog identify eating in one another, or in the bird? Is ingestion a behavior that species are exceptionally good at identifying in one another? What could be learned about the evolutionary relation of various behaviors from their cross-species identifiability?

case of transfer may seem more inevitable than impressive. However, there is a serious mistake in regarding the case as a standard example of transfer, explicable in terms of generalization. Normally, we speak of transfer when a subject has been taught a relation, say, $A-B$, and then chooses the same relation without training on A_1-B_1. In this case we have A_1-B_1, the association involving items for which there has been no training, but we appear to lack $A-B$, the trained relation. That is, her use of monkey pellets to obtain coffee is not properly viewed as transfer for there has been no word—referent relation from which to derive the transfer.

This problem could be overcome by acknowledging that classification—words versus nonwords, etc.—is not the only prerequisite for the formation of associations between specific members of the two classes. In addition to distinguishing between words and referents, the subject apparently forms a superordinate association between the two classes and only then proceeds to form associations between specific members of the classes. In the present case, we could define $A-B$, the association from which A_1-B_1 was derived, as an association between the class word and the class referent; in effect, any word can be used to obtain any referent. Then the pellet—coffee case could be seen as transfer—derived, however, from a class—class relation instead of from the usual class member—class member relation for, according to all the evidence, there were no specific or class member associations at the time.

If the subject learns different things in the early and late stages, classification in one case, associations in the other, perhaps the training should be adjusted to these differences. Methods optimal for the formation of associations may not be optimal for the development of classification. It would greatly strengthen the whole argument concerning differences in what might be learned in early and late stages if it were possible to show training procedures that would optimize one outcome rather than another. But my efforts in this direction have been largely unsuccessful.

Because my attempts to devise stage-specific learning procedures were unsuccessful and as a failure deepened my suspicions of the whole argument, I tried two entirely different approaches to the problem of accelerating early learning. One of these, which I now believe to be definitely on the right track, is the major substance of Chapter 15 and so is not discussed here. The other approach, which I describe here, is of little theoretical consequence although it may be of practical benefit.

ICON

Iconic relations are learned faster than arbitrary ones (e.g., Fouts, 1972) and in one of several attempts to accelerate early learning, we tried to exploit this fact. In the original design of Sarah's language we deliberately sought to eliminate iconism, to duplicate the presumptive arbitrariness of natural language in order to show that the chimp's capacity for symbols was not limited to the iconic case. Forcing chimpanzees to use a language based on a thoroughly arbitrary word–meaning relation is somewhat ironic in the light of recently revived evidence for sound symbolism in natural language. It will be amusing if the only language that preserves would-be classic arbitrariness turns out to be the artificial one designed for the animals.

Using icons to speed up learning is suggested by comparing the swift learning of match-to-sample, on the one hand, with the initially slow learning of words, on the other. Match-to-sample requires the subject to select from a set of objects those that it (and the experimenter) consider to be alike; typically the chimp learns to do this in one or two sessions. However, if the subject can rapidly associate like objects it should also be able to do so in that special case where one of the objects happens to be a word and the other a referent.

To train the subject in iconic words we found it easier to make the word like the referent instead of vice versa. Initially we planned to use plastic fruits as names for the fruits, but the trainers who were charged with the task of finding cheap artificial fruits cleverly took the opposite approach. They made the fruit like the words. Previously apple had been cut in small wedges, bananas in slices, etc. Now apple was cut in the shape of a small triangle and dyed blue with tasteless vegetable dye; banana was cut in the shape of a small square and dyed red, these being the shapes and colors of the words in question. We confined the tests to those cases in which the fruit could be easily made to conform to its plastic name. Apple and banana were one of the pairs we started with, cantaloupe and pear the other. We used one old and one new pair deliberately to see whether by chance the method would work better with a familiar than with an unfamiliar case.

Peony, Elizabeth, and Walnut were given match-to-sample training on apple–banana and later on cantaloupe–pear (cantaloupe was actually a substitute for coconut, which cut and dyed nicely but which was abandoned when Peony refused to eat it). A basic trial consisted, as before, of putting two words (say, "apple–banana") in the presence of one fruit (say, apple) and requiring the subject to choose the correct word. Peony and Walnut were willing to put the word on the board but Elizabeth, a generally skittish animal, was disturbed perhaps by the commingling of two procedures, words and match-to-sample. She was allowed simply to place the correct word in the trainer's hand and so to make a more explicit barterlike word–object exchange, which, in fact, was the earliest training procedure used with Sarah.

The subject's general proficiency on matching like objects carried over to this case, at least in part. On the noniconic cases Peony, Elizabeth, and Walnut had been correct 58, 53, and 56%, respectively. After 250, 245, and 100 trials, respectively, on the iconic cases, they were correct 72, 64, and 68%, respectively (all significant at $p < .01$). The improvement was probably not simply the result of increased training, for all the subjects were quite stable on the noniconic baseline when the iconic training began. Moreover, in the case of Walnut, at least, when trials on the noniconic cases were interpolated at an even later stage, he fell all too readily to chance. Why did all three subjects perform less well on these tests than on conventional matching? Perhaps because the plastic words and matching fruit were merely similar, whereas in conventional matching the sample and correct alternative are the same. If the difference between "same" and "similar" is the explanation the magnitude of the effect is surprising, for on simple matching they have typically performed at the 90% level.

Each animal was trained a bit differently in a manner suited to its progress; the overall results are summarized in Table 4.2. All three subjects survived the removal of the shape cue, involving such transitions as triangle to wedge in the case of apple, square to circle (banana slice) in the case of banana. For Elizabeth, color and shape were removed at the same time; for Peony and Walnut, color was removed after shape and was in both cases removed in two steps, first diluted and then eliminated. Although both Peony and Elizabeth survived the removal of color, Walnut did not. After color was restored, Walnut recovered at least part of his earlier gain. He was then given a number of iconic trials with interpolated noniconic ones, five of the latter in every block of 20 trials; his average on the noniconic trials was about 61% correct. Walnut was retired from further language training until months later, when conventional training was resumed and with ultimate success; he now has a vocabulary of about 15 words.

Of course, the objective of the iconic series was not merely to train in iconic words but to see whether doing so would facilitate the learning of noniconic words. Icons as such are inefficient (no one wanted to go on cutting and dying the fruit so that it would match the words) and worse, it is questionable whether such concepts as tense, logical connectives, or interrogative vs declarative submit

TABLE 4.2
Icon Training with Peony, Elizabeth, and Walnut

| Chimp | Base (%) | Icons[a] | | | |
		Complete icons (%)	Color; shape faded (%)	Shape faded; color fading (%)	Natural fruit (%)
Peony	58	72	70	77	76
		(250)	(314)	(285)	(59)
Elizabeth	53	64	–	76	75
		(245)		(629)	(306)
Walnut	56	68	69	76	61
		(100)	(206)	(110)	(120)

[a]Number of trials is given in parentheses.

to iconic representation. In principle, the facilitation could take either of two forms:

1. Having acquired the "general idea" of using specific words to obtain specific referents, the subject would go on to acquire noniconic words more easily.

2. No general advantage of the above kind would be conferred but at least the subject would retain the iconic words that were taught it even after their iconism was eliminated.

The latter would seem to have been accomplished with both Peony and Elizabeth, although not with Walnut. Unfortunately, we have no simple way of evaluating the realization of the more general facilitation.

5
Later Success:
Mapping a Social Transaction

Human giving is unrestricted both as to the agents that can participate as donors and recipients, and as to the items that can be transferred (apparent exceptions are demonstrably cultural not biological: limitations found in one place and time do not reappear in other places or times). This contrasts with the restricted form that giving appears to take in most other species. Characteristically, giving is confined to the transfer of food. In addition, the exchange is restricted to caretaker and young, although some species expand on this narrow form, allowing food exchange between adults. Certainly, this is a minor elaboration, however, compared to human giving where any agent can give anything to any other agent, including even other agents.

The generalism of human giving is not unique to giving but applicable to all human acts, even as the restrictions on giving in nonhuman species appears to be applicable to other acts of the same species. However, the lack of generalism in the acts of nonhuman species does not appear to be entirely uniform. Many nonhuman species appear to be specialists, having one or more generalized acts, their other acts being high restricted. Only in man is every act a relation subject to the possibility of being instanced by every conceivable argument. The degree to which the ape approximates man in this regard is not known, although the approximation appears to be exceptional.

It is also not known whether the transfer of goods in chimpanzees is accompanied by taboos comparable to those found in human giving. It is evident that in Western culture, at least, human giving does not confer full perogatives of ownership. For instance, you are not to pass on to another recipient something only recently given you, and especially not if the second transfer is likely to be discovered by the original donor. Although this constraint may be culture-specific, it seems reasonable to anticipate some form of constraint on giving in all human cultures. Whether there are comparable social constraints on chimpanzee giving is unknown at this time.

The act of giving is subject to variation at three points—object, donor, recipient, independently or in combinations—and we have so far varied only the object, changing the fruit from one trial to another and accompanying each such change with a change in the word or piece of plastic intended to serve as a word. This same procedure can be used to map the other perceptual classes in the give transaction. In principle the procedure is straightforward. Make only one change in the perceptual class at a time and accompany it with a change in the language element. Arbitrarily we turned next to the action class rather than to either the donor or the recipient. Fruit was no longer given when the subject wrote, say, "apple," but a two-word sentence was required, specifically, "Give apple."

In teaching Sarah the two-word sentence, the word "give" was placed before her as the only alternative. After she put "give" on the board she was offered the word "apple," which she already knew. With a little guidance, she put it below "give," forming her first two-word string, "Give apple" and was given the piece of apple. She was taught to write "Give banana" in the same fashion.

Then she was given choice trials with only one fruit present, along with the words "apple," "banana," and "give," requiring that she both choose the correct object name and use the correct word order. She chose correctly on 16 of 21 trials, about 76%, only slightly below her accuracy level of 80% correct in the simple choice between "apple" and "banana." The word-order requirement had a far more adverse effect on word choice in both Peony and Elizabeth (see page 78) Sarah made only three word-order errors, writing "Apple give" twice and "Banana give" once.

The fact that Sarah placed "give" in the appropriate location in the string did not, of course, justify assigning any meaning to the particle. If an organism sensed the correspondence between the behavioral elements, on the one hand, and the plastic pieces, on the other, it might conceivably have induced the meaning of the "give" particle. "Give" was not the name of either fruit, yet its use was a requirement for obtaining both fruits. In all likelihood, however, this information would be inadequate for even the most astutely inferring organism to arrive at the intended meaning of "give."

What evidence would justify making a semantic claim about the "give" particle? The best if not only evidence for this purpose is the kind used earlier in making semantic claims about the fruit names. We must teach Sarah the name for another action. Her ability to choose correctly between the two names would then support the claim that she knew the meaning of both particles. Ironically, in order to prove that the subject assigns a meaning to one particle, it must be taught meanings for at least two particles. The claim that it knows either particle is based on its appropriate choice between the two particles. Notice that this does not say that the subject who has been trained with only one particle cannot know its meaning. The problem does not lie with the subject. It is the observer's ability to know what the subject knows that seems to depend on a minimum of two alternatives.

To teach Sarah a second alternative in the action class, we put a can on the table along with the fruit, gave her a particle intended to mean "insert," and using the same procedure used with "give" induced her to write "Insert apple." When she did, we dropped a piece of apple in the can. Next we gave her the words "give" and "apple," making it possible for her to write "give apple," which she did. We then retrieved the piece of apple from the can and gave it to her. Sarah was not visibly disturbed by the delay but appeared to be at least somewhat interested in the trainer's shenanigans. This was true not only on this occasion but on the many similar occasions that arose in the course of the training.

We gave her a total of eight errorless trials on "Insert apple" and eight on "Insert banana" and followed each with the presentation of the words "give" and the name of the fruit, making it possible for her to request the inserted fruit. On the fourteenth such trial, the trainer removed only the word "insert," leaving "banana" on the board, and gave Sarah only the word "give." She put "give" above "banana" and was given the fruit. On the fifteenth and sixteenth trials, the trainer again removed only the word "insert" but this time gave Sarah both "give" and the name of the fruit, in a test to see whether she would take advantage of the word already on the board or would more or less mechanically write "give X," X being the name of the fruit. On both trials, Sarah responded in an economic manner, adding only "give" and producing the required "give X," much to the trainer's delight. Note, incidentally, that with these trials the range of "give" was extended. Originally "give" was applied only to objects that were visible on the surface; now it was applied also to objects that were invisible in a container.

We turned then to the question of interest: Did Sarah know the meaning of the verb particles? The can and a piece of apple or banana were placed before her along with the words "give," "insert," and one or the other fruit name. She wrote "Give X" on all ten trials. Although this could mean that she preferred direct to delayed receipt of the fruit and knew the difference in outcome associated with the action particles, it could also simply reflect the far greater number of times she had written "Give X" rather than "Insert X."

To cope with this problem, we added powered sugar to the can, so that when she wrote "Insert X," "Give X," she received a piece of sugared apple or banana. After 15 such trials, we repeated the former test, giving her "insert," "give," and one fruit name plus a piece of fruit and the sugar-filled can. In 15 trials she wrote "give X" 13 times and "insert X" (after which she was allowed to add "give") two times. This would appear to refute the conclusion that she knew the meaning of the verb particles, or it would certainly if she preferred sugared to plain fruit as we assumed. However, when we offered her a choice between equal pieces of sugared and plain fruit, we found that, contrary to our expectations, she did not prefer sugared fruit but was indifferent. In ten trials on sugared vs. plain fruit, her choices were six to four for apple and four to six for banana. Her use of "give" and "insert" (13 to two) was not concordant with her preferences; but that was confounded with frequency, which greatly favored "Give X" over "Insert X."

Despite the indeterminate test results, we adopted the sanguine position that Sarah probably knew "give" and "insert," and we added "wash" and later "cut" in the same way that "insert" had been introduced. In response to Sarah's successive commands—"Wash apple," "Cut apple," "Insert apple," etc.—a larger than usual piece of apple was first washed, then cut, inserted in sugar, and finally given to the subject.

The fact that the actions named were components in a sequence rather than independent alternatives explained much of the difficulty we had in obtaining the desired evidence. Members of the fruit class were independent alternatives, each of which could be requested by the appropriate word. But the actions were members of a sequence that always culminated in giving. Cutting, washing, and inserting were actions that Sarah tolerated, even with some interest, but only so long as they ultimately culminated in giving.

The whole problem was solved nicely at a later stage when we were able to use comprehension as well as production. Such instructions as "Sarah apple cut" or "Sarah apple wash" gave each act the status of an independent alternative, making the verification of semantic claims straightforward. In addition, we devised a procedure that made possible verifying semantic claims in the production mode. The trainer carried out an act (say, cut rather than wash) and the subject was required to describe the trainer's act, for example, "Debbie apple wash." These two procedures made it possible to assess semantic claims for action names in both modes. At this stage, however, Sarah was not yet trained in either procedure.

We made one last attempt to measure her knowledge of verbs before we moved on to a new topic. The measure sought to exploit the fact that the acts labeled were, as mentioned, members of a sequence. If the apple had been, say, washed but not cut, would Sarah show her knowledge of the words by requesting that it be cut rather than washed again, or inserted before it was cut? In brief, we brought the apple to various stages in the sequence, and at each stage gave Sarah a pair of words making it possible for her to request that the fruit be carried forward to the next step in the sequence instead of either repeating a step, skipping a step, or going back a step. We regarded the former as correct and indicative of a knowledge of both verbs and sequence and all of the latter as incorrect.

Sarah did not choose between the alternatives in a way that could be taken as evidence that she knew what word went with what action. On the contrary, her choices caused the sequence to skip, repeat, and retrogress—all the "violations" discussed above. Does this mean that she had not formed the desired associations?

If her choice of alternatives had consistently advanced the fruit one step, we could then have concluded that she had learned the desired associations. The converse does not follow, however, for it assumes that one sequence alone is admissible and that deviations from it can occur only from ignorance. That this assumption was untenable was shown during the course of the test. For instance, we considered it a major error (a sequence retrogression) to cause an already cut piece of apple to be dipped in water. But Sarah did not agree with our judgment. She ate fruit dripping with water as avidly as any fruit, and when this caused us to grimace, she took time off to look at us, before going back to her chewing. Although the test taught us little about Sarah's early verb knowledge, it did teach us something we should have recognized earlier. A sequence of action we considered to be inviolate was ordained by nothing more sacred than human preference. Rather than struggling further with the verbs, we left them and did not return to them until Sarah had been taught comprehension. Notice that the evidence collected to that time did not say that verb training had failed but only that we had no tests that said it had succeeded.

With Peony and Elizabeth, as with Sarah, we started with the object class in mapping the transaction of giving. The results for this phase, described in detail in the preceding chapter, can be summarized as follows: Peony was given 98 and Elizabeth 95 lessons on four consistently paired sets of fruit names—apple versus banana, orange versus grape, raisin versus date, and cantaloupe versus pear. Peony was given a total of 168 errorless and Elizabeth 228 errorless trials over the four pairs of words. From the beginning, Peony was shown a piece of fruit, with two words on the table in front of her, and was required to put the appropriate word on the board. Elizabeth's jitteriness was accommodated by requiring her merely to hand the word to trainer at first and only later to put it on the board. The disparity in errorless trials between the two animals is explained by the same factor. Hundreds of errorless trials were used in adjusting the emotionally unstable Elizabeth to carry out the "spooky" response of causing a piece of plastic to adhere to the board.

Following errorless trials on each of the four pairs, Peony made 825 errors in 2,097 choice trials and Elizabeth made 466 errors in 1,147 trials. Despite the protracted failure to learn specifically the word—referent relation, both animals finally mastered all the desired associations.

The first words had been trained as fixed pairs for hundreds of trials, offering a good chance to determine whether a deficit would result when the words were presented in new combinations. With Sarah we did relatively little fixed-pair training but on one of the few occasions that we did, we found a deficit when the words were recombined to form new pairs (see page 185). Perhaps this deficit depended on having contrasted a set of words for an unusually long period. Peony and Elizabeth provided an opportunity to answer this question, for some of their original food names were contrasted exclusively with one another for over 1,000 trials, longer by far than the contrast maintained between Sarah's color names. Nevertheless, when the food words were recombined to form three new pairs, Peony performed at the 75%, 80%, and 85% level compared to her previous average on the four fixed pairs of about 81%. Corresponding figures for Elizabeth were about 75%, 80%, and 80%, compared to about 79%.

TWO-WORD SENTENCES

In teaching Peony and Elizabeth the two-word sentence, "give" was placed on the board by the trainer and the subjects were required only to place the fruit name below it, a slight modification on the procedure used with Sarah. Peony was given 60 and Elizabeth 113 errorless trials on this procedure, using eight different fruit names. On some of the errorless trials a slightly different procedure was used; "give" was placed on the table, closer to the board than the other words, encouraging the subject to place it on the board first. Following the errorless trials, "give" was taken down from the board and added to the fruit names, and the subject was required both to choose the correct food name and to compose the order of the two-word sentence "Give X."

Peony and Elizabeth were trained first with only two-food alternatives, and then with three, the alternatives being drawn from a set of eight fruit names. On this early series Peony chose the correct food name 103 out of 115 and 82 out of 112 trials per total trials, or 90 and 73% correct on the two- and three-food alternative trials, respectively. Corresponding figures for Elizabeth were 118 out of 142 and 100 of 153, or 83 and 65% correct. Accuracy fell in both subjects with the addition of the third alternative but remained well above chance. Word-order accuracy improved with the addition of the third alternative, apparently more helped by practice than hindered by the increased alternatives. (Neither the length nor the complexity of the sentence, which remained a mere two-word string, was increased by the added alternatives, so there was no reason for word order to suffer from the added alternatives.) Peony made 21 word-order errors on the first 150 trials with two food–name alternatives and only four word-order errors on the next 112 trials with three alternatives. Corresponding figures for Elizabeth were 19 word-order errors with the first 140 trials and only 9 on the next 142 trials.

Because obtaining evidence on verb contrasts in an early training stage poses difficulties, we reserved this step for later and instead advanced to the three-word sentence by requiring that the recipient be specified. Peony was given 6 errorless trials and Elizabeth 40 errorless trials on sentences of the form, "Give X Peony" and "Give X Elizabeth," respectively. The errorless trials were carried out in two stages. After first being shown a piece of fruit and required to write

"Give X," where X was the name of the fruit, they were given either "Elizabeth" or "Peony" and required to add their names, thus producing "Give X Elizabeth (Peony)." Passive guidance was used to assure that they added their names appropriately to the bottom of the string.

Before being given choice trials on their names, they were made responsible for the word order on the three-word string. The proper names were added to the alternatives and they were required to write "Give X Elizabeth (Peony)." Only one food name alternative was present, along with "give" and the proper name, so that the only errors possible were those of word order. Peony made no errors in the five trials she was given; Elizabeth made two errors in 19 trials. In the next step, two food names were presented (along with "give" and the subject's name); Peony made seven errors in 31 trials; Elizabeth made 14 errors in 36 trials. Five of Peony's seven errors were of order and two were of choice; 13 of Elizabeth's errors were of order and one was of choice. The word order errors were as follows:

Errors	Frequency
"Give Peony X"	4
"X give Peony"	1
"Give Elizabeth X"	7
"X give Elizabeth"	3
"X Elizabeth give"	3

It is of interest that adding a second food name, and so introducing a choice requirement not present in the preceding phase, seriously impaired word order. The impairment occurred even though (1) the added alternatives did not in any way increase the complexity of the sentence called for—it remained a three-word string—and (2) the subjects made relatively few errors on choice per se. Notice that in discussing these results we find it convenient to distinguish between choosing the correct words, on the one hand, and arranging them in the proper order, on the other; however, the data suggest that the subjects do not themselves make a comparable separation of the two tasks. Although we did not explicitly teach them to separate the tasks, the general manner in which they were trained, different somewhat from that used with Sarah, would seem conducive to doing so. They were allowed to correct errors of order but not those of choice. That is, if a subject put correct words on the board in an incorrect order she was allowed to rearrange the words. However, once the subject put an incorrect word on the board, whether it was the first, second, or third word, all words were taken down and the trial was terminated. The penalty thus imposed on an incorrect choice should, it seems, have inclined the subject to make word choices "early"—before it has put any words on the board. If it did, this would be tantamount to separating the two tasks. If the tasks had been separated, however, word-order errors should not have arisen when new alternatives were added; because they did, there is no evidence that the subject separated the tasks.

In both subjects, the dominant word-order error, accounting for over 60% of all errors, was "Give recipient X" as opposed to "Give X recipient," an inversion between direct and indirect objects. This was Sarah's major error, too, as shown by the data discussed later in the chapter (page 97). Both orders are acceptable in English, and later in training we accepted both. In Sarah's case we were eventually forced to do so by trainers who succumbed to English, thus intruding the patterns of that language into Sarah's. When both orders were accepted, Sarah came to use both, although interestingly, with one trainer who never veered from the original restriction, Sarah used only the originally accepted word order.

FOUR-WORD SENTENCES

Word-order accuracy was burdened by the request to specify the recipient and declined in Peony from 96% correct word order on the two-word sentence to 75% correct on the three-word sentence. The decline was still stronger in Elizabeth, for whom the corresponding figures were 92 correct and 64% correct, respectively. Nevertheless, both subjects were advanced to the four-word sentence, requiring addition of the donor's name and thus arriving at the target sentence, for example, "Debby give X Peony," "Debby give X Elizabeth." Errorless trials took the same form as those on the previous occasion. "Give X Peony" was written on the board by the trainer, and Peony was given the word "Debby" on ten trials and "Amy" on ten other trials, assuring that she wrote both "Amy give X Peony" and "Debby give X Peony." Elizabeth was given the same training.

In the next step all helper words were removed from the board and given to the subjects, requiring them to produce the four-word sentence from scratch. The difficulty of these tasks was then progressively increased by adding alternatives as follows: two food names; two donor names (but with only one donor present); two food names and two donor names (but only one donor present); two food names and two donor names (and two donors present); and finally two food names, two donor names, two recipient names (and two donors present). Peony made negligibly few word-order errors and no choice errors until faced with two donor names in the presence of both donors; then she made five errors in 20 trials. When faced with the last and most difficult of all the alternatives in the series, she refused to participate. After making two errors in four trials, she whimpered and could not be coaxed into coping with so large a number of alternatives. Refusal to contemplate lessons of unconscionable difficulty was not unique to Peony. Each animal had its sense of what was reasonable and could not be coaxed beyond it. We once confronted Sarah with a comprehension task in which six sentences appeared on the board at the same time, the minimum number needed to establish whether or not she could determine who gave X to whom (see page 241). With the board fairly buried in words, she required only a glance at it before she leaped to the other side of the cage. The precise and unyielding nature of her refusal was Chaplinesque and we all laughed, but humor was all the lesson yielded. Only when all the sentences were removed from the board was she coaxed back to the lesson.

Elizabeth's performance in this early period was less certain than Peony's. When required to form a sentence from alternatives that included two food names and two donor names (along with the verb and her own name), she made 11 errors in 40 trials, both in choice of words and in word order. At the next higher level of difficulty, same alternatives but with both donors present, she made two errors in choice and four in word order in 11 trials. We withheld the still more demanding set of alternatives.

The word-order errors made by Peony and Elizabeth took the following form:

Errors	Frequency
"Trainer X give Elizabeth"	8
"Trainer Elizabeth give X"	4
"Trainer give Elizabeth X"	3
"Give trainer X Elizabeth"	1
"X Elizabeth give trainer"	1
"Trainer give Peony X"	1
"Trainer X give Peony"	1
"Give trainer X Peony"	1
"Give X trainer X Peony"	1
Total:	21

Seventeen of the 21 errors could be considered both grammatical and sensible in English, i.e., interpretable as a sentence in which the subject instructed the trainer to give her the desired item. Four of the 21 erroneous sentences violated this condition; "give" occurred before the trainer's name, so that the sentences could be read as the subject instructing herself to give X to the trainer—which is certain not to have been the subject's intention. Even though word-order errors were still frequent, it was encouraging that most of the incorrect strings approximated the target sentence. Moreover, practice on producing sentences over the course of this series apparently benefited both subjects. On two-, three-, and four-word sentences, Peony was correct on word order 96, 75, and 85%, respectively; corresponding figures for Elizabeth were 92, 64, and 71%. When the variation in chance level is taken into account, this may be seen as a striking improvement.

Despite their partial success on the four-word string, both subjects refused to continue producing them. Elizabeth flew into tantrums when told the sentence was wrong, and Peony sulked and refused to work. It is perhaps no surprise that both subjects refused to continue using the four-word string. The training given them so far did not involve the explicit mapping of all four classes. Only the object class had been explicitly mapped. "Apple" had been contrasted with "banana," "banana" with "orange," etc. Both subjects had passed choice tests on these words, proving that the object names were associated with specific referents. But the other three classes had not been mapped in this fashion.

If learning were determined strictly by input information, with little inference on the part of the subject, "give" could have no clear referent and would be tantamount to a nonsense word. "Give" had not been contrasted with anything but had been simply introduced as a particle that had to accompany the object name in order for the subject to receive the fruit. Actually, the requirement was a little more specific than that. The particle had to precede the object name, not merely accompany it, and was a universal requirement, that is, there were not some fruits for which it was required and others for which it was not. With such experience what is the "give" particle likely to have meant to the subject?

Although the recipient and donor classes were not mapped any more formally than the action class, they were helped by supplementary information. Agent names were hung around each agent's neck—trainers as well as chimps—and there was not one such particle, as in the case of "give," but exactly as many as there were agents. Therefore, in the three-word sentence, for example, "Give apple Peony," the subject could observe the similarity between the terminal particle in the string and the particle that she wore during language lessons. In the four-word string it was also possible to observe the correspondence between the first particle in the string, e.g., "Amy give apple Peony," and the particle worn by the trainer who handed over the apple. Moreover, during the training of the four-word string, errorless trials were given in which the particles "Debby" and "Amy" were associated with the giving of goods by Debby and Amy, respectively. Nevertheless, no choice trials had been given that could inform both the observer and subject whether or not the subject knew the associations between the agents and their names and, if they did not know them, help the subjects learn them.

In summary, only the object class was explicitly mapped, that is, rotated through a series of contrasts each associated with a specific language particle, followed by choice tests demonstrating formation of the desired associations. Action, recipient, and donor classes were not mapped in the same explicit fashion, although the training situation did provide information that an appropriately inferential subject might have used to arrive at the referents of the other particles. For example, although there were different fruits and a name for each and different agents and a name for each, there was only one action; likewise, there was only one action particle, "give," and it applied to all fruit names.

After Peony and Elizabeth refused to continue with four-word sentences they were dropped back to two-word sentences (with recipient names available) for two lessons. On the third lesson, after they had effectively ignored the recipient particle for two lessons, both subjects reintroduced the recipient name themselves, henceforth writing "Give X recipient" instead of just "Give X." On the fifth lesson, donor names were readmitted to the set of available alternatives. Neither subject consistently adopted the optional donor particle as they had the recipient particle, yet both subjects did write occasional four-word sentences, for example, "Debby give apple Peony," even though they were not required.

VERBS

Comprehension lends itself better to teaching verbs than does production. For example, to teach "wash" the trainer can write "Amy apple wash," wash the apple herself, then follow this immediately with the reciprocal instruction "Peony apple wash," and hand Peony the apple. If the subject failed to imitate the trainer's action, modeling could be supplemented by passive guidance. There was little need to use passive guidance, however, because all the actions labeled were already in the subjects' repertoire and had been carried out in free play (see page 92).

Basically, names for actions were taught by exposing the subject to a set of objects, inducing the subject to respond to the objects in a canonical way, and then teaching the subject a name for its own act. For example, at one point a plastic apple was made available as the object to be operated on, along with three instruments—a knife, bowl of water, and an empty container with a slotted lid. These objects led the animals to carry out cut, wash, and insert, although, of course, the chimpanzee form of the act did not coincide perfectly with the human one.

Although the acts were induced largely by the objects themselves, their reliable occurrence in canonical form depended, in addition, upon a certain arousal level. The desired level was assured by installing the animal with a bit of ceremony alongside the writing board. However, the animal could be released from the school room arousal level by fairly minor departures from normal vigilance. Sometimes the trainer had only to lean back in her chair, replacing her normal expression with something more lighthearted, for the animal to ascend to a higher level. Generally the first thing to go was the independent occurrence of the three acts. For example, Elizabeth and Peony washed the apple but, while it was still in the water, they also stabbed at it, thus combining wash and cut. In addition they violated the neat separation between instrument (knife, bowl, and container) and object (apple) that we had imposed upon the situation; they not only cut with the knife but also washed and inserted the knife. Thus, when in an intermediate arousal level the animals did not so much carry out new acts as combine old ones. Even the use of the knife as an object rather than an instrument was only partly new; the washing and inserting, which had been confined to the apple, was simply extended to the knife.

The animals could be returned to their original arousal level by a signal no more intense than the one that had released them; simply leaning forward toward them was generally effective. However, they could also be led to a still higher arousal by amplifying the original signal, for example, by slumping lower in the chair, allowing one's grin to pass into open laughter or most effectively perhaps by egging them on overtly with appropriate gestures. Then wash, cut, and insert, the decorous set, disappeared altogether and whole new acts emerged. On some occasions Elizabeth masturbated with the knife handle; on other occasions she stole glances at herself in the reflectant surface of the blade. The bowl of water was tipped over and worn like a hat (cf. Premack, 1975a, for a perceptual rather than motor hat transformation). Neither animal any longer inserted anything into the empty container; instead they sat on it and rocked, causing the plastic lid to crack and pop with their rhythm.

The schoolroom arousal level was needed not only to assure the canonical acts but also to make teaching the names of these acts possible. The subjects were unlikely to learn names except when in a suitable arousal level. This would seem to pose a problem in teaching the name of, say, masturbation and other acts of high arousal. When masturbating, the animal is unlikely to learn words and, conversely, when learning words, is unlikely to masturbate. Yet, of course, this word is known to people along with the names of kill, copulate, and the like. However, using the subject's own acts as referents for the names of the acts, as we did with cut, wash, and insert, is not an approach that could be used to teach "kill," "copulate," etc. Names for these acts must be taught through reading or conversation. One might accompany the text with a picture, or even perhaps refer to a previously observed act carried out by other agents—for example, "you remember what those dogs were doing? that is called 'copulation.' " But neither one's own act or even the direct observation of the act by another one could be used as the referent for teaching the names of acts in these cases.

The acquisition of verbs in both Peony and Elizabeth passed through a course rather like that for the nouns, although fortunately a less protracted one. The difficulty was concentrated in the first few cases. "Give," the first verb taught, was taught in comprehension. Training began with errorless trials on both "Peony give ball" and "Peony give keys"; each instruction was given with only one object present and with the trainer extending her hand to receive the object. The ball and keys were used to circumvent the motivational problem that might have arisen with more valued items. Following two errorless trials on each instruction, both instructions were repeated in random order in the presence of both objects, and the subject was required to give the designated object. The difficulty the subjects found in these early lessons was reflected in Peony's record. Eleven lessons, approximately 16 trials per lesson, were devoted to teaching "give." The alternatives were varied somewhat from lesson to lesson—ball/keys, spoon/keys, ball/spoon, clay/apple—and occasionally increased from two to three, for example, ball/keys/clay. Peony made 50 errors over the 135 choice trials. Finally, on the tenth and eleventh lessons, choosing between three alternatives, ball/keys/clay, she gave the trainer the correct item on 14 of 20 trials (significant at the .01 level for three alternatives).

Elizabeth showed a comparable although less protracted difficulty in acquiring "give." After four lessons of approximately 12 trials per lesson, each lesson opening with a pair of errorless trials on each alternative, Elizabeth attained the 80% correct level in choosing among three alternatives. Both subjects acquired the remaining verbs in notably fewer trials. For instance, the most recently taught verb, "touch," was acquired by both Peony and Elizabeth in one lesson of 10 and 14 trials, respectively.

In carrying out the verbs or action names, the subject's behavior only approximated that of man. For example, when instructed to "Wash X," the subject dunked the item in water, sometimes releasing it so that it bobbed to the surface, or if the item was absorbent used it as a sponge, filling and squeezing it out, often repeatedly. "Wash" therefore meant operate on with water; any cleansing, the main human meaning of "wash," was accidental. "Cut" was another case in which the animal and human behavior only partly overlapped one another. "Cut" tended to mean poke at the item with the point of the (dull) knife, although ultimately all three female subjects did use a knife in the human manner. Of course, we could have undertaken to bend chimpanzee behavior toward the human standard or else sought more accurate English translations, speaking of "immerse" rather than "wash," or "poke" rather than "cut," but nothing in our objectives required that we convert chimpanzee ways of handling objects into human ones. It was sufficient for our purposes to divide the motor space into alternatives that were well defined for the animal. So much the better if the acts were easily and enjoyably performed by the animal.

A few acts were unsatisfactory in their original version and had to be modified. For example, taking per se was an act with which Peony and Elizabeth appeared to have little experience. They took things well enough but did not stop there. After taking them they went on to eat, play, insert, etc., instead of taking them and doing nothing further. "Take" was apparently not a terminal member in a chimpanzee response sequence so much as an intermediate member in many sequences. The difficulty both subjects had in using take as a terminal response was made especially clear by Peony's slow, deliberate style. Peony displayed her knowledge of "Take clay," for example, by holding the clay in midair until relieved of it by the trainer. "Take" at this stage had a beginning but no end, and was defined negatively, as consisting of not inserting, not cutting, not washing, etc. Both animals were finally shown that "Take X" could consist of putting X in one's lap or on the table between one's legs. Because chimps often tuck objects into the crease between their thigh and body, it seemed strange that neither animal adopted this movement spontaneously or simply put the object down beside it, as Sarah did in fact. My impression is that Sarah distinguished between her space and the trainer's, between her side of the table and the trainer's, even dividing the board into the side on which she wrote and the side on which the trainer wrote. Trainers came to Sarah's home cage to give her lessons, whereas Peony and Elizabeth were taken to a "school," where they were given lessons and little else. It is possible that in the "school" they had no sense of their own space, and for that reason were reluctant to put items down beside them.

"Insert," another verb with a troubled beginning, started out as an act that involved picking up an object and depositing it in a can. The can's wide mouth offered no resistance to any of the small objects that were put into it. In watching the subject, one saw its great hand hover over the surface of the can and then rather aimlessly release the object into the can. The action struck one as aimless because the subject did not attend to its own behavior—there was no hand—eye coordination. Moreover, while waiting for the trainer to set up the next trial, the subject carried out acts of insertion with fine hand—eye coordination. Elizabeth pressed into the tile on the wall behind her pieces of banana and other material she found about her, mortaring up the small holes with meticulous care. It was not this between-trial's act, however, with its superb hand—eye coordination, that was being associated with a word, but the aimless dropping of an item into an unresistant entry. The problem was solved by fitting the coffee can with a plastic lid in which a cross was slashed, so that resistance was encountered when an object was inserted. "Insert" was then learned rapidly and interestingly, once learned, was transferred to containers that did not have resistant entries.

COMBINED NOUN—VERB CONTRASTS

The verbs taught Elizabeth and Peony included names for the actions of give, take, insert, cut, wash, tickle, kiss, and draw or mark. Some were taught as noun (or object) contrasts, for example, cut: apple/banana, and then transfered to verb (or action) contrasts, for example, cut/wash: apple, whereas others were taught as verb contrasts in the first place. Once Peony and Elizabeth passed the individual contrasts, the two kinds of contrasts were combined. Typically, the initial effect was a substantial increase in errors but one that declined over successive tests. Elizabeth's first exposure to the combined case involved the action names, "give," "take," and "insert," on the one hand, and the object's names "keys," "apple," and "banana," on the other. "Insert" was associated with an action that depended on the presence of a container but the other two verbs did not entail any identifying materials. All of the individual words were reasonably well known as judged by the standards of Elizabeth's generally spotty record. The impact of the combined alternatives can be appreciated by observing her performance on an immediately preceding verb contrast test. When given "give/take/insert: keys" for the first time, she was correct nine out of 12 times, which is well above chance, and when the test was repeated the following day she made no errors in five trials. Then a plastic apple was added to the keys and she was tested on "give/take/insert: apple/key." She made three errors in seven trials, with two errors on the action and one on both action and object. Despite her poor performance, we added a plastic banana, so that the materials before her included keys, plastic apple, banana, and a container, and then tested her on "give/take/insert: apple/banana/keys." She made two errors in three trials, with one error on both the object and the action. A partial repeat of this series failed to help much. When tested again at the end of the series on "give/take/insert: apple/banana/keys" she made five errors in ten trials, with three on objects and two on both. Although significant at the .05 level (for six alternatives), it was an unimpressive performance.

Instead of repeating the training, we decided to attempt to reduce its difficulty. One way of doing so, we thought, was to name each target object—keys, apple, banana—by pasting the name of the object on the object. With each object's name written on it there should be no problem in selecting the correct object; the difficulty of the task should collapse into that of a verb contrast. For instance, when told "Elizabeth, apple take, " she could match "apple" in the instruction (on the board) to "apple" attached to the actual apple and would then have only to decide whether to take, give, or insert the apple. As we might have guessed, however, this seemingly reasonable analysis did not apply to the skittish Elizabeth. When tested on "give/take/insert: apple/keys" with both keys and apple labeled, she made 12 errors in 15 trials, exactly chance. When tested the following day with only one object alternative "give/take/insert: apple," but that one labeled, she made 12 errors in 16 trials, whereas when retested in the same way but with the label removed she made only two errors in 12 trials. Labeling objects still seems a reasonable idea, a crutch by which at least some subjects benefit, although with such a subject as Elizabeth it is seldom possible to find effective forms of intervention.

A more clear-cut effect of combining noun and verb contrasts was seen in the data from Peony. Her first test of this kind was made with the verbs "take" and "insert," and the objects apple, crayon, and ball. The series proceeded as follows:

Instructions	Correct per total trials
1. "Take/insert: apple"	11/12
2. "Take/give: cup"	10/12

3. "Take/insert: crayon"	4/5	
"Take/insert: ball"	9/10	
"Take/insert: crayon/ball"	2/5	(two errors on action, one on object

Various portions of the series were then repeated as described:

Instructions	Correct per total trials	
1. "Take/insert: crayon"	4/5	
"Take/insert: ball"	5/5	
"Take/insert: crayon/ball"	4/5	
2. "Take/insert: crayon/ball"	8/12	(one error each on action and object and two on both)
3. "Take/push: crayon"	4/5	
"Take/push: ball"	5/5	
"Take/push: crayon/ball"	4/5	(error on action)
4. "Take/push: crayon/ball"	6/10	(two errors on action, one on both)

A second series, involving the actions cut, insert, wash, and take and the object's apple, banana, crayon, and ball, proceeded as follows:

Instructions	Correct per total trials	
1. "Insert/cut: apple"	8/12	
2. "Insert/cut/wash: banana"	9/12	
3. "Insert/take: apple"	11/12	
4. "Insert/cut/wash: apple"	17/20	
5. "Insert/take: crayon"	4/5	
"Insert/take: ball"	9/10	
"Insert/take: crayon/ball"	2/5	(two errors on action, one on object)
6. "Insert/take: crayon"	4/5	
"Insert/take: ball"	5/5	
"Insert/take: crayon/ball"	4/5	
7. "Insert/take: crayon/ball"	8/12	(one error on action, two errors on object)

A third series proceeded as follows:

Instructions	Correct per total trials	
1. "Wash/cut/insert: banana"	9/12	
2. "Wash/cut/insert: apple/banana"	9/10	
"Wash/cut/insert: apple/banana/sponge"	6/10	

A fourth series proceeded as follows:

Instructions	Correct per total trials	
1. "Push: marker/key/clay"	9/11	
2. "Push/take: crayon"	4/5	
"Push/take: ball"	5/5	
"Push/take: crayon/ball"	4/5	(error on action)
3. "Push/take: crayon/ball"	7/10	(two errors on action, one error on both)

A fifth and final series proceeded as follows:

Instructions	Correct per total trials
1. "Touch/insert: apple"	5/5
"Touch/insert: apple/banana"	9/10

On the first and third test of the series, the second being a repeat of the first, Peony performed at chance level on the combined tasks, although in both cases her performance improved with repetition. More important, on her subsequent exposure to new combined tasks, e.g., the third, fourth and fifth tests in the series, she performed significantly above chance. Therefore, although when first exposed to new combinations of established nouns and verbs she performed at chance, in later tests on equally new combinations she performed well above chance.

DESCRIBING THE TRAINER

Elizabeth and later Peony were taught to do productive description, that is, to watch the trainers carry out various acts and then to describe the act. The trainer's acts were simple: cutting a piece of fruit, dunking an object in water, inserting an object into a container—acts that in all cases the subjects had performed themselves in either free play, response to linguistic instruction, or both. The objective was to teach the subjects to describe with words acts carried out by the trainers, which acts they themselves had previously carried out in response to the trainer's words.

In an earlier phase, trainers had written, say, "Elizabeth apple wash," and Elizabeth had washed the apple. Now when a trainer washed the apple, Elizabeth was taught to write "Amy apple wash." Both subjects were taught in the usual way, by starting with trials on which they were given only the correct words— and so were responsible for word order alone—and then progressing to other trials on which they had to select the correct trainer name, action name, object name, and finally combinations of all three. All the sentences the chimps wrote on those occasions described the trainers' immediately preceeding behavior and could be said to answer the question "What did I do?" although the question was not actually made explicit. Both subjects mastered productive description, although for reasons that were unclear it was difficult to induce Peony to use language in this manner. She would request items reliably and generally answer questions, but she was least inclined to use language descriptively. Elizabeth showed no such reluctance.

SELF-DESCRIPTION

After Elizabeth became relatively proficient at describing the trainer's behavior, we wondered whether she could be induced to describe her own behavior. She was provided with two kinds of items: such behavior supports as a bowl of water, a knife, a can with a lid, and a plastic apple, on the one hand, and a set of words, including "Elizabeth," "wash," "cut," "insert," and "apple," on the other. So provisioned, she began by engaging in free play, cutting or actually stabbing the apple as it floated in the water. After a time, however, she became restive; the lesson situation was one in which she normally received food, and although tidbits were visible, so far she had not received any. Moreover, she could not request any of the food, for the words needed to make requests—for example, "give" as well as the name of the trainer—were not available to her. She turned to the word for apple, inserted it in the can, stabbed the plastic apple again, and, when the word "apple" was returned to her, inserted it again. These acts produced no food, however, and she was now close to a tantrum. At this point, the trainer pointed to the writing board. Elizabeth then wrote "Elizabeth apple." A moment later, she picked up the word "cut" but seemed not to know what to do with it, until the trainer again pointed to the board, whereupon Elizabeth added "cut" to the words already there, forming the sentence "Elizabeth apple cut." The trainer then gave Elizabeth a small piece of apple from the dish nearby and did so on all other occasions in the lesson when she made a complete sentence, whether it was an accurate description or not.

Elizabeth then carried out three trials on which she cut or stabbed the apple and following each such act wrote "Elizabeth apple cut." In the remainder of the lesson, Elizabeth washed, inserted, and cut the apple 20, 18, and 16 times, respectively. On two of the 20 occasions on which she washed the apples, she wrote "Elizabeth apple wash;" on three of the 18 occasions on which she inserted the apple, she wrote "Elizabeth apple insert"; and on six of the 16 occasions on which she cut the apple she wrote "Elizabeth apple cut."

All of the above sentences were written after the act was carried out, directly after. However, there were other occasions on which sentences were written and then an act followed the sentence with equal directness. For example, on one occasion she dunked the apple in water, after a moment wrote "Elizabeth apple cut" and then speared the apple with a knife. On another occasion, following an interval of undefined play (wild play that did not fit neatly into our code), she wrote "Elizabeth apple insert" and then inserted the apple. On a third occasion she wrote "Elizabeth apple wash insert," and then inserted but did not wash the apple. On a fourth occasion, she wrote, "Elizabeth apple cut wash," and then first washed, that is, dunked the apple and then cut it, or speared it with a knife.

Although the majority of her acts were not accompanied by linguistic behavior—54 acts and only 13 sentences—both the sentences that followed and those that preceded an act were accurately related to the act. All nine sentences that directly followed acts correctly described the acts they followed, and the four sentences preceding acts that directly followed described the acts correctly either in whole or in part.

Can we say that sentences which preceded the acts that followed were, in effect, a statement of her intentions? I suspect that this is the case but I can see no way to prove it. To put it bluntly, we can just as well say that having written the sentence caused her to act in a given way, as that an intention to act in a given way caused her to write a particular sentence. That is, how do we discount the possibility that as a result of having written a particular sentence she went on to act in a particular way? This interpretation may seem vulnerable to the criticism that it does not explain what has caused her to write a particular sentence in the first place. But notice that the intentional interpretation is vulnerable to the same criticism: It does not explain what has led her to have a particular intention in the first place. By no means do I wish to discount intention as a legitimate object for study, yet it is necessary to point out that the present data, although appearing to contribute to that study, do so only in a guarded way. All we can say legitimately is that some of her sentences have the quality of prediction; from them an observer can tell what she is going to do.

The films of Washoe that I have seen show considerable evidence of spontaneous self-description. For example, on one occasion she is shown slowly tumbling, putting her head into a hat as she tumbles, frequently signing "in" or "head in," both before and after the act. This kind of behavior, involving description of both completed and impending acts, is especially recurrent in the human child.

Nor does it abate in the adult, although in the adult it undergoes changes that make it more difficult to recognize as a form of self-description. First, there is an increase in the interval between the act and the speech (or speech and the act), second, the speaker is less likely to talk to himself than to a listener. Nevertheless, the frequency of self-description probably does not decline (and may even increase) in the adult. For example, often as the wife drives her husband home from the airport, he tells her what happened on his trip, that is, describes his past behavior. She reciprocates in a sense with a description of her own past behavior. When one points out the self-descriptive aspect of this kind of exchange to participating parties, they are often offended and seek to explain their behavior on other grounds, in terms of interest in the other one and certainty of the other one's interest in them. Whether true or not, however, this is aside from the point. The behavior is self-descriptive by definition—the individual does produce a description of his or her own prior behavior—and as such, the behavior can be seen as evidence for a disposition to repeat, that is, to produce equivalences between experiences in different forms. Moreover, it is equally certain that the husband while on his trip told more than one listener what he had said to and so and so yesterday, last year, 5 years ago and planned to say a week hence when he would see so and so. In music the repetition of themes is sometimes especially evident; even a dilettante such as myself can marvel at the degree of repetition in the several works of a composer. However, this is pale evidence compared to everyday life. I have no ethnographic data, but my impression is that each person lives his or her life thousands if not hundreds of thousands of times, repeating events day after day, year after year, throughout a lifetime. We seek interminably to produce equivalences, and the justifications we are prepared to give for doing so serve only to conceal from ourselves a disposition we do not presently understand.

PREFERENCE AND LANGUAGE

Suppose a child were handed a toy animal and told to put it either "in the basket," "on the table," or "under the chair." In fact, when children of 1 year 6 months to 2 years 5 months were given instructions of this kind, they proved to vary systematically in the accuracy with which they carried out the instruction. They did best on "in," next best on "on," and worst on "under." The data have been interpreted to mean that the child learns to comprehend the word "in" earlier than the word "on," and "on" earlier than "under" (Clark, 1974).

Preoccupied with language, the experimenter assumes that the child's performance has only one determinant, the instructions given it. However, that is only one of several determinants. What is the probability that the subject will carry out the several acts independent of verbal instruction? Suppose the child is given the toy animal but is told nothing—what will it do with the toy? Is it equally likely to put it in the basket, on the table, or under the chair? For the child who is unlikely to engage in free play at all the same kind of control data can be realized in a different way. The experimenter can model the three acts and then invite the child to copy. Will the child be equally likely to repeat each of the experimenter's acts?

When controls of this kind were belatedly carried out, the three acts proved not to be equally probable; the child was most likely to copy an act involving in, next one involving on, and least likely one involving under (Clark, 1973). In other words, the accuracy the child showed in carrying out the verbal instructions could be predicted from its preference for the three acts.

A subject's performance is never determined exclusively by instructions but always by a combination of instructions and preference or response bias. Therefore, in all tests of comprehension one needs as control data the probability of the subject's carrying out the instructed acts independently of the instructions. The lack of this kind of data is most apt to lead to erroneous conclusions, specifically with children and chimpanzees. They, more than a human adult, are the subjects likely to harbor preferences of a kind that the experimenter, another human adult, has difficulty imagining. No experimenter would starve a subject, place food on the right, instruct the subject either to "turn right" or "turn left," and then treat the subject's penchant for turning right as evidence that it learned "right" before it learned "left." Yet this is exactly the kind of error that is made in interpreting children's data (e.g., Clark, 1974), simply because certain preferences in the child are not evident to the adult investigator.

Interestingly, in the matter of in, on, and under, children and chimpanzees appear to have similar preferences. When Peony and Elizabeth were given the opportunity to place a variety of common objects either in a bowl, on the desk, or under the desk, they showed the same bias or preference the children showed when urged to repeat the model's act. Elizabeth put the object in the bowl 12 times, on the desk eight times, and under the desk not at all. For Peony the corresponding figures were nine, four, and zero ($p < .01$). Why do children and chimpanzees prefer to put objects in a container? To get at one of the possible determinants, we drew a chalk circle about 4 in. in diameter on the desk, left the bowl on the desk, and gave the subjects the same objects as before. Both subjects inspected the circle, using tongues followed by fingers, which would seem to be the customary receptor order for inspection in young laboratory chimps. The inspection over, for Elizabeth the circle proved to have almost as much motive force as the bowl. She put the objects in the bowl, in the circle, on the desk (but not in the circle), and under the desk, 10, 20, 0, and 0 times, respectively. Peony found the circle less compelling; for her the corresponding figures were 20, 0, 2, and 8. We have since given both subjects the opportunity to place not only objects in a small circle but themselves in a large circle (see Figure 5.1). Both subjects carry out both acts and do so with considerable affect; we are attempting now to establish the possible relation between the acts (Premack, 1975b).

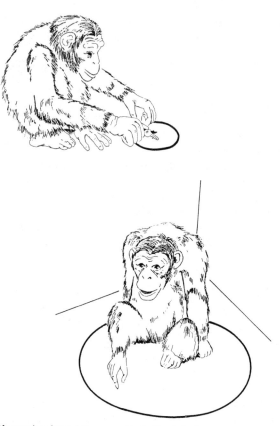

FIG. 5.1 Elizabeth putting keys into a small chalk circle in one case and herself into a larger chalk circle in another. (From Premack, 1975b. Used with the permission of M.I.T. Press.)

To date we have taught Peony and Elizabeth "on" (see page 108) but have not yet tried either "in" or "under." When we do try, it seems reasonable to anticipate "in" to be learned more rapidly than "under." In learning "on" Elizabeth proved to be slower than Peony, (see page 109), again because of preference, although preference in this case to carry out the relation one way rather than another. Elizabeth preferred to put keys on clay rather than vice versa—in contrast to Peony, who had no such preference—and for many trials erred on the instruction "(Put) clay on keys."

EFFECT OF PREFERENCE ON PRODUCTION

The examples above all concern the effect of preference on the apparent comprehension of language. Consider now the relation between preference and language production. To test for this possibility we use two steps. First, we determine what preference if any the subject may have to engage in certain acts; second, we require the subject to describe these same acts as they are carried out by another party. If preference affects production, then the acts which the subject should be most likely to describe (or describe accurately) are those acts which the subject prefers to engage in itself.

In the first step, Peony and Elizabeth were seated alongside materials that made possible such simple acts as cutting, inserting, washing, pushing, taking and, of course, giving to the trainer. The materials included a knife, container of water, empty container, and an apple—all materials that had been used in teaching them the verbs "cut, insert, wash," etc. Two sessions of this kind showed that Peony's preference order was cut, insert, wash, whereas Elizabeth's was wash, insert, cut ($p < .05$). The results, summarized in Table 5.1 show, for example, that on two sessions Peony cut the apple a total of 18 times, inserted it 13 times, and did not wash it at all.

In the next step, the trainer took over the subject's role and pretended to play with the same material the subjects had played with earlier. Actually, the trainer's play was programmed: in each of two sessions the trainer cut the apple, washed it, and inserted it, more or less imitating chimp style, doing each equally often and in counterbalanced order. The chimps sat at the writing board, watching as the trainer performed. Their task was to describe the trainer's behavior with such simple sentences as "Amy apple cut," "Debby apple wash," etc. The words available to them included either "Amy" or "Debby" plus "apple," "cut," "insert," and "wash." They had passed noun—verb contrasts on all the object and action names and were familiar with all the words.

The results for the second step are shown in Table 5.2. The words are listed in the order in which the acts named by the words have been preferred by the subjects in the free play sessions, e.g., cut, insert, wash for Peony. Actions refer to the acts carried out by the trainers. In each cell the number is the frequency with which the subject has used either "cut," "insert," or "wash" in describing the trainer's act. For instance, the number 3 in cell cut—cut in Peony's table indicates that on three occasions when the trainer cut the apple Peony correctly described the act as "Trainer apple cut"; the number 2 in cell wash—cut indicates that on two occasions when the trainer actually washed the apple Peony incorrectly described it as "Trainer apple cut."

TABLE 5.1
Peony and Elizabeth's Preference Order in Free Play

Peony	Session 1	2	Total	Elizabeth	Session 1	2	Total
Cut	9 + 9		18	Wash	5 + 9		14
Insert	4 + 9		13	Insert	3 + 8		11
Wash	0 + 0		0	Cut	3 + 2		5

TABLE 5.2
The Relation between Accuracy Description and
Preference for the Act Described

		Action					Action			
Peony		C	I	W		Elizabeth	W	I	C	
W	C	3	1	2	6	W	W	6	2	2	10
o						o					
r	I	1	3	0	4	r	I	0	4	2	6
d						d					
	W	1	1	3	5		C	0	0	1	1
		5	5	5	15			6	6	5	17

$$\chi^2 = 6.1$$
$$\alpha = .25$$

$$\chi^2 = 8.92$$
$$\alpha = .075$$

Both subjects showed a tendency to describe the trainer's action in keeping with their preference for the action, Elizabeth more so than Peony. For example, on all six occasions when the trainer washed the apple, Elizabeth accurately described the act. However, on only one of the five occasions when the trainer cut the apple did Elizabeth accurately describe it—and washing was Elizabeth's most preferred act, cutting her least preferred act. Therefore, what Elizabeth described the trainer as doing was determined in large measure by what she preferred to do herself. The combined significance level for the two chi squares was borderline ($p < .07$). The tests need to be repeated, more revealingly perhaps with delay between the observation and description. In the present test the chimps typically described the trainer's act even as the trainer carried it out. Seemingly this should lead to the greatest accuracy, yet even in this circumstance the description tended to be influenced by the subject's preferences for the acts described. The relevance of these data to the classic topic of the evidentiary status of testimony seems straightforward (see Münsterberg, 1925). The data also point up the control typically lacking in classical treatments, viz., the witnesses' preferences for the acts about which they are called upon to give testimony.

SARAH: WORD ORDER

In the early training, Sarah's grasp of sentence structure or word order was uncertain. In addition, several months had passed since she had produced any sentences. She had been taught "same–different," as well as several versions of match-to-sample, and had spent the interum answering implicit questions by filling in the blank space between the like or unlike objects with "same" or "different." However, she had had little opportunity to produce sentences from scratch or to request items. To strengthen her uncertain word order we gave her a long series of unusually simple lessons, requiring only that she request either of two fruits, apple or banana in one session, orange or grape on the alternate session. A piece of either apple or banana was placed before her along with the words "give," "Sarah," "apple," and "banana," and she was required to write "Give apple Sarah," or "Give banana Sarah." On alternate sessions, a piece of grape or orange was placed before her along with the words "give," "Sarah,"

TABLE 5.3
Frequency of Some of Sarah's Word Orders

	Orange/grape
Frequency	Type
2	Sarah give
6	Sarah orange give or Sarah grape give
1	Sarah orange grape
1	Sarah orange give grape or Sarah grape give orange
8	Sarah give grape or Sarah give orange
10	Give orange grape Sarah or give grape orange Sarah
179	Give grape Sarah or give orange Sarah
11	Give Sarah grape or give Sarah orange
3	Give Sarah orange grape
3	Orange give Sarah grape
1	Orange grape
1	Give grape Sarah orange

	Apple/banana
Frequency	Type
1	Sarah give
5	Sarah banana give or Sarah apple give
0	Sarah banana apple
0	Sarah banana give apple or Sarah apple give banana
8	Sarah give banana or Sarah give apple
0	Give banana apple Sarah or give apple banana Sarah
151	Give banana Sarah or give apple Sarah
11	Give Sarah banana or give Sarah apple
2	Give Sarah banana apple
2	Give banana Sarah apple
3	Give Sarah
0	Banana give Sarah apple
0	Banana apple

"orange," and "grape," and she was required to write either "Give orange Sarah," or "Give grape Sarah." No errorless trials were given, simply 16 choice trials per session. The object names were at least somewhat known to her, "orange" and "grape" less so than "apple" and "banana" but well enough, we thought, so that the emphasis could be primarily on word order. In a later stage we accepted both "Give X Sarah" and "Give Sarah X" and they came to be in free variation, but in this early stage we were more strict and accepted only "Give X Sarah."

The results, presented in Table 5.3, show each of the different word orders she has produced on each session and the frequency with which she has produced them. In all, she produced 11 different word orders—a prolixity, however, that rapidly converged on only one word order. The rate of convergence was faster for the better known pair of words. With "apple–banana" she eliminated all incorrect word orders by the sixth session, and with "orange–grape" this did not occur until the eleventh session (see Table 5.4). At her worst, she produced six different incorrect strings with "apple–banana," compared to ten different incorrect strings with "orange–grape."

Sarah's word orders were not random, however, but were distributed in a way that approximated the correct order. For example, of the 409 total strings, 373, or 91%, began with "give," 32 with "Sarah," and only four with the object name. Twenty-seven took the blatantly incorrect form "Sarah X give" and "Sarah give X," compared to a total of 372 that took either a correct or an approximately correct form: "Give X Y Sarah," "Give Sarah X," or "Give X Sarah." Such forms as "Give apple banana Sarah," or "Give orange grape Sarah,"

TABLE 5.4
Sarah's Errors in Word Order and Word Choice

Sessions	Apple–banana		Orange–grape	
	Order	Choice	Order	Choice
1	12	9	16	8
2	11	6	11	6
3	8	10	5	6
4	5	8	3	4
5	3	8	0	3
6	2	7	1	4
7	0	5	0	3
8	1	7	0	5
9	0	2	0	2
10	1	2	0	0
11	0	2	0	0
12	0	2	0	2
13	0	0		
14	0	0		

in which both objects were requested, were not, strictly speaking, incorrect as to word order, although we scored them as incorrect. Should they be scored as incorrect with regard to word choice? At a later stage we invited just such strings. We put out not one fruit but several of them and were quite pleased to accept, say, "Give apple banana Sarah," a more economical form than "Give apple Sarah" and "Give banana Sarah." Nevertheless, at this early stage, we rejected sentences of this kind because only one fruit was before her and the terms of the lesson were that she could request only items that were before her. Given our early rejection of such sentences, it is noteworthy that Sarah did not abandon the form but persisted, trying the form at various times until finally we accepted it.

Despite producing a large number of incorrect word orders, Sarah nonetheless eliminated errors of word order more quickly than errors of word choice. For instance, she ceased to make errors in word order by about the fourth and sixth sessions on "banana–apple" and "orange–grape," respectively, but continued to make errors in word choice for at least another six sessions in both cases (see Table 5.4). The two kinds of errors were not independent. For instance, if Sarah used correct word order in writing "Give Sarah orange" or "Give Sarah grape," the probability that she would also use the correct word was .8, whereas if her word order were incorrect, the probability of her chosing the correct word was only .43. On the other side of the coin, if Sarah chose the correct word the probability of her using correct word order was .8, whereas if she chose the incorrect word the probability of her using correct word order was only .45. The conditional probabilities, and therefore the dependence between the two kinds of errors, appeared to be somewhat greater for orange–grape than for apple–banana, although chi squares computed on the two contingency tables were highly significant in both cases. $\chi^2 = 11.8478$ ($p = .9994$) for orange–grape and $\chi^2 = 6.7195$ ($p = .99905$) for apple–banana.

The conditional probabilities discussed above were based upon data averaged over the first three sessions only, because errors became too infrequent in later sessions to analyze their dependence. In a path analysis (Wright, 1934) which was made next, we considered the same kind of dependencies but specifically over successive sessions.[1] There are four possible relations, two dealing with like effects and two with mixed or cross-effects. First, there are the effects of errors of word order in a given session on errors of word order in the next session, as well as the effect of word choice in a given session on errors of word choice in the next session. Second, there are the cross-effects, the effects of errors of word order in a given session on errors of word choice in the next session, and vice versa.

When the data are treated over successive sessions in this manner, word order emerges as a decidedly stronger factor than word choice. The magnitude of the

[1] I am greatly indebted to Marg Cruise, Center for Advanced Study in Behavioral Sciences, Stanford, California, for expert statistical advice and computation.

TABLE 5.5
Summary of Path Analysis Results

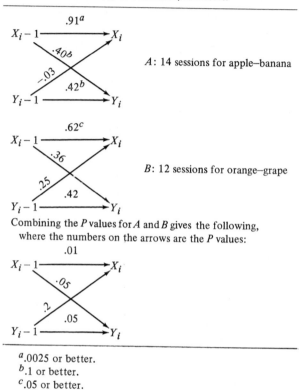

Combining the P values for A and B gives the following, where the numbers on the arrows are the P values:

[a].0025 or better.
[b].1 or better.
[c].05 or better.

effects is shown in the diagrams in Table 5.5, each containing four arrows, horizontal ones showing like effects and diagonal ones showing mixed or cross-effects. The top arrows give the effect of word order on word order, the bottom arrows word choice on word choice, and the diagonals the appropriate cross-effects. The diagrams show apple–banana and orange–grape results separately, and in the diagram at the bottom, the p values for the two separate analyses are combined and the numbers shown on the arrows are the p values themselves.

The p values can be used to estimate the effect because they are proportional to its magnitude. By far the strongest effect was that of word order on word order. Sarah's accuracy in word order on any given session was strongly affected by her accuracy in word order on the preceding session. In addition, her accuracy in word choice on any given session was affected by her accuracy in word order on the preceding session. This mixed or cross effect was weaker than the direct effect but nonetheless determinate and significant.

In contrast, although her accuracy in word choice on a given session was affected by her accuracy in the same factor on the preceding session, this within-factor effect was no stronger than that of the previous cross-factor effect. In other words, word order had as much effect on word choice as word choice had on itself. Finally, word choice had no significant effect on word order. Briefly, then, as regards her session by session progress, word order in one session had not only a strong effect on word order in the next session but also a weak effect on word choice, whereas word choice had only a weak effect on itself and no effect on word order.

Why was word order the stronger factor? The outcome may be seen as compatible with the view that grammar, in this case word order, is a stronger factor than the semantic one. This is a common assumption and these data, simple as they are, may be considered to support it. But this assumption needs to be qualified in at least two ways. First, the same results might not be produced by another subject, or even by Sarah in another period. Although Sarah's results were the same in both tests, they were both obtained in the same time period and may be specific to a certain stage in language learning. Second, it is not clear that word order and word choice are equated for difficulty.

One might suppose word order to be the more difficult factor because there were six possible word orders and only two possible word choices. However, on every trial the same word order was correct and correct in an absolute sense. In contrast, the choice of a word was correct conditional on the fruit present on a trial, so that word choice depended on a relation between the word and an extralinguistic state of affairs. If there was any dependence of this kind in the case of word order, it was invariant and simple. Sarah wanted the piece of fruit, we can reasonably assume, and the grammatical character of her sentence encoded that fact. The grammatical requirements could be made more sensitive to the world. Not at this stage, but later with increased linguistic competence, the subject could be required not only to request things but also to describe them and to ask about them as well. The same sentence type would not then be appropriate on every trial—some would call for an imperative sentence, others for a description or a question—and this arrangement might force the subject to manage its grammatical resources in more nearly the way Sarah was forced to manage her semantic resources in the present lessons. In brief, although it is interesting to find word order taking precedence over word choice, the difference cannot be interpreted without further tests.

It is of interest to ask how Sarah distinguishes corrections for order from those for choice. In correcting Sarah, the trainers used the same admonishment for both kinds of error. Trainers disapproved sentences that were incorrect for either reason and then removed them from the board. Occasionally the trainers sought to induce Sarah to correct her own errors, by pointing to either the incorrect word or the incorrect word order, but there was no basis on which Sarah could distinguish one kind of pointing from the other. Quite likely, when Sarah made both kinds of errors in the same sentence, or made an error after a long period without errors, or made a markedly ungrammatical sentence, the trainers amplified their disapproval. However, this would not provide a basis for distinguishing between disapproval for errors of order and that for errors of choice. How then did Sarah learn which factor to correct on a given trial?

Notice that after she had made no errors in word order, Sarah was corrected 12 more times in the case of "apple–banana" and six more times in the case of "orange–grape," all corrections being for errors of word choice. How did Sarah know these corrections were not for order and were for choice, however, or even perhaps not for both? One might suppose that the effect of these corrections would be to cause unlearning of the word order; yet clearly that was not the case. To understand the differential effect of the correction, it seems necessary to assume that Sarah has a sense of which of the two factors she has faulted. Perhaps when two factors are acquired at different rates, as choice and order have been in the present case, it is easier to discriminate one kind of error from the other. In any case, Sarah's data suggest that a subject may reach a point at which it can accurately judge for which of two factors it is being corrected and so not correct for the inappropriate factor.

Although Sarah might be considered slow in acquiring word order, once she acquired it she retained it well. In learning subsequent words, errors in word order were rarely other than a minor factor. An example of her mastery of word order was provided in a lesson given shortly after the present training. She was taught the names for jam, peanut butter (one word in her language), honey, cracker, and bread in the production mode, having to request the item by writing either "Give X Sarah" or "Mary give X Sarah."[2]

The five new object names were introduced in pairs, starting with "peanut butter" and "jam," each of which was then contrasted with "honey." Next "bread" and "cracker" were paired and finally all five words were brought together in the concluding lessons of the series. Standard errorless trials were followed by choice trials. In the presence of a jar of peanut butter, she was given the words "give," "Sarah," "Mary," and the new word "peanut butter." When she wrote "Mary give peanut butter Sarah" or simply "Give peanut butter Sarah," Mary gave her a spoonful of the requested item. Comparable trials were used to introduce "jam" and likewise "honey." A jar of the item was placed before her,

---

[2] Use of the donor name was optional at this early stage. Although we frequently included donor names in the set of alternatives given her, she rarely used them, no more than about once every twentieth trial on the average, and for a time we did not press her to do more. Typically only one trainer was present, making the use of his or her name gratuitous. However, even in this early period she was occasionally confronted with a comprehension trial, an instruction requiring her to, say, "Give cracker Mary." These occasional comprehension sentences, along with the few sentences in which she specified the donor herself, kept the donor names alive. Later, when several agents were present in the same session, use of the donor's name was made obligatory.

the new word was added to the already known words, and she was required to produce "Give jam Sarah" or "Give honey Sarah" as the case might be, following which she received a spoonful of the item. She was given eight errorless trials on both "peanut butter" and "jam" and four such trials on "honey."

Choice trials were then given in which either jam, peanut butter, or honey was placed before her. She was given the words "give" and "Sarah" and a pair of object names, "jam" and "peanut butter" for the first four trials, "jam" and "honey" for the second four trials, and "honey" and "peanut butter" for the last four trials. She made only one error in the 12 trials. On the following session all three object names were presented as alternatives; "cracker" was introduced with four errorless trials and then added to the other object names, making four alternatives among which to choose; finally two comprehension trials of the form "Give cracker Mary" were interpolated, requiring that she give the designated item to the trainer. She made no errors on the 12 trials; most impressive, she correctly and swiftly carried out the instructions to give the trainer a cracker.

The last of five new words, "bread," was introduced with four errorless trials in the next session. Then she was given 12 sessions, 9–20 choice trials per session, with the words "Mary," "Sarah," "jam," "peanut butter," "honey," "bread," and "cracker" as alternatives. On the choice trials, either one item or all five items were present. If only one item was present, she was required to write a sentence designating specifically that item, for example, "Give jam Sarah." Alternatively, if all five items were present, she was required to write a grammatically correct sentence and then point to the item that was requested in the sentence. Therefore, she could get, say, jam in either of two ways: by writing "Give jam Sarah" when jam alone was present or by writing the same sentence when all five items were present and pointing to the jar of jam. In addition to trials requiring that she produce the appropriate sentence, eight comprehension trials, of the form "Give cracker Mary" or "Give bread Mary," were interpolated among the production trials, requiring that she give one or the other to the trainer (it was impractical to require Sarah to dish out the jam, honey, or peanut butter).

On the overall series dealing with the five new words, she was correct on 142 out of 160 trials, or 89% correct, an impressive level of accuracy that probably reflected her good interest in such things as jam and honey. Of greater interest was her performance on word order. In the 160 trials in the series she made only eight errors on the word order, all of the form "Give Sarah X" rather than "Give X Sarah," which, as already noted, was a form we later accepted. On only six out of the 162 trials did she use the donor's name, producing the four-word sentence "Mary give X Sarah," although she was correct on all six such trials both as to word order and as to word choice, possibly indicating a good attention level. Her 5% word-order error on this series was representative of her general accuracy on word order.

SARAH'S PERFORMANCE AS A DONOR

When required to serve as a donor, for example, "Sarah give cracker Mary," Sarah often displayed behavior other than what was taught her. The present series yielded at least one trial of this kind, although she was unusually compliant on this series, giving the trainer either bread or cracker on five of the six occasions she was requested to do so. On one trial, however, she cried and did not hand the trainer bread but handed her her own name, the plastic word "Sarah" taken from the pile of words before her. In general, her performance on instructions that required she give something to the trainers fell into three categories:

1. She carried out the instruction with consummate obedience.

    She had a mild tantrum, refusing to carry out the instruction, and moved away from the board, disrupting or terminating the lesson.

3. She refused, but instead of simply moving away from the board, she operated on the words in unique ways that had not been taught her.

Perhaps the least innovative of these ways was simply to remove the words from the board and to hand them back to the trainer, although even this was mild improvisation, for erasing the board was the responsibility of the speaker not the listener, and Sarah's intrusion of erasure from the position of a listener was an illegal and disruptive act, one in which she did not engage except in the present circumstance. A more interesting operation was the one just described, handing the trainer her own name, which she did on several occasions. Interestingly, she did not attempt to insert it into the sentence herself, that is, to remove the trainer's name and insert her own, perhaps because she had been taught not to modify existing strings except in prescribed ways. Some potentially interesting innovations might have been quashed by the restraint of this kind but it was necessary in order to maintain one-to-one substitution as a training method.

Probably the most dramatic use she made of her name was to apply it vigorously to the foodstuffs before her. On one occasion when requested to give fruit to the trainer, she acquiesced on the first two trials but when the request was repeated a third time she took her name from the pile of words before her and slapped it down vigorously on the pieces of fruit she was requested to give. It does not seem unreasonable to suggest that in applying her name in this way she was saying something comparable to "Mine mine!" She had no possessive pronouns, no other way of saying "Mine!" The closest parallel to her behavior I know of in human behavior is that of the young child who, when a guest attempted to help himself to the toys, shouted "Mize! mize! . . ." (his version of "mine"). The child screamed its possession, whereas the ape realized a comparable emphasis by the force and repetition with which it applied its name to the fruit. Neither scene was photographed, unfortunately, but in my recollection the protest registered by the hominid and pongid were equivalent in character, roughly equivalent in intensity, and different only in form.

SENTENCE PRODUCTION ORDER

In learning to produce sentences from scratch, Sarah passed through three stages, in only the last of which did she produce the sentence in its final order. Unlike Sarah, trainers always produced sentences in their final order. If the instruction given Sarah by the trainer was to be "Sarah apple take," the trainer wrote "Sarah" first, "apple" next, and "take" last. Although Sarah had ample opportunity to observe the trainers she nonetheless developed her own different, although equally systematic, production order. Notice that there is no requirement that the sentence be written in any particular way. Grammar is concerned only with the final order of the sentence, not with the order in which the sentence is produced.

Before she converged on the trainer's production order Sarah passed through two stages, both of which are illustrated in Table 5.6 with the use of a representative sentence, "Give apple Sarah," and the later form, "Mary give apple Sarah." In Phase I, which lasted approximately 2 months, Sarah began by placing the name of the object on the board. Below it she placed the verb, always "give" in this earliest period, and then added her own name to the head of the string. The result is shown at the top of Table 5.6 in the leftmost column, numbered according to the order in which she placed the words on the board. In the next column we see the first of two transformations she performed on the string. She moved "give" from its terminal position to the head of the string, producing "Give Sarah apple," which was not an acceptable string in that period. In a second rearrangement, she then moved "Sarah" from its middle position to the end of the string, forming "Give apple Sarah," which was the string we required. She maintained this form of sentence production, with its two rearrangements, for at least 3 months.

In the second period, she started by putting the verb on the board, her name below it, and then finished by placing the object name below her own name. It may be seen that the resulting string corresponded exactly to the product of her first rearrangement in Stage I. In Stage II, therefore, she began with a string that previously had cost her one transformation. Her next step was to move "Sarah" from its middle position to the end of the string, producing the results shown in the third column. This first rearrangement of Stage II is also recognizable; it corresponds exactly to her second rearrangement in Stage I. "Give apple Sarah," the resulting string, was acceptable, although in this period we added the donor's name, making it optional on some occasions and mandatory on others. Whenever she added the donor's name she did so by appending it to the head of the string, in what could be considered the second transformation of Stage II. She maintained this sytem for about 10–12 months, before finally dropping all rearrangements and additions. She then put words on the board exactly in their final order as the trainers had done from the beginning. However, whenever stressed, by photographers, unexpected trainers, or even difficult lessons, she returned to Stage II.

TABLE 5.6
Sarah's Sentence Production Order, Early, Middle, and Late Stages

Stage	String		Operation	String	Operation	String
Early	Sarah	(3)	S	Give	G	Give
	Apple	(1)	A	Sarah	S	Apple
	Give	(2)	G	Apple	A	Sarah
Middle	Give	(1)	G	Give	Mary	Mary
	Sarah	(2)	S	Apple	+	Give
	Apple	(3)	A	Sarah	G	Apple
					A	Sarah
					S	
Late	Mary	(1)				
	Give	(2)				
	Apple	(3)				
	Sarah	(4)				

Table 5.7 shows her system for producing the complex sentences requiring the specification of two objects or, on an alternative view, one object and its modifier. This is the sentence of the previous lesson in which she has been required to specify the receptacle and the spread, for example, " ... honey bread," in a fixed order. Column I shows that she began by putting the words on the board in a manner similar to that used at Stage II: verb first; her own name next; and then, departing somewhat from Stage II, the modifier at the head of the string and the receptacle at the bottom of the string. In her first rearrangement, she moved the modifier word from Position 1 to Position 3. In her second rearrangement, she moved "Sarah" from Position 3 to Position 4. Her composition in this case involved two rearrangements, as it did in Stage I above, but was otherwise like that of Stage II. Both rearrangements involved moving words down the board, both words were moved only one position, and the movement of "Sarah" was exactly the same as that of Stage II.

Peony and Elizabeth did not use the same productive system as Sarah, perhaps because they were trained somewhat differently, although all three subjects

TABLE 5.7
Sarah's Production Order on a Complex Sentence,
Middle Stage

		Operation	String	Operation	String
Honey	(3)	H	Give	G	Give
Give	(1)	G	Honey	H	Honey
Sarah	(2)	S	Sarah	S	Bread
Bread	(4)	B	Bread	B	Sarah

showed some similarity. Like Sarah, Peony and Elizabeth began by forming a string of generally correct words on which they then operated. The major operation was rearrangement, with the addition of a particle a distant second. Spontaneous or self-initiated deletion was never seen; all three animals could be induced to remove an incorrect word by the trainer's pointing to it and sometimes even to replace the incorrect one with a correct one, but they did not initiate deletion themselves. Most although not all rearrangements were downward on the board; most involved moving the word one position; and the same word was rarely if ever operated on twice.

Because trainers never used any transformations in the production of their sentences, I deliberately refrained from calling their attention to their production so as not to disturb it. For a long period one could observe the striking difference in the manner in which the two species produced their sentences. One species wrote all sentences in final order, the other never did but instead formed a string which it then rearranged one or more times. It was only after substantial training that Sarah transcended the species difference and regularly produced sentences without rearrangement. Sarah's achievements were more noteable than the trainers'. They, after all, were merely translating already existing English sentences into the plastic pieces, whereas the sentences Sarah produced without rearrangement were not translations but original compositions.

PREPOSITIONS

Sarah was taught "on" in the comprehension mode with the use of 2 × 4 cards that varied in color, a procedure made possible because she had meantime been taught the names of colors (see Chapter 9). On the errorless trials only one of the two colored cards was given to her, the other card being placed on the table before her. When the trainer wrote "Red on green," therefore, it was not difficult to arrange that Sarah place the red card (which she held) on the green one already on the table. The trainer guided Sarah on the first trial, leading her to arrange the cards so that they overlapped in a way that left the bottom one visible. This was an easy arrangement for Sarah and after the first demonstration she required no guidance. Following three errorless trials of the first kind, the cards were reversed, the red one placed on the table and the green one given to Sarah. The trainer now wrote "Green on red," and Sarah again carried out the desired arrangement.

Sarah's knowledge of color names made it possible to use semantically neutral materials, such as 2 × 4 cards, in which neither arrangement had any edge over the other. That is, red on green is no more compelling than green on red, in contrast to, say, "horse on fly," which an organism may be less willing to carry out than "fly on horse" even with toys or pictures. Moreover, by teaching "on" with items that were capable of playing the top and bottom roles with equal facility, we assured that if Sarah learned "on" at all it would necessarily be on a syntactic basis and not a semantic one. With the child, this may not be the case, for its early exemplars of "on" tend to consist of smaller items on top of larger ones, for example, dish on table, child on bike, food on plate, etc., such that for the child "on" may include a size relation as well as one of juxtaposition.

After six errorless trials on both "Red on green" and "Green on red," both cards were given to Sarah and she was given three lessons instructing her to put either "Red on green" or "Green on red." Having no verb for "put" at that time, we relied on the context to carry the force of the instruction. She was correct on 8 out of 11, 3 out of 5 (a reluctant student), and 13 out of 16 trials, respectively, or 75% correct.

Despite the borderline performance we gave her a transfer test, identical to the choice lessons except for the addition of blue and yellow cards. Twelve different instructions were made possible by combining the new colors with the old ones. We gave her 10 of these and she made two errors, with none on the first five.

Her use of "on" had been confined to comprehension up to this point. On the first production test, the words "on," "green," and "red," were given to her, the trainer placed the red card on the green one, and Sarah was required to write a sentence conforming to the trainer's arrangement. She correctly described the trainer's placement of the cards on seven of nine trials, being incorrect on the first and third trial of the series. Lessons consisting of fewer than the usual number of trials can bespeak lack of interest, difficulty, or both. The difficulty of the present material for Sarah was reflected in the slowness with which she worked, on comprehension as well as production. Unfortunately, we have no latency measures but the reader can infer at least a crude index of difficulty by comparing the number of trials realized per session on the various topics.

On the next session, a yellow card was added to the green and red ones, and she was given four words per trial: "on" and the three color names. We warmed her up with four comprehension trials followed by 13 production trials. She was correct on all four comprehension trials but made five errors on the production trials. She chose an incorrect color name on two occasions, which was now possible with the addition of the third color name, and made three errors of order. The latter were interesting. Twice she wrote "On green red" when "Green on red" was correct, and once "On red yellow" when "Red on yellow" was correct. Notice that her errors of order preserved all the information in the grammatical string and in a sense were more iconic than the grammatical ones. The ungrammatical strings did not separate the words "red" and "green" with the "on" particle but put them into immediate juxtaposition as their referents were in the world. In a more relaxed atmosphere, the jungle rather than a laboratory, the two forms would very likely be in free variation.

Sessions continued with five additional lessons of essentially the same kind, a block of four to ten comprehension trials followed by a block of four to 13 production trials. Three words were available to her on each production trial and three cards on each comprehension trial, and transfer was tested further by the use of colors not previously used in production. Her scores on these combined comprehension–production tests were: 4 out of 4 and 3 out of 4; 7 out of 10 and 5 out of 7; 9 out of 10 and 9 out of 12; 6 out of 7 and 6 out of 8; 8 out of 10 and 5 out of 6 correct per total trials on comprehension and production, respectively. The series was rounded off with one lesson that consisted of 12 productions trials, with no warmup on comprehension, and that introduced the word "orange" along with an orange card, which had no prior use in either production or comprehension. She was correct on 10 out of 12 trials, with one of the errors on "orange."

Peony and Elizabeth learn "on."   In teaching "on" to Sarah we assumed that the cards were neutral, that she would be as likely to put a red one on a green one as vice versa; but with Peony and Elizabeth, instead of assuming semantic neutrality we tested their tendency to put one item on another. Peony was again sluggish, battling *Giardia,* so we started with Elizabeth. In a free play setting Elizabeth was given all possible pairs of sponge, clay, magic marker, and ring of keys, each pair for approximately 60 sec. Although she at first put the keys on the sponge twice, she soon found more interesting things to do. She sniffed the magic marker, stabbed the clay, and tried unsuccessfully to get the keys off the ring. These acts took priority over *on* to such a degree that after the first two instances, *on* never reappeared.

Although done with a fine proprietary sense—it is nobler to test for preferences than to assume their absence—the test was not an unqualified success. Certainly the results could not be taken to prove that among the objects given her Elizabeth had no preference as to which went on top of which. The results showed only that *on* was a weak form of behavior relative to the other response alternatives and that to discover her preferences with regard to *on* it would be necessary to suppress or eliminate the other alternatives. The failure of the tests notwithstanding, we moved to the language training.

Elizabeth was given a lesson in the comprehension mode essentially like the ones given Sarah, with keys and clay substituted for the colored cards. Either the keys or the clay was placed on the table and the other object was given to Elizabeth. The trainer wrote either "Key on clay" or "Clay on key" and, with only one trial of passive guidance, induced Elizabeth to carry out the instructions. After five errorless trials on both instructions, she was given a choice test. Both objects were placed on the table, so that when the trainer wrote "Clay on keys" on some trials and "Keys on clay" on others, Elizabeth had to decide which object to place on which. She made six errors on 15 trials, four on the first five trials, five of six errors by placing the keys on the clay. This bias also showed up in subsequent lessons, indicating that she definitely had preferences in the case of *on,* concealed in all likelihood in the earlier tests by the other response alternatives. Interestingly, the "school situation" quelled the other alternatives. With the transition from free play to the language lessons, Elizabeth abandoned sniffing, stabbing, and wrestling with the key ring. She confined her behavior to the one operation for which the lessons called.

We continued the training with two errorless trials on each instruction, followed by 15 choice trials. Elizabeth made five errors, with one in the first five trials. An additional errorless trial was given on each instruction and then another 15 choice trials. She made 6 errors, with one on the first 5 trials, for a total of 11 errors in 30 trials or 70% correct. The lesson was repeated twice on subsequent weeks and she made 3 errors in 15 trials and 6 errors in 15 trials on the first and second lesson, respectively. Five of the six errors in the second lesson consisted of incorrectly placing keys on clay; these were the first five errors of the session. A transfer test would have been a clever thing to interpose at this point: change to items for which she had no preference and with these items demonstrate that in all likelihood she knew "on"; then return to clay and keys where she would still give the impression of not knowing "on." Instead we continued to use keys and clay, to see how long it would take for verbal instruction to overcome preference. We repeated the choice test twice. On the first test she made six errors in 15 trials, five of them on keys on clay, but on the second test she made no errors on ten trials. The keys and clay were retired, along with their names, and a shoe and a piece of monkey chow were introduced for the transfer test. These were both familiar and, of course, named items, although she had not been given them before as a pair. The trainer wrote "Shoe on monkey chow" (one word in her language) and "Monkey chow on shoe" in a mixed order, requiring her to decide which of the two objects to place on the other. She made only one error in ten trials, passing the first transfer test.

"On" with Peony.   Peony was still phlegmatic, having finished another round of medication for *Giardia* during the early part of the "on" training. Even when well she was a desultory student, working for peanuts rather than the pleasure of the lesson. A string of errors caused her to do little more than whimper, in contrast to both Sarah and Elizabeth, who were most dangerous when they failed. Sarah screamed and flailed about with her powerful arms; Elizabeth screamed and rocked wildly. Trainers fled as promptly as possible. Yet after every failure Elizabeth and Sarah returned for another try, basically attracted by the lessons. Peony neither protested when she failed nor showed visible excitement when she succeeded. Occasionally, during markedly phlegmatic periods, lessons were inaugurated by giving her a large pot of goods from which two items were removed when she failed and one added when she succeeded, but without notable effect.

We repeated the free play sessions with Peony, using the same objects and procedure used with Elizabeth. Peony put the clay on the sponge once but otherwise, as the trainer's notes describe the sessions, " . . . spent all the time trying to figure out what we want her to do. She tried give, stab, lots of push.

Did no playing. Ended up doing nothing and whimpering." Next, free play was tried with the wooden blocks, objects intended to increase the likelihood of *on*. She carried out only one act of *on;* the rest of her behavior was coded as *push.*

She was given four language lessons in the ensuing 2-week period, in the comprehension mode, essentially like those given Elizabeth. Following standard errorless trials, she was given choice trials instructing her either to put "Clay on keys" or "Keys on clay." She was correct on 11 out of 17, 9 out of 15, 12 out of 15, and 9 out of 10 trials per total trials on the four lessons, respectively. The keys and clay were replaced by magic marker and sponge, and she was given a transfer test. The words "magic marker" (one word in her language) and "sponge" were known to her, but because she had not used them recently we first refreshed her on them, telling her "Insert marker" on some trials, "Insert sponge" on others. Because she made no errors on four such trials, she was given the transfer test in the same session, being required to carry out either "Marker on sponge" or "Sponge on marker." She made two errors in ten trials.

Because her transfer performance was weak, she was given three additional transfer tests, the first simply repeating the "Marker on sponge" versus "Sponge on marker" distinction and the next two substituting monkey chow and shoe for the marker and sponge. She was correct on 7 out of 10, 8 out of 10, and 10 out of 10 trials per total trials on the three lessons, respectively, and made no errors on the first five trials of any lesson, thus passing the transfer test at about the 85% level.

When a subject is given an *on* instruction in the presence of only two items, it can respond correctly merely by attending to either of the two objects named in the instruction. If it attends to the first word, it can perform correctly by taking the object associated with that word and placing it on top of the only other object present. If it attends to the last word in the instruction, once again it need only respond to one object name.

The addition of a third alternative forces the subject to respond to both words. If told, say, "Sponge on clay," when the alternatives are sponge, clay, and monkey chow, the subject must attend to both object names in order to put not only the correct item on top but also the correct item on the bottom. Peony was tested in exactly this way, sponge, clay, and monkey chow as the alternatives, making six possible instructions and three items to choose among on each trial. She made three errors in nine trials on the first lesson and two in eight trials on the second, or 70% correct (compared to chance expectancy of about 16%). She was slowed down, relative to the two-alternative cases, but performed well above chance. Elizabeth has yet to be tested in this way. Sarah's successful performance on the three-item case was described earlier.

6
Transfer

Beyond a certain point in training, transfer became an invariable property of the data, occurring on every possible occasion and in that uncanny diversity of forms which is possible only in such a system as language. Yet the outstanding feature of transfer is not its ultimately invariant occurrence, to which we became accustomed all too readily, but its almost complete absence in the earliest stages of training.

From our adult perspective on language, we were unprepared for the totality of the early failure. A pair of nouns well learned with one verb failed to transfer to a new verb. Words learned in comprehension failed to transfer to production, and vice versa. Astounded by these failures, we wondered whether they were not the diagnostic differences we had been looking for, differences that would distinguish chimpanzee from child. In this mood, we were inclined to reduce the significance of the transfer failures, supposing them to be peculiar to the chimpanzee.

This proved to be an ethnocentric reaction not well supported by evidence. Although the overall evidence on this issue is slight indeed, such evidence as exists supports the opposite conclusion. Children, too, in the earliest stages apparently do not show transfer. As Bloom (1974) has observed, for example, the first words comprehended by the child are not the first words it produces. This is suggestive of a failure in transfer from comprehension to production, of a kind that can be shown openly with the chimpanzee. Moreover, Guess (1969) and Guess and Baer (1973) report a similar failure in transfer in their training of language-deficient children. More important, however, than the snippets of evidence linking early child incompetence to early chimp incompetence is the fact that in both species the failure is confined to the earliest stages. Ultimately, nouns learned with one verb transfer to all other verbs; verbs learned in a contrast with one noun transfer to all nouns; words learned in production or comprehension transfer perfectly to the other mode.

The facts that need explanation, therefore, are not so much the differences between the species—which must exist in any case—but the difference between early and late language performance, which is common to both species. What structures distinguish the beginner, be it child or chimpanzee, which shows no transfer, from the later learner in which there is no discernible limit to the transfer? Comprehension and production appear to begin as independent systems. They end up in both species as highly interdependent systems if not, indeed, one system. What structures are acquired that account for these changes?

The number of kinds of transfer that can be studied in the context of language is very large indeed, provided the subject has acquired a fair degree of language. For the early subject, however, there are really only two kinds of transfer that can be reasonably studied: (1) new word combinations, and (2) shifts from comprehension to production and vice versa. New word combinations are mainly of two kinds: nouns, or more accurately object names, that are taught with one verb or action name and are then transferred to new verbs, and the reverse, verbs that are taught with one set of nouns and are then transferred to new nouns. The two cases can be combined, requiring the subject to use nouns that have been taught with one verb in conjunction with a verb that has been trained with another pair of nouns and never used otherwise, thus combining the initial transfer experience of both the nouns and the verb.

The change in modality is the other major kind of transfer suitable to the early subject. With only a slightly more advanced subject, the modality change can be looked at in a richer way. The more advanced subject will be able to produce descriptions as well as requests and, likewise, to comprehend descriptive as well as imperative sentences. Transfer may be greatest for the overlapping cases, for example, from producing a demand to understanding a demand, and from describing a condition to understanding a description; and perhaps least for the cross products, for example, from producing a demand to understanding a description, and from producing a description to understanding a demand. Transfer may also be enhanced by overlap in content as well as in form and so be greater if the demand made on the subject is one it has made of others and if the description it has been required to comprehend is the same as one it has itself produced earlier.

THREE TRANSFER HYPOTHESES

In the area of word combinations, we can entertain three major transfer hypotheses—call them sharing, generalization, and configurational. The configurational hypothesis holds that the subject may not discriminate the individual words from the word combinations in which they appear. For example, if the subject never saw "apple" and "banana," but only "Cut apple" and "Cut banana," it might fail when told "Wash apple" simply because it did not recognize "apple" as a separate unit. Indeed, the first transfer test may provide the very conditions which are needed to teach the subject to discriminate the separate words—and therefore the first transfer test is perhaps better seen as the condition that prepares the animal for subsequent transfer tests. For instance, after a subject was trained on "Cut X" and "Cut Y" and failed to show transfer on "Wash X" and "Wash Y," it should show transfer on all further tests in which X and Y were combined with new verbs. In general, this hypothesis would seem more applicable to vocal or even gestural language, where dividing the verbal stream into morphemic units may be more of a problem; pieces of plastic are rather well-defined entities. Moreover, in the present case, we first taught the animals "apple" and "banana," and only later combined these words with "cut," "give," and other verbs. (It is really the verbs that have had no history of independent occurrence, because from the beginning the subjects have never been told just "cut," "give," or "wash" but always to cut, give, or wash something.)

The generalization hypothesis is recommended by its extreme simplicity. In this view, if a noun does not transfer from the verb with which it has been taught to the first new verb with which it is combined, it should be trained with additional verbs and then tried again. Transfer, on this simple view, is some increasing function of the amount of generalization training. One can dress up the stark simplicity of this view by noting that in a transfer test the subject must respond exclusively on the basis of linguistic cues. In normal language use, language is highly redundant with the overall context; words are only one of the elements in the set of cues to which the subject responds. When successful, however, the transfer test eliminates the normal redundant cues, forcing the subject to respond to linguistic cues alone. The subject is likely to have to learn how to do this; especially successive transfer tests but also generalization training can teach it to do so.

The sharing hypothesis, which is the last we consider here, is a more complex specialized version of the simple generalization hypothesis. This hypothesis observes that in the early stages of training, each verb tends to be associated with a small restricted set of nouns. For example, "give" may occur primarily with fruit names and "take" largely with inedible objects, such as ball, key, clay, and the like. Each verb can actually be trained with an independent set of nouns but we do not require so extreme a separation to recognize that some approximation of it is likely to hold in the beginning. As training proceeds, two changes take place. The number of nouns associated with each verb increases but also, more interesting, nouns associated with different verbs overlap. "Give," which began with a few fruit names, is applied not only to new fruit names, but also to inedible objects, for example, ball, key and clay. Likewise "take," which began with inedibles, becomes associated not only with new inedible objects but also with edible ones. Moreover, the number of verbs having nouns in common increases, as does the number of nouns shared by the different verbs. It is not difficult to relate these factors to transfer, specifically with respect to novel noun–verb combinations.

A simple transfer hypothesis can be stated in terms of the paradigm that underlies the test on noun–verb combinations. If two verbs V_1 and V_2 share nouns, then when a new noun is trained with either of them, it transfers to the other one. Conversely, if there has been no overlap in the nouns associated with the two verbs, a new noun trained with either of them does not transfer to the other one. The hypothesis need not be stated in an all-or-none fashion; the likelihood of transfer can be made some function of the number of nouns the two verbs shared. In addition, we could complement the primary transfer of the simple hypothesis with a secondary form of transfer (and the secondary with a tertiary, etc.). Verbs 1 and 2 share nouns and are therefore in a state of primary transfer. However, V_1 also shares nouns with V_3, as does V_2 with V_4. Although Verbs 3 and 4 do not share nouns, nouns trained with either of them nonetheless transfer to the other. Verbs associated with opposite members of a pair of verbs that are in a state of primary transfer are themselves in a state of secondary transfer; verbs associated with opposite members of a pair of verbs in a state of secondary transfer are in a state of tertiary transfer; etc. Transfer is greatest for the primary case and proportionately less as the indirection increases.

To test the simple version of the transfer hypothesis we first chose two verbs, "wash" and "insert," which had shared nouns in the histories of both Peony and Elizabeth. At the time in question, three object names had been used successfully with both verbs and, as shown below, two of the three nouns were the same:

Wash	Insert
Apple	Apple
Banana	Banana
Cantaloupe	Clay

Given two verbs that shared nouns, we introduced into the test a third verb "push," which shared a noun with "insert" but did not share any with "wash." As things stood, therefore, "push" and "insert" both shared a noun and were in a condition of potential transfer, whereas "push" and "wash" shared no nouns and were not in such a condition.

Next, we taught two new object names, "marker" and "keys," using them with both "insert" and "push," so that these two verbs shared three nouns, viz., "clay," "marker," and "keys." Finally, we added the new object name "sponge," associating it with both "insert" and "wash," so that as shown below three conditions were realized: (1) "wash" and "insert" both shared three nouns ("apple," "banana," and "sponge"); (2) "insert" and "push" both shared three nouns ("marker," "key," and "clay"); and (3) "wash" and "push" did not share any nouns:

Wash	Insert	Push
Apple	Apple	Marker
Banana	Banana	Key
Sponge	Sponge	Clay
Cantaloupe	Marker	
	Key	
	Clay	

Before we continued with the test, we stepped outside of language for a moment, returned to the world of play and physical objects, and gave both Peony and Elizabeth the opportunity to engage in free play with four unnamed objects—monkey chow, doll, gumdrop, and shoes. These were the four objects which were to be named and their names, combined with the appropriate verbs, would form the basis of the transfer test. The readiness with which a subject learns a name for an object or for an action depends, we know from previous data, on its preference for the object or action (see page 91). More important, the likelihood of the subject's responding correctly to an instruction depends in part on the probability of its responding in that way independently of any instruction. For instance, if a subject likes to wash apples, it is more likely to respond correctly when told "Wash apples" than if it does not like to wash apples. Conversely, if it dislikes inserting gumdrops, it is less likely to respond correctly when told "Insert gumdrops" than if it does not dislike inserting them. In brief, to test the accuracy of a subject's response to instructions requires appropriate base data, specifically the probability of the subject's carrying out the acts independently of the instructions.

Because both subjects showed only moderate preferences among the objects, names were taught for all four of the objects using the verb "push." This training was carried out in the usual way, starting with errorless trials in which the instruction, say, "Elizabeth monkey chow push," was given in the presence of monkey chow alone and "Elizabeth doll push" in the presence of a doll alone. The instructions were then repeated in the presence of both objects. The same procedure was applied to all four objects and continued until both Elizabeth and Peony achieved their customary criteria on all four object names.

The transfer hypothesis was tested by combining the four new object names with the verbs "wash" in one case and "insert" in the other. All of the combinations so formed were novel. According to the hypothesis, however, the subjects should have done better on those involving "insert" than on those involving "wash," for "push" and "insert" did share nouns, whereas "push" and "wash" did not.

The test content, order, and results are shown separately for each subject in Table 6.1. Elizabeth failed both of the tests on which the hypothesis predicted success and passed one of the two tests on which the hypothesis predicted failure. Peony, in contrast, performed in perfect accord with the hypothesis. She showed transfer when the nouns were combined with "insert" and not when they were combined with "wash." Although the outcome is less than heartening, I can think of one even less heartening that requires no change in results, only an exchange between the subjects receiving them. Peony is the less erratic subject. Elizabeth does several things of interest with the language that Peony does less well, but she is emotionally unstable and at her worst in a transfer situation.

An alternative view of the results is expressed in the recalculation of the data shown below. Because four out of five errors in one case and four out of four in another consisted of the choice of the same item, I assumed they were not simply errors but more likely the expression of preference. Accordingly, I eliminated all such trials and then, partly because of the reduced data, combined the outcome for the two subjects. On this treatment, there is only one transfer failure, viz., wash: monkey chow/shoe. Why should there be a failure in "wash" and not in "insert"? Simply because, as the record shows, there has been more generalization training with "insert" than with "wash." That is, more different nouns have been trained with "insert" than with "wash" before the present test has been made and, on the generalization hypothesis, the likelihood of transfer is some increasing function of the number of nouns with which a verb is combined. We cannot rule out this hypothesis with the data at hand, and it is recommended by its extreme simplicity in any case.

Data Recalculated to Eliminate Effects of Preference

	Insert: doll/gumdrop	Insert: monkey chow/shoe	Wash: monkey chow/shoe	Wash: doll/gumdrop
Elizabeth	10/15	4/6	8/15	15/16
Peony	14/15	9/10	9/10	14/20
Total	24/30	13/16	17/27 NS	29/36

At a later stage in training, all verbs had shared at least one noun and most of them several, and, of course, the amount of generalization training or number of nouns trained with each verb had increased. In Table 6.2 we list 11 cases for each subject in which nouns taught with one verb have been paired with another

TABLE 6.1
Early Transfer Results for Elizabeth and Peony

	Correct/trials	ρ
Elizabeth		
1. Wash: doll/gumdrop	15/20 (4 errors = doll)	.05
2. Insert: monkey chow/shoe	4/10 (4 errors = shoe)	NS
3. Insert: doll/gumdrop	10/15	NS
4. Wash: monkey chow/shoe	8/15	NS
Peony		
1. Insert: doll/gumdrop	14/15	.01
2. Wash: monkey chow/shoe	13/20	NS
3. Wash: doll/gumdrop	14/20	NS
4. Insert: monkey chow/shoe	9/20	.05

verb for the first time. The paradigm underlying the test is:

$$\frac{\text{Training}}{\begin{array}{l} V_1: \ N_1/N_2 \\ V_2: \ N_3/N_4 \end{array}} \qquad \frac{\text{Test}}{V_1: \ N_3/N_4}$$

The information given in each line answers two questions: (1) with what nouns (N_1/N_2) has the test verb (V_1) most recently occurred? and (2) with what verb (V_2) have the test nouns (N_3/N_4) most recently occurred? Consider Item 2 for Elizabeth. The first line in the left column shows that Elizabeth has last encountered "insert" in the instructions "Elizabeth apple insert," "Elizabeth banana insert," and "Elizabeth orange insert." The second line shows that she has last seen the test nouns "marker" and "sponge" in the instructions "Elizabeth marker give" and "Elizabeth sponge give." In the test, shown in the right column, she received the novel combinations "Elizabeth marker insert" and "Elizabeth sponge insert" and was correct on 8 out of 10 trials, with one error in the first five trials.

Almost all of the words were both trained and tested in the comprehension modality. In a few cases, as noted, the noun–verb combinations were accompanied by a modality shift; nouns were taught in production and then tested for the first time in comprehension. Items 9 and 10 for both Elizabeth and Peony were of this kind, "round" versus "square" and "red" versus "yellow" having been introduced in production with the verb "give" and then tested in comprehension with the verb "insert." Other cases deviate from the base paradigm in minor ways. For example, as many as four nouns were sometimes presented with a test verb, all four being new to the verb in several cases and only one or more forming a new combination with the verb in other cases. The items are listed in the order in which the tests have been given; the interval between tests and the amount of training interpolated between them is highly variable.

Both Elizabeth and Peony were generally successful in dealing with novel combinations of the present kind. In 11 such tests Elizabeth failed two and Peony failed three. Interestingly, Elizabeth passed both tests (Items 9 and 10) in which a modality shift was superimposed on the novel combination. The tests Peony failed made special demands. One involved a modality shift, whereas the other presented not one but two instructions at the same time, a form of training used in introducing the negative particle (see page 157). These results affirm that, at an intermediate stage of training, both Peony and Elizabeth have been able to respond correctly to novel combinations of verbs and nouns.

MODALITY SHIFT

The ideal way to study the transfer relations between the modalities could not be done with the child. We could not teach a child independent lexicons, A for production and B for comprehension, and after the child was expert in each observe its ability to produce in B and comprehend in A. Moreover, the very fact that production depends on a long course of phonological development all but assures that opportunities for comprehension precede those for production.

With Peony and Elizabeth, we approximated the experiments that could not be done with children. Restricting certain words to production and others to comprehension, after each set of words was mastered in its respective mode, we tested the subject's ability to use the words in the modality in which the words had not yet been experienced. Although the first formal tests of this kind were made with Peony and Elizabeth, the first suggestion of difficulty in transfer from one mode to the other actually came from Sarah, at an extremely early period in her training during which production and comprehension were combined in the same lesson. On half the lessons, Sarah was required to request one of three clothes items by writing "Give X," where X was either "hat," "purse," or "shoe." In the other half of the lesson she was required to respond to the instruction "Take X," where X had the same meaning. On the production trials, one item of clothing lay before her along with the names of two of the items; she was to choose the word that matched the item. On comprehension trials, the problem was reversed: whereas the trainer's sentence "Take X" presented her with only one name, the world offered two items and she had to choose the item corresponding to the word on the board. Over 30 lessons were given, during which she hovered at chance on both production and comprehension. Finally, she began to show evidence of learning in production, reaching almost to 78% correct on six consecutive lessons (where chance was 50% with two alternatives).

TABLE 6.2
Transfer Results on Noun Contrasts for Elizabeth and Peony

Training (comprehension)	Test (comprehension)	Correct/ trials	Correct/ first five trials	p
Elizabeth				
1. Wash: apple/ball Give: cantaloupe (in prod.)	Wash: cantaloupe/apple	15/20	(4/5)	
2. Insert: apple/banana/orange Give: marker/sponge	Insert: marker/sponge	10	(4/5)	
3. Push: keys/clay Give: marker/sponge	Push: marker/keys/clay	7/10	(4/5)	
4. Wash: apple Give: marker/sponge	Wash: sponge/apple/banana	14/20	(4/5)	
5. On: key/clay Push: shoe/monkey chow	On: monkey chow/shoe	9/10	(5/5)	
6. On: keys/clay Give: marker/sponge	On: sponge/marker	2/6	(2/5)	NS
7. Insert: apple/banana/orange Spoon: take	Insert: spoon/crayon	5/5		
8. On: key/clay Take: crayon/spoon	On: crayon/spoon	12/12		
9. Insert: apple/banana/orange Give: round/square (in production)	Insert: round/square	8/10	(5/5)	

#	Production	Comprehension	Score		
10.	Insert: apple/banana/orange Give: red/yellow (in production)	Insert: red/yellow	13/16	(4/5)	
11.	Touch: doll/cup	Touch: apple/banana	7/10	(2/5)	NS
Peony					
1.	Insert: apple/banana/orange Give: marker/sponge	Insert: marker/sponge	9/10	(5/5)	
2.	Insert: apple/banana/orange Give: keys/clay	Insert: keys/clay	8/10	(4/5)	
3.	Push: keys/clay Give: marker	Push: keys/clay/marker	9/11	(4/5)	
4.	Wash: apple Give: sponge	Wash: sponge/apple Wash: sponge/apple/banana	9/10 6/10	(4/5) (3/5)	
5.	On: key/clay Give: marker/sponge	On: marker/sponge	8/10	(4/5)	
6.	On: keys/clay Push: monkey chow/shoe	On: monkey chow/shoe	10/12	(5/5)	
7.	Insert: apple/banana/orange Give: spoon	Insert: spoon/crayon/ball/clay	12/16	(5/5)	
8.	Take: cup/key Give: spoon/clay	Take: spoon/clay/crayon/ball	4/11	(2/5)	NS
9.	Insert: apple/banana/orange Give: red/yellow (in production)	Insert: red/yellow	11/12	(5/5)	
10.	Insert: apple Give: round/square (in production)	Insert: round/square	10/17	(4/5)	NS
11.	Touch: doll/cup	Touch: apple/banana	8/10	(4/5)	

Nevertheless, in this same period she showed no improvement on comprehension, remaining at the 53% level. It was not possible to carry this failure to a more determinate conclusion; too many lessons had already been devoted to the same items and boredom was producing a reluctant subject. Moreover, this evidence is mainly of interest only because of the early stage from which it dates and because transfer has failed even though production and comprehension trials have been carried out back-to-back in the same session. In a more important sense, however, the evidence is indeterminate: learning is not well shown in either mode. Unless learning is truly shown in one mode, its failure to transfer to the other mode is not conclusive. This problem does not apply to later evidence.

Conclusive evidence for failure of transfer from production to comprehension was obtained with both Peony and Elizabeth in about equal force. The first 11 object names were all taught in the production mode, by the subject writing "Give X" in the presence of the appropriate item. Subsequently, both Peony and Elizabeth were taught the verbs "take" and "insert" in the comprehension mode, with the usual combination of imitation and passive guidance. For instance, the trainer wrote "Debby take X," carried out her own instruction, and then immediately followed this with "Elizabeth take X"; when necessary, she passively guided the subject through the target act. "Take" and "insert" were both taught with "ball" and "block." The latter pair of words had never been used with "give" and, like "take" and "insert," was taught in the comprehension mode. Both subjects quickly learned to follow the instructions "Take ball" versus "Take block" as well as "insert ball" versus "Insert block." Their grasp of the 11 object names learned with "give" included some of the first words they had learned—indeed, there were no words they knew better.

A transfer test was made by requiring Peony and Elizabeth to apply "take" and "insert" to the 11 object names. Because the object names had been used only with "give" in the production mode, and later "take" and "insert" had been used only in the comprehension mode, the test demanded two kinds of transfer. Nouns learned with one verb had now to be used with a second verb. In addition, words used only in production had now to be used in the comprehension mode. The basic test trial consisted of writing either "Insert X" or "Take X," where X consisted of one of the 11 object names. On each trial the instructions were accompanied by just two of the objects, say, apple and banana; the subject was required to take the designated object on some trials and to insert it on other trials. Peony made 74 errors in 177 trials, or 58% correct; Elizabeth made 120 errors in 292 trials, or 59% correct.

An outcome of this kind is quite shocking to the unprepared. The subject has correctly written "Give apple," " ... banana," " ... cantaloupe," " ... pear," " ... orange," " ... apricot," etc., on hundreds of trials. Likewise, when told to "Take ball" or "Take block" it had responded correctly hundreds of trials. When told "Take apple," " ... banana," " ... cantaloupe," etc., however, it responded at chance.

In both examples, the modality changes were confounded with changes in words. "Give X" in the production mode was contrasted with "Take X" in the comprehension mode. Therefore, the failure might be attributed either to the change in modality and/or to the fact that nouns trained with one verb were paired with a new verb. Fortunately, we have one case for both Peony and Elizabeth in which the same sentence "Give X" was used in both modalities.

"Give" was first introduced in the production mode, along with the fruit names, which were the first words learned by Peony and Elizabeth. Whenever a piece of, say, banana was set before them, they could obtain it by requesting "Give banana." Later "give" was used in the comprehension mode as a means of introducing the words "ball" and "keys." The trainer placed one object or the other on the table, wrote alternately "Give ball" or "Give keys," and extended her hand to receive the designated item. With this use of "give" in the comprehension mode, Peony and Elizabeth were exposed for the first time to the request that they give rather than receive; ball and keys were chosen deliberately to forestall the motivational problems that could be anticipated with more valued objects.

After the subjects had learned "ball" and "keys" and so were successful in responding to "give" in the comprehension mode, a plastic banana and apple were placed on the table and the trainer wrote alternately "Give banana," or "Give apple," extending her hand as before to receive the designated item. Both subjects performed at chance, six errors in 15 trials for Peony and six in 13 trials for Elizabeth. Although the fruit names had not previously been applied to plastic fruit, nevertheless, as we established in advance, both subjects could match the plastic and real fruits, and both had been allowed to discover that the plastic fruits were not edible. More to the point, neither subject showed any reluctance to hand over the plastic fruit, for which they were rewarded in the usual way, no more reluctance than in handing over the ball or keys.

The simplest interpretation is a failure to transfer from one modality to the other. When either banana or apple was placed before the subjects, they correctly wrote either "Give apple" or "Give banana," requesting the fruit that was present. When a trainer wrote the same sentences, however, requesting that she be given one of the fruit, neither subject consistently handed over the correct fruit. The failure was in no way comparable to their original failure to carry out the role reversal entailed by the modality shift. Both subjects were now fully competent in comprehension per se. Moreover, with only a little training on the same material, both subjects learned to respond accurately; we speak of a failure in transfer exactly because such training was required. In summary, both subjects had produced "Give apple" and "Give banana" accurately yet, when required to read sentences exactly like those they had already written, they performed at chance.

It is important to keep in mind that at a later stage all three subjects routinely transferred from one modality to the other and that in this chapter we are focusing on early failures. Consider now two examples from Sarah, one in which she was wholly successful and a second more special case in which she was at least partly successful.

TAKE VERSUS GIVE:
TRANSFER FROM PRODUCTION TO COMPREHENSION

The verb "take," which had been taught earlier with a standard combination of imitation and passive guidance, was applied to the five object names ("jam," "honey," "peanut butter," "bread," and "cracker") that Sarah had learned in an earlier series. "Take" had been introduced with fruit names. The trainer wrote "Mary take apple," carried out her own instruction, and then followed this immediately with "Sarah take apple." If Sarah hesitated, as she sometimes did on the first trial, the trainer passively guided Sarah through the act. Typically, Sarah did not need more than one such trial to carry out the act herself on subsequent trials.

The point of applying "take" to the new object names was twofold: first to determine whether words recently acquired with the verb "give" would transfer to the verb "take"; and second to examine transfer from production to comprehension.

Sarah was given three kinds of tests with "take." The jam, honey, and peanut butter were taken out of the jar and for the first time spread on crackers, which were laid out before her so that she could now take these items rather than have them given to her. In the first lesson, five kinds of canapes were spread before her: jam, honey, and peanut butter on cracker, along with plain cracker and plain bread. No errorless trials were given. Instead, the trainer wrote one of five instructions on the board and Sarah was required to take the item designated in the instruction. Five different instructions were given, in keeping with the five canapes available on each trial: "Sarah honey take," "Sarah jam take," "Sarah peanut butter take," "Sarah cracker take," or "Sarah bread take." She was correct on 13 out of 14 trials. On one trial, late in the lesson, when told to take bread she correctly pointed to but did not take the bread; we credited her with a weakened appetite but a correct choice.

In the next lesson, the three spreads were put on both bread and crackers, making six canapes, and the complexity of the instructions were increased commensurately. Because honey and the other spreads were now to be found on both bread and cracker it was necessary to have a way in which to differentiate these cases. "Take honey," or "Take jam" would no longer do, for now it was necessary to distinguish between, say, "honey—bread" and "honey—cracker," etc. With the spread name used essentially as a modifier, Sarah was given one of six instructions on each trial: "Sarah honey—bread take," "Sarah honey—cracker take," "Sarah jam—bread take," "Sarah jam—cracker take," "Sarah peanut butter—break take," or "Sarah peanut butter—cracker take." In the first lesson of this kind, she was not confronted with all six alternatives but was required to choose between only two alternatives. Peanut butter on cracker was contrasted with peanut butter on bread; then the same contrast was made with jam and then with honey. She was correct on eight of nine trials. Her alternatives were increased to four, and she was correct on seven of eight trials.

In the next three sessions, when confronted with all six canapes, she showed the added burden on the first session, doing only ten of 18 correct (still greater than chance expectancy of three with six alternatives). When the lessons were repeated twice, she quickly recovered her accuracy and was correct on 12 out of 15 and 11 out of 12 trials, respectively.

Next she was given six lessons identical to the preceding ones, except that instructions were now given in pairs. Rather than being told, say, "Sarah jam—cracker take," she was told "Sarah jam—cracker take" and, say, "Sarah honey—bread take." There were no restrictions on the possible pairs and they were written side by side. Her performance suffered a bit on the first lesson but recovered on the remaining five: 9 out of 14, 11 out of 14, 15 out of 19, 12 out of 12, 10 out of 14, and 8 out of 10 trials correct per total trials, respectively. These paired instructions could not be considered a paragraph even in a weak sense, for there were no restrictions on the order in which the two sentences were to be processed; nor, interestingly, did she show any preference for order. Over the whole series she was correct on 98 out of 128, or 76%. This is a commendable performance level given that for the most part she was choosing from six alternatives.

The above series was directed at two questions: (1) the transfer of nouns from one verb to another and (2) the transfer from the production to the comprehension mode. All six nouns introduced with the verb "give" were transferred without intervening errorless trials to the verb "take"; in addition, she had no difficulty using combinations of these new words, for example, "honey—bread" and "honey—cracker," and in distinguishing between combinations of the new objects. Incidentally, the latter indicates that she could equate, say, jam in a jar with jam spread on a cracker, an identity not likely to trouble chimpanzees but apt to trouble lesser species.[1]

The data on transfer from production to comprehension were equally decisive. The only qualification comes from the six or eight prior uses of "give" in a comprehension mode. In the preceding series, Sarah was occasionally instructed to "give cracker Mary" or "give bread Mary" and was largely successful in doing so. Of course, this is itself evidence of transfer from production to comprehension. Further and more extensive evidence of the same kind comes from the

---

[1] We are so quick to impose identities that it can only profit us to work with lesser species. Their failure to impose the same identities can help to awaken us to the full inventory of perceptual transformations that we take for granted.

words "honey," "peanut butter," and "jam"; they had no previous use whatever in the comprehension mode. Therefore, three words came to the test untouched by use in comprehension, two only slightly touched. She was about equally accurate in her use of both sets of words.

TRANSFER OF WORD ORDER
FROM COMPREHENSION TO PRODUCTION

In the next series we examined transfer in the opposite direction, from comprehension to production, a special case of it concerned with word order. Could Sarah transfer to her own production word order that was originally shown her in the comprehension mode? Recall that in her previous instructions the name of the spread invariably preceded the name of the receptacle, e.g., "Sarah honey–bread take," "...honey–cracker," "...jam–bread," etc., never "bread–honey," "cracker–jam," etc. Now she was called on to request the same items herself. Would she employ in her own sentences the same adjective–noun order that was shown her in the trainer's sentences?

One item, honey spread on bread, was placed before her and she was given only the words needed to form the sentence: "give," "honey," "bread," and "Sarah." Instead she wrote "Give bread Sarah," probably in keeping with the large number of times she had written that sentence in her earlier training. Encouraged to correct she wrote "Give bread honey Sarah." Finally, she wrote "Give honey bread Sarah" and was then given the honey bread. The same testing on jam–cracker produced "Give jam Sarah" and then "Give jam cracker Sarah." On the third trial she was again given a honey–bread canape but now the incorrect words "jam" and "cracker" were added to the words already available to her. She chose the correct words but repeated her order errors exactly, i.e., she wrote successively "Give bread Sarah," "Give bread honey Sarah" and finally "Give honey bread Sarah."

She was then given eight trials on which each of the six canapes was placed before her one at a time along with a pile of 12–15 words, of which only "give," "jam," "cracker," "bread," "honey," "give," and "peanut butter" were relevant. She was required to request the prescribed item by writing "Give X Y Sarah," where X was the name of a spread and Y the name of the receptacle, either bread or cracker. The irrelevant words were added because we felt that her knowledge of the key words was now sufficient to bear the strain of a more difficult test. From about this stage of the training on we regularly added five to ten irrelevant words to any set of alternatives given her on a production test. Irrelevant words were varied both within and between sessions, so that words that were relevant on one lesson, that is, occurred in prescribed sentences, became irrelevant on a subsequent lesson. The attempt to increase difficulty in this manner was of doubtful success. The records show that Sarah never used an irrelevant word. Whereas this reflects her grasp of the training material, it must also reflect the inherent simplicity of nearly all lessons. Lessons were typically devoted to a small well-defined topic. A search of her extensive data reveals perhaps a dozen lessons that took up several topics and shifted freely from one to the other, but most lessons dealt with only one topic. There was one set of alternatives, e.g., the six canapes, or five fruits, or three donors, or occasionally combinations of donors and objects, but always the lesson concerned a well-defined set of alternatives. The words and even the sentences germane to each lesson also made up a well-defined set. The boundedness of the lesson, in both its verbal and its nonverbal alternatives, could not but have helped Sarah discover the topic of the lesson—and in that way have helped her to discriminate relevant from irrelevant words.

Moreover, Sarah's scrupulous disuse of irrelevant words suggested that the simple structure of the lesson was not wasted on her. Quite likely there was a real sense in which she could be said to have discovered the topic of each lesson; how better to explain her impeccable record on the nonuse of irrelevant words? Unfortunately, we did not prepare Sarah for the possibility of being interviewed after a lesson. Had we trained her appropriately, it might then have been possible to ask her what in fact she considered to be the topic of the lesson.

On the eight sessions she was correct on 4 out of 6, 4 out of 5, 6 out of 7, 6 out of 7, 8 out of 8, 5 out of 7, 5 out of 6, and 6 out of 6 trials per total trials, respectively, or 84% correct. Of her nine errors, three were errors of choice and six errors of order, all of these YX rather than XY, for example, "bread–honey," rather than "honey–bread." In brief, she produced the correct word order on 50 of 56 four-word sentences, which compared favorably with her earlier performance in the series devoted to word order.

Her opening use of "Give bread Sarah" to request the bread–honey canape, as well as her subsequent "Give jam Sarah" to request the jam–cracker canape, were scored as errors of word order, although they involve omission of a word rather than incorrectly ordered words. Moreover, the omission is defensible. When the world offers only one canape it can be identified exhaustively by referring either to its receptacle or to its spread; reference to both receptacle and spread is redundant.

Notice how few trials she carried out in each of these lessons, an average of only about seven, approximately half her customary number. Although sessions were typically scheduled for 20 trials, they were often shorter and only occasionally longer, depending on the subject's willingness. The occasional short lesson was not indicative of anything: barking dogs, working men in the hall, or the subject's bad mood. However, a string of short lessons, such as in the present case, was typically indicative of difficulty. Sarah evidently found it demanding to produce four-word sentences with the present fixed word-order requirement. The demand did not impair her accuracy (84% correct) but reduced by about 50% the number of sentences she produced in any lesson.

SUCCESSFUL TRANSFER OF "ON" FROM COMPREHENSION TO PRODUCTION

Like Sarah, Peony and Elizabeth were taught "on" in comprehension and successfully transferred to production. A detailed account of the original training is given elsewhere (pages 108–110); here we look only at the transfer. In the comprehension training, the trainers wrote such sentences as "Keys on clay" for which the subjects indicated comprehension by placing the keys on the clay. After they were fully proficient in the comprehension mode, the trainer reversed the process. One item was placed on another and the subjects were required to produce sentences describing the arrangement.

In the first test of this kind, the items used were keys and clay, two of the items used in the comprehension training, and the words given Peony and Elizabeth were "keys," "clay," and "on." Previously they had responded to such sentences as "Clay on key" by placing one designated object on the other; now they were required to produce the same sentences as descriptions of the trainer's arrangement. On the first lesson of this kind, Peony was correct on nine of ten trials, with one error in the first five trials. Elizabeth was given only five trials but was correct on all five. Next, the alternatives were changed and increased to monkey chow, sponge, and shoe, and the words given the subjects were changed accordingly. The trainer then carried out five of the six possible arrangements and Peony correctly described all five. Elizabeth had more difficulty with the increased alternatives; she was correct on 11 of 17 trials, which was well above chance, however, with six alternatives. Therefore, the same subjects that performed at chance in an earlier period when transferred from one modality to another now transferred successfully.

TRANSFER AND REDUNDANCY

A fully successful transfer test eliminates all the redundancies that are a basic factor in especially the child's use of language but even in the adult's use as well. In the natural setting, the child is not told "Pick up your clothes" in the presence of its scattered toys, nor "Pick up your toys" in the presence of its scattered clothes. Neither instruction would be given in the same tone of voice in which the child is, say, called to dinner. Neither, moreover, is the child likely to be given either instruction when engaged, for example, in putting something away in the refrigerator. Instructions do not come out of the blue but are more commonly part of an existing structure. Speech joins with other factors in carrying the child another step forward in an ongoing sequence, or perhaps in bringing a straying child back to the sequence in progress. Although it is difficult to measure the redundancies in the use of natural language, we have reason to believe that they are considerable. Ten years ago as a small first step toward such measurement, we recorded the lunchtime conversations of mothers and children, categorizing their speech in terms of six semantic classes appropriate to children, for example, school, friends, sports. We found that over 93% of what the mother said to the child repeated the semantic topic of the child's previous utterance (Premack & Anglin, 1973).

In the transfer tests described above, all of the following redundancies were eliminated. First, there were no intonational cues; this was true, of course, not only in the transfer tests but in the routine use of the plastic words, so in effect the instructions to "Cut apple," "Wash apple," etc., were given in the same tone of voice. Second, the instructions were not given in the presence of only those implements that were appropriate to the act but in the presence of both kinds of implements (in some cases, the joint occurrence of the implements was itself new, so that the transfer test introduced novelty both inside and outside of the sentence). Third, each instruction was essentially a nonsense instruction, not a part of an existing structure and not predictable from previous or current factors in the situation. The requests did not even invite the subject to do things they were much interested in doing, so there was little if any coincidence between the instructions and the subject's motivational state, which is a frequent source of redundancy.

In pointing to limitations in Sarah's use of language, Brown (1973) described what Sarah did as processing " . . . a sentence when it arrives as the crowning problem in a pyramid of training . . ." and contrasted this with human language use, which he described as processing " . . . a sentence which comes to you as simply one from the infinite possibilities of language. . . ." Is Brown's characterization quite correct, or has he overlooked the redundancies that obtain in normal language use? How would the human language user fare if, in fact, he did not confront sentences as more or less crowning elements in a redundant structure but rather as simply one among the infinitely possible sentences? We cannot tell from the normal use of language for there sentences are not experienced in the way Brown describes. However, it is possible to get some idea from the laboratory, which is perhaps the only place where a sentence is ever experienced as one among the infinitely possible. A recent experiment by Bransford and Johnson (1972) is relevant, not because they have used especially unpredictable sentences but because, even with normal material, they have been able to show how much comprehension depends on nonlinguistic factors. The subjects were required to comprehend sentences with and without being shown pictures illustrating the topic of the sentences. The addition of pictures produced a significant gain in comprehension. The adult reaction in reading this may tend to be, "Well, that is the case for children; they are after all rather like chimpanzees." However, the subjects that Bransfeld and Johnson tested were not young children but college students.

I point out some of these factors in specifically this context because, in comparing the chimpanzee with the child—and wondering if even the naive child may not show far more transfer—one must not use as a basis of comparison the child's performance in a natural setting. The redundancies there, although difficult to measure, are nonetheless certain to be very large. Ask, rather, how the child and chimpanzee would compare if the child too were being asked to comply with nonsense instructions.

7
Early Concepts:
Same — Different, No,
and the Interrogative

Same–different is an exceedingly simple judgment from the human point of view, so basic to our theorizing that we have difficulty describing events in the world without it. We use it unthinkingly, both in describing our own behavior, where the description may be correct, and in describing the behavior of lesser species, where it may be less correct. For instance, in watching a pigeon select grain from a set of particles, we rather automatically describe the behavior in terms of same–different judgments. We assume that the bird judges each new particle to be the same as one it has already eaten (in which case it eats the particle), the same as one it has already rejected (in which case it avoids the particle), or different from either (in which case it tries out the particle). Although same–different is obviously vital to this account, an alternative account can be given in which it plays no role whatever—fortunately, for there is reason to believe that pigeons are incapable of same–different judgments.

On the alternative account we assume that the bird simply approaches and eats instances of, say, smooth red particle, and avoids instances of, say, rough grey particle, thus responding to the absolute character of each particle rather than to a relation between successive particles. Which account is correct? The behavior in this example is too simple to force a decision between the two accounts. To determine whether or not the bird is capable of making same–different judgments we must use a more demanding task.

A decision could be made by presenting the bird the same particles but in a different format. Give it two red particles on some trials and a red and a grey particle on other trials, and require that it peck on the left when given the former and on the right when given the latter. Pigeons can learn to do this, i.e., to respond differentially to $A-A$ and $A-B$. However, when given $B-B$, or comparable cases instanced by new elements, e.g., $C-C$, $C-B$, $C-A$, they respond at chance. The stimuli we have used (corn, wheat, pebble) may be inappropriate, and birds may succeed when given comparable tests with more salient stimuli. For the stimuli we have used, however, pigeons do not make same–different judgments.

Zentall and Hogan (1974), Lubow (1974), Honig (1965), Malott *et al.* (1971), and others have tested pigeons on match to sample and similar paradigms in a number of clever ways, by and large with negative results. What may be needed now more than cleverness is doggedness, e.g., a test in which pigeons are given not one or two but, say, 20 different matching problems. Such tests would make the pigeon's experience more nearly comparable to that of the primate. Typically, pigeons are given only two or three different matching problems, whereas chimpanzesss and children may receive 10 different problems before being tested for transfer. The reason for this disparity is simple. The primates may learn the 10 training cases as well as pass the transfer test in one session, whereas the pigeon requires hundreds of trials and many sessions to learn even one problem. Yet precisely because the pigeon is slow would it seem desirable to give it the benefit of at least as many exemplars as are given the more facile primate. On the other hand, although this simple test is definitely needed, there is no guarantee or even suggestion that the dogged experimenter would not have better spent his time on some other project. For pigeons learn arbitrary or so-called symbolic problems (if sample is red, take blue alternative) at the same rate they learn matching problems (if sample is red, take red alternative), and show no savings at all in learning the second or even third matching problem in a series of such problems.

Matching to sample and responding differentially to A–A versus A–B make logically equivalent demands, so it is reasonable that if the bird fails one test it would fail the other. Both require that responding be associated not with absolute physical features but with the features of sameness and difference. To respond correctly, the bird must be able to observe not only that the relations between A and A is same, as that between C and C is same, but also that the relation between A and A is the same as that between C and C (or that C–C, A–$A, \ldots , N$–N instance same, whereas C–B, B–$A, \ldots , N$–X instance different).

Generalized match to sample illustrates in a uniquely simple way the minimum computational power that a species must have in order to acquire language. First, the species must be capable of responding to relations, for even the simplest sentence contains markers for both relational and absolute concepts. Consider such sentences as "Daddy home," "Mommy purse," "Bill hit Mary," and "Mommy take flower." In the last two cases, the relational terms—"hit" and "take"—are explicit, whereas in the first two the relations are not explicitly marked, and we interpret strings of this kind as sentences by inferring the relations. In the first case, we may infer a locative type relation between daddy and home, e.g., "daddy is home," and in the second, convert the two word string into a sentence by interpreting the string as a genetive relation, e.g., "Mommy's purse." These examples suggest that a sentence could be defined, in the weakest possible sense, as a string of words in which there is an implicit or explicit dependence among the words of a kind that can be represented by the relation between a predicate and its arguments. The point of this definition is to stress that a sentence is inconceivable without a relational term, either implicit or explicit. A species that could not fulfill this weak condition could not possibly fulfill the inordinately stronger conditions imposed by adult sentence structures.

Second, it is not sufficient that the species be capable of responding to relations; to acquire language it must be able to respond to relations between relations. Consider the following predicates all of which have the same logical status and differ only in the complexity of their arguments.

▨	Same	▨
Apple	Name of	▨
Red	Color of	Apple
Sarah drop glass	⊃ (if–then)	Glass break

In "same–different," the simplest case, the arguments are things; whereas in the conditional particle or "if–then," the arguments are not only linguistic entities, but sentences.

To acquire these predicates in the generalized sense that is indispensible for language, the subject must in each case respond to a relation between relations. For example, to acquire "same–different," the subject must first recognize that the relation between, say, apple and apple is $same_1$; likewise that the relation between, say, banana and banana is $same_2$; and finally that $same_1$ is the same as $same_2$. It must make a comparable judgment in the case of the other predicates:

1. The relation between, say, "apple" and apple is the same as that between, say, "banana" and banana, i.e., $name of_1$ is the same as $name of_2$.

2. The relation between, say, red and apple is the same as that between, say, yellow and banana, i.e., $color of_1$ is the same as $color of_2$.

3. The relation between, say, dropping the glass and the glass breaking is the same as that between, say, tipping the glass and the water spilling, i.e., $\supset_1$ is the same as $\supset_2$.

"Same–different" was therefore not singled out arbitrarily but is demonstrably representative of the kind of predicate a species must be able to acquire in order to acquire language.

We are in a position to extend the list of preconditions for language. In addition to being able to recognize representations of itself, a species must have the capacity to respond to relations between relations. Without this capacity it could not acquire language; each time a predicate occurred with a new argument the species would have to be retaught the predicate.

A standard rebuttal to this argument is to diminish the phenomenon by calling it nothing but generalization. However, even if the phenomenon is viewed as generalization, it is nonetheless not a kind of generalization that is open to most species. Accounts of language such as the one by Skinner (1957) are wide of the mark in large part because they treat all species as being essentially of the same intelligence. Only by ignoring species' differences would it seem possible to base a theory of language on data derived from a species that is almost certainly incapable of acquiring language.

Moreover, the bird's failures on generalized match to sample is not incompatible with its success in discriminating between man and nonman, water and nonwater, and other cases of this kind. The latter do not require that responding be associated with the feature of sameness or difference, but only that the bird code the physical stimuli in terms of some features and then respond in an absolute fashion to instances of the coded features.

An apparent ability to imitate or repeat the behavior of a model may appear to evidence a capacity for same–different judgments—we describe the behavior as doing the same thing the model does—but in fact it does not, even when social facilitation is successfully ruled out. The standard imitation experiment is too weak a test on which to base a decision. There is no question but that the rat and other nonprimates can form associations on an observational basis. For instance, a rat may observe a conspecific bar press for food and on this basis form associations between food and features of the cage and/or even food and features of the model's behavior. These associations could increase the incentive value of the environmental and/or behavioral features, thus making the observer more likely than a control to engage in behavior like that of the model. However, the features in terms of which the associations are formed may be of the standard kind and need not involve same–different judgments.

Because the foraging behavior of a conspecific is apt to be a salient cue, we can use it as the stimulus basis of a test that is strong enough to determine whether or not the rat has the capacity in question. The subject could be required to respond in one way when two conspecifics both foraged for food in the same way $(A-A)$, and to respond in a different way when the conspecifics did not forage in the same way $(A-B)$. If the rat could not only learn this discrimination but also generalize it to new As and Bs, it could be said to have the capacity in question. Obviously we find it highly convenient to use the predicates of same–different in describing behavior; e.g., the rat behaves the same way as the model. The description is harmless as such. But the danger lies in the fact that predicates primates use in describing the rat may come to be imputed to the rat.

We must distinguish closely between behavior that instances a predicate—that causes the describing organism to use a predicate—and behavior the discriminative control of which is the same as that of the predicates used to describe the behavior.

Although only primates may be capable of same–different judgments, by their standard the judgments are primitive and they can make them at an early age. In Chapter 13, as background for the quantifiers, we review some work on the ability of young children to assign a number to sets of objects. The sets were small—two, three, or four members—so that counting was not necessary. When the sets were homogeneous, even $2\frac{1}{2}$-year-old children assigned a number to them. But when the sets consisted of a mixture of objects, young children no longer assigned a number to the whole set. They subdivided the set and assigned a number to each subset. Subdivisions of this kind already presuppose a judgment of sameness and difference.

In addition to the primitive character of the judgment, the words "same"–"different" that are to be associated with the judgment make a good starting point. The words can be applied to objects that are not themselves named. For instance, to call two bananas "same" or a banana and an apple "different," neither object need be named. Therefore, "same–different" has no linguistic prerequisites and in this sense can be contrasted with, for example, "name of" (which is a relation between an item and its name) or the still more demanding "if–then" (which is a relation between sentences).

Complex forms of matching (such as those dealt with in Chapter 10) need not be used in order to decide whether the species can make those judgments for which "same" and "different" are the appropriate linguistic markers. Can the subject match "like" objects and transfer this disposition to nontraining items? If the answer is yes, then it is sensible to attempt to teach the subject "same" as a label for items which it considers to match, and "different" as a label for items it does not consider to match.

The first matching procedures taught Sarah involved simple object matching. Ten pairs of objects were used: cup, spoon, clothespin, rubber band, postage stamp, pipe, cotton ball, key, paper clip, and blue bead. The first sample given her was a cup, with cup and spoon as alternatives. Her hand was placed on the correct alternative and physically guided so that she moved the cup to the sample. Then the position of the alternatives was exchanged, and the guiding procedure was repeated. More elaborate shaping procedures were necessary with Peony and Elizabeth but not with Sarah. She was given 12 trials with the cup as sample and the cup and spoon as alternatives, and then 14 trials with spoon as sample and the same alternatives. She made three and five errors on the first and second arrangements, respectively.

Then a transfer test was given using the other eight items listed above. The eight new items were combined with the two training items, each one being used at least once, both as a sample and as an alternative. Sarah made six errors in 22 trials, one in the first five trials. The results suggested that she had learned to match not only items used in training but nontraining items as well.

Having established that Sarah was capable of matching like objects, we introduced the words "same" and "different" (in the latter case without bothering to teach an oddity judgment to establish that she was capable of the judgment of difference). The same two cups used in the matching procedure were placed before Sarah at a small distance from one another, she was given a piece of plastic intended to mean "same" and was required to place it between the cups. After four trials of this kind, she was given a cup and a spoon, plus a second language element intended to mean "different," and was required to place it between them. She was given 14 trials, seven of each kind.

Choice trials were then used to establish whether or not the desired association had developed during the errorless training. The stimulus arrangement was identical with the earlier one. Two cups were set before her on some trials and a cup and spoon on others. However, now she was given both "same" and "different" and was required to choose between them. She made four errors in 20 trials, with one in the first five trials. Errors on the use of "same" and "different" were one and three, respectively, a harbinger perhaps of the consistently greater difficulty she would subsequently show in learning negative or marked forms.

Summarizing the standard training procedure, which we are to encounter over and over, the first step is the errorless trials; this is followed by choice. If the subject failed the choice test it was then returned to an earlier step, but if it did not fail it was given the third and last step in the standard procedure, a test of transfer.

Sarah's ability to transfer was tested on new combinations of old items (members of the set of ten items used in the original match to sample), some entirely new items, and some nontraining items for which names had and had not been previously taught. These experimental niceties proved to be in vain, however. She made so few overall errors that one condition could not be differentiated from another. These are characteristic transfer results, as the rest of the book testifies. Although Sarah had difficulty learning certain complex and/or ill-taught words, despite her difficulty in learning them she never failed a transfer test on any of them.

In principle, Sarah could have moved about the cage, picking up pairs of objects and labeling them "same" or "different." Whether her ability to label like and unlike pairs of objects may actually dispose her to do so is something we have not tested. In this phase of the research we were concerned with her ability to acquire language, not yet with her ability to use it. Match-to-sample established that she could identify instances of sameness for an apparently unlimited range of objects and the transfer data suggested that she could apply the words over a comparable range of objects. That the acquisition of language maps existing capacities can probably offer no simpler example.

It would be surprising if the transfer data for matching and for labeling were to disagree, and Sarah did not occasion any such surprises. However, the agreement between the two would be more impressive if instead of being perfect at both procedures the subject were imperfect at one and then showed corresponding imperfections in the other. By luck, we have data that meet these specifications.

In the early stages of training, Sarah was taught fruit names with the use of pieces of fruit. Apple, banana, orange, etc. were always cut into slices or wedges; even the peanuts were shelled and offered one piece at a time. Any use of a fruit name in that period resulted in a piece of fruit, therefore, never the intact fruit. Given this correlation, it is reasonable to ask, did "apple" mean to Sarah what it does to you and me, a compact, round, red object typically with a stem, or did it mean a wedge of wet, grainy, whitish material? Likewise, did "banana" mean a mildly curved cylinder, yellow with blackish streaks, or a small round slice of mushy material? These were reasonable questions, not only because the words were consistently associated with the pieces and never the intact fruit, but also because in that period, preparation of the fruit took place outside of Sarah's view. Therefore she had few if any opportunities to observe the relation between the various pieces of fruit and their source.

To answer these questions, we used match-to-sample, in one procedure with the name as the sample and two intact fruits as the alternatives, and in the reverse procedure with the intact fruit as the sample and the names of two fruits as alternatives. The fruits tested were apple, banana, orange, and pear. Sarah failed the test conclusively except for orange where she was above chance both when the name was used as the sample and when the intact fruit played that role. On all other fruits she performed at chance; for example, she selected apple as often as banana when the sample was "banana" and vice versa. Perhaps her success with orange was owed to the fact that there is more color overlap in this case between the intact and the cut fruit; or possibly she had eaten more oranges outside of the test situation than other fruits and in this way had learned to associate the inside and outside of the fruit.

The results distressed us at the time, far more than they would now with our revised view of the relation between knowledge and words (see Chapter 15), for at the time we saw them as a specifically linguistic failure, indicative of what was to be expected with an ape or any other species of slight linguistic capacity. Yet even in that early period of confused thinking it was possible to correct the interpretation and show that the failure was in no way linguistic. This was done in the next test: Words were removed altogether and the materials used were only intact fruit and pieces of fruit. In this second test, the intact fruit was again the sample on some occasions and the alternatives on others; but now pieces of fruit were substituted for the words, so that Sarah was required to match only fruit to fruit—part to whole or whole to part. Sarah failed this test no less conclusively than the preceding one. As before, she performed above chance only on orange, showing about the same level of accuracy in matching a piece of orange to an intact orange as she had shown in matching the word "orange" to an intact orange.

At a later time, after a period in which fruit was routinely prepared in Sarah's view, the same tests were repeated, changed only by the addition of several new fruits—peach, grape, and fig—which in the meantime had been added to her vocabulary. On this second round of tests she was successful both in matching pieces of fruit to intact fruit and in matching names of fruit to intact fruit. There was a complete parallel, therefore, between the perceptual and the linguistic results. At a time when she could not associate a piece of fruit with the whole fruit, she was unable to match the name of the fruit to the whole fruit, names having been trained exclusively with pieces of fruit. Later, when capable of matching pieces of fruit and whole fruit—having meanwhile been given an opportunity to discover the source of the pieces—she was also able to match names and whole fruit (even though there had been no change in the language training, and fruit names were still applied exclusively to the pieces).

"SAME—DIFFERENT" WITH PEONY AND ELIZABETH

Peony and Elizabeth learned match-to-sample far more slowly than Sarah. Nevertheless, the difference did not prepare us for the magnitude of the difficulty that they subsequently encountered in learning "same—different." For a time it looked as though their belated success at matching, on the one hand, and still more stubborn failure to learn "same—different," on the other, would constitute a clear disconfirmation of the mapping hypothesis. Ultimately, however, they did learn to label as well as to match.

Can we explain the disparity in the rate at which they mastered the two procedures? Unfortunately, the explanation cannot come from the mapping hypothesis itself, for it is not a quantitative hypothesis from which one can predict that if the subject learns matching in N trials it can go on to learn labeling in X trials. Predictions of this kind are not possible because there is no way to equate the efficiency of the procedures for teaching matching and labeling. Moreover, there is good reason to believe that the procedure for teaching labeling in the case of "same—different" is notably inefficient. Peony and Elizabeth were not the only subjects who learned matching with relative ease and then took hundreds of trials to learn labels for these same judgments.

Many children, trained in a manner comparable to that of the chimps, showed the same pattern.[1]

On simple matching, Peony reached a 75% correct level in five lessons; Elizabeth, invariably more excitable, reached a 68% level in nine lessons. Both were then trained on "same–different" in a manner comparable to that of Sarah. That is, exemplars for "same" and "different" were the same objects used in the simple matching; errorless trials were given on both "same" and "different," and these were followed by choice trials. However, both Peony and Elizabeth required more explicit shaping on the simple mechanics of the procedure. With Peony two lessons were spent teaching her to place "same" between two cups and "different" between cup and spoon. With the skittish Elizabeth, 20 lessons were devoted to the same objective. Previously, she had placed all words in the trainer's hand, a kind of direct barter that was accepted because of her uneasiness in the test situation. Now, however, she was required to place the word between a pair of objects. Physical guidance could not be used with Elizabeth in that period: she would not allow her hand to be picked up and moved. Although on some occasions she would take the trainer's hand, it was not until months later that she shared the prerogative, allowing the trainer to take her hand. Indeed after a year's work with Elizabeth, we realized that our procedures could be used not only with chimpanzees and autistic children but also with an autistic chimpanzee.

After she had been successfully shaped, Peony was given 20 errorless trials followed by seven lessons consisting entirely of choice trials. The first three lessons were confined strictly to cup–cup and cup–spoon; she made a total of nine errors in 30 trials. Then she was given four transfer sessions, each involving a new pair of objects, and made only 10 errors in 47 trials. Although not an outstanding performance, 80% correct on the transfer test was nonetheless acceptable and we assumed that she would improve with further training.

[1] The 2-year-olds who, along with Peony and Elizabeth, failed "same–different" all typically formed a position habit. In contrast, six-year-old children who failed did not form position habits. When a new pair of objects was introduced, they typically formed a one-trial association between the objects and "same" or "different"; so that it was only the transfer data that revealed that the 6-year-old had not really learned "same–different." With one-trial learning and relatively few transfer trials per training trial, rote memory, which some of the older children appeared to use, could be a favorable strategy. Introducing new pairs at a higher rate may make the strategy less favorable, and this is something we have not yet tried. Interestingly, no child adopted a memorization strategy on the simple match-to-sample; all subjects, including the 2-year-olds and Peony and Elizabeth as well, were able to learn that problem in the normal number of trials. Does the disparity between simple matching and "same–different" require that we abandon the thesis that prelanguage tests can be used to predict subsequent learning of linguistic markers? Instead of abandoning that thesis, I prefer to recommend that the prelanguage and language tests be made as alike as possible. Using the matching format to teach "same–different" to Peony and Elizabeth, which is described later in the chapter, was an attempt to carry out that recommendation.

Instead, a small change, made for reasons discussed later on, had unexpectedly adverse consequences. An interrogative marker was placed between the two objects, so that she no longer received say, cup–cup, but cup–?–cup; she was required to remove the question mark before replacing it with the word "same." She was given 36 errorless trials to accustom her to this small change, and then 22 lessons requiring her to remove the interrogative marker and replace it either with "same" or "different." Although all the lessons were limited to the original materials, cup–cup or cup–spoon, she made 103 errors in 333 trials, or 67% correct. Her performance fluctuated from 50 to 80% correct and showed no positive trend. Interestingly, in the same period she continued to learn the names of new objects and also to observe order requirements in the sequences of words she produced in requesting these objects.

With Elizabeth the approach was even more cautious. After 121 errorless trials, 65 with "same" and 56 with "different," we advanced to an intermediate form of errorless training, which we called "geometric errorless." Both alternatives were presented but the incorrect one was placed off to the side, farther from the sample than the correct alternative. She was given 118 trials of this kind, 60 with "same" and 58 with "different." This was followed by five choice lessons, all confined to cup–cup and cup–spoon; she made 17 errors in 52 trials, or 67% correct. As a last shot, we combined fadeout with geometric errorless. The alternative that was correct on a given trial was placed 3 in. farther to the side than the correct alternative for one session, 1.5 inches on the next session, and none on the third. Elizabeth made 3 out of 20, 5 out of 16, and 10 out of 17 errors per total trials on the three sessions, respectively. In the same period she continued to progress on other lessons; she acquired new object names and requested them with sequences of words that observed the order requirements.

With both Elizabeth and Peony we then abandoned Sarah's format and adopted a new procedure for teaching "same–different," one closer in form to the matching procedure. On each trial the subject was given two identical match-to-sample formats, one accompanied by the word "same" and the other by the word "different" (see Figure 7.1). In contrast to Sarah's procedure, in which the subject operated on the words—placing "same" between like objects and "different" between unlike objects—in the new procedure the subjects no longer operated on the words but merely observed them and then operated on the objects, moving the matching one to the sample in the presence of the word "same," and the odd one in the presence of the word "different."

The logic of this new arrangement is recognizably equivalent to that of so-called conditional discrimination, a procedure used extensively by Harlow and his associates (e.g., Harlow, 1950). Moreover, the equivalence is not limited to this case; there is a general similarity between conditional discrimination and the early methods we used to teach words. The overlap is understandable on the grounds that words are inherently conditional. Their use is not correct or incorrect in an absolute sense but is correct conditional on given conditions.

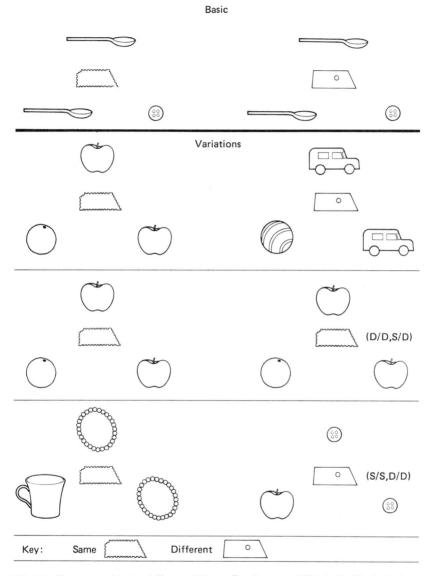

FIG. 7.1 Format used to teach "same–different" to Peony and Elizabeth. The basic format is at the top and three variations below.

Simple training cases, such as those used to teach names of objects or agents, bring this out clearly. For instance, requesting banana with the word "banana" is correct when the fruit present is banana and incorrect otherwise. Likewise, in the request "Debbie give Peony apple," "Debbie" is the correct agent name to use providing it is Debbie who is present. (Later methods used to teach words were not structurally equivalent to conditional discrimination; the similarity held only in the beginning and only for simple cases. For example, after the subject had been taught "name of," words were introduced by explicit instructions, e.g., "fig name of" the object fig.)

Given the equivalence between conditional discrimination and the present early methods for teaching words, it is puzzling that the historically extensive use of conditional discrimination did not lead to a study of language. There are doubtless many reasons why. One of them is suggested, I think, in a simple yet basic procedural difference between conditional discrimination and the present approach. Traditional conditional cues were an intrinsic part of the apparatus, and so the subject had no way in which to operate on the conditional cues. For instance, in a typical arrangement, a green board required the subject to match, a red board to do oddity. If instead the experimenter had cut the board into pieces, giving the subject both a piece of red wood and a piece of green wood, the subject could then have used these pieces in the productive mode, for example, to place green pieces between like objects, red pieces between unlike objects. The pieces of wood would then have been functionally equivalent to words, the green piece meaning "same" and the red piece "different." Traditional contextual cues were therefore potentially more like words than might have met the eye. Their peculiarity lay in the fact that although wordlike, they were words known to the subject only in the comprehensional mode. Traditional conditional discrimination training is comparable to teaching a subject to understand instructions without at the same time teaching it to produce the instructions.

Peony and Elizabeth were given a series of lessons in which each trial consisted of two match-to-sample formats as shown in Figure 7.1, one with the word "same" and the other with the word "different." Therefore, each trial required the subject to carry out both matching and oddity, for example, to match button to button in one of the formats and spoon to button in the other. Objects, consisting of beads, rings, toy cars, etc., were varied from trial to trial. Elizabeth was given three lessons of this kind and Peony four, all lessons consisting of ten trials, with two choices per trial. Elizabeth performed at the 72% level and Peony at the 67% level. Because a middling performance with no hopeful sign of improvement often seemed associated with inattention, we increased the salience of the stimuli. Toys were replaced by pieces of fruit. Now the trainers were busy, indeed, inducing the subjects to perform matching and oddity with items that were meant for eating; but there was no longer any suggestion of inattention. On 20 trials or 40 choices of this kind, Peony advanced to the 75% level, where Elizabeth remained at about the 73% level.

The next lessons were aimed at progressively eliminating certain features of the test that were constant but logically irrelevant. For example, on every trial the two match-to-sample formats had been the same. That is not a logically necessary condition for making a sameness–difference judgment. But did the subject recognize as much? To find out, it was necessary to remove the feature. Accordingly, the match-to-sample formats were varied so that one might consist of apple as the sample, with apple and orange as alternatives, and the other of toy car as the sample, with car and ball as the alternatives.

The second constancy had to do with the instructions given on each trial. Formerly, "same" had always been given with one format and "different" with the other, requiring the subject to do matching with one format and oddity with the other. This was changed to include all combinations "same" and "same," "different" and "different," as well as the original "same" and "different," as shown in Figure 7.1. Finally, in a third test series, we combined both changes, i.e., gave variable instructions in conjunction with match-to-sample formats that were alike on some trials and different on others. Elizabeth survived all three changes, responding at 80%, 87%, and 77% correct on the first, second, and third series, respectively. Peony weathered the first change at the 74% level but succumbed to the second one, at 56% correct, and was not tried on the third one.

In view of Peony's failure we returned her to the original condition, in which both match to sample formats were the same but continued to present all combinations of words. In addition, we replaced the fruit with new objects, two of them named (clay and spoon) and two unnamed (stick and button). She made 12 errors in 40 choices, or 70% correct, with no advantage for named objects. We then removed the last constraint, constant objects within a trial, and tested her again with still another set of four new objects. Again she performed at the 70% level.

Elizabeth, who had succeeded where Peony failed, was given five transfer tests, with no constraint on either objects or words and with great variation in the objects used. Eight named objects, such as monkey chow, ball, and toy dog, were used along with unnamed objects of a comparable kind. She made 30 errors in 100 trials, or 70% correct, with no advantage for named items. We considered both animals to have "learned," although within obvious limitations. The criterion was weak and the range of conditions restricted. The knowledge was fragile and would need strengthening.

The peculiar character of adult knowledge can lead to spurious claims about the knowledge of young organisms, children or chimp. We say the child knows arithmetic or the chimp knows "same–different." It is inconvenient to characterize knowledge in more specific terms and, given the nature of adult knowledge, inconceivable that it should be necessary to do so. Yet some initial learning is absurdly specific. The child doing sums with white chalk fails when the chalk is colored. The chimp doing match-to-sample when the sample faces it and the alternatives are distal fails when the sample is distal and the alternatives face it.

Peony and Elizabeth, with their apparently frail grasp of "same–different," offered an excellent opportunity to check the generality of their grasp of this distinction. They had failed to learn the distinction with Sarah's format and then acquired it, albeit weakly, with the new format. Could they go back and use "same–different" in Sarah's format? This would require that they use the words in production, whereas so far they had been taught them only in comprehension. In general, how context dependent was their grasp of "same–different"?

To answer this question and also simply to improve their performance, we gave them a series of tests in which the configural characteristics of the original training were first changed and then eliminated. For example, in the first test, we simply gave them one matching format per trial instead of the customary two. This flummoxed both of them. Both Elizabeth and Peony made 6 errors in 15 such trials. However, their recovery was immediate; on the next lesson they returned to their formal level: Elizabeth made 7 errors in 27 trials and Peony made 4 in 22 trials. In all subsequent tests in this series we then continued to use one matching format per trial instead of the previous two.

In the next test we reversed the position of the matching format. As shown in Figure 7.1, the two alternatives were originally proximal to the subject and the sample was distal; now the sample was proximal to the subject and the alternatives were distal. This change did not disturb either subject: Elizabeth made four errors in 16 trials and Peony two in 16. Interestingly, both subjects moved the sample to the alternative, thus operating on the proximal object. The rule we had in mind was move the correct alternative to the sample; their rule had nothing to do with this distinction but concerned which object was closer.

In the next test we introduced a change that was intended to close the gap between Sarah's format, in which words were operated on, and their format, in which words were comprehended but not operated on. They were given a standard matching format, that is, a sample and two alternatives, but the word "same" or "different" was not placed in its usual position inside the format. Instead, one or the other of the words was placed off to the side, requiring the subject to insert this word into the matching format—so that it was clear what was to be done with the format—and then to carry out the specified operation. In other words, the subjects were required to play a bit of the trainer's role along with their own customary role. After receiving a format without an instruction, they were to add the instruction themselves, either "same" or "different," and then to carry it out. This change also gave no difficulty to either subject. In fact, Elizabeth, after only one error in eight trials of this kind, moved spontaneously into Sarah's format. Instead of carrying out two separate operations, bringing in the word and then operating on the objects, she managed to place the word strategically, more between the like objects if the word was "same," more between the unlike ones if it was "different." In that way she converted a two-step into a one-step procedure. Henceforth we gave Elizabeth only a pair of objects, like or unlike, along with the words "same" or "different" which she placed between the two objects, thus officially converting her to Sarah's format. Her first test on Sarah's format was incorporated into the present series, and she made one error in seven trials.

Peony had no more difficulty than Elizabeth with the intermediate form but because she did not drift spontaneously into Sarah's format, we took a different approach with her. With one stroke we wiped out all former configural properties, simply throwing out before her three objects and two words, with only one constraint, two of the objects were alike. Peony's response to this challenge took several forms, as shown in Figure 7.2, all of them profoundly reassuring as to the nontrivial character of pongid intelligence.

1. She put two spoons together (did nothing with the word "same," as though it were redundant) and put the word "different" on top of the piece of clay.

2. She put clay next to the word "different," the two spoons together, and the word "same" on top of them.

3. She put two pieces of clay together and the word "same" on top of them (and did nothing with "different" and the spoon).

4. She wrote out in a linear fashion "Clay same clay different spoon," that is, A same A different B.

On subsequent lessons, she was given a large variety of objects in the same configurationless way. Most of the forms that appeared in the first lesson disappeared, including, regrettably, her linear format: A same A different B. By and large, she settled on only one of the several forms that had appeared in her first lesson: she superimposed the two like objects insofar as possible and placed the word "same" on top of them; then she placed the word "different" either on or alongside the odd object. One form she did not use was to bring together the two unlike objects and place the word "different" on them, perhaps because to have done so would have left no way to deal with the remaining object and the word "same." Peony's behavior suggested that to her "same" meant an object with a twin, whereas "different" meant the condition in which an object did not have a twin; this was a construction altogether compatible with the terms of her training.

Peony's success in ignoring the configural properties could be likened to that of a human subject who correctly answered the question: What are the necessary and sufficient conditions for labeling objects "same" or "different"? Even a child trained in as rigid a way as Peony might have mistaken some of the configural properties of the training for necessary conditions, thus answering the question incorrectly, i.e., that the objects had to be laid out so and so. From Peony's behavior we can conclude that she did not mistake this irrelevant aspect of training for a necessary condition.

Subjects seem to vary greatly in this aspect of intelligence. Sarah and her cagemate Gussie, another African-born female, were once temporarily returned to my care during a vacation of their trainers. Both animals sat at my feet,

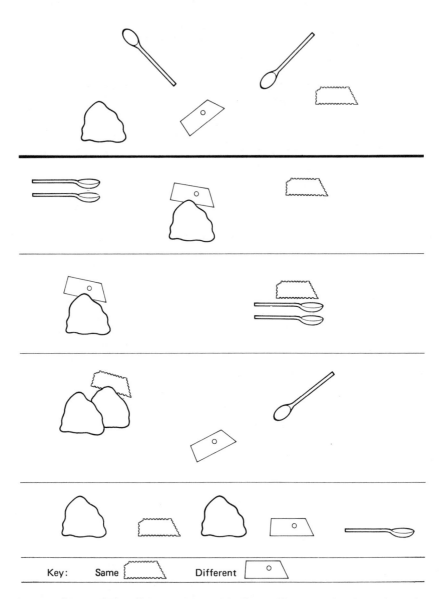

FIG. 7.2 "Same–different" formats invented by Peony. The top section shows the random arrangement of the five items–two spoons, one lump of clay, and the words "same" and "different"–as they were thrown out before the subject. The four sections below show the different arrangements Peony imposed on the material.

patiently awaiting the preparation of their bottles. Although over 2 years old at this time, they were still given milk from bottles, compensation for the late weaning they would have known had they not been taken from their mothers. With the bottles finished, I placed each one roughly in the vicinity of the waiting animal, and then took up the cleaning. Glancing down, I found Sarah drinking, but Gussie still sitting alongside the upright bottle, empty handed. Her appetite was always as good as Sarah's and she had given fine evidence of it earlier in her close observations of the preparations. However, now she was not drinking a bottle that stood no more than about 6 inches from her. Moreover, when I handed her the bottle she took it and drank immediately. Had Sarah learned a general approach response—take the bottle wherever it may be—and had Gussie learned some restrictive association, and was it only this accidental test that revealed the difference? Tests of the hypothesis were not very gratifying. On the next feeding session, even though I placed the bottle behind her, Gussie took it without difficulty. Yet on the first occasion she had definitely sat alongside the bottle, not drinking, while alongside her Sarah greedily emptied hers.

Factors that impose barriers on generalized action need not be cognitive, of course. In an experiment with 5- to 6-year-old children, a pinball machine was placed alongside a candy dispenser, and the children were first told and then shown that they could use both items as they wished. They could shoot the pinball machine and then step 3 or 4 inches to the side and scoop up a candy from the ever filled dish, or vice versa. Most children negotiated the slight distance between the two devices with the greatest of ease, many carrying out a kind of rhythm—two or three shots and then a piece of candy, two or three pieces of candy and then a shot, etc. But some children got stuck. They played the pinball machine or ate candy but could not negotiate the few inches separating them from the other device. Glancing ever more longingly at the device across from them, they could not pass through an invisible barrier that had risen alongside them.

INTERROGATIVE

In the "same—different" training the subjects were already being asked a question. The same procedure with English-speaking subjects would almost certainly have included instructions along the following lines: "What is the relation between the two objects—are they the same or different?" However, Sarah and the other two subjects were asked this question or its equivalent without an explicit interrogative marker. The only marker they had thus far was the implicit one of the space between the objects, into which they were to insert their answer, and the fact that a trial did not end until they had completed the construction by adding the third item.

The question could be made explicit by any of the three standard linguistic devices: inflection, word order, or an interrogative particle. We chose the latter as the simplest, both in the sense of involving the least change for the subject and of being the most compatible with the present physical system. So we simply added an interrogative marker to the construction Sarah was already receiving. For example, where we had previously written

$$A \qquad\qquad\qquad A$$
$$\text{``same''} \qquad \text{``different''}$$

we henceforth wrote

$$A \qquad\qquad ? \qquad\qquad A$$
$$\text{``same''} \qquad\qquad \text{``different''}$$

This is the same construction (see page 140) that, for unknown reasons, appears to have derailed Peony. It had no such effect on Sarah, however, nor has it troubled other subjects with whom it has been used, including global aphasic adults (Velettri-Glass, Gazzaniga, & Premack, 1973) and various language-deficient children (De Villiers & Naughton, 1974; Premack & Premack, 1974).

The basically simple nature of the question is obscured by the variation in mechanical devices that are used by natural languages to identify an utterance as a question. Any completable construction is a potential question. It becomes a question once it suffers one or more missing elements. That is the structural view. From the psychological point of view, we must add that a question arises when a speaker finds himself unable to complete certain constructions and has at hand a listener whom he regards as a probable source of the missing elements. If this analysis is correct, then the ontogenetically earliest context in which to introduce the question—and with great didactic benefit to all subsequent training—is that offered by the simplest possible completable construction. "Same–different" is such a construction because, as already pointed out, it can be introduced as a relation between unnamed items and so has no linguistic prerequisites.

Because questions derive from missing elements, with a two-term relation such as "same–different" two question forms can be generated directly: one by removing the predicate ("same" or "different") and another by removing one of the objects instancing the predicate (A or B). A third form can be generated indirectly by appending the interrogative marker, which itself stands for missing element, to the head of the construction and then requiring that it be replaced by a further element—specifically, by either "yes" or "no." Examples of all three question forms are shown in Figure 7.3.

FIG. 7.3 Examples of (a) four *wh-* and (b) four *yes–no* questions with English paraphrases. However, "different" would be more accurate paraphrase than "not same," because a negative particle was not used. (From Premack, 1971. Copyright 1971 by The American Association for the Advancement of Science.)

What is A the same as?| A, B   What is A not the same as?| A, B

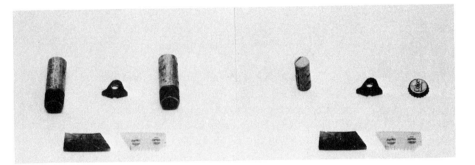

What is A to A?| same, diff.   What is A to B?| same, diff.

FIG. 7.3 (a)

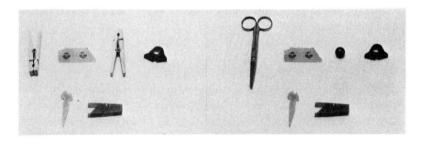

Is A the same as A? yes/no   Is A the same as B?| yes/no

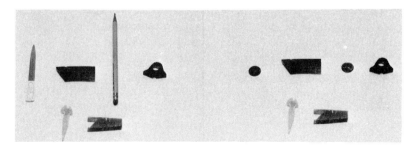

Is A not the same as B?| yes/no   Is A not the same as A?| yes/no

FIG. 7.3 (b)

An example of two versions of *wh*-type questions is shown in the upper panel of Figure 7.3. They can be paraphrased as "*A* is what to *A*?" and "*A* is what to *B*?" The alternatives for both versions are "same" or "different" and the subject's task in both cases is to replace the interrogative marker with the word appropriate to the case.

Two versions of a second type of *wh*- question are shown in the lower panel of Figure 7.3; they can be paraphrased as "*A* is the same as what?" and "*A* is different from what?" Now the alternatives are no longer the words "same" or "different" but the objects themselves. Sarah's task remained essentially the same: to replace the interrogative particle with the appropriate object and thereby complete the construction.

The first two question forms involved only one new term, the interrogative marker itself. The use of this particle, its removal and replacement by the particle or object that completed the construction, was taught by direct intervention. Sarah was already thoroughly experienced in placing either the word "same" or the word "different" into the space between the two like or unlike objects. Adapting her to the interrogative particle required only placing her hand on the particle, which was located between the two objects, and guiding her to move it out of the string, leaving the familiar *A–A* or *A–B* (letters represent objects), which she then proceeded to complete as usual with "same" or "different." Her formal training on the use of the interrogative particle consisted of no more than that.

Next she was given 20 questions of the *wh*- type in which not the predicate but one of the two objects was replaced by the interrogative particle, for example, "? same *A*" or "? different *A*." On each trial her alternatives consisted of two objects. She was slow to start work, perhaps because she had never seen such a construction before, and was primed by again placing her hand on the interrogative particle and leading her to move it out of the string. She then chose correctly on the first six trials, and on ten of the remaining 14. Three of her four errors were on "different."

Aside from the "balk" on the first trial, which may have been a mild emotional reaction to a novel form, there was evidence of transfer from the first to the second *wh*- form. The transfer cannot be ascribed specifically to the interrogative particle, for she may have done as well without it. Indeed, it seems unlikely that the interrogative particle can be a prerequisite for transfer, because in the *wh*-type question the "?" is a redundant device, serving merely to give the blank space better definition than it has otherwise. The main point, in any case, is the transfer Sarah showed from one form of the *wh*- question to the other.

YES–NO QUESTION

The *yes–no* question, the third form that can be generated in this context, is shown in four versions in Figure 7.3. They can be paraphrased as: (1) "Is *A* the same as A?"; (2) "Is A different from A?"; (3) "Is A different from B?"; and (4) "Is A the same as B?" These questions were formed not by removing any item from the sentence but by adding the interrogative marker to the head of the sentence. Five linguistic items were involved in questions of this form: "same," "different," "yes," "no," and the interrogative marker itself. Of the five, Sarah was already familiar with the predicate, the interrogative marker (introduced in the wh- forms) and "no," the negative particle that was taught her earlier as an injunction against carrying out the action called for by a sentence. We will discuss her training on the use of negation in the next section of this chapter.

Because of the five linguistic items involved in the yes-no question all but one could be said to be known, we elected to treat the yes-no question itself as a strict training procedure for the introduction of the one unknown item, viz., "yes." Sarah was given explicit training on the first two forms of the yes-no question shown in Figure 7.3. Then she was tested without prior training on the other two forms. Could she transfer from one form to the other? That was the point of training her on two forms and withholding training on the other two.

Training started with the question "? A same A" (Are A and A the same?), where A represents any of the several objects used in the original match-to-sample. The only alternative given her was "yes," the one word in the yes-no construction that was unknown to her. She displaced the interrogative marker, forming the sentence "Yes, A same A." Next she was given the question, "? A different A" (Are A and A different?). Now the only alternative given her was "no." Using it to displace the interrogative marker she formed the sentence, "No, A different A." She was given seven errorless trials on each of the two forms.

At step two, she was given the same questions but with both the words "yes" and "no," and was required to choose between them. She made two errors in 15 trials, one on the first five trials. Ordinarily at this point we would have given her a transfer test, new items being substituted for training items. Instead, she was tested on the other two forms of the yes-no question, forms she had not yet seen. The four forms of the yes-no question were intermingled and she was asked them in more or less random order. As before, her alternatives were "yes" and "no" and the objects substituted for A and B were those used in training.

On the questions shown in Figure 7.3, she made the following number of errors per total number of trials: 6 out of 33, 11 out of 43, 2 out of 27, 11 out of 51. Errors were concentrated in the forms in which the word "different" appeared. She made 25 errors in 94 trials on "different" questions and only 8 errors in 60 trials on "same" questions. Otherwise her error distributions were about the same. She made approximately the same number of errors on the two new forms introduced in the transfer test as on the two familiar forms on which she had been taught from the beginning (new, 13 out of 78; old, 20 out of 76). And she made about the same number of errors on questions requiring "Yes" answers as on those requiring "No" answers (yes, 17 out of 78; no, 16 out of 70).

The data indicate that Sarah did not learn the "different" and "same" questions in the same manner. Apparently she learned the "different" question simply as a correlation: write "No" whenever the word "different" appears. This too simple rule failed, however, when the second form of the question was introduced in the transfer test, for once both forms were present "different" questions could no longer be answered with "No" but required both "Yes" and "No" answers (as did "same" questions). This explains why, after making virtually no errors on the "different" question in the original training, she went on to make numerous errors on the same question when the second version was introduced.

Although she could just as easily have learned "same" questions in the same mechanical way, viz., write "Yes" whenever "same" appeared, she apparently did not. The introduction of the second form of the "same" question did not occasion a large number of errors; on the contrary, she learned both versions of the "same" question at the same rate and at her usual high level of proficiency. Linguists distinguish between marked and unmarked forms of antipodal terms, such as "big–small," "high–low," "up–down," etc. One form is considered primary and the other secondary; the latter is felt to be produced by adding a marker to the primary form. The unmarked form is considered simpler and there is some evidence that in children the unmarked forms are learned earlier (e.g., Donaldson & Wales, 1970). We might account for the present data by extending the same hypothesis to Sarah. In the human case "same" is thought to be the unmarked form, and we could make the same assumption for Sarah. Then, however, two additional points need to be considered. First, in originally learning the predicates "same" and "different" she did not make more errors with one than with the other (although she tended to make somewhat more errors with "different" than with "same" in learning the two forms of the wh- question). Second, in the yes–no question the difference appeared to be more basic than merely learning one form faster than the other. She learned the questions with different strategies: as a blind correlation, so to speak, in the case of "different" and with understanding in the case of "same."

The absence of differences in her learning in the original predicates might be explained by noting that these cases were taught by strict training procedures, and training of this kind should eliminate or at least minimize errors. In contrast, the wh- questions were not taught by strict training procedures. In teaching the yes–no question we again abandoned this approach, specifically to find out whether or not she could transfer from two versions of this question on which she was trained to two other versions on which she was not trained. The training was not of a kind to minimize errors; in fact, it would have to be judged poor on the grounds that it more or less invited learning to take an inadequate form—a correlation between "different" and "no," on the one hand, and "same" and "yes," on the other. The striking thing is not that learning took this inadequate form in the case of the "different" question but that it apparently did not take this inadequate form in the case of the "same" question.

ARE THESE EXPRESSIONS QUESTIONS?

Consider three objections to calling the above expressions questions. First, each case has the form of one-to-one substitution: the interrogative particle was removed and replaced by a single item. Human interrogation obviously does not suffer from any such limitation because in the human case answers can be of any length. We give a more extended reply to this in a latter section but for the moment consider that, even at this tender stage, the present system is not restricted to one-word answers. Already there were counterexamples in which answers consisted of more than one word. For instance, when the question asked Sarah was "*A* ? *B*" (what is the relation between *A* and *B*?) and the alternatives given her were "no" and "same"—rather than the usual "same" and "different"—she answered "no same." Although laconic, this is nonetheless a two-word answer and is therefore a case of many-to-one rather than one-to-one substitution.

Second, she answered but did not ask questions. This would be a serious objection if she failed to ask questions when given an opportunity to do so. The omission was in the training program, however, not in the subject. In the beginning we could not find a simple condition in which to make the test; then we were diverted from the matter by other issues and ended up by (conveniently) forgetting it. Moreover, on more than one occasion, apparently bored by excessive drill, she stole all the words before her—retired to the floor where her position was less vulnerable—and wrote out and then answered all the questions taught her. Hunching over the plastic pieces, passionately arraying them in sequences taught her, she offered one of the few displays not only of her ability to learn but of her ardent desire to use what she had learned. The display also bespeaks one of our main failures, a failure to interdigitate the motivational pressures that make language valuable with the cognitive program teaching it. In fact, we did not locate Sarah or the other subjects in a world, such as the child's, where increasing command of language provided increasing command of the world.

Third, a quite different kind of objection might be made on the grounds that the questions were not themselves genuine. In human affairs, a question is often taken as evidence of (1) the speaker's ignorance and (2) his assumption that the listener is less ignorant. For example, a person may ask "What time is it?" because he does not know and believes that his listener does know. It is clear that none of the above questions asked Sarah belong to this paradigm.

It is just as clear, however, what paradigm they do fit and also that the above paradigm is only one of several that figure in human interrogative behavior. Another widely used paradigm is based on exactly the opposite assumption about the distribution of knowledge; it is the mainstay of the teacher's business and it is the paradigm applicable here. The teacher knows the answer to the question and therefore asks it of the student to find out whether he also knows the answer. For example, a father may ask his son "What time is it?" thereby determining whether or not the boy can tell time. Although the distribution of knowledge is now the opposite of that in the first case, the utterance is no less a question.

CHILD VERSUS CHIMP

Observations by Klima and Bellugi (1966) suggest that the order in which English-speaking children acquire the *wh-* and *yes–no* forms of the question is the opposite of that in which they have been taught to Sarah. That is, the child learns the *yes–no* question before it learns the *wh-* form, whereas in Sarah's case the *wh-* form was taught first. This does not establish a difference between child and chimp, however, for it was not the case that the chimp, after being given an opportunity to learn both forms, learned the *wh-* first, unlike the child. Instead, the experimenter found it more convenient to teach the one form before the other. In natural language the *yes–no* question can be marked simply by a rising intonation—which is the form taken by the child's first *yes–no* question—but there is no counterpart of this simple intonational device in the plastic system. Moreover, we do not mark grammatical distinctions by inflection. Because changes in word order were also ruled out as too complex, only the interrogative particle remained as a way in which to mark the question. Once that decision was made, the *wh-* question had to be taught first. It alone provides a direct and simple way of introducing the interrogative particle which, once defined, can be added to the head of a sentence to form the *yes–no* question. The *yes–no* question cannot itself be used to introduce the interrogative particle. In this case, therefore, the differences between the child and the chimp appear to reflect differences in the surface properties of the language systems rather than species differences.

QUESTIONS AS MISSING ELEMENTS

How general or abstract was Sarah's conception of "missing item"? Was it specific to the same–different construction in which it had been taught, or would she be able to use the interrogative marker as a general particle in any known construction? Suppose her definitions had not been abstract. Then it could have been necessary to introduce as many different interrogative markers as she had recognizably different constructions. However, there was no problem of this kind. Ultimately, the same interrogative marker was used in all possible constructions. Moreover, it was ultimately used not only in sentences where, as in the case of "same–different," some of the elements were actual objects but also in sentences consisting solely of linguistic elements. To leap ahead of our story for a moment, it was possible to ask her such questions as "? color of apple?" (What is the color of apple?) or "? red is on green" (Is red on green?) using the same interrogative particle that was introduced in the same–different constructions. This suggests that Sarah had a generalized concept of missing elements, not one restricted to specific constructions. Moreover, her abstract definition of the interrogative particle was not unique but was in keeping with the rest of her transfer data.

Can the human form of interrogation be encompassed by the simple notion of missing elements? At first glance it may seem not; questions in natural language take forms in which there does not appear to be any simple blank space. This impression is misleading, however; a confusion of form with what underlies form. In fact, it seems that most questions can be rewritten without loss so as to comply with the missing element format. Consider some examples. "How old are you?" can be written as "Henry is ? years old," where "Henry" is the name of the person in question and a necessary substitution for an organism that lacks personal pronouns. "What time is it?" can be rewritten as "The time is ?" and "Does Henry know whose car we're taking?" as "? Henry knows whose car we're taking," etc. In each case the English form was rewritten to conform to the format used with Sarah. The format allowed answers to be constructed without either rearrangement or deletion, requiring only insertion of the missing element at the marked location in the string. In fact, the trainer's questions were kept on the board before Sarah not simply to avoid memory problems—this could have been achieved by a number of formats—but mainly to allow her answers to take this extremely simple form.

QUESTION-INDUCING OCCASIONS

How valid is the notion of the question as an incomplete construction? Consider the other side of the coin, not sentences that are recognizable as questions but situations likely to cause organisms to utter such sentences. Consider a subject who is indisputably qualified in the question; in what circumstance is it likely to raise a question? Here, too, the answer seems to turn on incompleteness or missing elements. For instance, suppose an organism that was habitually fed at a given time and place failed one day to receive its food. If the organism does not merely assault the trainer but behaves verbally as well, the thing it is most likely to say is, "Where is my food?" Situations in which expectancies are disconfirmed are extremely likely to generate questions. These are situations in which expected elements fail to materialize. Questions as incomplete constructions and incomplete situations as question-inducing occasions represent other instances of the general parallel between language, on the one hand, and states of affairs that language maps, on the other.

NEGATIVE PARTICLE

"No" was taught Sarah as an injunction against carrying out an action. Small pieces of bread and cracker were spread with peanut butter, jam, or honey and the cocktail party generated by this 2 × 3 factorial was arrayed before her in six columns of about five canapes each. On perhaps 20% of the lessons, she seized the goods and the lessons proceeded no further. On the other 80%, however, she took only those things she was instructed to take despite the fact that the trainer looking at her across the canape-laden table was essentially powerless to restrain her. This obedience was not so much taught as generated by the social relation between her and the trainers. Her apparent reinforcement by their approval was a critical part of the motivational basis of the training and, in fact, made it possible.

Pairs of sentences were written on the board instructing her to take a specific two of the six kinds of canapes available. Initially both instructions were positive, that is, "Sarah jam–cracker take" and "Sarah honey–bread take." Once she was proficient in carrying out the two instructions, however, the negative particle was appended to the head of one of the constructions. An example is shown in Figure 3.3. A literal translation of the two sentences is "no Sarah honey–cracker take" and "Sarah jam–bread take." (In the beginning Sarah was taught with the verb in the terminal position, but this rule was violated so often by her English-speaking trainers that we also accepted the normal English verb position, for example, "Sarah take jam–cracker." The two forms ended up in free variation, with this exception. One trainer insisted on the terminal verb position and, with this trainer, Sarah used only the terminal position.) "No" or more credibly, "don't" was then taught her simply by staying her hand whenever she reached for an item referred to in a sentence to which a negative particle was appended. This simple procedure was extremely effective not only with Sarah, but also with other subjects, global aphasics (Velettri-Glass, Gazzaniga, & Premack, 1973), language-deficient children (Premack & Premack, 1974), and both Peony and Elizabeth, who have also learned "no" or "don't." The trainer frequently managed to catch Sarah's hand in flight. An arrested gesture is evidently a highly discriminable event, one with which a word can be readily associated. The positive sentence that was always given along with the negative one, as well as the trials on which both sentences were positive, were not necessary but simply a means of making obedience easier.

On earlier lessons, one trainer in particular used the procedure of occasionally italicizing the new word in a construction by pointing to it, and Sarah may have been mimicking this gesture when on her own she adopted the practice of pointing to the sentence she was working on. By pointing, she in effect told us which of the two positive sentences she was carrying out, making it possible to judge her accuracy on the basis of an individual sentence rather than on the basis of a pair of them. Also, her pointing to the sentence on which she was working made it possible to anticipate her reaching for an interdicted item. After no more than five or six "arrests" she ceased even to point to th _s sentence to which the negative particle was appended and, of course, on those occasions did not reach for the item in question.

We might have required her to process the sentences in a fixed order, say, left to right, but her use of pointing removed this necessity. It also made it possible to discover that she did not observe a fixed order herself. There was some tendency for a preferred item to be chosen first, but her preferer e among the six canapes was fortunately not strong. Her uninstructed disincl nat on to use the same sentence twice in a row was interesting. After operating on one of the instructions, she proceeded to the next one instead of returning to the same sentence. Perhaps this was merely because "new" items were always more interesting, although pieces were deliberately kept small; it is hard to say whether this behavior was the result of a rule of her own, response to subtle cues from the trainer, or simple preference for "new" items.

We debated inserting the negative particle into the sentence, for example, "Sarah no take jam—cracker" (as we did later on), so as to direct its force specifically on the verb but decided, I now think incorrectly, that initially the effect would be clearer if the particle were appended rather than inserted. At this stage, being very hesitant about the certainty of Sarah's understanding, we noted that to append the negative particle would leave the base sentence intact whereas to insert it would not. I think we attributed more fragility to her understanding than was called for. I dwell on this point because in appending rather than inserting we violated one of our own rules. Do not introduce quasi-acceptable forms that are later regarded as infantile and are superceded by fully acceptable forms. That was another objective of the training program. If particles are introduced in a proper order, there should never be a need for quasi-acceptable forms that are later abandoned. In the present case, there was actually no such need and only our own hesitation about her comprehension led us to violate the rule.

NEGATION TRAINING

The negative was taught in the comprehension mode. With six different canapes arrayed before her, Sarah was given a pair of instructions, one of them negative, for example, "Sarah jam—cracker take" and "No Sarah peanut butter—bread take." Positive sentences varied over trials, but to make things easier, negative sentences were consistent within a session and varied only between sessions. She was correct 10 out of 10, 10 out of 12, 11 out of 12, 8 out of 12, 8 out of 10, 9 out of 10, 7 out of 8, and 10 out of 10 trials, respectively. Of her 11 errors, only one consisted of choosing a countermanded item.

Next, she was given 11 sessions like the former except that in addition to the pairs of positive and negative sentences she received other pairs in which both sentences were positive. In these tests also the negated item was constant within the session but no longer consistently negated; sometimes in a pair of positive sentences she was called on to take the previously negated items. She was correct on 10 out of 10, 9 out of 10, 8 out of 10, 8 out of 10, 9 out of 12, 8 out of 12, 9 out of 10, 10 out of 10, 9 out of 10, 9 out of 10, and 10 out of 12 trials, respectively. On this series she made only two errors on the negated item; her overall performance on the negative series was 180 out of 210, or 86% correct. The still more difficult task in which the negated item varied from trial to trial was to be dealt with later, although we got caught up on other topics and never got back to it. The test has since been done with Peony and Elizabeth, both of which readily acquired the negative particle through a comparable procedure.

NEGATION VERSUS INJUNCTION

The original training with the negative particle might be said to have given it a meaning close to "don't," a sense removed from the one required in the yes–no questions. Indeed the injunctive and negational senses may overlap so little that Sarah may have learned a new and unrelated particle as "no" in the yes–no question as readily as she has learned to adapt the old negative particle to this purpose. That seems doubtful in view of her performance on the "same" questions but we have not tested the matter directly.

In fact, Sarah was taught negation, but not until after she had already been taught the yes–no question. Hence, we cannot ask whether training on negation has facilitated learning on the yes–no question. However, we can ask the opposite, whether use of the negative particle in the yes–no question has facilitated acquisition of negation. Unfortunately, because of an unforseen problem, we must settle for a merely suggestive answer.

In teaching negation, four questions were used, actually two questions, each with two alternatives: (1) "A ? A," with "same" and "no" as alternatives; (2) "A ? A" with "different" and "no" as alternatives. (3) "A ? B" with "same" and "no" as alternatives; and (4) "A ? B" with "different" and "no" as alteratives. Sarah was not given explicit training on any of the forms but was tested directly on the first two forms to determine whether or not she had benefited from the use of "no" in the yes–no question.

The task confronting her was to recognize that the equivalent of "same" could be formed by properly combining "no" and "different." When asked "A ? A" (What is the relation between A and A?) and given "same" and "no" as alternatives, she was to answer "same." When given the same question but with the alternatives "different" and "no," she was required to produce "same" by negating "different," that is, "no" + "different" = "same."

The test was ill conceived or at least premature. Critical trials required that she substitute two particles for one interrogative marker, an act for which she was not prepared by previous experience. She was hesitant about making such a substitution—her occasional blind obedience was not always helpful—and in the necessity of having to shape her to this act, we lost most of the information we were after. In retrospect it is clear that she should have been taught to make substitutions of this kind in another context; the necessity of training in this act may not then have confounded the present test.

After coaxing her (in English) for several trials, we instated a time rule. Three seconds after we presented a question, we informed her whether or not her answer was correct and did so for all questions in the exercise. For example, if in answering "A ? A" she inserted either "no" or "different" but did not add the second word within the 3-sec limit, she was marked wrong, although the trainer was lenient on the first three or four trials.

In the course of six sessions, about 16 trials per session, devoted exclusively to the first and second forms, she made 13 errors on each form, respectively. Her errors on the second form were understandable; she was hesitant about adding the second particle and often failed to meet the time criterion. However, her errors on the first form were puzzling and indicative of confusion. She did not err by writing "A no same A" instead of "A same A," as might be expected, but by writing "A no A," which is an altogether perplexing form since it had no previous history. Nevertheless, 11 of her 13 errors were of this kind. Does the outcome suggest a strategy of answering the first form with a one-word answer, the second with a two-word answer? If so, "same" would have been a better one-word answer than "no." In fact we do not understand the basis of this peculiar error. In any case, on the sixth session, she made no errors in 16 trials and we then added the other two forms and gave a series of six lessons on all four forms combined.

On Questions 1, 2, 3, and 4 she made the following number of errors in the course of the six sessions: three, eight, eight, and nine, respectively. Her errors were confined mainly to the first three sessions. Overall she made the following total number of errors per total trials on the four question forms: 16 out of 79, 20 out of 77, 8 out of 37, and 9 out of 35, respectively. Although the data do not establish that she has learned negation through her experience with the yes—no question, they do show that she is ultimately capable of negation. Also, comparison of her performance on Questions 2 and 3 suggests that training on the production of "same" through the negation of "different" (Question 2) has transferred to the opposite case, benefitting her production of "different" through the negation of "same" (Question 3).

Did the two senses of the negative particle—injunction and negation—overlap, or should we have introduced separate particles for each? Whether they over-lapped in a helpful way could be determined by a comparison between her learning to negate "same" and "different" with a new particle and her learning to do negation with an old particle the history of which included an injunctive use. The same comparison could be made between her learning of a new "no" in yes—no questions and of an old "no" that had been used injunctively. Moreover, despite the apparently primitive quality of injunction, there is no hard rule saying that it must precede negation. Therefore, the question could be asked in the reverse. Does the use of "no" in negation facilitate its subsequent acquisition in injunction? Intuitively we considered the two senses to overlap and did not therefore introduce separate particles. However, we have no data on the matter. One of the larger issues to which this question relates is polysemy, the multiple meaning that is a general characteristic of words in natural languages. (Consider "spring" which can be metallic, liquid, seasonal, a bodily act, etc.) The two meanings of the negative particle were probably our most explicit case of polysemy. Sarah's language was otherwise largely a one-to-one mapping (although there were a few accidental synonyms) rather than a many-to-many mapping, and this might be the single major difference between her language and a natural one. Perhaps, however, the more appropriate comparison is suggested by this question. How much polysemy is there in the language of the young child?

MISSING ELEMENTS AND WELL-DEFINED CONSTRUCTIONS

"Same–different" has been the only predicate in which we have introduced the question. Could it not be introduced equally well with other constructions? More specifically, what are the necessary and sufficient conditions for introducing the interrogative particle? If the question derives from missing elements, it seems necessary only to use constructions in which the fact of a missing element is conspicuous. However, it is not hard to show that this is a necessary but not a sufficient condition.

For example, nonsense strings, such as "red large take," "apple blue orange," etc., could be presented over and over until held together firmly by familiarity. After the strings were well memorized, one of the words in them could be eliminated and replaced with an interrogative particle. The subject could be taught to replace the interrogative particle with the missing word, thus restoring the well-memorized nonsense string to its familiar form. Now the question is whether familiarity can serve as the basis for introducing a generalized interrogative marker.

We could reasonably expect transfer to "new" nonsense strings, that is, well-memorized nonsense strings not used as training exemplars in introducing the interrogative particle. We could also reasonably anticipate transfer to highly familiar sensible strings (provided the subject did not on its own decide to restrict the interrogative particle to nonsense strings). However, we would have no basis for anticipating transfer to nonfamiliar sensible strings. For example, if the subject had experienced "A same A," "B same B," etc., but not "L same L," it would be unable to answer the question "? same L" (What is the same as L?).

Likewise, if it had encountered "Red color of apple," "Red color of cherry," etc., but not "Red color of ball," it would be unable to answer the question, "? color of ball"; and similarly for all novel constructions. In brief, if the interrogative particle were introduced in well-memorized nonsense strings, no matter how conspicuous the missing word for which the particle was substituted, there would be no basis for anticipating transfer to sensible but unfamiliar constructions. When the "?" is introduced with "same–different" (or other sense-making constructions), however, transfer should not depend on familiarity. It should occur to any incomplete but potentially sensible construction, whether novel or familiar.

8
"Name of" and Metalinguistics

"Name of," the relation between a word and its referent, was taught on the basis of two positive and two negative exemplars. The positive exemplars were "apple" and the object apple and "banana" and the object banana. The negative ones were "apple" and the object banana and "banana" and the object apple, formed simply by recombining the positive ones. Although nearly all words have been introduced with the use of both positive and negative exemplars—and these have been sufficient conditions for introducing words—we cannot yet say whether they are necessary ones (see page 269 for suggestive evidence on this point). To exemplify "name of" it was not necessary presumably to have used specifically the relation between an object and its name. The relation between an actor and his or her name or that between an action, for example, giving, cutting, etc., and its associated name might have been used as well. Nothing is more convenient, however, than the permanent and highly docile object. Apples and bananas can be moved from one location to another without complaint and replenished as needed.

In teaching "name of" we followed the basic steps illustrated earlier with "same–different." The word "apple" and an actual apple were set slightly apart and Sarah was given only one alternative, the piece of plastic intended to mean "name of." In placing the only available piece of plastic between the two slightly displaced items, she produced a string that can be read as "Apple name of object apple." This was the first positive instance of "name of," just as the two cups given her earlier formed the first instance of the predicate "same."

We formed "not-name of" by gluing the negative particle to the name for the positive case. This made "not-name of" (Figure 8.1) no less a single particle than "name of" and made possible using one-to-one substitution in the training of both. That is, in both cases the training sentences could be completed by putting one word into one blank. At a later stage, the two words were separated, "not"

"Apple" is the name of apple

FIG. 8.1 An example of "*X* is the name of *Y*" and "*X* is not the name of *Y*," formed by gluing the negative particle to the predicate "name of." (From Premack, 1971. Copyright 1971 by The American Association for the Advancement of Science.)

"Banana" is not the name of apple

was given as a separate particle, and the subject was itself required to negate the positive term to form "not" + "name of."

The first negative instance given her was the pair "apple" and the object banana, followed by "banana" and the object apple. In both cases her only alternative was "not-name of," which she placed between the items in each pair, forming strings that could be read as "Banana not-name of object apple" and "Apple not-name of object banana." She was given 20 trials, five each on the two positive cases and five each on the two negative cases.

On the second step, we repeated the material given her on the first step but now gave her both alternatives, "name of" and "not-name of"; she made three errors in 17 trials, with one on the first five and all three errors on the negative form. Because she had already been taught the interrogative, we took advantage of that form in further assessing her learning. Following the choice trials, she was asked all four versions of the two *wh-* questions as well as all four versions of the *yes–no* question. For instance, she was asked "Apple ? object apple" (What is the relation between the word "apple" and the object apple?); as well as the negative version of the same question, viz., "Apple ? object banana" (What is the relation between the word "apple" and the object banana?). Her alternatives were "name of" and "not-name of."

In the other versions of the *wh-* question, she was required to make substitutions not on the predicate but on the names of the objects in one case and on the objects themselves in the other. For instance, she was asked "? name of the object apple" (What is the name of the object apple?) along with the corresponding question in the case of banana, for which her alternatives were "apple" and "banana." In addition, she was asked questions of this kind: "Apple name of ?" ("Apple" is the name of what?) and the corresponding question in the case of banana for which her alternatives now were the actual fruits apple and banana. On the first type of *wh-* question involving predicate substitution ("name of" versus "not-name of") she made four errors in 18 trials. On the questions involving substitution of names ("apple" versus "banana") she made three errors in 16 trials, and on the questions involving substitution of objects (apple vs banana) she made two errors in 14 trials, or 81% correct overall.

In addition to the *wh-* questions, she was asked questions of a *yes–no* form. For instance, she was asked "? banana name of object banana" (Is "banana" the name of the object banana?), the corresponding question in the case of apple, as well as the negative version of both questions, for example, "? banana name of the object apple" (Is "banana" the name of the object apple?). Her alternatives in these cases were the words "yes" and "no." She made five errors in 17 trials.

On the transfer tests, nearly all of these questions were repeated, changed only by the replacement of the training items with words and objects not used in training. The first transfer test included the pairs "apricot"–apricot, "raisin"–raisin, "apricot"–raisin, and "raisin"–apricot, cases that were not used in training but that also involved fruits or edibles. On questions of this kind, involving both the *wh-* and *yes–no* forms, she made 4 errors in 21 trials with no errors on the first five trials. Next, questions of the same form were directed at semantically unrelated material, for example, at the pairs "dish"–dish, "pail"–pail, and the two negative combinations, and on this material she made 4 errors on 19 trials with 1 error on the first five trials. She made a total of 6 errors on the negative cases as opposed to 2 on the positive, which was in keeping with her generally poorer performance on the negative. In brief, she performed as well on the transfer material as on the training material and showed no advantage when there was an apparent semantic overlap between the transfer and the training material.

Two kinds of cases were omitted from the transfer test, both of which, however, could be included if the test were to be redone. The first concerned such pairs as "red"–red, or more generally the relation between the name of a property and an instance of it. There is no reason to exclude cases of this kind from the set "name of," although instancing this kind of relation with individual exemplars is a difficult matter; "red" and other property names do not have physically isolable referents, as is discussed at length in Chapter 9.

The other case not included in the transfer set was the verbs, pairs consisting of the name of an action and the action. Their exclusion was based on the difficulty implied earlier, actions are transient and more difficult to represent than objects or agents. Incidentally, agents, too, were left out of the transfer set, forgotten rather than deliberately excluded. In practice, therefore, "name of" was restricted to the subset objects and their names, a transfer test more restricted than most and more than it would have been had we been more thoughtful.

METALINGUISTICS:
TEACHING NEW NAMES WITH "NAME OF"

The practical reason for introducing "name of" was to be able to use it productively, that is, to generate new instances of itself. The first item we named metalinguistically was figs, which happened to be in season at that time, were well liked by Sarah, and were not yet named. The old way of naming figs would have been to introduce them into a situation of a kind that was already mapped, such as giving, and then arrange for her to use "fig" in a sentence the other words of which were known. For instance, by placing a fig before Sarah and inducing her to write "Mary give Sarah fig," she could have been taught the name for fig. But the concept "name of" made possible introducing new names in a more direct manner. With "name of" the new word need not be used in a sentence but could be introduced by the explicit statement "X is the name of fig."

We placed a fig before her, a piece of plastic intended to mean "fig" slightly apart from the object, and then placed the word "name of" between them. Next we placed a second piece of plastic slightly apart from the fig and placed the word "not-name of" between them. Had Sarah attended to the lesson? In order to answer this question we resorted to the interrogative, giving both the *wh-* and *yes–no* forms of the question. She was asked first "Fig ? object fig" (What is the relation between "fig" and the object fig?) and then the negative version of this question, for which the alternatives, in both cases, were "name of" and "not-name of." Next she was asked "? fig name of object fig" (Is this piece of plastic the name of fig?) and the negative version of this question for which the alternatives were "yes" and "no." On the *wh-* questions she was correct on 14 of 17 trials and on the *yes–no* questions on 10 out of 12, or 82% correct. This level of accuracy made it reasonable to move to the last step, which required that she show her comprehension of the new word by using it appropriately in a sentence.

The materials set before Sarah were a fig and a number of words: "fig," the piece of plastic she had been told was not the name of fig, the names of two other fruits, "give," "Sarah," and "Mary." Sarah was given the fig when she produced the sentence "Mary give fig Sarah," which she did correctly on 8 of the first 10 trials. She was equally proficient when later exactly the same procedure was applied to Crackerjack, peach, and other items. Notice that the negative trials, on which she was told X was not the name of Y, served to rule out the possibility that the name was conferred simply by geometry, by the physical contiguity between the language element and the object. Both when it was asserted that X was the name of Y and when it was denied, the spatio-temporal relation between the language element and the object were identical. Yet only in the case of assertion did the subject go on to use the language element as the name of the designated referent.

Even at this stage of training it seems reasonable to guess that the language elements had taken on a classlike character. They all conformed to a special conjunction of features, not found in any other elements of Sarah's world: hard, shiny, metal backed, adhesive to the board, nonedible, etc. Indeed, it is no longer necessary to treat this as a guess; we now have evidence (see Chapter 4) from both Peony and Elizabeth that one of the first things they learn are the class properties of a word. Long before they learn what word goes with what referent, they can tell a word from a nonword. This fact must have been an advantage to the instruction "*X* name of *Y.*" Presumably, if a proposed name did not have the properties of the word class, the instruction would either fail or require many more trials to be learned. This presumptive effect could be likened to the difference between offering a child as a name for an unnamed object a sound that did belong to the language as opposed to one that did not.

INFORMAL NAMING PROCEDURE

At a much later stage of training, new words were introduced in a far less formal way. The trainers simply held up both a piece of plastic and an object and called attention to the pair. Sarah went on to use the piece of plastic as the name of the object to which it was paired no less effectively than she used names introduced by the formal procedure. A great many words were introduced in this way, in fact, all object names after a certain period. The procedure might have worked from an earlier time but we did not try it until late in training, not until after Sarah had already been taught property names, the compound sentence, etc. The effectiveness of the informal procedure indicated that, as suggested above, Sarah recognized the plastic and nonplastic objects as being members of two classes, classes moreover that took the relation "name of" with respect to one another. This is a reasonable inference because the plastic piece was always the name of the other item, never vice versa, and "name of" was the only relation members of the two classes took with respect to each other. (Names of properties and actions could be considered exceptions because with them the pieces of plastic named not the object or agent but only an attribute of the object or agent. We never undertook to name either properties or actions in this informal manner.) The presumptive instruction of the implicit naming procedure could have been made ambiguous by holding up together either two pieces of plastic or two objects. Then it would have been unclear which was to be the name of which, whether they were synonyms (in the case of two pieces of plastic), or whether some predicate other than "name of" was intended. We resisted the temptation to confront Sarah with these ambiguous cases because they might have confused her.

What did "name of" mean to Sarah and how could we substantiate the claim? At this early stage we had no illuminating alternatives with which to contrast "name of." Later we were able to ask her whether, for example, "banana" was "name of," "color of," "size of," or "shape of" the object banana. Yet even her ability to answer correctly with this expanded set of alternatives did little to help define "name of." Although her saying that, for example, "name of" was not the same as "color of" was gratifying and increased our confidence in her general language ability, it was not particularly clarifying of either concept. "Name of" and "color of" are not semantically "close" and so are not likely to be mistaken in the first place. As with any primitive, "name of" can be made no clearer than the distance between it and its closest competing concept. There is the obvious fact that "name of" is defined by the use to which words were put in the first step, e.g., by the fact that "Give apple" resulted in one outcome, "Cut apple," in another. Is it necessary that the use include both comprehension and production? For example, does it contribute as much toward defining "name of" to use a word in a declarative sentence (for example, "Apple is red") as to use it in an imperative one (for example, "Give apple Sarah")? We have not confined any word to comprehension alone, or to the declarative mood alone, etc., and then asked whether or not the relation between a word and its referent, experienced under restricted usage, qualifies as an instance of "name of." Tests of this kind may reveal that "name of" is divisible into components which covary specifically with use. Alternatively, and more reasonably, the "correspondence" in Sarah's mind standing as the basic definition of "name of" may prove to be unitary—contributed to equally by all of the different possible language usages. This does not mean that she may not have been given separate vocabularies, for example, one for comprehension and another one for production, and have been taught different words for "name of," specific to the two main uses of language. But that is quite a different issue.

The difficulty in finding words in close semantic contrast with "name of" suggests that perhaps we have been looking in the wrong place. The closest alternative to "name of" may not be a word but an object. Consider the contrast between, say, cracker and "name of cracker." The referent in the first case is a cracker, in the second case a piece of plastic. The key distinction in the case of "name of" would thus appear to be that between an object and its name; a subject who could give evidence of knowing that distinction could be said to understand (at least part of) the meaning of "name of."

An interesting test, for which we are indebted to H. Gleitman, provided a way of testing Sarah's ability to distinguish between the name of an object and the object itself. In this test we placed before Sarah a number of pieces of cracker and a number of tokens of the word "cracker." A dish was present into which she was to place the instructed alternatives. The instructions given her were of two kinds: (1) "Sarah insert cracker dish" and (2) "Sarah insert name of cracker dish." In the first case, she was to put a piece of cracker in the dish, and in the second case, a C-shaped, red piece of plastic, which happened to be the name of cracker. She made two errors in 11 trials, one on the first five.

The test was increased in difficulty by adding a green dish to the red one already present and by augmenting the instructions to accomodate this further contrast. She was then given four different kinds of instructions, of which the following three are examples: "Sarah insert cracker red dish," "Sarah insert name of cracker red dish," "Sarah insert cracker green dish." She accepted only six such instructions, apparently finding them demanding, but made only one error and none on the first five. The results added substantially to our confidence in Sarah's knowledge of "name of." This evidence may be considered to compensate for the lack of a close semantic contrast, although it is not clear what kind of tradeoff there is between the two kinds of tests.

Given Sarah's success in contrasting X with "name of X," we considered generalizing this test and applying it to, for example, "Insert apple" vs "Insert color of apple," or " . . . shape of apple," " . . . size of apple," etc. These contrasts are less satisfactory, however. When a subject is told to operate on an object in one case and, say, the color of the object in the other, the subject can respond correctly by operating on the object in both cases. That is, if you are told to insert apple in one case and color of apple in the other, by inserting apple you are doing both. This ambiguity does not arise in the case of "name of," where in operating on the object you definitely are not operating on the name of the object.

Because of this ambiguity we tested Sarah's ability to distinguish between an object and a property of the object in a different way. The test consisted of questions of the following kind: (1) "? color of the object apple" (What is the color of the object apple?); (2) "? color of apple" (What is the color of apple?); (3) "? color of object orange" (What is the color of the object orange?); (4) "? color of orange" (What is the color of orange?); (5) "? not color of orange"; etc. The alternatives given her were the words "red," "orange," "green," and "blue." (In this language the color orange and the object orange are named by different words.) Why did we use specifically "green" and "blue" rather than two other incorrect color names? Just these colors were used because they were the color of the word "apple" and of the word "orange," respectively. They therefore offered Sarah the possibility of confusing the word "apple" with its referent, that is, of answering the question, "? color of apple" not with the word "red" but with the word "blue," the latter being the color of the word "apple" rather than the object referred to by the word. However, Sarah was not at all confused by this possibility and made no errors in seventeen trials. Interestingly, she made no use of "green" and "blue" whatever, not using them even when to do so would have been quite acceptable.

For example, she was asked the negative questions "What is not the color of orange?" and "What is not the color of apple?" To these questions she answered "red" in the first case, and "orange" in the second. She would have been equally justified in answering either "blue" or "green" but she did not. Her answers suggest she strictly contrasted apple with orange, whether they were represented by the objects or by names of the objects, and at no time contrasted (or confused) names of objects with objects.

A still more revealing test, which might have been carried out but was not, would be one requiring a contrast between the name of an object and the color of the name of the object. Here the instructions could be: (1) "Sarah insert name of apple dish" versus (2) "Sarah insert color of name of apple dish." In the first case, she should put a blue triangular piece of plastic in the dish and in the second case, a clear, crescent-shaped piece of plastic, the first piece being the word "apple" and the second the word "blue." One reason for not carrying out this test was the possible ambiguity of the sentence "Sarah insert name of color of apple." Without a conjunction marker, and none had been introduced at the time, the sentence could have been read in either of two ways: (1) put the color of the name of apple in the dish or (2) put the color of and the name of apple in the dish. As Sarah's language stood, we had no certain way of differentiating the two.

WHEN IS A PIECE OF PLASTIC A WORD?

How do we know when a piece of plastic is a word? The traditional answer to this question is that the piece of plastic is a word when it is used as a word—when it occurs along with other words of appropriate grammatical class in sentences and when it occurs as the answer or part of the answer to questions. For instance, we consider the small piece of blue plastic to be the name for apple because (1) it was the word Sarah used when requesting apple, that is, "Give Sarah apple," and (2) it was the answer given when she was asked, in effect, "What is the name of apple?" This is a standard and unobjectionable treatment to which, however, we may be able to add. We may say in addition that the piece of plastic is a word when in the presence of it alone the subject can give what amounts to a description of the referent that has been associated with the piece of plastic. We can determine whether or not this condition obtains in a direct and simple way.

FEATURES ANALYSES OF APPLE AND "APPLE"

With match-to-sample procedures we can obtain independent features analyses of both the word and its referent. In the first test of this kind, Sarah was presented with an actual apple as a sample and with pairs of alternatives that did and did not instance some feature of apple. Four pairs of alternatives were used in the first test: a red plaque versus a green plaque, a square with a stemlike protuberance versus a plain square, a plain square vs a circle, and a square with a stemlike protuberance vs a circle (see Figure 8.2). This first test was intended to

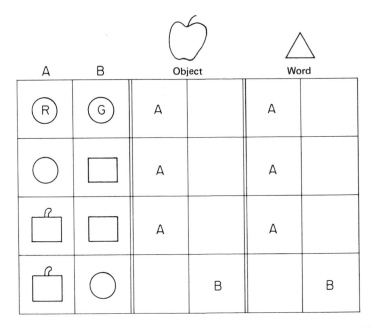

A	B	Object		Word	
(R)	(G)	A		A	
○	▢	A		A	
▢	▢	A		A	
▢	○		B		B

FIG. 8.3 Features analysis of the object apple and the word "apple" (Premack, 1970).

answer a question preliminary to that of symbolization. Can the chimpanzee analyze an object into its features? More operationally, can match-to-sample be used to answer this question? With certain lesser species, e.g., the pigeon, we get a negative answer, one that it is not clear how to interpret: (1) the species cannot analyze objects into their component features and (2) the more agnostic position that match-to-sample is too demanding for the pigeon. We need to find a methodologically less demanding procedure in order to answer the question. The chimpanzee does not leave us in this quandary.

Sarah's features analysis of the apple accorded nicely with the human analysis. She chose red over green, round over square, square with a stemlike protuberance over plain square, and for the most part round over square with a stem. Two tests of 20 and 22 trials, respectively, were given, with approximately five replications of each pair of alternatives per test presented in a mixed order. She was consistent in her choice of three features and inconsistent on the fourth, choosing round over square with a stem on seven of ten trials and square with a stem on the other three. The inconsistency is not an error, of course, but simply reflects the apparently greater weight she assigns to roundness than to stemness, the other positive features with which it is contrasted. Moreover, all of her choices were acknowledged with tones of approval and, in addition, on every fifth trial she was given an opportunity to take goodies from the tray.

The test was then repeated exactly except the object apple was replaced with the word for apple. Once again Sarah was required to indicate whether or not the sample was red or green, round or square, etc., although now the sample was a small blue triangular piece of plastic rather than a red apple. Nevertheless, she assigned the same features to the word "apple" that she had earlier assigned to the object apple. On two tests of 20 trials each, she deviated from her previous choices on only one trial, when she chose green rather than red, through inattention I would say (even though she was approved of for this choice as for all others, she did not choose green again). The agreement between her analysis of the object and of its name included the same seven to three split on round vs square with stem.

CARAMEL AND "CARAMEL"

On a subsequent analysis of this kind, the word "caramel" was tested, specifically because it had been introduced by informal pairing. Although there was not the faintest suggestion that the status of a word depended in any way on which of the three methods had been used to introduce it—(1) embedded in a sentence, (2) "name of," or (3) informal pairing—still it was of interest to substantiate this impression by a features analysis test. "Apple," the first word analyzed, had been introduced in the old-fashioned way, that is, by being embedded in some of her earliest sentences, whereas "caramel" was one of many later words introduced by informal pairing.

The caramel of Sarah's experience was the old-fashioned brown cube of candy wrapped in cellophane. To test her ability to describe the candy on the basis of its name, we used four pairs of alternatives: a wooden cube versus a wooden disk of the same size, a white disk versus a brown one, an unpainted large triangle versus an unpainted triangle of the size of a caramel, and two pieces of paper, one smooth and the other crumpled. The intended features were shape, color, size, and texture of the covering. She was given 20 trials, five replications on each pair of alternatives in a mixed order. On the first and third sessions the sample was the word "caramel" and on the second and fourth session the sample was an actual caramel. The counterbalancing was done to rule out the unlikely possibility that on the former test she had simply memorized the alternatives for apple and then applied them to "apple."

The features Sarah chose accorded with the human analysis and were approximately the same for the word and the object. In her analysis of both the word and the object she chose on most trials the cube, the brown disk, the triangle of appropriate size, and smooth paper. With the word as the sample she deviated from the human analysis on four occasions, choosing crumpled paper once, large triangle once, and noncube twice. With the object as the sample she deviated on five occasions, choosing crumpled paper three times and noncube twice. All of these deviations must be considered errors; i.e., none of them was a case in which one positive feature was pitted against another. This still left her with 90%

correct on the word, with about 87% correct on the object, and with an impressive agreement of better than 94% between the features she assigned to the word and to its referent.

On a later occasion we made a features analysis of "apple," using words rather than objects as alternatives whenever possible. She had no word for stem, but she did have the words "red" and "green" as well as "round" and "square." She was given four 20-trial sessions, the first and third using the word "apple" and the second and fourth the object apple. Her agreement between the analysis of the word and the object was better than 96%, essentially the same as for the earlier test in which the alternatives were objects.

REVERSING THE QUESTION:
FROM REFERENT TO NAME

In both the test on "apple" and the test on "caramel" Sarah was asked to display her knowledge of the word by "describing" its referent. In the next test we turned the question around, asking her to display her knowledge of the referent by describing its name. That is, rather than giving the word and asking her to describe its referent, we gave the referent and asked her to describe its name. Once again apple was used as the sample, but this time with alternatives that were irrelevant to apple and relevant instead to little blue triangle, the name of apple. She was given 15 pairs of alternatives, both words and objects, with the first five consisting of wood blocks and the second ten of words. The first five alternatives were: square versus triangle of equal size, triangle versus circle of equal size, large triangle versus small triangle, and small circle vs triangle of equal size. The second ten alternatives were: "big" versus "small," "square" versus "triangle," "round" versus "triangle," "green" versus "blue," "red" versus "blue," "big" versus "small," "triangle" versus "round," "triangle" versus "square," "blue" versus "red," big" versus "small," and "triangle" versus "square." She made one error in 15 trials, choosing "big" over "small." On this test, unlike the others, we disapproved of her erroneous choices and she did not repeat this error. Therefore, Sarah selected features descriptive of "apple" in the presence of apple, even as earlier she had done the reverse.

The two kinds of tests Sarah passed are comparable to using a dictionary in both directions. From the word "apple," she selected alternatives compatible with apple and conversely, from apple, alternatives compatible with its name. Both descriptions were done in the absence of the item that was described, thus introducing a need for memory or internal representation. In the presence of the word, she provided a description of apple; and in the presence of apple a description of the name of apple. The first test would require an internal representation of the referent and the second one of the name. (These results are massively corroborated in Chapter 15.)

Similar tests could be made in natural language, for example, by giving a child an object and asking it to describe its name or by giving it a name and asking for a description of its referent. The latter is straightforward. Given the word "apple," the child could be asked to choose between the same alternatives used with Sarah. The reverse test is also possible, although the alternatives used with Sarah can no longer be used; they must be modified to suit the change from a language based on pieces of plastic to one the written form of which is based on letters. This change reaffirms a point noted earlier: In natural language words and referents are unlikely to be confused; they have little dimensional overlap. This holds even for written words. Features that are appropriate to an analysis of orthographic units have little to do with the features appropriate to an analysis of the referents. It is only in the present language that words and referents can both be, say, red or round or small, etc.

Previous attempts to answer the question of when an item is a word (noniconic symbol) have been uniformly unsuccessful (see Morris, 1946). In a first attempt, an item was said to be a word when the subject responded to the word in the same way as it responded to the referent of the word. However, pies are made with apples not with "apples" (and sentences are made with "apples" not with apples). An attempt was made to circumvent this problem by amending the key phrase respond "in the same way" to read respond "in a similar way." "Similar" was given several interpretations, the most plausible being that one responded to, say, "apple" in a way that was anticipatory of apple. For instance, one might salivate upon hearing "apple" in anticipation of the more copious salivation that occurred when one actually ate an apple. This "corrected" view is, if anything, worse than the first one, for where the first one was grossly wrong, this one gives the impression of being on the right track. Actually, the whole approach is misguided.

"Apple" and, say, "hot dog" are not as alike in meaning as one could mistakenly assume by equating meaning with the anticipatory responding associated with each word. One could salivate upon hearing both words and yet respond altogether differently to any of a host of questions concerning the two words, for example, what grows on trees? what, is an animal product? what has seeds? what is sometimes covered with caramel? what is generally found in a bun? All attempts to explain meaning by comparing either overt or covert responding to the word, on the one hand, with responding to its referent, on the other, overlook the major function of a word. When in the presence merely of the name of an item, the language-competent subject can answer as many questions about the item, as when in the presence of the item itself. The ability to use words in this manner does not depend upon anticipatory responses, upon having a mouth that is inclined to salivate. One need not be hungry for apples in order for the word "apple" to serve as an information retrieval device for apple.

The properties Sarah assigned to the word "apple" showed that her analysis of the word was based not on the physical form of the blue piece of plastic, but on the object that the plastic represented. Therefore, "apple" can be considered a symbol of apple. Do we know the necessary and sufficient conditions for this effect, or even the specific point in training when the effect first becomes demonstrable? Strictly speaking we do not. There are a number of intermediate possibilities, but consider two major alternatives:

1. In the course of acquiring language the organism learns how to symbolize.

2. Symbolization is an integral property of perhaps all learning and makes language possible.

If the latter were true and symbolization were a more primitive disposition than we have supposed, what form would symbolization take in lower organisms? What form would it take in a pigeon, for example?

HOW TO TEST FOR SYMBOLIZATION IN THE PIGEON

Consider a multiple schedule in which a vertical line is associated with the opportunity to eat corn and a horizontal line with the opportunity to eat wheat. The test would begin by first requiring the bird to do a features analysis on each food. For instance, with wheat as the sample, the bird would be offered a choice between such alternatives as brown versus yellow, oblong versus round, a wheat-sized square versus ones both larger and smaller than wheat, etc. A similar test would be given on corn, with the alternatives adjusted to accommodate features that are applicable to corn. The bird's choice of alternatives on these tests would identify the features it could associate with each food and so could itself use to distinguish between the foods. If the bird's analysis accorded with the human one, as for example Sarah's analysis of apple accorded with the human one, the bird would select, for example, brown and oblong as features of wheat, yellow and round as features of corn.

In the next step, we would associate the vertical line with corn, and the horizontal one with wheat, perhaps in the context of a simple multiple schedule. Pecking in the presence of the vertical and horizontal lines would result in wheat and corn, respectively. The simple correlation between the two line orientations and the two foods is comparable to that between two pieces of plastic and their respective referents. Indeed, the multiple schedule offers as much opportunity to learn the correlation between the lines and their associated foods as the language training offers to learn the correlation between pieces of plastic and their associated referents. The presence of the vertical line would permit the bird to anticipate or expect the opportunity to eat corn and the presence of the horizontal line, the opportunity to eat wheat. As far as I can see, the two kinds of training do not differ in any essential way: Both offer the opportunity to associate a nonpreferred item with a more preferred one. The fact that one organism pecks at the stimulus and the other puts the stimulus on a board seems wholly inconsequential.

The essential difference, if there is one, is not between the procedures but between the species—their capacity to process the information that is contained in the procedures. Moreover, if we seriously believed the procedures to be important, we could reverse them, applying the multiple schedule to the chimpanzee and the language training to birds. My conjecture is that species and not procedure is critical: The chimpanzee will process the information in the same way in both procedures, and so will the pigeon. The question is whether the way in which one species processes the information is the same as that in which the other species processes it.

The question can be answered by the third and last step in the experiment, in which we return to the match-to-sample format, now, however, replacing the wheat and corn with the two line orientations. The bird would be asked the same question concerning the two lines that Sarah was asked concerning the small blue triangle. Can the bird, when in the presence of the vertical line, select features appropriate to corn and, when in the presence of the horizontal line, features appropriate to wheat? (Sarah, when in the presence of the small blue triangle, selected features appropriate to apple.) If the bird can do this, then the two lines are no less names for wheat and corn, respectively, than the blue triangle is a name for apple. If the bird cannot do this then the two lines are merely discriminative stimuli; they do not have the information retrieval capacity of the pieces of plastic. At this point, if the exposition has been clear, the reader should see that every word is a discriminative stimulus, but not every discriminative stimulus is a word. That is, every item that can be used as an information retrieval device for its associated referent can also be used to set the occasion for a response; but not every item that can be used to set the occasion for a response can be used as an information retrieval device. Moreover, as I have already conjectured, which stimulus function is realized is determined not by the experience per se, but by the nature of the species that is given the experience.

Is the pigeon capable of both stimulus functions or can it acquire only discriminative stimuli? At the moment we cannot answer the question definitively. The main thing we have learned so far is that the pigeon is unable to do a features analysis on simple objects, such as a picture of a grain of wheat or a kernel of corn, let alone on a would-be symbol of an object. The pigeon is apparently incapable of match-to-sample on color, and perhaps on any dimension. It can peck the red rather than green alternative when the sample is red, the green when the sample is green; but when a new color is introduced its performance drops to chance. If this inability were restricted to color, we could agree with Cumming and Berryman (1965) that the problem lay in the use of inappropriate hues, in the fact that the pigeon divides the spectrum differently than we do. However, the bird's failure to abstract the matching principle, to do other than respond to specific training cases, appears to apply to form no less than to color and presumably to other dimensions that we have not yet tried. In brief, because we cannot teach the bird to do features analyses on objects, we cannot take the next step and determine whether the bird can use a stimulus to retrieve the features of an object with which the stimulus has been associated.

The pigeon's failure on matching is puzzling for we know that it is capable of distinguishing, say, man from nonman and water from nonwater (Herrnstein & Loveland, 1964; Siegel & Honig, 1970). However, it is premature to link the bird's success in the one case and failure in the other to differences in type of concept or conceptual operation, for procedural differences divide the cases also. For example, match-to-sample requires the subject to reverse its choices, to pick red when the sample is red but not when the sample is green. Evidence for such concepts as man and water does not require reversal but only that the subject respond correctly to new (nontraining) instances of man and water. It remains to be seen whether procedure alone can account for the differences, or whether a conceptual explanation may be necessary. If we can pinpoint the bird's failure it may be as instructive as the chimpanzee's success (see Chapter 7 for bolder guesses concerning the basis of the bird's incapacity).

How primitive a mechanism is symbolization? Is the use of one item to retrieve a representation of another an integral component of all learning or a mechanism more or less restricted to primates? Our inability to measure this capacity in the pigeon may mean that the bird lacks the capacity or, the agnostic alternative, that an answer depends on less demanding test procedures, although it is not clear what they may be. For a species that does symbolize, such as the chimpanzee, it is reasonable to assume that symbolization is an integral part of learning, in no way instilled by the training. Symbolization, like transfer, lies at the heart of language learning. It is not instilled by training but is a capacity that is exploited by the training.

9

Properties and Property Classes

Teaching names for properties and actions can be expected to pose difficulties not posed by names for objects and agents. The word "apple," for example, applies to the whole apple, even as "Mary" and names of other agents apply to whole individuals. In the case of properties and actions, however, the arrangement is less convenient. It is not possible to divide the world into pieces that correspond to either a property or an action. In talking about the world we give the impression of such pieces, for example, "a red patch," "a square," "an act of giving," "a good jump," but one has only to attempt to teach the words "red," "square," "give," or "jump," to discover that in fact there are no such pieces.

For instance, to teach "jump," we cannot point to a jump—as we can point to an apple or a Mary—but only to a jumper. Likewise, in attempting to teach "red," "square," or "large," we cannot point to a red, a square, or a large, but only to, say, an apple, a cracker, and a watermelon. In teaching "jump," we must somehow assure that the subject abstracts specifically the action of the jumper and not any of numerous concommitants, such as the cry the jumper may emit, his flapping garments, or the dust that rises when he lands. Similarly, in teaching "red" by pointing to an apple, we will at the same time point to an instance of round, shiny, hard, small, etc., and must somehow assure that the subject abstracts specifically the color and not any of the accompanying properties. We distinguish names of objects and agents from those of properties and actions by saying that the former have referents, whereas the latter are instanced by the world. However, *instance* is a logical relation and does not identify the psychological process that makes the relation possible.

To learn names for actions and properties a subject must be able to attend selectively, to analyze objects into features and complex events into components. If a species could respond to objects and events only as indivisable wholes and under no circumstance analyze them into components, it could not learn the names for properties and actions. The chimpanzee, like other species, may very well perceive items as gestalts but, when required to do so, it can also analyze them into components. This was shown by two facts. First, Sarah had already been taught names for actions. Second, she had passed match-to-sample tests of a kind requiring that she match two different objects in terms of a common feature. For example, her choice of red and round, both with apple and the word "apple," was of interest originally because of the comment it made on her symbolic capacity. But the very fact that she could match the red and round alternatives to an apple shows that she could abstract features from objects, and so should have had available the kind of perceptual event that was needed for the labeling of properties.

Although the few tests we made of this kind with Sarah were limited to showing the agreement between the features she assigned to the referent and to its name, with Peony and Elizabeth we carried out a large series of feature-matching tests, not in the context of symbolization but strictly for its own sake. Peony and Elizabeth were required to analyze the features of four pairs of nonsense objects, blocks of wood cut into a variety of shapes, with holes drilled in at various points, nails pounded in to varying depths, jagged or smooth edges, some painted and some natural. The features tested were color, shape, size (separate tests for larger and smaller), and detail, the latter consisting of the holes, nails, and jagged edge.

On each trial, the subject received either of two nonsense objects as the sample along with a pair of alternatives, planometric forms one of which instanced a feature belonging to the sample and the other of which did not. Four different pairs of nonsense objects were used, one pair for each of the four features studied. The number of redundant features present in each alternative was varied over the test series. For example, in the first series both the correct and incorrect alternatives were fully redundant; only the correct alternative was the same, say, color as the sample but both the correct and incorrect alternatives had the shape, size, and detail of the sample. Over the course of the series the redundant features were progressively reduced; finally the correct alternative matched the sample in only one feature and the incorrect alternative matched it in no feature whatever. Interestingly, this variation had little effect on the performance of either subject; therefore, the results were averaged over all the redundancy conditions. The use of nonsense objects and planometric alternatives was deliberate, intended to make the tests more difficult than would be expected with familiar or sensible objects and three-dimensional alternatives. Delayed matching was done as well as nondelayed.

Both animals proved to be able to analyze nonsense objects into their features. Simple as this act may seem it is not one that can be done by all species. Indeed, although we have had some preliminary success with dogs (Premack, 1973a), the only solid data come from primates. Peony did about equally well on color and on shape, whereas Elizabeth performed below Peony on color and about the same as she on shape. These results conform with the performance of the two animals on sorting tasks (see Chapter 11). Peony was as likely to sort objects on the basis of color as on the basis of form and shifted spontaneously from one criterion to the other. Elizabeth definitely preferred shape and did not use color as a sorting criterion unless forced to do so by the removal of all shape differences. These same differences reemerged later when Peony and Elizabeth were taught names for colors and shapes (see pages 187–188). On the size feature, both animals tended to choose the larger of the two alternatives. As to delay, the 5 sec we used had little effect on either color, size, or shape; but even this short delay had an adverse effect on the detail feature (the hole, nail, or jagged border). Differences in detail may have been smaller than those in the other features, although this seems unlikely, for example, nail versus no nail; instead, features of this kind may be more difficult to retain or represent in short-term memory.

The results of this extensive series corroborated Sarah's earlier data. They left no doubt that the chimpanzee can match different objects on the basis of individual features and can attend selectively to features per se. Therefore, the chimpanzee should have available for labeling the kind of perceptual events that underlie "red," "round," "large," and the names of other features.

METHODS FOR TEACHING PROPERTY NAMES

As we have seen, the problem in naming features is to direct the subject's attention to the target, or conversely to functionally eliminate all the incorrect or nontarget features. In the method of *single differences* we attempted to solve this problem by using two objects that were identical except for the pair of features to be named. For example, in our first attempt to teach Sarah the names of red and yellow, we dyed two little pieces of apple red and yellow, respectively, with tasteless vegetable dye. "Red" was to be associated with the color of one piece of apple, "yellow" with the color of the other piece. How does this method assure that the subject associates the words specifically with the colors and not with some other properties? Because there are two words to be learned and only one property that is represented by two values, if the subject successfully associates the two words with the two objects, it can only be with the color values. The words cannot be associated with, say, the size or shape features, for the pieces of apple are alike in size and shape and, indeed, in all respects except color. In brief, in the method of single differences, all the features the two pieces of apple share are irrelevant; it is the features they do not share that are to be named. A subject can reach that conclusion by an astute glance, observing that only color is present in two values, or can learn the same thing by trial and error, trying shape, size, position, etc., only to find that the only difference with which the words can be uniquely associated is the difference in color.

Sarah was given one piece of apple and the appropriate words in a standard errorless approach. In the presence of a yellow piece, she was required to write "Give yellow" and in the presence of a red piece, "Give red," after which she was given the piece of apple and promptly ate it. Choice trials were then used to assess the effectiveness of the errorless trials. They revealed that she had learned nothing. Moreover, they did not succeed in teaching her the desired associations any more than the errorless trials. After 84 errorless trials and over 200 choice trials, she performed at the 53% level. When given a piece of yellow apple she was as likely to write "Give red" as "Give yellow" and likewise when given a red piece of apple.

In view of the apparent simplicity of the method of single differences, her failure was a great surprise and we sought refuge in a flurry of hypotheses. Perhaps she was not attending to the color or any other aspect of the fruit but was simply popping the apple into her mouth. Why should she look closely at the pieces when the fruit did not vary from lesson to lesson and taste did not vary with color? Although this may be as good a guess as any, it is not hard to find evidence against it. For example, chickens sated on yellow corn resume eating when offered red corn, and the birds seem to have had no more cause to inspect their food than has Sarah. But chimps not being birds may not combine looking and eating in a birdlike way, so we have tested the hypothesis.

PIECES OF APPLE AS NAMES

To force greater attention to colors, we attempted to use the pieces of apple not as objects instancing the features to be named but as names themselves. We selected gumdrops, a liked but so far unnamed object, to be named by the red piece of apple, and cupcake, an equally liked but also unnamed object, to be named by the yellow piece of apple. This was the one and only occasion on which we violated the word class, attempting to set up as a word an object other than the special metal-backed piece of plastic. However, the pieces of apple did preserve one essential relation. Like the plastic words, they were less valued than their referents. That is, we chose gumdrops and cupcake deliberately, to offset the fact that Sarah liked the pieces of apple as such. She does not like them as much as the gumdrops and cupcake, however, and the absolute value of a word is probably unimportant so long as it is less than that of its referent. In a language in which referents and words are equally tangible, and words are preferred to their referents, words are unlikely to be used in wordlike ways.

Training took the usual form. The cupcake was set before Sarah on some trials, along with the words "give" and "cupcake" (the latter consisting of the piece of red apple). Since the apple would not adhere to the board, she was required to write "Give cupcake" from left to right on the workbench alongside the cage. On other trials, the gumdrop was set before her along with the words "give" and "gumdrop" (the latter consisting of the yellow piece of apple). After 15 errorless trials on each of the two cases, she was given the usual choice test. With only one object before her but all three words, she was required to write "Give gumdrop" or "Give cupcake," depending on which object was present. She made 13 errors in 27 trials, doing no better with the pieces of apple as would-be names, therefore, than when the pieces of apple were used to exemplify the properties to be named.

A simple object discrimination was used to test for color blindness, a possibility we could no longer suppress. She was presented with a piece of red and a piece of yellow apple, red arbitrarily being designated correct and yellow incorrect. If she chose the yellow piece she was given nothing. If she chose the red piece, she was given the words "give" and "chocolate" and could write "Give chocolate"; following this she was given a piece of chocolate, which she preferred to apple. A correct choice therefore made available to her words with which she could request and receive chocolate, whereas the incorrect choice made available nothing. (We used this arrangement, instead of simply giving her chocolate when she chose the correct piece of apple, to forestall the possibility that the red piece of apple would come to be the name for chocolate, or to have the meaning of "Give chocolate.") She made only three errors in 26 trials, eliminating color blindness as the problem.

Why was she able to pass this test and not earlier ones? In addition to having been given later, the simultaneous discrimination does not have a conditional component and so may be simpler. Red is "correct" and yellow "incorrect" in an absolute sense, whereas in the conditional discrimination red is correct for cupcake (but not gumdrops), and yellow is correct for gumdrops (but not cupcake). Needless to say, this does not explain why she has been capable of learning the names of objects, agents, and actions, which also involve conditional discrimination.

Another hypothesis is that the procedure fails because apple, the receptacle for the two different colors, is an already named entity. We should have instanced the two properties either with an unnamed entity or, if we use a named entity, have made the name explicit. Instead of requiring Sarah to write just "Give red" or "Give yellow," therefore, she should have been required to write "Give red apple" and "Give yellow apple." We have yet to introduce the property name as the modifier on an already named object, but we have tested the other suggestion, viz., to instance the properties with unnamed objects.

My daughter combined a junior highschool cooking class with a contribution to science by baking a large batch of cookies differing only in shape, some round and some square. The same procedure tried earlier with the words "red" and "yellow" was now tried with "round" and "square," the only difference being that, unlike apple, cookie was an unnamed entity. A round cookie was placed before Sarah, she was given the familiar word "give" and the unfamiliar one "round," and she was required to write "give round." On other trials a square cookie was placed before her, she was given the words "give" and "square," and she was required to write "Give square." She wrote both sentences without hesitation and was given the round and square cookie, respectively, which she ate promptly.

On a total of 162 choice trials, she was correct only 53% of the time, with as many errors on the ninth and last session as on the first. She showed a strong preference for the word "round," which was larger than the word for square, choosing "round" 117 times, "square" 39 times, and both of them six times.[1]

THE RELEVANCE OF IRRELEVANT DIFFERENCES

Because Sarah learned names of actions without difficulty but had so far failed to learn those of properties, we had to ask in what way these two categories differed. We have already brought them together by contrasting both of them with agents and objects, noting that names of actions and properties have a more complex relation to the world and depend on selective attention. However, we must now separate actions and properties so as to understand Sarah's success on one and failure on the other.

A moment's reflection shows that property names impose one unique requirement. The essence of naming a property lies in attending to one and only one feature. Actions do not impose this requirement because most, if not all, actions differ from one another on a multidimensional basis. In this respect, agents and objects are like actions; they also do not require names based on single features. Until required to learn property names, Sarah had not been required to associate names with individual features, and there was no evidence that she had done so. A subject who associated "apple" with round (in a contrast with banana) and "cherry" with red (in a contrast with orange) would be unable initially to distinguish between "apple" and "cherry"; round would apply to cherry (and apple) and red to apple (and cherry). But Sarah had no such difficulty. Fruit names were taught her in restricted pairs, setting up the opportunity for feature-specific learning; yet when she was subsequently required to contrast each fruit name with all others, she was successful from the beginning. Therefore, at least part of her difficulty with feature names might have come from the fact that she had no prior experience in associating words with single features.

---

[1] Her illegitimate choice of both words recalls a warm afternoon in 1955, in Orange Park, Florida, when I tested a chimpanzee for the first time. I offered Alf, a large imposing male, a choice between a black and white plaque, beneath one of which was a slice of banana. He studied both me and the discrimination problem for a moment and then calmly pushed back both plaques, an outcome for which my rat experience had not prepared me.

A second source of difficulty may have come from the method of single differences itself, which assumes that the subject can exploit the category of irrelevant differences, quickly learning to ignore the irrelevant features that are shared by the two pieces of apple. However, Sarah had little if any previous experience with irrelevant differences per se. In the items she had previously named, all the features that distinguished one item from another were likely to be relevant (with the possible exception of size). The method of single differences may be unhelpful to a subject who has little experience with irrelevant differences. It may be important instead to teach such a subject about irrelevant differences, to acquaint it with the category. The method of sets, to which we turn now, has been devised for this purpose.

METHOD OF SETS

To teach "red" and "yellow" we abandoned the pieces of apple and collected two sets of six objects each. All members of the one set were red and all those of the other set were yellow, but color was the only property common to all members of each set. Otherwise every item in the red set—marble, cherry, toy car, etc.—differed from every other one, just as every item in the yellow set—flower, Cheesit, box, etc.—differed from every other one. On errorless trials, Sarah received the word "red" in the presence of each member of the red set, the word "yellow" in the presence of each member of the yellow set. On these trials, Sarah had the opportunity to discover the common property that united each set. She could observe that the items associated with "red," like those associated with "yellow," had many variable and therefore irrelevant properties but only one common and relevant property, viz., color—red in the first case, yellow in the second.

In this same period, we also tried iconic cues and introduced "blue" and "green" by placing the former on a blue card, the latter on a green one. In this way Sarah could match the word on the blue card to the blue objects and the word on the green card to the green object, even though these words were achromatic pieces of plastic like all other color names. Except for the iconic cards, which were reduced in size over the course of the lessons until only the words remained, the training for "blue—green" was like that for "red—yellow." "Blue" was represented by a set of six items, the only common property of which was color, and "green" by a comparable set of items. In the beginning "red—yellow" and "blue—green" were trained in separate lessons, but later they were combined in the same lessons.

One object from the red set was consistently paired with one from the yellow set, and likewise one from the blue set with one from the greeen set. She was given four to six errorless trials per pair. For example, a plastic bow, one of the objects in the blue set, was placed before her along with the words "give" and "blue," the latter on a blue card. After she wrote "Give blue," the bow was handed over to her for a brief inspection. There were several food items in both sets, for example, cheese and cherry in the yellow and red sets, respectively, and she was allowed to eat them when they were correctly requested. With the nonfood items, she was given fruit cocktail and yogurt when correct, in addition to the opportunity to explore the item.

On choice trials she was given one of the training items in the presence of the word "give" and the two color names either "red–yellow" or "blue–green." Each session consisted of 16 trials, all of them confined to one pair of items. Typically, two sessions were given a day, one on each pair of colors. She made fewer errors in learning the blue–green distinction than the red–yellow distinction, possibly because of the iconic crutch. In learning "red–yellow," she showed a definite preference for one of the words, a characteristic that sometimes emerged when she had difficulty in learning. Of her first 56 errors only four were based on the incorrect use of "yellow" (not all of the remainder were based on "red," however; many of her errors consisted of the illegitimate use of both color names, for example, "Give red yellow," and also "Give blue green"). In learning "blue–green," she showed no preference for either word.

In both cases, after she learned the color names she showed clear transfer over the different pairs of objects, ultimately succeeding on pairs of objects that differed only in color. For example, she correctly applied "red" and "yellow" to red and yellow cards, as well as "blue" and "green" to blue and green wires. In thus naming the color of objects that differed only in color, she succeeded in doing what she had been unable to do in the first procedure.

After she learned the two pairs of words, she was given sessions in which "yellow" was contrasted with both "green" and "blue," and "red" with both "blue" and "yellow." About two-thirds of the trials were based on the new pairings and one-third was based on the original ones. On each trial one of four objects was present (as opposed to one of two objects in the previous sessions) and she was given the words "give" along with either "yellow–green" or "red–blue" and required to write "give X," where X was the color of the object present. She was given a total of five sessions, with approximately 16 trials a session and a different set of four objects on each lesson. On the second session, a transfer test was incorporated by using all new objects. She was correct on 13 out of 16, 14 out of 16, 11 out of 16, 11 out of 15, and 12 out of 14 on the five lessons, respectively. Errors came mainly from the new pairs of words–14 out of a total of 16 errors–divided more or less evenly over the four cases. She therefore performed at about the 72% level on the new pairs vs. 96% level on old pairs. On the second session, the use of new objects produced no decrement, indicating that she could selectively attend to the color of a new object as accurately as to that of an old object (we cannot say "as quickly" because we have no latency measures). Her difficulty came not from objects per se but in choosing between words that had not before been paired. This suggested that in learning property names the features of the words she used were not altogether independent of those of the paired word. Suppose a pair of words differed greatly in size; this might incline the subject to assign a greater weight to size than otherwise. Later, when a word identified on the basis of its size was paired with a new word of roughly equal size, the subject would have difficulty discriminating between them and would be forced to modify the features it used. Although this is a hypothetical example, the uncharacteristic errors she showed when color names were combined in new pairs suggests a similar process. In more than one respect, property names gave Sarah more difficulty than any other lexical class.

On the last test given on color names, her alternatives consisted of honey, dyed one of four colors with tasteless vegetable dye and smeared thickly on cracker. In addition to these new alternatives (which differed by color alone), all four words were available on each trial. Her accuracy fell somewhat at first but then returned to its former level. She was correct on 14 out of 21, 9 out of 14, 6 out of 10, 15 out of 16, 17 out of 21, 8 out of 12, and 15 out of 16, respectively. On the first two sessions she continued to err more on what could be considered new pairs than on old ones, for example, choosing "red" when the correct choice was "brown," and vice versa. But this trend disappeared over the course of the seven sessions.

SETS APPLIED TO SHAPE NAMES

Because she failed to learn "square" and "round" when these words were applied to cookies differing only in shape, we arranged two sets of objects with disparate members, each set alike in only one regard, squareness and roundness, respectively. Jar lid versus curry can, Reagan button versus box, transparent ball versus yellow block, round wooden red ball versus plastic block, vanilla wafer versus raisin bread square, and onion cracker versus plain bread square were the pairs of objects used in training. When she performed correctly she was given food, either the edible items from the training pairs or other food.

She was given eight sessions on toys alone, three sessions on food alone, and seven on food and toys combined. Each session consisted of 20 trials and dealt with one pair of toys, one pair of foods, or a pair consisting of a toy and a food. She learned to apply "square" and "round" to the shapes of foods more readily than to the shapes of toys, perhaps merely because the shape difference was more clearly realized with food. With toys she responded at the 45% level after 100 trials and with foods at the 85% level after only 30 trials. In the sessions combining trials on food and toys she performed as follows: 90%/55%, 100%/60%, 100%/70%, 100%/80%, 100%/55%, 100%/60%, and

100%/95%—percent correct food/percent correct toys—respectively. She passed a transfer test that combined two new foods with two new toys at the 95 and 80% levels on food and toys, respectively.

LARGE–SMALL

"Large" and "small" were learned with the fewest errors, perhaps simply because they were taught last. Some of the objects used were bottle cap, uninflated balloon, and grommet in the small set and sponge, wood block, and plastic bottle in the large set. The range of things called "large" and "small" reflected her caged existence. She did not have access to cars, trees, houses—objects we might have labeled "very big" had the occasion arisen.

After four to six errorless trials on the members of each pair, she was given six sessions of 20 choice trials each, ten per training pair. She made 12 out of 20, 16 out of 20, 17 out of 20, 18 out of 20, and 17 out of 20 correct responses per total trials on the six sessions, respectively, with a total of 4 errors on "large" and 16 on "small" ($p < .05$). The tendency to make more errors on "small," the so-called marked form, than on "large" was seen again in the learning of "size of" (where she also made more errors on "small") and was reminiscent of her greater difficulty in acquiring the *yes–no* question when it concerned the difference rather than the sameness between two objects. In the transfer test she was given pairs of pieces of bread and of white paper cards, in both pairs of which the objects differed only in size (about four to one), and made only three errors in 26 such trials.

In summary, Sarah succeeded when the contrast was between sets of unlike objects, each of which was unified by a common property, but failed when the contrast was between two objects that were alike except for one feature. If the earlier guess was correct and the use of sets taught her about irrelevant features, henceforth it should have been possible to teach her other feature names with the use of single differences. Although there was no lack of other features with which to test this prediction, we turned to other matters.

There was a further and more substantial reason for suppressing further speculation about Sarah's failure. It was not replicated by either Peony or Elizabeth. They both learned names of properties with the method of single differences and did so from the beginning. Although this leaves Sarah's results shrouded in mystery, it is a reaffirmation of parsimony for it is hard to conceive of a simpler approach to the naming of properties than the method of single differences.

Both Elizabeth and Peony were taught, first, color and then shape names with the same method of single differences. After wedges of apple were dyed either red or yellow with tasteless vegetable dye, the same training procedure used with Sarah was applied to Peony and Elizabeth.

Training began with standard errorless trials. The words placed before Elizabeth were "Amy," "Elizabeth," "give"—all known words—and either "red" or "yellow," the unknown words. One piece of colored apple or the other was placed before her and she was required to write "Amy give red Elizabeth" or the alternative. After this she was given the apple, which she ate with lip-smacking grunts and an inward eye that marked all of Elizabeth's eating, making the feeding part of Elizabeth's training a pleasure both to Elizabeth and to the trainer.

After four errorless trials on each new word, she was given 32 choice trials—in the course of two lessons—in which both the words "red" and "yellow" were present and she was required to choose between them. Elizabeth performed at chance, with 13 errors in 32 trials. Certainly we would have interpreted this failure as a replication of Sarah's failure—and an indictment of the procedure—if we had not happened to have trained Peony on the same procedure a day earlier. Peony had succeeded where both Sarah and Elizabeth failed. On 27 choice trials, given after a total of 11 errorless trials, Peony made only five errors, or 82% correct.

This contrast between Peony and Elizabeth recalled two earlier problems in which a similar contrast had arisen. Both on the simple sorting of objects and on the features analysis of nonsense objects, Elizabeth had performed poorly on color; she only sorted objects on the basis of color when forced to do so by the removal of other cues; also, in analyzing features she was markedly poorer in selecting those for color than those for shape, size or even detail. Peony, in contrast, used color as well as she used shape and all the other features.

In view of Peony's success in learning color names and Elizabeth's known difficulties in using color discriminatively, we shifted Elizabeth from color to shape, substituted round and square sugar cookies for the dyed apple wedges, and reapplied the same procedure. Now on an errorless trial the words given Elizabeth were "Amy," "give," "Elizabeth," and either "round" or "square." The square or round cookie was alternately placed before her, and she was required to write "Amy give Elizabeth round" or the alternative, after which she was given the cookie. (She dispatched the sweet crunchy cookie with so deep an inward eye that onlookers laughed and praised her style.) After only two errorless trials each on "round" and "square," both new words were made available at the same time and she was given 73 choice trials in the course of five lessons. She made 14 errors in the 73 trials, with four errors in 15 trials on the first lesson, or 81% correct overall. After failing to learn names for the color distinctions, therefore, she went on to learn names for the shape distinctions.

Before we returned Elizabeth to the color problem—to see whether her success with shape features might have helped her with those for color—we tested her ability to transfer the shape names to new instances of round and square. Items used in the transfer test were fig newton, banana slices, Oreo cookies, and crackers, Items 2 and 3 instancing "round" and 1 and 4, "square." Elizabeth failed the first two transfer sessions—four errors in 11 trials and five errors in 10 trials, respectively—but passed the third session—no errors in 11 trials. The failure may have been attributable to the fact that the test material made special perceptual demands. The training pairs, round vs. square cookies, differed only on shape, whereas the transfer pairs, for example, fig newton versus banana slice, differed on a number of features. Given that the latter differed in terms of design, color, size, and smell, as well as shape, Elizabeth may not have attended to the transfer pairs specifically in terms of the appropriate features; her initial failure may therefore have been more perceptual than linguistic. In any case, she subsequently passed other transfer tests that were made on new items, some differing only in terms of shape but others differing on a number of features additional to shape.

Her success with shape names encouraged a second try at teaching her color names. Using the same procedure as on the first try, she was given two errorless trials on both "red" and "yellow," followed by 27 choice trials. This time she made only four errors, 85% correct. She was given a transfer test the following day and made three errors in 18 trials, or 83% correct overall. Red and yellow jellybeans, red and yellow gumdrops, and red and yellow M&Ms were the materials used in the transfer test; like the training materials, these pairs differed only in the color feature (we neglected to look into the possible source of her difficulty on the transfer test on shape, as we might have done by pairing, say red gumdrop and yellow M&M, etc.)

We made a further test by combining the four new words—"red," "yellow," "round," "square"—giving her items that varied either in shape (but not in color), for example, square and round cookies, or in color (but not in shape), for example, red and yellow jellybeans. She was required to request the item presented by writing "Amy give Elizabeth red (yellow, square, round)," depending on the item present. She made two errors in 12 trials, using the incorrect feature but never the incorrect dimension. That is, on no occasion did she request round or square objects by using "red" or "yellow," or request red or yellow objects by using "round" or "square."

Because the production mode had been used in teaching Elizabeth both the color and shape names, we had yet another opportunity to test her ability to transfer from production to comprehension. A container was placed before her along with a pair of objects, one of them round and the other square. The objects included the familiar sugar cookies as well as items that had not previously been used in this context, for example, poker chips, ring, box, and block, thus adding to the test for transfer. The trainer wrote on the board "Elizabeth round insert" or "Elizabeth square insert," requiring Elizabeth to select the object corresponding to the key word and to insert it in the container. She made 2 errors in 10 trials, with none on the first 5 trials.

The shape test was followed by a comparable one on the color names, in which new items were also used, for example, building blocks, bowling pins, and toy monkeys. Now the instructions were "Elizabeth red insert" or "Elizabeth yellow insert." She made 3 errors in 16 trials, performing at the 80% level in both tests.

In the earliest stages of training, all of the subjects dealt with comprehension and production as though they were distinct and unrelated tasks. A word taught in the production mode and well known in that mode was nonetheless responded to at chance in the comprehension mode. If the present tests had been made early in training, we would expect Elizabeth—after correctly using the words "red," "yellow," "round," and "square" in the production mode—to be utterly befuddled when required to comprehend them. We would expect her to choose designated items at chance level. This, in fact, was how she and the other subjects behaved when required at an early stage of training to show transfer on names of objects and actions (and there is no reason to suppose that the names of properties would have escaped this difficulty). Yet, at a later stage of training, a functional equivalence develops between the two systems; words trained to a given level of accuracy in one mode are immediately responded to at the same level of accuracy in the other mode. This conclusion was formerly based on names of objects and actions; the present results make it possible to extend the conclusion to the names of properties.

PROPERTY CLASSES

Having taught Sarah "red—yellow," "round—square," and "large—small," we were in a position to turn to the names of the class relations "color of," "shape of," and "size of." In each case, the class name was introduced as the relation between a property and an item instancing that property. As shown in Figure 9.1, the items instancing the properties were actual objects in some cases and names of objects in other cases. The occasional use of objects was forced by limitations in Sarah's lexicon. The fact that a property could be instanced by the name of an object no less than by the actual object was, of course, highly encouraging. It was among the first unqualified suggestions that the pieces of plastic had the referential function of words.

We led into the new predicates "color of," "shape of," and "size of" with a review of "name of," which we planned to contrast with the new predicates. Exactly where in semantic space "name of" stands with respect to, say, "color of" is not easily said. Nevertheless, the contrast between, say, "Red is the color of cherry" and "Cherry is the name of the object cherry" is not vacuous or totally uninformative. If a subject can make this contrast we can be additionally confident of its knowledge of the key words. The most compelling evidence in evaluating a subject's knowledge is its ability to contrast neighboring words. What constitutes semantic neighbors is not always evident. The dimensional predicates "color of," "shape of," and "size of" are an intuitive cluster, standing

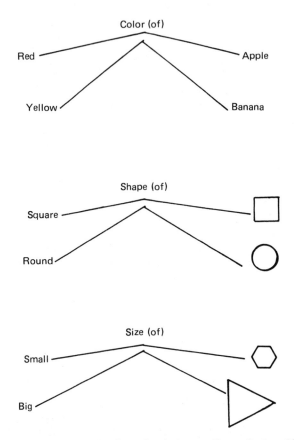

Fig. 9.1 Materials used to teach the dimensional class predicates "color of," "shape of," and "size of." Words were used to instance property values in first case and objects were used in the other two cases (Premack, 1971).

somewhat apart from "name of," but the distances between them is not so great that a subject's ability to make the contrast is wholly uninformative.

"Name of"

Because "name of" had received little use in the preceding period, we gave six review lessons on it before starting on the new predicates. The objects used were chocolate, nut, and cracker, along with their respective names, paired so as to form *wh-* questions, for example, "Nut ? object nut" and "Nut ? object cracker" for which "name of" and "not-name of" were appropriate answers, an equal number of each. She was correct on 62 of the 73 questions given on the six review sessions; all 11 errors were on the negative form.

"Color of"

She was given a total of ten errorless trials in an irregular order of the following questions.

1. "? color of apple" (What is the color of apple?)
2. "? color of ✐" (What is the color of the object apple?)
3. "? color of banana" (What is the color of banana?)
4. "? color of ✐ " (What is the color of the object banana?)

Next she was given ten errorless trials on the following questions:

1. "? not color of apple" (What is not the color of apple?)
2. "? not color of ✐ "
3. "? not color of banana"
4. "? not color of ✐ "

Her alternatives were either "red" or "yellow" depending on the question asked. Notice that the instructions are atypical in that the new word, "color of," was placed in the string and the already existing words "red" and "yellow" were used to complete the string. Ordinarily the words in the string were established ones and the word used to complete the string a new one.

The effectiveness of the errorless instruction was assessed by nine questions of the following kind:

1. "Red ? apple" (What is the relation between red and apple?)
2. "Yellow ? banana"
3. "Red ? banana"
4. "Yellow ? apple"

Her alternatives were "color of" and "not-color of" plus the usual four or five irrelevant words. The lesson was more complex than the typical one in that she was required to shift from substitution of "red" and "yellow" in the errorless training to substitution of the predicates "color of" and "not color of" in the choice trials. She was correct on seven of nine trials.

The assessment continued in the next lesson by asking her all of the above questions plus four others produced by substituting the objects banana and apple for the respective words. For example, "Red ? ✐" and "Red ? ✐ ," etc. Her alternatives remained the same, "color of," and "not-color of," and four or five irrelevant words. She was correct on 20 of 24 trials; three of four errors were made on the words "apple" and "banana," only one on an object. She was then asked the following six questions:

1. "? color of apple" (What is the color of apple?)
2. "? color of grape"
3. "? color of banana"

4. "? not color of apple"
5. "? not color of grape"
6. "? not color of banana"

"Green" and "grape" were her first transfer items in this series. Her alternatives were "red," "yellow," "green," and four or five irrelevant alternatives. She was correct on 17 of 21 trials, two of five errors occurring on grape. Interestingly, when told "no" to her incorrect answer "green not-color of grape" she corrected not by changing the color, say, "green" to "red" but by substituting "color of" for "not-color of."

The transfer assessment continued in the next lesson with the following questions:

1. "red ? apple" (What is the relation between red and apple?)
2. "red ? chocolate"
3. "brown ? chocolate"
4. "brown ? apple"

"brown" and "chocolate" being the second transfer item. Her alternatives were "color of," "not-color of," and four or five irrelevant alternatives. She was correct on 20 of 23 trials, with only one error on "chocolate" and "brown."

In the next lesson, "name of" and "color of" were combined for the first time. She was given the following questions:

1. "Banana ? ⬭ " (What is the relation between banana and the object banana?)
2. "Yellow ? ⬭ " (What is the relationship between yellow and the object banana?)
3. "Apple ? ⬭"
4. "Red ? ⬭ "

Her alternatives were "name of" and "color of" plus four or five irrelevant words. She was correct on eight of nine trials.

The test was repeated with the following questions:

1. "Banana ? ⬭ " (What is the relation between banana and the object banana?)
2. "Chocolate ? △"
3. "Yellow ? ⬭ "
4. "Brown ? △ "

She was correct on 19 of 24 trials.

She was then given three different question forms in the same lesson, each form in a block:

1. "? color of apple" (What is the color of apple?)
2. "? not color of apple"

3. "? color of banana"
4. "? not color of banana"

with relevant alternatives "red" and "yellow."

1. "Red color of ?" (Red is the color of what?)
2. "Yellow color of ?"
3. "Yellow not color of ?"
4. "Red not color of ?"

with "apple" and "banana" as relevant alternatives.

1. "? red color of apple" (Is red the color of apple?)
2. "? red not color of apple"
3. "? yellow color of banana"
4. "? yellow not color of banana"

with "yes" and "no" as relevant alternatives. She was correct on 15 of 17 trials.

The assessment continued with two lessons of blocks of the following *yes–no* questions:

1. "? red color of apple" (Is red the color of apple?)
2. "? red not color of apple"
3. "? red color of banana"
4. "? red not color of banana"
5. "? yellow color of banana"
6. "? yellow not color of banana"
7. "? yellow color of apple"
8. "? yellow not color of apple"

with "yes" and "no" as relevant alternatives. This was followed by *wh-* questions of one form:

1. "? color of apple" (What is the color of apple?)
2. "? not color of apple"
3. "? color of banana"
4. "? not color of banana"

with "red" and "yellow" as relevant alternatives, and then by *wh-* questions of the other form:

1. "Red color of ?" (Red is the color of what?)
2. "Red not color of ?"
3. "Yellow color of ?"
4. "Yellow not color of ?"

with "apple" and "banana" as relevant alternatives. She was correct on 22 out of 25 and 21 out of 25 trials, respectively, with a total of five of seven errors on the negative form.

On the next day she was given a further transfer test:

1. "? color of orange" (What is the color of orange?)
2. "? not color of orange"
3. "? color of apple"
4. "? not color of apple"

with "red" and "orange" as relevant alternatives. (The color name "orange" was not the same as the object name in this language.) She was correct on 17 of 20 trials, all three errors being on apple. The transfer test was completed with the following three blocks of questions. First:

1. "? color of ○ " (What is the color of the object orange?)
2. "? not color of ○ "
3. "? color of ⊘ "
4. "? not color of ⊘ "
5. "? name of ⊘ "
6. "? name of ○ "
7. "? not name of ⊘ "
8. "? not name of ○ "

her relevant alternatives being "red," "orange," "apple," and "orange." She was correct on 16 of 20 trials, with three of four errors on the negative form. Second:

1. "? color of ⊘ " (What is the color of the object apple?)
2. "? color of ○ "
3. "? color of ⊘ "
4. "? color of ○ "
5. "? not color of ○ "
6. "? not color of ⊘ "

with "red" and "orange" as relevant alternatives. Third:

1. "? red color of apple" (Is red the color of apple?)
2. "? orange color of orange"
3. "? red color of orange"
4. "? orange color of apple"

with "yes" and "no" as relevant alternatives. She was correct on 17 of 17 trials. The transfer tests on "grape–green," "chocolate–brown," and "orange–orange" were interpolated among the trials on the training items "apple–red" and "banana–yellow." There were 39 transfer trials; she made six errors, none on the first transfer trial in any case. The results for this series and those for the other relational predicates are summarized in Table 9.1.

TABLE 9.1
Summary of Sarah's Results on Relational Predicates

	Relational predicates			Transfer, Correct/ total
	Correct/ total		Errors on negative/ total errors	
Name of	81/94	86%	9/13	Review
Color of	199/234	85%	22/35	33/39 85%
Shape of	134/151	82%	8/17 (square)	31/42 81%
Size of	88/113	78%	15/25 (small)	16/20 80%

Successive sessions (correct/total)

Name of

13/15, 6/6, 15/19, 12/14, 13/15, 22/25

Color of

7/9, 20/24, 17/21, 20/23, 8/9, 19/24, 15/17, 22/25, 21/25,
17/20, 16/20, 17/17

Shape of

14/14, 19/20, 18/24, 16/20, 9/12, 19/20, 22/24, 17/17

Size of

10/15, 14/18, 8/14, 19/20, 11/13, 17/20

"Shape of"

The training of "shape of" was comparable in most respects to that of "color of" and the main results are summarized in Table 9.1. Instead of giving a blow by blow account, I will concentrate on four aspects of the training unique to this predicate. First, the negative "not-shape of" was not used at all in the original training. This was managed by contrasting two positive forms, "Round shape of ○ " with "Square shape of ☐," rather than a positive and a negative form, say, "Round shape of ○" with "Round not-shape of ☐." Moreover, the training sentences took the form "? shape of ○ " rather than "Round ? ○ ," so that Sarah completed the string by adding the known word "round" rather than the unknown word "shape of." This is exactly analogous to the training in "color of" where also she was required to add "red" to "? color of apple" rather than "color of" to "Red ? apple." The success of this variation of the standard procedure shows that in order to learn a new word Sarah need not actually use it, i.e., need not pick it up and place it in the sentence. It is sufficient if the new word merely occupies a position in the sentence, and is observed by Sarah when she adds an old word to the sentence in the course of completing it.

Second, contrasting "round" with "square"—rather than "shape of" with "not-shape of"—did not interfere with her subsequent ability to correctly use "not-shape of." In the choice tests, she was given *wh-* questions requiring the substitution of "shape of" and "not-shape of" as well as *yes–no* questions in which both "shape of" and "not shape of" appeared. For example, she was asked such questions as "Round ? ☐ " (What is round to ☐ ?), given "shape of" and "not-shape of" as alternatives, and "? square not shape of ☐ " (Is square not the shape of ☐ ?), given "yes" and "no" as alternatives. Interestingly, she made no more errors on the negative than on the positive forms in this case, one of the few exercises in which the negative form did not lead to more errors.

Third, although she passed at the usual level of accuracy (see Figure 9.1), these tests were necessarily limited to round and square objects not used in training and were not applied to other kind of shapes as "round" and "square" were the only shape words she knew.

Fourth, because she now knew three relational predicates she was given tests in which all three appeared as alternatives. In the most interesting version of the several tests of this kind, she was given either a red ball or a yellow cracker and asked to state the relation between these objects and the words "red," "yellow," "round," "square," "ball," and "cracker." Representative questions are:

1. "Round ? ball" (what is the relation between round and ball?)
2. "Red ? ball" (what is the relation between red and ball?)
3. "Ball ? ○ " (what is the relation between ball and ○ ?).

Her alternatives were "color of," "shape of," and "name of." Although the test was simplified by the exclusion of all negative cases, her 22 correct on 24 trials is still impressive. Yet, in another sense the test only confirms what we already know. The chimpanzee is capable of sorting the same objects on the basis of different criteria, according to form on one occasion, color on another. In indicating that the relation between red and ball was color and that that between round and ball was shape, therefore, Sarah merely provided a linguistic corroboration of an already demonstrated perceptual capacity. If this test adds to the perceptual one, it is in the relation between, say, "cracker" and ☐; it is not clear how to test for the perceptual equivalent of "name of" on a nonlinguistic basis.

"Size of"

The training of "size of" took a completely standard form and the main results are summarized in Table 9.1. It is of interest that she made more errors on "small" than on "large"—15 versus 10, overall—resulting from a tendency to

answer "large" when the correct answer was "small." This tendency was especially clear in the initial choice sessions. Her first seven errors were all of this
kind, as were 12 of her first 16 errors. No bias of this kind was seen in the other
cases. Errors on the use of "round" and "square" were about equal (eight vs
nine) as they were in the use of "red" and "yellow." Also, in the case of both
"name of" and "color of" more errors occurred on the negative than on the
positive forms, 9 versus 4, and 22 versus 13, respectively; this was not the case
with "shape of" and "size of," however. Of the adjectives used in this series, the
marked—unmarked distinction is applicable to "large—small" but not to either
"round—square" or "red—yellow," the pairs used in teaching shape and color. If
we combine the errors on "small," the presumptive marked form, with those on
the negative forms, which are visibly marked forms, we find that they account
for 63% of the total errors ($p < .01$).

Although children learn unmarked forms of polar adjectives earlier than
marked forms, it is not altogether clear why. The child's speech sample is biased
because in adult speech unmarked forms outnumber marked forms and it is the
former that the child learns first. Sarah's training did not suffer from the usual
parental bias, the two forms being counterbalanced in most lessons. Should we
conclude, therefore, that her data support the markedness theory? Interestingly,
in going over old data, I find a definite bias in favor of the positive forms, not
simply in favor of unmarked adjectives as in the case of the child, but in favor of
forms that do not use the negative particle. As noted earlier (Chapter 6), Sarah
was aversive to questions that required a "no" answer and to the use of the
negative in general. The stalling and sometimes unruly behavior that the negative
occasioned was bothersome to her trainers. They apparently compensated by
setting up lessons in which two positive forms were contrasted rather than a
positive and a negative. For example, "name of" was contrasted with "color of,"
rather than "color of" with "not-color of." Moreover, I can find no lessons
devoted exclusively to negative forms, e.g., "not-name of" vs "not-size of." With
the autistic child now being trained with Sarah's procedure, we are often forced
to adopt this same approach. There are periods in which the child simply refuses
to work with negative forms; in these periods we deliberately introduce new
positive forms by contrasting them with another positive form rather than with
their negative.

MULTIPLE ALTERNATIVES

At a later date, a series of tests were given in which the dimensional predicates
were contrasted with one another, both two and three at a time. The primary
aim was simply review, as several months had passed without their use, but the
tests also served to demonstrate that Sarah could readily discriminate among the
predicates. Moreover, because about a quarter of the objects used were new and
her performance on new and old cases was indistinguishable, the results could

not be attributed to memory and were the more impressive. Another peculiarity of these tests is that they dealt only with the positive forms, for reasons already suggested. The following is a list of the tests in the order given along with her errors per total trials: "name of" versus "color of" (six out of 35), "color of" versus "shape of" (zero out of 17), "size of" versus "name of" (two out of 14), and "name of" versus "shape of" versus "color of" (zero out of seven). Once again there was the firm suggestion that well-practiced words were well remembered.

NONATOMIC APPROACH TO PROPERTY CLASSES: "SAME COLOR OF" VERSUS "COLOR OF"

In naming the class relations "color of," "shape of," etc., we first taught "red," "round," etc., arguing that these class members were appropriate and necessary exemplars for teaching the class names. Is this strictly the case? Consider an alternative approach in which we introduce class names without first teaching the names of class members. We have already seen that one can use either a word or an object to instance a property, for example, either "Red color of apple" or "Red color of ⬛ ." Perhaps we might also omit "red" and substitute for it a red object. In that case we would have not "Red color of ⬛" but " ⬛ color of ⬛ ." If the latter proved to be effective then it would appear we could indeed introduce the names of property classes without first naming their members. In fact, we might then use the property names to introduce the names of class members, reversing the order of the procedure actually used.

There is not much doubt that if the word "color of" is already known, strings of the form " ⬛ color of ⬛ " can be informative. But that is after "color of" has been learned. Could such strings also serve as a teaching device, as a means of introducing the word "color of"?

Suppose we used a red slip of paper as the first term, attempting to say in effect that what the paper and apple have in common is called "color"—there would be no assurance that the subject would single out specifically color rather than some irrelevant property, for example, the smoothness of both the paper and the apple skin. We may cope with this problem by using a series of objects as the first term rather than one object, a series designed to reveal that all properties except color are irrelevant. For instance, a second slip of paper might be rough, although still red, etc. In addition, a second series consisting of, say, a banana and a series of yellow objects, designed like the first series to converge on color as the only shared property, might help the subject abstract the intended relation. Between the apple and its series and the banana and its series, we could then place one and the same piece of plastic—to encourage the subject to see that the relation instanced in both cases was the same.

Following these two positive cases we might use at least one or perhaps two negative cases. These could be provided by pairing the banana with the apple series and the apple with the banana series. These pairs would now have in common a nonsameness in color—banana paired exclusively with red objects and apple exclusively with yellow ones. Moreover, we could use a piece of plastic different from the first one to identify this relation, the same piece for both the apple—yellow object series and the banana—red object series.

What are these pieces of plastic likely to mean? Skipping details, their most likely meaning is "same color of" or "same in color," and the negative thereof, say, "not-same color." If these meanings are likely to be the explicit products of this procedure why is it not then acceptable as a training procedure?

The relation taught by the above procedure is nonatomic, being divisible into two components "same" and "color," each of which can be taught individually. In general, we reject training procedures yielding relations that are divisible into components that can be taught individually; sooner or later the components must be separated.

10
Productivity:
Use of Concepts to Generate
New Instances of Themselves

After Sarah learned "name of," the instruction "X name of Y" was an effective way in which to introduce new names. Henceforth, X, a previously unused piece of plastic, became the name of Y, a previously unnamed object. Sarah produced such sentences as "Give X Sarah" and comprehended such others as "Sarah insert X dish," showing in this way and others that she knew the meaning of X. So used, the word *name of* served to generate new names, and so new instances of itself.

Productivity is what I will call the ability of a concept to generate new instances of itself. Although this property first entered the language with "name of," it is in fact a general property of language, not limited to "name of" or any other specific words. For example, "color of," "shape of," "size of"—indeed, all the dimensional predicates—are no less productive than "name of"; they can be used to generate new color, shape, or size names quite as "name of" can be used to generate new object names. Nevertheless, there are limits on productivity—not all words can be used in this manner, and in this chapter I discuss the conditions a word must meet in order to qualify as well as provide examples of the cases that have been realized with Sarah.

Productivity may be confused with transfer, to which it bears a superficial resemblance, but the two can be readily distinguished. Although both give evidence of the conceptual structure that the organism brings to the language training, they do so in different ways. In transfer the organism must recognize instances of a concept that have not been used in teaching it a name for the concept. For instance, after we had used "apple" and the object apple (as well as "banana" and the object banana) to teach Sarah "name of," she was subsequently queried about the relations between "apricot" and apricot on the one hand, and "apricot" and raisin on the other. She recognized the first case as an instance of "name of," the second as an instance of "not-name of," thus passing the transfer test.

Notice that the transfer test did not generate any new words. "Apricot" and "raisin," the transfer cases, were established names, a fact that made their use in the transfer test possible. Sarah had already produced sentences involving "apricot" ("Give apricot Sarah") and comprehended others ("Sarah take apricot"); presumably it was exactly these numerous previous uses of "apricot" that made it recognizable as an instance of "name of," even though it was not itself used as an exemplar in teaching "name of."

Productivity goes beyond transfer, for with it existing names are not merely recognized as instances of a concept; new names are generated. The trainer takes out a new piece of plastic, one that has the class properties of a word but is not yet a word, and by placing it alongside "name of" and an appropriate object brings the piece of plastic into the language. When the instruction is successful, the piece of plastic becomes the name of the object. Henceforth, it functions in all of those ways that serve to identify a piece of plastic as a word. Suppose there were a species that could not learn "name of." For members of this species, an item could become a word only by being directly associated with its intended referent in one linguistic context or another; e.g., by being used to request an object, to designate an object for which some operation was specified, or to designate an object that was part of a description. There would be no way to circumvent all this use, all this heavy traffic in which language and operations on the world are combined.

The distinction between transfer and productivity has to do with actual and positive instances of a class, as is shown in Figure 10.1. Transfer is a property of actual words, whereas productivity concerns possible words. Of the words that exist at a given moment in time, some will be used as exemplars in teaching "name of" and others will not. Transfer concerns the latter, existing words not used as training exemplars. Productivity, in contrast, does not apply to existing words at all but concerns possible ones, unused pieces of plastic that can be introduced as words once "name of" has been taught and the subject's understanding of the word has been assured by a successful transfer test. Therefore, transfer and productivity differ in their effect on the subject's lexicon. Transfer has no effect on it at all, whereas productivity increases it.

NEW COLOR NAMES

Productivity is no more unique to the property classes "color of," "shape of," etc., than it is to "name of," although it is especially easy to illustrate with property classes. Certainly it is an interesting fact that a class name, such as "color," can be introduced on the basis of no more than two values, for

TRANSFER vs. PRODUCTION

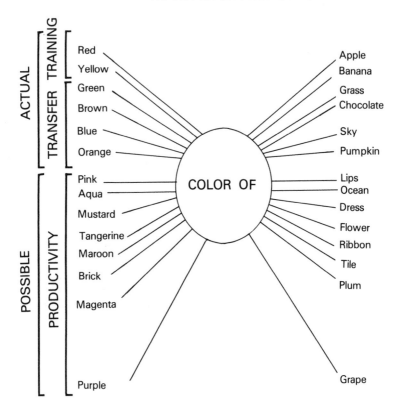

FIG. 10.1 The distinction between transfer and productivity diagrammed with the predicate "color of."

example, "red" and "yellow," after which "color" can be used to generate indefinitely many new instances of the class.

For example, Sarah was taught the new word "brown" with the sentence "Brown color of chocolate." "Color of" and "chocolate" were both established words, whereas "brown" referred to a so far unused piece of plastic that was to become the name for brown through the given instruction. Training took the usual errorless form. Sarah was asked, "? color of chocolate" (What is the color of chocolate?) and was given "brown" as the only alternative. Replacing the interrogative marker with the only alternative available to her, she formed the sentence "Brown color of chocolate." Next, she was given the question, "? color of grape" (What is the color of grape?) along with the alternative "green," leading to the sentence "Green color of grape." Because "green" was an already established word, the sentence involving it was introduced simply to provide the usual contrast in teaching "brown." The two negative exemplars, given following the two positive ones, were "? not-color of grape" (What is not the color of grape?) and "? not-color of chocolate" (What is not the color of chocolate?). The alternatives given her were "brown" and "green," respectively, with which she formed the sentences, "Brown not-color of grape," and "Green not-color of chocolate."

At step two she was given the same questions as before but now in the presence of both "green" and "brown," requiring her to choose between them. Correct on eight of the first ten trials, she was advanced to the transfer test in which she was required to apply these same words to nontraining items. Because there were no further brown or green objects for which she had been taught names, the transfer tests were confined to objects. For example, she was asked, "? color of" 2 X 4 brown card and "? color of" 2 X 4 green card, in effect, What is the color of the brown card and What is the color of the green card? With "brown" and "green" as alternatives, she answered 17 of 20 questions correctly, with no errors on the first five questions.

Notice that transfer tests of this standard kind leave open the question whether, in addition to being able to apply words to nontraining items, she could also use them in a grammatical context different from the training one. "Brown color of" 2 X 4 brown card is a hybrid string consisting of both words and nonlinguistic objects, whereas "Brown color of chocolate" is a pure string consisting only of words; nevertheless the two strings are structurally the same.

To determine whether she could understand "brown" in a sentence structurally different from the training one, we gave her the instruction, "Sarah take brown," at the same time confronting her with four colored wooden disks, only one of which was brown. We followed this with the more complex "Sarah insert brown (in) red dish," where now a red and a green dish were present along with the four wooden disks. In both cases she operated on the brown disk in a manner appropriate to the instructions, establishing that her comprehension of the word was not limited by syntactic context. The same point was made by other tests, which showed the reverse, viz., that after learning a property name in a nounlike usage, for example, "Mary give Sarah red," she could subsequently understand the word when it was used as a modifier, for example, "Insert apple (in) red dish." Although these are early tests rather than final ones, we have yet to find any evidence that the comprehension of a word is restricted to the syntactic context in which it is originally learned.

A more exacting test could have been arranged if all four disks had instanced a property characteristic of chocolate but only one of the four was brown. Suppppose that in Sarah's experience chocolate was not only invariably brown but also invariably of a unique shape, size, crenalated border, etc. Then one of the four disks should have been of the distinctive chocolate shape, another of its size, another of its border, and another of its color. If each alternative instanced some property of chocolate, the subject's ability to take specifically the brown disk would have established that she was responding not just to any property of chocolate but specifically to its color. In the test given, Sarah's choice of the brown disk proved only that she was responding to some property of chocolate but not necessarily its color. The test was actually better suited to the less specific instructions, "Brown is a property of chocolate—take brown." We did not try Sarah on the more discriminating test, for the niceties of this argument did not occur to us until after Sarah had become sexually mature and difficult if not dangerous to test.

Even though the present test did not establish that in choosing the brown disk she relied specifically on the exact meaning of "color of," it by no means ruled out that possibility. Moreover, earlier tests had already established that she distinguished "color of" from the other dimensional predicates. For instance, when she was asked questions about the relation between, for example, red and apple, round and apple, and large and apple, as well as the word "apple" and the object apple—with "color of," "shape of," "size of," and "name of," as alternatives—she answered correctly, substantiating her ability to distinguish one property relation from another.

DISPLACEMENT

The above result involves a simple case of what has been called "displacement" (Hockett, 1959), that is, talking about things that are not present. Displacement has been cited as an important design feature of language, which it would certainly seem to be, although no more so than productivity. Interestingly, although the two properties can easily be distinguished, in the present example they happen to be combined. "Color of" was used productively in generating "brown." However, the use also qualified as a case of displacement, for when Sarah was given the instruction "Brown color of chocolate," no chocolate was present. That is, neither chocolate nor grapes were present when the original instructions were given, nor were they at hand later when she was given the instruction to "Take brown." In selecting the brown disk under these conditions Sarah had to be able to generate an internal representation of the meaning of "chocolate" and to be able to match it or some aspect of it with the brown disk. The ability to generate internal representations of a referent on the basis of its name alone appears to be the psychological function that underlies displacement (see Chapter 15). This capacity is evidently not unique to man, as has been claimed. In Chapter 15 we find abundant additional evidence for the capacity; more important, we see that displacement is merely a special outcome or symptom of a general mnemonic capacity and can be expected whenever the memory capacity of the species reaches a certain level.

NEW SHAPE NAME

"Triangle" or "triangular" was introduced through the productive use of "shape of" in the same way "brown" was introduced through the use of "color of." The case did not qualify as displacement, however, because a triangular cracker was used to exemplify the property. The use of an object was dictated by Sarah's lexicon, which did not include the name of an object with a characteristically triangular shape. The training was standard. She was given two positive instances, "? shape of" triangular cracker and "? shape of" round cracker, and supplied the new word "triangle" in the first case, the old word "round" in the second. Both constructions were hybrid strings, her answer to the first question, for example, "triangular shape of" triangular cracker, consisting of two words and a cracker, the three elements lined up from left to right, with the cracker spaced off from "shape of" in the same way that "shape of" was spaced off from "triangular." (Without exception, the objects used in hybrid strings were dimensionally comparable to words. It was never the case that the words stood alongside, say, a watermelon or a horse; if there was a need to use objects that were not themselves dimensionally appropriate, we used a visual representation.)

The positive instances above were combined with standard negative ones to form such questions as "? not-shape of" triangular cracker (what is not the shape of the triangular cracker?). She was given "round" as the answer to the question. Next, she was given the question "? not-shape of" round cracker (what is not the shape of the round cracker?) and given the word "triangle." She formed the sentences "round not-shape of" triangular cracker, and "triangle not-shape of" round cracker.

By repeating the previous questions while giving her both "round" and the new word "triangle" between which to choose, she was tested in the usual way. She made three errors in 14 trials. Transfer tests were necessarily confined to objects, for we had yet to name any specifically triangular objects, although we used several figures that were right triangles as opposed to the equilateral one used in training. Finally, we broadened the test to include square forms as well as new round and triangular forms, adding the word "square" to the words "round" and "triangle" already present as alternatives. In effect, she was asked a series of questions of the form, What is the shape of X? where all the given alternatives were correct on some occasion and X was either a round, a square, or a triangular object. She made two errors in 16 trials. Unfortunately, we did not try the productive use of "size of," through which Sarah might have acquired "medium," "tiny," or "gigantic," but given that she acquired "size of" without difficulty, there is no reason to suppose that she could not have used it in the same way she used the other logically comparable predicates.

DEFINITIONAL ALTERNATIVES

Words can be taught either ostensively, that is, by pointing to nonlinguistic items, or by relying only on other words. We taught nearly all words ostensively, by associating the pieces of plastic with nonlinguistic items, such as "apple" with an actual apple and the like. Not only names of objects but also those of agents, actions, and properties were taught in this manner.

For words that are defined linguistically, we can distinguish several approaches: one in which the definition is explicit, another in which the word is defined by the productive use of a predicate, and a third in which it is taught by being used in sentences, that is, by example. The discussion of displacement contains an example of a word defined solely through the use of other words. In the introduction of "brown" through the instruction "brown color of chocolate," only words were used. Interestingly, the productive use of "name of" is not strictly comparable, for in "apple name of" apple, as in all cases involving "name of," a nonlinguistic item is present, making these cases a form of ostensive definition.

Although we had no occasion to use full explicit definitions, we used several approximations. For instance, strawberry and cantelope were successfully distinguished as "red fruit" and "yellow fruit," respectively, which is all the occasion required, and there is reason to believe that these elliptical forms could have been expanded into complete definitions such as "cantelope is large round yellow fruit" if the occasion had demanded.

The only method we have not used is teaching words by example. This is almost certainly the most important source of words in the acquisition of natural language, especially for abstract words. The word "idea," for instance, could probably not be taught except through example. One cannot point to an exemplar of idea in the sense that one can point to an apple. Neither can "idea" be taught by explicit definition. Almost any explicit definition of "idea" will involve sentences so abstract as to be comprehensible only to someone who is well advanced in language (and already knows the word "idea"). The remaining alternative is to use "idea" in simple sentences of a kind the beginning subject can understand.

"Idea" might be introduced by telling the subject that "Mary has lots of good ideas," "John never has any ideas," and "Bill is full of bad ideas." These are sensible sentences to use provided the teacher and subject are thoroughly familiar with the agents in question. The sentences will be effective to the extent that the subject associates with "idea" generally the same aspects of Mary, John and Bill's behavior that the speaker associates with "idea."

Assume, for example, that the speaker and subject often approach Mary, especially when they are bored, for she frequently proposes interesting things for them to do. In contrast, they never approach John except for food and money. They also seldom approach Bill, for, although he suggests many things for them to do, they are rarely things they wish to do.

The effectiveness of the above sentences can be judged by waiting until the subject uses the word "idea" in his own speech, and observing the errors the subject makes. New sentences can then be chosen accordingly, to counter the errors and sharpen the definition. For instance, the subject may confuse having ideas with being talkative; this could be resolved by referring to still another agent Henry, known to both the teacher and the subject, "who talked alot but had no ideas."

There was no difficulty in teaching Sarah both "want" and "prefer," even though, like idea, they too refer to psychological states. "Want" and "prefer" are strongly linked to easily modulated external conditions, however, deprivation or satiation in the first case, and stimulus parameters in the second. "Want" was taught by withholding cookies while making marshmallows plentiful. She was asked "Sarah? cookies" along with "Sarah? marshmallows" and was supplied the answer "want" in the first case and "no want" in the second. After passing the choice test, three errors in 16 trials, she was given a transfer test on nuts and chocolate, items for which she was also deprived and sated respectively, which she passed, with one error in 14 trials. Later the deprivation conditions for cookies and marshmallows were reversed and she was asked, "? Sarah want cookies" and "? Sarah want marshmallow." On these *yes–no* questions she made only 2 errors in 18 trials. More subtle psychological state words such as "hope," "think," believe," "guess," are far less operationable than "want" or "prefer." Moreover, explicit definition of these words is well known to lead to horrific abstractions. There would seem to be no alternative but to teach these words by example, using them in appropriate sentences.

ARE ALL CONCEPTS PRODUCTIVE?

Are all concepts productive? If not, what are the special characteristics of those that are? "Same–different" as we have used them so far cannot be used productively, whereas "color of" can. In what way do they differ? Although "color of" and "same–different" are both two-term relations they differ in that in the former one of the two terms must be represented linguistically, whereas in the latter neither term need be so represented. That is, "same–different" has been used as a relation between objects; "color of" has been used as a relation between a property and an object instancing that property, where the property must be named and the object may but not need be named. Therefore, a necessary condition for productivity is that at least one of the terms in the relation be represented linguistically. This is hardly a surprise. Because productivity concerns new words, if neither term of a two-term relation is a word, the concept can hardly be used to generate new words.

But linguistic representation of at least one term is not a sufficient condition. Even if "same" or "different" were to be applied to words rather than objects, they could not be used productively. For example, suppose we were to try to introduce the word "chair" by the instruction "Chair different from table." We could then test the effectiveness of the instruction by confronting the subject with a set of alternatives and telling her "Take chair." If the alternatives consisted of four tables and one chair, the astute subject would choose correctly, suggesting perhaps that "different" had been used productively. But this impression could be dispelled by replacing the chair with a footstool or magazine rack. Then the same strategy that led to the correct choice of chair would lead to the incorrect choice of footstool or magazine rack. Not all nontables are chairs, and the predicate "different" is not exclusive enough to protect the subject against that fact. It is not that the instruction "Chair different from table" is devoid of information but that the information is not sufficient to differentiate "chair" from other nontables.

Overinclusiveness is a problem that confronts the would-be productive use of other predicates, such as the connectives "and," "or," and "if–then," which can also be regarded as predicates that take words, phrases, or sentences as their arguments. For instance, a subject who did not know the word "cat" could not be taught it by the instruction "Cats and dogs fight" because the opponents of dogs are not limited to cats. Similarly, "snake" could not be taught by the instruction "If you are bitten by a snake, stay calm," since this is good advice for bites from bats, rats, and other nonsnakes. The clever subject could use these instructions to narrow down the alternatives, to make astute guesses, in some cases correct ones. They are the kind of instruction that can be used to study the *inferential* capacity of a species, a topic that needs attention and to which we may hope to turn if the chimp can achieve enough linguistic power to make the study worthwhile. But productivity should not be confused with inference. If a word can be used productively it is because of the meaning of the word, the subject's understanding of that meaning, and not because of the inferential capacity of the user.

Consider next the word "is" in the sense of class membership, for example, "Apple is (a) fruit," or "Sweet is (a) taste." The copula was ultimately taught Sarah and we discuss it in detail in Chapter 11 but at this point we consider only the fact that like "name of" and "color of," it too can be used productively. With "name of" we generate new names, with "color of" new colors, with "shape of" new shapes, etc. What is generated with "is?"

With "is" it is possible to generate the names of new classes. In principle, class names could be generated for all cases in which the subject knew the names of class members but not the name of the class to which the members belonged. For example, suppose the subject knew the words, "red," "green," and "blue" but did not yet know the word "color." It could be taught "color" by the instruction "red is (a) color." The effectiveness of the instruction could be tested with the standard approach, a set of alternatives only one of whose members was colored. For example, if given three achromatic disks and a fourth one that was colored but not red and told "Take (a) color," the subject should choose the colored disk. The subject can also be tested linguistically by asking it, e.g., "What is blue, green, yellow, etc.?" to which it should reply "Color."

"Shape," "size," "texture," "taste," "temperature," and all other property class names could also be introduced through the productive use of "is," the requirement being the same as in the case of "color," viz., that the subject know the names of class members. For instance, if the subject knew "sweet," "sour," "bitter," but did not yet know "taste," "Sweet is (a) taste" should serve to introduce "taste." Similarly, if it knew "hot," "cold," "tepid" but did not know "temperature," "Cold is (a) temperature" should serve to teach it "temperature." And a similar argument should hold for teaching "shape" through "Round is (a) shape"; "texture" through, say, "Rough is (a) texture"; etc. Prerequisites are the names of class members and of course a knowledge of "is."

Except in the case of color, which is a peculiar property in some respects, nonlinguistic tests could not be used to gauge the effectiveness of the above instructions. We cannot place before the subject a set of alternatives none of which has a shape, texture, size, temperature, weight, etc. With color this is a possibility insofar as we agree to treat black and white as noncolors. It might also be done with taste if, before we granted that a substance had a taste, we demanded a certain minimum of stimulation. In fact, we do talk of tasteless substances even as we talk of colorless ones.

Because nonlinguistic tests require alternatives that are nonmembers of the class, and because such alternatives are not possible in the case of shape, texture, size, temperature, etc., language is required in these cases to test the effectiveness of the instruction. If the subject is told that, say, "Hot is (a) temperature" or that "Rough is (a) texture," the effectiveness of the instruction can be tested by asking the subject to classify, say, "red," "square," "cold," "smooth," and "bitter." If it applies "temperature" only to "cold" and "texture" only to "smooth," the instructions have been effective, and we can conclude that "is" has been used productively to introduce the class names "temperature" and "texture."

PRODUCTIVITY IS ASYMMETRICAL

Notice that "color," for example, which can be used to generate the names of new colors, cannot be used to generate the names of objects that instance the colors. Likewise, although "is" can be used to generate the names of classes, it cannot be used to generate the names of class members. Productivity is asymmetrical. Productive predicates can be used to generate one of their arguments but not both.

Suppose, for instance, we attempt to introduce the word "fudge" with the instruction "Brown color of fudge." We test the instruction in the usual way, by presenting a set of alternatives and telling the subject to "take fudge." Because not all brown objects are fudge, however, the instruction is too inclusive. Although the subject should not choose nonbrown alternatives, it would not be protected from choosing brown ones that were not fudge. A comparable problem arises if we try to use "is" to generate the names of class members instead of the names of classes. Then, too, the information provided is sufficient to eliminate some false alternatives but insufficient to permit positive identification. For instance, suppose we attempt to introduce "fig" with the instruction "Fig is (a) fruit." We would be met with the familiar problem of overinclusiveness. When told to take "fig" the subject should avoid all nonfruit but would be as likely to pick an incorrect fruit as the correct one. Pomegranate, apricot, persimmon, indeed all fruits for which the subject had not yet learned names, could be mistaken for fig.

Notice that the limitation is on the predicate and not on the word or kind of word that is to be introduced. Although "fig" cannot be introduced productively with "is," it can be introduced productively with "name of" and in Sarah's case it was. "Fudge" too could be introduced with "name of."

The word "brown" also shows that the limitation is on the predicate not the word. Like "fig" and all other class members it cannot be generated by "is." Fig is (a) fruit" and "Brown is (a) color" are both overinclusive instructions, protecting the subject against nonfruit and noncolors, respectively, but not at the same time directing it to the target. Nevertheless "brown" can be introduced productively with "color of" and with Sarah it was.

"Is" can generate "color" but not "red," whereas "color" can generate "red" but not "apple"; and "name of" can generate "apple." Does it follow that there is no limit on the words that can be introduced productively and that it is only a matter of locating the appropriate predicate? This possibility goes beyond any that I can prove. Notice that in the examples of productively introduced words, none has been the name of a relation; all have been absolute terms, names of nonrelational classes. Does it follow that relational terms cannot be introduced productively? That does not seem necessary; to introduce a relational term productively seems only to require a predicate at least one of the arguments of which is itself a relational term. There must be such words, although presently I cannot think of any.

SYNTHESIZING CONCEPTS

One way to approach the dependence of transfer and productivity on underlying structures that predate language training is by picturing how one may *synthesize* such structures in the hypothetical organism that does not have them. Picture, for example, an organism that lacks the concepts of color and taste. Consider that the deficiency is conceptual, not sensory. That is, the organism can see colors and experience taste and can acquire color names, "red," "yellow," etc., as well as taste names, "sweet," "sour," etc. Indeed, not until the organism was required to carry out conceptual operations was the deficiency even disclosed. Then it was found that it could not place "red," "yellow," and the other exemplars of color in one bin, "sweet," "sour," and the other exemplars of taste in a different bin. That is, the conceptually deficient organism did not see red and yellow as the same kind of thing, different from sour and sweet, which it also did not see as the same kind of thing. Additionally, it could not impose distance functions on either tastes or colors. When forced to make similarity judgments it found red closer to bitter than to yellow.

Such a subject may be taught that, say, red and yellow are referred to by the common name "color," but it then has no basis for transferring "color" to blue or orange and should be as likely to apply "color" to "sweet" as to "green." Can the subject be taught that red is to apple what yellow is to banana? If the subject lacks not only color and taste but essentially all class concepts it seems unlikely that it can be taught the relation of analogy, $X-Y$ same $A-B$. In any case, one of the most obvious exemplars for teaching analogy is the relation between classes and their respective members.

Consider now how we may attempt to synthesize the missing concepts in the case of such a subject. We start by teaching names for both properties and classes and by informing the subject to which class each property belongs. For example, we teach "salty" and "sweet" as instances of "taste," "red" and "yellow" as instances of "color," "rough" and "smooth" as instances of "texture," etc. We can then test the effectiveness of the instructions by giving the subject four disks, varying in color, texture, etc., all of which are tasteless except for one that has been dipped in quinine. The subject is told to "Take (the) taste."

A clever subject who had benefited from the instructions could base its choice on an inspection that was appropriate to the class. In the present case, therefore, before choosing, it should put each disk to its mouth. Shape, texture, size, temperature, etc., cannot be tested in quite the same way because clearly we

Unique values

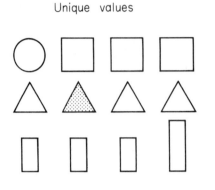

FIG. 10.2 A unique value in each row, in shape, texture, and size, respectively.

cannot provide noninstances of these classes. However, we need make only a slight modification to test these cases. The subject can be given a set of alternatives in which there is only one class represented by a unique value (see Figure 10.2) and told to "Take the distinctive or unique X," where X is shape, color, texture, etc. As shown in Row 1 of Figure 10.2, shape is represented by a unique value when three of the disks are of one shape and the fourth is of a different shape. With this arrangement, when told to "Take the distinctive shape," the subject should choose from the first row and, when given comparable instructions with regard to texture and size, it should take from the second and third rows, respectively. In each case, the basis for the subject's correct choice should be reflected in the appropriate inspection it has applied to the stimuli. The exaggerated form the inspection is likely to take itself suggests that the subject is proceeding from "unnatural" training.

Even classes belonging to the same modality can probably be differentiated by exploiting differences in the procedures that can be used to identify class members. Color might be singled out from other visual properties in that whereas some visual properties could be discriminated in the dark, color could not. In other words, some visual properties are exclusively visual, whereas others, such as shape and size, are visual and tactual. Further refinements might differentiate shape and texture, the former being detected by palpating the outline of a figure, the latter by its surface; the subject might exploit possible differences in threshold, using hands for shape, cheek or lips for texture. Even size might be distinguished by a test based on a graded series of apertures through which objects were pushed in order to find the unique one. If mutually exclusive procedures could be devised for each class, the subject could apply them to the stimuli in some strategic order until it found the one test that yielded a unique value (rather than four like values, or four different values, etc.). In this way, the conceptually deficient subject could select the unique shape, color, etc., even though the specific values used in the test were not previously identified as a shape, color, etc.

Classes synthesized in this fashion could go only so far, however. First, it is not certain that mutually exclusive tests could be designed for each class. For example, with a synthetic taste class the subject would fail tests in which, although the distinctive alternative could be detected only with the tongue, the sensation was nonetheless not an instance of taste. A disk that extruded a pin or changed radically in temperature when contacted by the tongue but that did not so react when contacted by any other appendage would be mistaken for a taste. Moreover, an affective qualification, such as "tongue sensations that are more or less pleasant," would not eliminate the nonmembers because clearly not all tastes are pleasant.

Second, even if mutually exclusive tests were possible, the subject would still fail tests that went beyond mere class detection and required ordering members of the class. If asked to make similarity judgments on individual tastes so as to establish distances among them, the subject would fail. It could tell all tastes from all colors, as well as discriminate each taste (and color) from the other, but it could not order the tastes (or colors) in any way. Remember that the tastes share nothing except their detectability by a common test procedure and, furthermore, do not vary with respect to this shared property. That is, the items in this world either are or are not detectible in the way that tastes are; those that are are tastes, whereas the others are not. All this points up that, although we can conceive of a hypothetical organism that is capable of distinguishing tastes from nontastes but cannot at the same time impose a distance function on the tastes, in nature there are no such organisms.

Third, a closer look at this problem suggests that we have grossly underestimated the incapacitation that follows from a conceptual deficiency of the kind discussed. If a subject cannot make similarity judgments on two different colors, should we assume that it can recognize one color, seen on different occasions, as the same color? Having granted the hypothetical organism normal sensory capacity, we can just as arbitrarily grant it the ability to match an earlier instance of a sensation with a later one and so to judge them same or different. In hindsight, however, it seems clear that similarity judgments must derive in a fairly straightforward way from same–different judgments and therefore that the inability to see, say, red and green as the same kind of thing is likely to follow from a deeper incapacity—the inability to see two instances of red as the same kind of thing. If so, a common detection procedure could not be substituted for the missing conceptual process. The hypothetical organism would be unable to recognize, as the same kind of thing, repeated instances of the same detection procedure.

11

Class Membership

"A visitor entered wearing a soft wool skirt; Sarah touched the skirt, looked at the visitor, then ran to the crib and felt her (similarly textured) blanket." " . . . Sarah, touching my tongue, looked at me, at her hand, and then stuck out her own tongue and touched it." These entries are from a log kept by Dr. Rosemary Cogan, Sarah's first surrogate mother, dated March 27, 1965, when Sarah was estimated to be 18 months old. Not yet trained in language, Sarah could acknowledge the match between the skirt and blanket only in the way she did, by contacting both items in the same interval of time. Had she been trained in language, she need not have rushed from one item to the other, but could have acknowledged the relation between the skirt and blanket by touching the skirt while saying "blanket." Whether the subject says "blanket" while touching the skirt, or rushes from skirt to blanket, the same triumph is celebrated: the discovery of an equivalence.

The separation of a collection of items into groups is a precursor of the ultimately hierarchical classification systems that are the underpinnings of human knowledge. Even hunter–gatherers, the technologically most primitive human group, classify consanguinous relations as well as the plants and animals of their region, often into hierarchical systems of at least three levels (Berlin, Breedlove, & Raven, 1973; Berlin & Kay, 1969). The clearest evidence for classification lies, of course, in language. Pointing to a plant, the native informant may give the ethnologist the folk equivalent of a genus name, a second name identifying the plant as either usuable or "weed," and in some cases even a third name specifying the nature of its use, food, dye–cosmetic, or both. Nevertheless, the brute fact of a classification system can be revealed without words--despite the laboriousness of doing so--by sorting actual plants instead of their names. For example, the informant might introduce the notion of plant by placing some number of them on the ground and then contrasting the notion of plant with that of animal by placing animal exemplars elsewhere on the ground.

At the next level, plants might be separated into usable and weed (and the same division made with the animals) and at a still lower level usables divided into food and nonfood, again for both main categories. Whether each level should be represented by common members—as in Figure 11.1—or simply by a prototype is a matter merely of convention or the availability of a prototype (cf. Rosch, in press). The point is not to claim that this is done or, except in a laboratory, ever likely to be done, but simply to show that classification can have a visual or preverbal form.

Sorting or preverbal classification, of the kind illustrated in Figure 11.1, is an immediate precursor of verbal classification. Probably it should be distinguished from discrimination, which would seem to be a more distant precursor. All species show discrimination in one form or another, but it is not clear that this is the equivalent of sorting. For example, dogs, along with other mammalian species, respond differently to conspecifics on the basis of both age and sex. As every dog owner knows, if the dog approaching in the distance proves to be either a puppy or a member of the opposite sex, one can breath easily. This is evidence for discrimination, but is it equally evidence for sorting or preverbal classification?

Because the dog does not bury all objects, it may be said to discriminate between bones and nonbones. Similarly, because it is more likely to invite play with some conspecifics than with others, it evidently distinguishes between young and old, and between like and unlike sex. But classification does not consist merely in burying one set of items and not another, in growling at one set and not another, or in eating one set and not another. Classification, like sorting, is a superordinate form of responding that can be made to all stimulus classes. Species that classify or sort stimuli do so in addition to responding to them in stimulus-specific ways. They not only eat food, play with mates, flee and attack predators but also divide these items into groups and then make no further response to them. For instance, when eating is not prepotent, chimpanzees place fruit in one location and candy in another (later, when taught the words, they can distinguish between the same items by labeling some "fruit" and others "candy"). Similarly, when motor exploration is at low ebb, they place one kind of toy in one container and another kind in a different container. Lying with its nose pressed to the rug, the dog may dispassionately sort out in its mind all the objects before it. It would be premature to say that there are no stimuli with which it carried out disinterested classification. We lack all evidence that this is so, however, and the contrary is definitely possible. Although all species respond discriminatively, only primates may sort the world, i.e., divide it into its indeterminately many classes and then make no further response to them. To sort or classify requires, in the first place, the capacity for same–different judgments, and it is not clear that any species below the primates has this capacity.

Beyond the simple fact that sorting or preverbal classification occurs, we know little about it. What is the base level at which chimpanzees, or any other species,

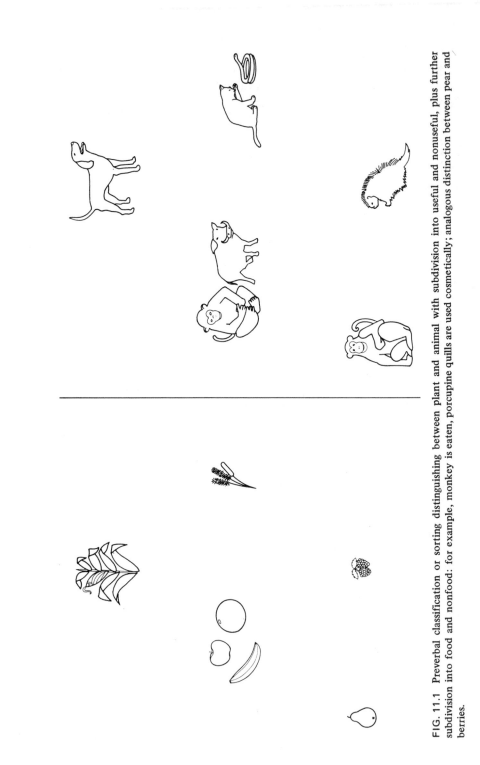

FIG. 11.1 Preverbal classification or sorting distinguishing between plant and animal with subdivision into useful and nonuseful, plus further subdivision into food and nonfood: for example, monkey is eaten, porcupine quills are used cosmetically; analogous distinction between pear and berries.

engage in this behavior? What is the basic underlying disposition: to bring order into a disorganized space; to carry out an act or organization, whether or not the space is already organized; or to put "like" items together, even though this may involve substituting one class for another so that there is no resulting change in the overall organizational level? Nearly all the sorting we have observed has taken place with regard to unordered items, suggesting that the first alternative may be correct. But the suggestion is not supported by anything more serious than default; for the most part, we have not given the subjects already organized items to see whether this quells the disposition to organize or whether they reorganize.

Similarly, we do not even know whether the subjects prefer binary contrasts, as we apparently do, for nearly all the problems we have given them have been of this kind. Nor do we know what the limit may be on the number of contrasts they can use at the same time. With blocks that vary in both color and shape, a 2 X 2 factorial, we have yet to give Peony and Elizabeth four bins, to see whether they can use all four cells. From other tests we know that Sarah is capable of using a conjunction of three features to identify objects (see page 280), suggesting that she can sort items into at least three piles.

CLASSIFICATION AND RECLASSIFICATION

When given 16 blocks that differed in both color and form—red and yellow triangles and red and yellow squares—Peony typically first sorted the blocks into two boxes on the basis of color. After the experimenter praised her, reassembled the blocks and gave them back, Peony shifted criteria, sorting them into the same boxes on the basis of shape. In 20 trials, she shifted criteria 14 times. We have not tried to induce her to recombine the items herself and then sort them again, but when the trainer has carried out the intermediate step (recombined the separated items) Peony has readily resorted the items, changing spontaneously from one criterion to another. Elizabeth needed no guidance to sort on the basis of shape but typically did not shift spontaneously from shape to color. Sometimes she did not shift even when guided by samples from the trainer. Although the trainer put one of each color in the two boxes, on four of 20 trials Elizabeth ignored the exemplars and sorted on the basis of shape; on the other 16 occasions she did follow the trainer's samples. However, the simplest way to induce her to sort on the basis of color was to eliminate the shape feature. She never refused to sort blocks that differed only in color.

In addition to shifting the sorting criterion from one feature to another with the introduction of new items, both Peony and Elizabeth combined items they had previously separated. For example, in some studies on visual metaphor, we first established that both Peony and Elizabeth could sort items on the basis of what man would label plant versus animal. Given leaves, stems, seeds, and flowers, on the one hand and fur, teeth, hair, and bones, on the other, Elizabeth and Peony sorted these items into piles corresponding to the human plant–animal division at about the 78 and 80% level of accuracy, respectively. In a later step, erasers, pins, buttons, paper clips, and the like were added to the above items, and both subjects were led to resort according to a new criterion. The previously separated plant and animal items were now combined and contrasted with hairpin, button, etc. Although we do not know the features the chimps used in making this separation (which would be called animate versus inanimate in man), we need not know them to recognize the cognitive flexibility, the chimp's ability to contrast A with B on one occasion, then to combine A and B on another occasion and contrast their conjunction with C.

TIME AND SPACE AS SORTING CRITERIA

A substantial body of data reported by Hayes and Nissen (1971) and Kohts (1935) shows, as do the data above, that the chimp can sort items into different locations. For example, Peony and Elizabeth distinguished between two colors and between two shapes by placing them in two different containers.

Can the chimpanzee shift from spatial to temporal sorting and vice versa? The answer is yes, as we found out in the first place largely by accident. On one occasion Peony was negligently given only one box in which to sort the blocks that she had previously sorted into two containers. Even though given only one box, Peony could nonetheless have continued to sort on a spatial basis. She could have put the square blocks in the container, leaving the round ones on the outside. Likewise, she could have dispensed with both boxes, placing square blocks on the right, round blocks on the left. In fact, she repudiated all spatial options and shifted to the use of time. With only one container, she first put in most of the red blocks and then followed them with most of the yellow ones. Her separations were not perfect, although the first run typically included about 83% of the items in one category. The inaccuracy came from nothing more serious than slovenliness, a tendency to ignore blocks that were farther from reach until reminded of them by the trainer. Elizabeth also shifted immediately to time when given only one container; and back again to space when given two containers. At first, neither subject used time when given two containers or space when given only one container but, with repeated exposure to the procedure, both subjects abandoned the nice separation and mixed time and space sorting without regard to the number of containers. For example, Peony sometimes appeared to time sort in one container, making no use of the second container, and then switched to the latter and put only one kind of item in it. Like Peony, Elizabeth's first run generally included about 85% of the items in one category, although this percentage was increased to 100% on two occasions by carefully placing all the blocks close to her. The view that chimpanzees cannot comprehend a vocal language because they cannot process temporal pattern is not disproved by these data; however, it is not entirely compatible with them either, not with the ease with which these subjects shifted to the use of time in their own production. Other species may also interchange space and time. Some monkey species, long considered territorial, were recently found to violate this generalization. Groups A and B were observed feeding in the same groves; but A consistently fed in the morning, B consistently in the afternoon (J. Smith, personal communication, 1974). The separation produced by time was no less effective than the one ordinarily produced by space.

SEMANTIC CLUSTERING

In retrieving a list of items, it is more efficient to recall the items in terms of the categories to which they belong than to ignore this information. Human subjects show so-called semantic clustering, producing the names of, say, plants together, as well as those of animals, cities, people, etc. (e.g., Bousfield, 1953; Cofer, 1973; Miller, 1956). Also, they show an apparently related phenomenon on lists that do not have obvious categories. When read lists of unrelated items, human subjects reproduce the list in a more or less fixed order from trial to trial, even though the list has been read to them in a different order from trial to trial. Evidently the human subject imposes his own organization on the material, forming idiosyncratic categories, so-called subjective organization (e.g., Tulving, 1962).

Can we find semantic clustering in chimpanzees? To adapt the question to apes we shifted from recall to reproduction and from words to objects. Like most, if not all, linguistic phenomena semantic clustering could also have a visual or nonlanguage form. Suppose a subject were first shown a set of objects and then was required to identify the same objects in a substantially larger set of objects. Consider that the objects shown the subject belonged to conventional categories, such as fruit, toys, candy, and the like. If we observed not only the accuracy with which the subject selected the previously shown items but also the order in which it selected them, we might find that the subject identified, say, all the fruit first, then the animals, etc., in which case it would be showing the equivalent of semantic clustering, now, however, carried out with objects rather than words.

To make tests of this kind, we needed only to elaborate match-to-sample, specifically to accustom the animal to a sample consisting of not one item but of many. Starting with one-item samples, two-item alternatives, and no delay, we moved progressively to 12-item samples, 20-item alternatives, and up to 20 sec delay. All three subjects were capable of tasks of this kind, although Peony and Elizabeth, who were less than $3\frac{1}{2}$ years old at the time of this training, performed much less well than Sarah, who was already 9 or 10 years old.

The sample of, say, nine items was placed in a box and dumped out before the subject to assure a nonsystematic arrangement of its content. Then the items were gathered up and removed from the subject's view. Five to 20 sec later, a box of up to 20 items was dumped out in the same manner and the subject was required to select from the up to 20 alternatives the nine items that had previously been shown it. The test amounts to nothing more than delayed match-to-sample with a multiple sample. However, we were interested not only in the items the subject chose but also the order in which it chose them, order being the basis for judging semantic clustering.

The categories used were fruit, candy, and doll's clothing, categories we thought likely to be familiar to the chimps in view of their laboratory experience. With Sarah there was good reason to be confident about her knowledge of the items; she had previous experience with items of a similar kind and indeed already knew names for some of them. With Peony and Elizabeth the items were best guesses, the closest we could come to possible categories. For example, all three subjects had had dolls as playthings and knew something about their clothes; Sarah had also worn clothes herself in an earlier stage, although the other two had not.

Neither Peony nor Elizabeth provided evidence of semantic clustering, either because of limitations in their use of the items or perhaps for more fundamental reasons. For them candy and fruit were seductive items: their prepotent response was not identification or classification. Trainers were continually on guard to assure that the subject did not eat the stimuli. This preoccupation not only overrode classification but might also have been responsible for the low accuracy that both young subjects showed on this task. For example, neither Peony nor Elizabeth got much beyond the 60% level of accuracy even on the fourth and last trial in the series.

Sarah also showed dishonorable intentions with regard to the stimuli, but her preoccupation with food was not so intense as to blind her to a cognitive opportunity. On a total of eight problems, consisting of nine-item samples, 18-item alternatives, and 5-sec delay, her accuracy was 89, 89, 100, and 100% on the first through fourth trials, respectively. Of greater interest to the present discussion, she showed reliable evidence for semantic clustering, an overall average of about 28% compared with chance expectancy of about 1.21%.

OPERATING PRINCIPLES:
DISPOSITIONS THAT OCCUR FOR THEIR OWN SAKE

Semantic clustering and subjective organization are typically discussed as utilitarian strategies. By reducing the memory load, they can contribute to the overall accuracy of problem solving. One need not dispute this interpretation to consider that the same dispositions may also occur strictly for their own sake. Indeed, the more vital a strategy to the cognition of a species, the more likely it may be that the strategy exists as an operating principle, that is, as a disposition sustained by intrinsic consequences. The whole behavior sequence comprising the strategy or independent components of it—which are knit together in the development of the organism—may have this status, so that one should be able to observe a base frequency independent of extrinsic consequences either for the whole sequence or for its components.

That semantic clustering may have this status was first suggested to us by accident. To help acquaint the subject with all the items in the sample, we trained them to pick up the items one at a time, look them over if they liked, and then hand them back to the trainer. After a while we began to record not only the order in which the subjects selected the items from the larger set of alternatives but also the order in which they handed them back when they were first shown them. One could not speak of any pressure of memory at that time, for there was no larger set of alternatives from which the sample was to be identified. Indeed, there was no such thing as a correct or incorrect item, only the requirement that the subject pick up the items and hand them back one at a time until all the items had been returned.

On trials of this kind, Sarah showed even stronger evidence for semantic clustering than she did in the experiment proper, about 62% before the test began versus 28% in the test proper. She was therefore classifying before the experiment began and was more successful at it than in the test proper when she was required to duplicate the sample from memory by selecting it from the larger set of alternatives.

CLASSIFICATION AS A SUBSTITUTE
FOR SPECIES-SPECIFIC RESPONSES

When the disposition to classify food is not preempted by eating, a person may discuss the character of different foods, comparing one ethnic menu with another. While awaiting dinner, people often discuss food, sometimes to an elaboration that unnerves the hostess; she cannot combine in one meal all the foods of the world. Eating is not the only behavior for which classification can be a surrogate. Once, during a lively professional discussion with a colleague, the exceptional backside of a barmaid came prominently into view. My speech faltered and I stared fixedly. My colleague turned about, exploring the source of my derailment, and laughing, turned back to me. Soon we were discussing with all the fervor of a moment ago the intensity of the male response and its bizarre proportionality to certain almost ineffable qualities of the female configuration. We sought desperately to delineate a system, one that would explain why a millimeter here or there could have such an effect.[1]

---

[1] In this case, classification was not only a surrogate for a more direct response but a welcome one. Classification does not immobilize its victim with a punishing refractory period as other responses do after the organism attains a certain age. Moreover, the expertise of the judgmental machinery, its subtlety, and its success in sharpening distinctions reach a peak at about the same time as the species-specific forms of response decline. The time curves for the two forms of behavior may cross benevolently.

CLASSIFICATION AND EVALUATION

We typically consign only certain classes to an evaluative domain, viewing other classes as discriminable on one physical dimension or another but not in terms of value. For example, in psychophysical experiments, subjects are asked to make judgments about weights, temperatures, hues, and the like or are requested to report which is heavier, which temperatures are equal, into which categories they wish to sort the hues. We do not ask them which weights they prefer, which temperatures they like equally well, or to sort the hues in terms of how well they like them. Yet when we did ask subjects exactly these questions, first in a preliminary study on weights and later in an elaborate study on hues, they were quite able to answer. In 1964, Walter Kintsch and I asked subjects to categorize Munsel color cards by hue and by their preference for hue, counterbalancing for order, and found that, although the amount of information transmitted through the value categorization was less than that transmitted through the more customary system, it was nonetheless substantial. The average amount of information transmitted by 16 subjects by categories of hue and value was $T_{XY} = 3.21$ and $T_{XY} = 2.27$, respectively (Garner & Hake, 1951).

Cultures specialize in the classes they submit to evaluation and find it peculiar when classes outside their areas of specialization are dealt with evaluatively, as we find it peculiar to make value judgments for weights. Yet what is outside one culture's evaluative domain may be inside another's, and I suspect that no classification escapes evaluation, although the intensity may be enhanced or diminished by cultural specialization.

Elaborate judgmental discussions of the kind I have been suggesting go beyond simple classification, though not necessarily in any basic way. They presuppose simple classification, the sorting of stimuli into either different places or times.

VERBAL CLASSIFICATION

Actual physical sorting is not likely to be a necessary condition for verbal classification, merely a hopeful sign of the kind of cognition on which such classification depends. It is also a hopeful sign if a species has an endogenous disposition to divide items into groups and engages in sorting without human intervention. These hopeful signs invite the next question: Can the species be taught to label the relation of class membership and so be inveigled into some of the endless classification in which man engages, for example, red is a color, apple is a fruit, eat is an action, "Sarah" is a personal name? Other questions assume that the chimpanzee can indeed mark the relation of class membership and go on to attempt to exploit the capacity. For instance, if it can mark the relation of class inclusion, can it also be taught syllogistic reasoning? All chimps are mortal,

Sarah is a chimp, therefore. . . . Or if not, why not? Still other questions simply express curiosity as to how the chimpanzee may handle ethologically interesting cases such as the classification of facial expressions of conspecifics, man and other species.

THE FIRST STRATEGY

There are at least two strategies that can be used to introduce a marker for class membership, the first of which is entirely straightforward. By this time, the animal has a long experience in requesting individual fruits with such sentences as: "Mary give apple Sarah," ". . . give banana," ". . . give orange . . . ," etc., sentences in which the variable term is the name of the individual fruit. If we remove all fruit names, providing as a substitute the new word "fruit," the subject can be led to request the same items previously requested with the individual names by simply writing ". . . give fruit. . . ." This should serve to establish a functional equivalence between "fruit" and the already known words naming the individual members of the potential fruit class.

The same procedure repeated with, say, "chocolate," "caramel," "gumdrop," and "M & M," another set of words used to request individual items, should serve to establish another class word. "Candy" should become the functional equivalent of its member words in the same way "fruit" has for its member words. Then with both "fruit" and "candy" at hand, "is," or any other device one selected as a marker for the class membership relation, could be introduced in the following way:

1. "Apple banana is fruit"
2. "Chocolate caramel is candy"
3. "Apple banana not-is candy"
4. "Chocolate caramel not-is candy"

This set of sentences realizes all the features of the standard training procedure for introducing a new word. "Is," the new word, is the only unknown in the strings; other words—"fruit," "candy," and all names of members of the two classes—having been taught earlier. In addition, the sentences provide the customary two positive and two negative exemplars, the latter being formed by recombining the former in a manner that so to speak closes the circle, that is, x is a, y is b; x is not b and y is not a. Finally, the training sentences are not only grammatical but sensible; that is, they describe nonlinguistic states of affairs that are both true and well known to the subject. Although we did not use this procedure with the chimps, we have used it, exactly as described above, in teaching the copula to a markedly language-deficient autistic child (Premack & Premack, 1974).

THE SECOND STRATEGY

The strategy we actually used in introducing a name for class membership, although ultimately successful, ran into trouble from the beginning, I think, because earlier we had neglected to mark "of" or the genitive relation. We had the words "color of," "size of," etc., but not the class names "color," "size," etc. "Color of" had been taught earlier as the relation between apple and red, "Red color of apple," using a single particle to stand for "color of." Ideally we should not have introduced "color of" before having first taught "of." Then "color" could have been introduced as a separate particle and used in the desired way, as a class name. Given this mistake, we could have retraced our steps and introduced a genitive particle. Instead, we ignored the need for such a particle and simply used "color of," "shape of," and "size of" to stand for "color," "shape," and "size" in the new copular constructions. In the old string "Red color of apple" and in the new one to be trained, "Red is (a) color," therefore, "color of" and "color" would be represented by the same particle; the subject would have to learn to interpret the particle differently depending on its context.

Aside from the difficulty with the genitive particle, the actual form of the training used to teach "is" was otherwise routine. We began with the question "Red ? color (of)" (What is the relation between red and color?). The only alternative given her was the new word "is," with which she replaced the interrogative marker, forming the sentence "Red is color." We repeated the procedure with "Round ? shape" (What is the relation between round and shape?), leading her to form the sentence "Round is shape." After the usual five trials on the two positive exemplars, she was given the same number on each of the negative ones. For example, she was asked "Red ? shape" (What is the relation between red and shape?), as well as "Round ? color" (What is the relation between round and color?). In both instances the alternative given her was "is-not." Later "is" and "not" were given as separate particles, but the appended form—"not" glued to "is"—was the standard treatment of the negative at this stage of training. She displaced the interrogative particle, forming "Round is-not color" and "Red is-not shape."

At step two, she was asked the same questions as before but, being given both "is" and "is-not," was required to choose between them. Her response to this standard step was to make 10 errors in 22 trials. All of her errors were caused by the same failure, a refusal to use "is-not," resulting in such blatantly incorrect answers as "Round is color" and "Red is shape." A reluctance to use the negative form, or an overuse of the positive form, were not new forms of behavior; only the degree of the reluctance was new. The trainer offered Sarah the opportunity to correct her incorrect sentences, which had also been done on other occasions. Especially for errors that were blatant or simple, immediate correction seemed the best didactic course. Sarah refused the offer, however, apparently preferring to leave the sentence in its uncorrected state rather than to replace "is" with "is-not."

Following this unprecedented failure at Step 2, we could think of nothing more astute, short of calling a halt and sidetracking to teach her the genitive particle, than more of the same. Accordingly, we retreated to Step 1, gave five more trials on each of the "is-not" cases, and tested her again on choice trials. This time she made 14 errors, 11 of them on "is-not." Determined to teach this simple marker by brute force if necessary, we returned once more to Step 1, gave only two trials on each of the negative cases, and retested her on choice trials. On this third and final test, she made no errors in 18 trials, a testimonial perhaps to the ultimate power of drill.

But it was not yet clear what the drill had accomplished. Had she learned to mark the relation of class membership or simply to memorize the four strings, for which she would seem to have had more than enough trials? The question was settled by the transfer test, on which she was asked all of the former questions with the words "yellow" and "triangular" substituted for the training words "red" and "round." For instance, she was asked "Yellow ? color" (What is the relation between yellow and color?), "Triangular ? shape" (What is the relation between triangular and shape?), as well as the negative versions of these questions, for example, "Yellow ? shape" (What is the relation between yellow and shape?), and, as before, was required to choose between "is" and "is-not." She made only three errors on 26 such questions, none on the first five trials. Despite her many errors in acquiring "is," therefore, she nonetheless transferred "is" successfully to nontraining items. The reader will note later a case of the same kind in the concept of "if–then," which was also acquired with an atypical number of errors but was then transferred to nontraining items with customary success (see pages 236–238).

PLURALIZATION

Pluralization, in keeping with the rest of the system, was introduced in the form of a separate particle rather than as an inflectional change. Because it was mechanically awkward to pluralize both nouns and verbs, we arbitrarily restricted pluralization to the verb. For example, we wrote "Red green is pl color" ("is" + "pl" = "are") but did not write "Red green is pl color pl," where "pl" after a word is the plural marker. Although this procedure precluded studying verb–object agreement, it permits studying the more basic subject–verb agreement. Ultimately we will pluralize both grammatical classes, although not necessarily with the same particle.

A simple way to teach the plural would be to contrast it directly with the singular form, for example, "Red is color" with "Red yellow is pl color." However, because Sarah already knew the singular version of the sentence, it was possible to make an interesting test of her ability to learn to distinguish between two forms when the two forms were not explicitly contrasted during the training of either one. She had already been taught the singular without being shown the plural; we had now only to attempt to teach her the plural without explicit reference to the singular in order to complete the experiment. Later, of course, we tested her on exactly those contrasts that were not included in the training.

The first sentence given Sarah in the training of the plural was "Red yellow is ? color" which largely defies translation into English. The only alternative given her was the plural marker "pl" with which she displaced the interrogative marker, forming the sentence "Red yellow is pl color? (Red and yellow are color). Next she was given the comparable sentence with respect to shapes, viz., "Round square is ? shape," which is no more translatable than its counterpart in color. Displacing the interrogative marker with the only alternative given her, she formed the sentence "Round square is pl shape" (Round and square are shapes).

The two negative instances given were "Red yellow is-not ? shape" and "Round square is-not ? color." Now she displaced the interrogative marker with "pl," forming the sentences "Red yellow is-not pl shape" and "Round square is-not pl color" (Red and yellow are not shapes and Round and square are not colors). Notice that the training departed from standard format in giving the same alternative, "pl," on both positive and negative trials. This was so because we appended the negative particle to the verb, that is, "is + pl" = "are" and "is-not + pl" = "are not," rather than to the negative marker, that is, "pl-not," which we rejected as making little sense.

The choice trials were modified to accommodate the above departure and consisted of putting two interrogative markers in the same sentence, indicating thereby a need for two words, and of offering three alternatives to chose among rather than the usual two. For example, she was asked "Red yellow ? ? color," and given the alternatives "is," "is-not," and "pl." She displaced the two interrogative markers with the particles "is" and "pl," more often in the right order than not, forming the sentence "Red yellow is pl color" (Red and yellow are colors). She was equally successful at displacing the two interrogative markers in the sentence "Round square ? ? color," with "is-not" and "pl" forming the sentence "Round square is-not pl color" (Round and square are not colors). On 14 such trials, she was correct 10 times, was helped three times, and used the incorrect "pl + is" once. The use of double interrogative markers may have been an unnecessary crutch. After only 4 such trials, we reverted to the use of a single interrogative marker. Although now required to substitute two words for one interrogative particle, she made no errors in 15 such trials. Her successful replacement of one interrogative marker with two words was a departure from the one-to-one substitution that had characterized most of her training. We viewed this use of many-to-one substitution as a step toward the eventual achievement of answering questions not with a word but with a complete sentence.

Before we moved on, we added a few trials on sentences in which the subject of the sentence consisted of three items instead of two, simply to forestall the impression that pluralization was specific to two-item subjects. The sentences given her were "Red yellow blue ? color" and "Red yellow blue ? shape." The alternatives were "is," "is-not," and "pl." She answered all eight of the questions given her correctly.

Her last test in this series consisted of seven sentences with only one interrogative marker, which had to be replaced by one word on some occasions and by two on others, thus demanding that she use one-to-one and many-to-one substitution in the same lesson. In addition, we included in this lesson her first test of a direct contrast between the singular and plural forms, each of which had been taught separately and which were now presented together for the first time. The questions included: "Yellow ? color" (Is yellow a color?), "Yellow ? shape" (Is yellow a shape?), "Yellow red green ? color" (Are yellow, red, and green colors?), "Red green ? shape" (Are red and green shapes?), "Circle triangle ? color" (Are circle and triangle colors?), etc. She was correct on all seven.

PLURALIZATION AND KNOWLEDGE OF THE SUBJECT

Although by itself pluralization is a minor distinction—a language may leave this property unmarked and suffer little—the contrast between plural and singular can be used to raise a searching question. Specifically, did Sarah understand what constituted the subject of a sentence? In the lesson above, Sarah appeared to have pluralized whenever the subject was compound, that is, it consisted of two or more items. However, we could equally well say that she pluralized whenever there were two or more words to the left of (actually in her case above) the copula. For instance, in the sentence, "Red yellow is pl color" she might pluralize because "red" and "yellow" constitute a plural subject or simply because "red" and "yellow" are two words.

To test this point we need only offer such sentences as "Red apple ? fruit" or "Big cracker ? round." Although in these sentences also there are two words to the left of the copula, the subjects are singular, and the sentences should not take the plural. The first of the two sentences above would offer an especially searching test because it is analytic and provides no nonlinguistic cue. The second sentence is synthetic and therefore would be accompanied by a nonlinguistic state of affairs, in the present case by a single large round cracker, which Sarah could observe and use as a cue for pluralization. That is, with the synthetic sentence pluralization has two cues, one inside and one outside the sentence. With the analytic sentence, however, there is no extralinguistic cue, and one must decide whether or not to pluralize strictly on the basis of one's understanding of the sentence.

At a later stage of training, having meanwhile been taught "and" and some additional sentence structures—but with no further training specifically on pluralization—she was tested with sentences of the following kind: "Apple ? red and round," "Apple and orange ? fruit," "Banana ? yellow fruit," "Round apple ? fruit," and "Cookie and cracker ? bread stuff." Her alternatives were "is" and the plural marker. She made 6 errors in 37 trials, with one on the first 5, or about 82% correct. Although it is important to extend these tests to additional cases, their results are highly encouraging, more so than others that may be thought more dramatic. Sarah apparently induced the correct rule, or some effective approximation of it, on the basis of training that did not make the rule explicit. Induction of a rule from weak exemplars is always more impressive: the stress is then on computation by the organism rather than on structure imposed by the training.

DIRECT INTRODUCTION OF CLASS NAMES

With the introduction of "is," we could assert, for example, that "Apple is a fruit," or "Chocolate is a candy," and no longer had to rely on exemplification or indirect ways of teaching class names. Notice the parallel between the indirect and direct approaches to naming objects, on the one hand, and classes, on the other. The indirect approach amounts always to exemplification, using a word in such a way that it becomes a name of an object or class of objects, whereas the direct approach amounts to using a word that has the force of asserting that such and such is the case. The words in question are "name of" for objects and "is" for classes of objects. Consider, for example, "Fig name of object fig" and "Chocolate, M & M, caramel is candy." In these sentences "fig" is introduced as the name of an unnamed object, "candy" as the name of a new class. Therefore, "is" can play the same productive role in naming classes as "name of" played in naming objects (see Chapter 10 for further discussion of this point).

In fact, we had no difficulty teaching Sarah object classes, the first three of which were "fruit," "breadstuff," and "candy," taught in that order. We contrasted "fruit" with "breadstuff" (a class invented for the occasion), with standard errorless trials, using as exemplars "Cracker is ?" (Cracker is what?) and "Banana is ?" (Banana is what?). The only alternatives given on these errorless trials were the new words "breadstuff" in one case and "fruit" in the other, with which she displaced the interrogative marker, forming the desired sentence "Cracker is breadstuff" and "Banana is fruit." Corresponding trials on the negative cases led her to write "Banana is-not breadstuff" and "Cracker is-not fruit." She was given five trials on each of the positive cases and two on each of the negative ones.

In the standard test that followed she was given the same questions, but with the requirement that she choose between "breadstuff" and "fruit." She made only one error in 15 trials, none of the first five. Then she was given a transfer test, "cookie" and "bread" being substituted for "cracker" and "grape" and "peach" for "banana." Questions took the form: "Grape is ?" (Grape is what?), "Grape is-not?" (Grape is not what?), "Bread is ?" (Bread is what?), "Bread is-not?" (Bread is not what?), etc. She made seven errors in 46 trials, only one error on the first five trials.

If she had failed, how should we have interpreted it? Having been taught that banana is a fruit, suppose Sarah should choose not to call peach or grape a fruit; in what sense can she be considered in error? In the present exercises, she was not asked *yes–no* questions, which would indeed have required that she decide whether or not, say, peach was a fruit; but was merely asked *wh-* questions, which required only that she decide whether a peach was more like a fruit or a breadstuff. Errors in this test are ambiguous. They could mean that she had failed to learn the words or, alternatively, that she classified differently than we do.

However, her performance level of 85% correct did not suggest either that she classified differently than we do or that she failed to learn the desired associations. Interestingly, the rather atypical fruit, banana, which was one of two defining exemplars of "fruit," did not prevent her from deciding that peach and grape belonged to this class rather than to the one defined by cracker. The outcome may have been different, however, if "breadstuff" had been defined by a suitably mushy cake or pie; then peach and grape may not have been classified as "fruit."

Next we introduced "candy," using "chocolate" as the training exemplar, with only one positive and one negative sentence and with no further exemplars. The sentences used were "Chocolate is ?" (Chocolate is what?) and "Chocolate is-not ?" (Chocolate is not what?). The answers provided were "candy" and "fruit," respectively, leading her to write "Chocolate is candy" and "Chocolate is not fruit." She passed the standard choice test at the 85% level and then was given transfer tests in which candy was contrasted not only with "fruit" but also with "breadstuff," a class with which candy had not been directly contrasted. For example, she received such trials as "Gumdrop is ?," "Peach is ?," and "Cracker is ?," as well as the corresponding negative forms and was given all three class names—"fruit," "candy," and "breadstuff"—among which to choose. She made only four errors in 36 trials, with none on the first five. Even though she was not told that, e.g., peach (or fruit in general) is not candy, therefore, she apparently did not contemplate that possibility on her own. She had been told, of course, that peach, etc., was a fruit, and perhaps it was a part of her thinking that if an item had been assigned to one class it would not belong to another. The training program might be considered to encourage that conclusion because it did not include multiple assignments for any items. That is, in her experience no item was assigned to more than one class.

The object classes were then combined with the plural and she was given a number of questions of the form: "Peach banana is pl ?" (Peach and banana are what?), "Cookie bread cracker is-not pl ?" (Cookie, bread, and cracker are not what?), etc. She made no error in 10 such trials, after which she "requested" the words, as she did on nearly every lesson, and then wrote without assistance "Cracker bread is pl breadstuff" and "grape banana is pl fruit."

On a subsequent lesson, many of the present words were made available to her and she wrote on her own "Grape is ?," "Cookie is ?," "Bread is ?," "Banana is ?," "Grape is ?," "Grape is-not ?," "Banana is ?," "Bread is ?," and "Peach is ?," in effect asking herself a series of questions which she went on to answer, her relevant alternatives being "breadstuff," "fruit," and "candy." She always answered one question before writing another one. Although she seldom answered her own questions incorrectly, in the present exercise she erred on the first and seventh questions. Notice that despite her aversion to the negative form, she did ask herself one negative question, "Grape is-not ?" and answered it correctly, "Grape is-not breadstuff."

In a subsequent lesson she was given a few trials requiring that she select the correct negative alternative from multiple alternatives. For example, "? is-not fruit" (What is not fruit?), "? is-not breadstuff" (What is not breadstuff?). Her alternatives were "banana," "peach," and "cracker" in the first case and "cookie," "cracker," and "banana" in the second. She accepted only seven such questions and made two errors. Her difficulty was also reflected in her generally slow performance.

Still another lesson brought together object and perceptual classes that had so far been kept separate. "Peach is ?," "Triangle is ?," "Bread is ?," and "Red is ?" were asked her in a mixed order with "breadstuff," "fruit," "color," and "shape" as relevant alternatives. She made four errors in 16 trials, with none on the first five. The lesson was notable because it was one of relatively few in which the semantic content was not monolithic.

In teaching her the object classes the information given was actually not sufficient for her to have answered the transfer questions as she did. Instructions of the kind "Apple is fruit," "Chocolate is candy," "Apple is not candy," and "Chocolate is not fruit" are compatible with two conditions: (1) no fruit is a candy and no candy is a fruit and (2) some candy is not fruit and some fruit is not candy. That is, the information given her was compatible not only with Condition 1 but also with Condition 2, the intersection between the two classes. Accordingly, when asked in the transfer test whether or not, say, peach was a fruit or a candy, the information given her would accept either answer. That this problem did not arise is of some interest, for it suggests that Sarah was not independently disposed to think of the intersection condition, even though the information given her was compatible with that possibility.

Notice that "is" was taught with perceptual exemplars (color and shape) and then used to introduce not names of new perceptual classes, e.g., texture or taste, but names of object classes. This suggests that she learned the object classes "fruit," "candy," and "breadstuff" essentially as analogies to the perceptual classes, "color," "shape," etc. In fact, I have tacitly assumed that the perceptual class is primitive and that the object class is a derived notion. A direct test of this assumption could be made by introducing "is" with perceptual class exemplars in one case and object class exemplars in the other, and by then examining the transfer that each would allow to the other. If "is" had been defined by the relation between apple and fruit—"apple is fruit"—how effective would "is" have proved to be in introducing "color"? How would the efficiency of this strategy compare with that of defining "is" by the relation between red and color—"red is color"—and then using "is" to introduce "fruit." This is the comparison we need in order to determine whether either the property or the object class is more primitive than the other.

MEANING OF "IS"

It is difficult to say what exactly "is" meant to Sarah because we did not teach her any other concept with which to contrast "is." Concepts might be said to come in clusters. Only by teaching at least two members of any cluster is it possible to say what either one means. This is not a new point but a methodological stricture that we have adhered to in all previous cases:

1. From the beginning, no object, agent, or action class was given only one member. In mapping the original transaction, "apple" was contrasted with "banana," "orange," etc.; "Mary" with "Randy," etc.; "cut" with "give," etc.

2. We taught not one property class but "color," "shape," and "size," largely for the same purpose.

3. The logical connectives as discussed in Chapter 12 are an unfinished cluster—the meaning of "if–then" being destined to remain in doubt until Sarah passes tests on "and" and "or."

All these cases differ somewhat from "is," however, in that in these cases it is intuitively clear what constitutes contrasting alternatives. It is less clear what constitute semantic neighbors for the relation of class membership or, indeed, whether this relation has any neighbors. Suppose, for instance, Sarah were asked to state the relation between apple and fruit and answered "Apple is fruit" rather than, say, "Apple color of fruit." We would not be too impressed by this correct reply, for "is" and "color" would not belong to the same cluster.

Moreover, the subject's successful performance on a transfer test cannot substitute for its ability to discriminate between neighboring concepts. Sarah passed the transfer test on "is" by writing, for example, "Yellow is not shape" and "Yellow is color," "yellow" being a nontraining item. This established that, on her own, she assigned to "yellow" and "color" the same relation that she was taught to assign to "red" and "color." Unfortunately, however, it did not tell us what that relation was. That information can come only from the subject's ability to discriminate a word from close alternatives.

However, we cannot treat the successful contrast of semantic neighbors as a necessary condition for granting meaning to a term. On that requirement any concept for which there was no semantic neighbor would be judged meaningless. Is the world neatly divided into semantic neighborhoods, such that if class membership is a legitimate concept neighboring concepts will turn up, and until they do this concept must remain suspect? Perhaps we should concede that semantic neighbors are after all only a convenience: they permit interrogating a subject in a revealing way. Whenever a subject chooses correctly from a set of close alternatives the experimenter is handed a reassuring kind of evidence. The evidence is less reassuring when the alternatives are widely spaced; then it is possible that closer alternatives can be found, and when they are the subject must fail. Yet to whom are closely spaced alternatives an advantage? Does the subject require them in order to learn the distinction in question? Or is the advantage to the experimenter, in enabling him to overcome his doubts and to have confidence in the claims he has made about the subject's knowledge?

ANALYTIC VERSUS SYNTHETIC USE OF "IS"

The questions used in teaching Sarah "is" were of the form "? red is color" (Is red a color?) and "? round is shape" (Is round a shape?), all of which can be answered without so much as a glance at the world. Indeed, if an individual who was asked such questions were to search about in the world—looking to see whether or not red was a color, or round a shape—we would know there was a problem, a trivial one if it could be cleared up by articulating the question more clearly, a serious one otherwise. Answers to questions of this kind depend only on a knowledge of the meaning of the words; which is to say, the "is" initially taught Sarah was strictly analytic.

This was not the first use of training sentences that did not require any inspection of the world. Other sentences of this kind were those used to introduce the dimensional classes. For example, in learning "color of" as the relation between red and apple—"Red color of apple"—or "shape of" as the relation between round and cracker—"Round shape of cracker"—the new words were sensible in light of the already known meaning of the other words in the string; no further contribution was needed or made possible by an inspection of the world.

On other occasions this was not the case: the new words could be learned only by keeping a close eye on both the world and the words. For example, to learn "on," Sarah and the other subjects had had to watch both world and words and to consider the agreement between them. In proving that she comprehended an *on* sentence, the subject had to construct a specific arrangement in the world, say, put a red card on a green one. Likewise, in producing *on* sentences, that is, in describing *on* relations that existed in the world, the subject had to take cognizance of the arrangements that existed, for example, observe that red was on green, and produce sentences in conformity with the observed arrangement. However, in learning "is" Sarah was not required to inspect the world at all or to consider the conformity between it and the training sentences in any way.

Following the exclusively analytic use of "is" as described above, Sarah was given a 13-item *yes–no* test in which at least some of the cases were clearly synthetic. They were synthetic in the sense that the question could not be answered correctly without considering the conformity between the question and the world. Some of the questions given Sarah on her first exposure to the synthetic use of "is" were the following: "? pail is yellow" (Is pail yellow?), "? chocolate is brown" (Is chocolate brown?), "? cookie is round?" (Is cookie round?), "? carmel is square" (Is carmel square?), "? nut is green" (Is nut green?), "? banana is yellow" (Is banana yellow?), "? nut is triangular" (Is nut triangular?), and six others of a like kind. In each of these cases the question was accompanied by a nonlinguistic state of affairs, for example, by a pail that was yellow, chocolate that was brown, a cookie that was triangular (instead of round), etc. She was correct on the first four uses and on a total of ten out of 13, just below her customary 80% level.

Having been taught "is" in a context where there was no need to consider the match between the sentence and the world, nor any sense in attempting to do so, she went on to use "is" in questions that could only be answered correctly by considering a match between the world and the words:

1. What mediated the transfer between the analytic and synthetic cases?
2. Would it have been sensible to introduce separate markers for the analytic–synthetic distinction?

Consider the last question first.

For our purposes it could be sufficient to distinguish synthetic and analytic on the grounds suggested, in terms of the necessity either to consult or not to consult the world before answering the *yes–no* question. Moreover, in order for a distinction to be incorporated by language it is by no means necessary that the distinction be logically immaculate. The distinction in Spanish between permanent (*estar*) and contingent characteristics (*ser*) hardly seems water tight, yet it survives, partly on rational grounds as a learnable rule, but partly by custom, through rote memory. The same could hold for "is" and "tis" the markers we might have used to distinguish between the analytic and synthetic cases. If the distinction were instilled with clear cases, presumably it could have been made strong enough to survive the inevitable unclear cases. Given the puzzlement that has surrounded the analytic–synthetic issue, it may have been a nice move to have given the chimpanzee a possibly clearer head on this issue than English-speaking organisms are likely to have in advance of philosophical therapy.

The analytic use of "is" involved statements of either class inclusion, e.g., "Apple is fruit," or *instance of,* for example, "Yellow is color" (the exemplars given Sarah did not disambiguate these interpretations), whereas the synthetic use of "is" involved the ascription of properties, for example, "Banana is yellow." How did Sarah transfer from the former to the latter? The two are sometimes equated by reducing the ascription of a property to class inclusion. For instance, the statement "Banana is yellow" can be seen as "Banana is a member of the class of yellow things." Evidently all "*X* is *Y*" statements can be rewritten as "*X* is a member of a class with the property *Y*" (although the classes that have to be invented in order to sustain the equivalence do not seem comparable to those that occur in natural statements of class inclusion). Alternatively, the meaning of statements of the kind "Apple is red" and "Pail is yellow" can be assimilated to that of statements of the kind "Red is color" and "Apple is fruit" by treating the former and latter as two successive steps up an abstraction hierarchy. (I am indebted to Martin Braine, personal communication, 1975, for this point.)

The transfer results suggest that a common conceptual primitive may underly both cases. This primitive is, I think, the notion of possession or belonging, which can be realized either by an item that belongs to a class or a property that belongs to an item (and in other ways as well, such as psychological possession, for example, a space that belongs to an individual). Regrettably this suggestion cannot be sustained by the present data. They further the need for a study of the several senses of "belong" and their possible interrelation.

The fact that Sarah apparently found enough in common between the two kinds of statements to transfer from one to the other does not mean that she found no difference between them. It is important to keep in mind that in all the present tests transfer does not mean that the subject has been incapable of discriminating between the cases for which transfer is shown. In the present instance, therefore, transfer does not mean that if tested appropriately Sarah cannot discriminate property ascription from class inclusion, for example, "Banana is yellow"-type statements from "Yellow is color"-type statements.

It was a shortcoming of all our tests that they did not include either the option in which all alternatives were incorrect (or unsatisfactory to the subject) or a device with which the subject could express a similarity function. The yes–no question is a perfect example of the limited alternatives within which Sarah has been forced to operate. In addition, the response of not responding, or no response, was not itself an accredited alternative. On a few occasions she forced this alternative on us, when she not only refused to respond but did so persistently. Then the alternative of no response was more or less entered into the data but only in a semimysterious status, demanding an interpretation that was essentially clinical. These oppressive boundary conditions have since been importantly expanded by McClure (1975), who has added, first, the options in which the alternatives are either all correct or all incorrect—as opposed to the conventional correct and incorrect—and second a well-defined device for obtaining a similarity function overcoming the limitations of a two-valued system.

In McClure's system, which is best described in the context of match-to-sample, the subject is required to operate on all the alternatives presented and not only on one of them, as is conventional. If two alternatives are given, some correct and some incorrect, the subject makes one response to the correct item and a different response to the incorrect one, e.g., places matching items alongside the sample, but puts nonmatching items in a pan that is then handed out to the experimenter. Trials include all possible combinations: all alternatives are correct, all are incorrect, and the one on which tradition has fastened—some are correct and others are incorrect. The only alternative not so far included as a well-defined entity is that in which the subject elects to make no judgment—because the decision is either too difficult, or too easy and so not to be taken seriously, or too risky, etc. Actually, it is quite important to work out a way of giving this alternative a well-formed status. One suspects that man has a basic predilection to render a judgment and that strong counterfactors have to be introduced, e.g., harsh penalty for incorrect judgment, to restrain this predilection. Another way of saying the same thing is that man cannot suspend judgment until the act of suspending judgment becomes so nicely elaborated or ritualized that it can itself substitute for judgment. All species may not be as strongly constrained to make judgments as man apparently is. To find out whether or not they are, we need to make nonjudgment a well-defined alternative.

The devices for obtaining similarity functions are still in the planning stage but take two forms. One is to allow the space between the sample and the correct alternative to function as a metric, similarity being inversely proportional to the distance between the sample and where the subject locates the correct alternative. Another possibility is to use sequence rather than distance and to derive similarity by combining correct and incorrect. For example, placing an item by the sample equals correct, placing it in the pan equals incorrect, but placing it by the sample and then in the pan equals similar, i.e., similar = correct + incorrect. Degrees of similarity could be obtained by the use of frequency; for example, two incorrect plus one correct would be less similar than one incorrect plus two correct. Finally, it will be of interest to try to establish a conversion factor between the two ways of expressing similarity.

12

Toward Logical Connectives
and the Concept of Causality

In teaching Sarah "if–then" we did not use preverbal tests to study the conceptual structure underlying "if–then" and the other logical connectives but used the preverbal period to build in a kind of experience which, if it were described with words, would require the use of "if–then" or some equivalent phrase. In a preliminary step, we gave her a series of choices between pieces of apple and banana; she chose apple 28 times in 66 trials, confirming, as we suspected, that she did not have a marked preference for either fruit. In the more important next step we arranged a contingency between the choice of apple and the receipt of chocolate. She preferred chocolate to both fruit and, with the contingency in effect, chose apple 26 times in 30 trials.

Sarah's behavior during the contingency could be described by such sentences as "If Sarah took apple, then Mary gave her chocolate." Sarah could have come close to describing her own behavior, for the description depended on four simple or atomic sentences which she already knew, viz., "Sarah take apple," "Sarah take banana," "Mary give Sarah chocolate," and "Mary no give Sarah chocolate." These sentences needed only to be joined with "if–then" to form the appropriate pairs:

1. If Sarah take apple   then   Mary give Sarah chocolate.
2. If Sarah take banana then   Mary no give Sarah chocolate.

Because the words marking the conditional relation were the only words not known to Sarah, the conditional sentences themselves could be used as a strict training program for introducing "if–then." "If–then" is two words, however, and these are words that occur discontinuously. The discontinuous constituents that natural languages use to mark the conditional relation pose an interesting problem, although not one we have needed to grapple with at this time.

236

Reserving the problem for a later time, we marked the conditional not with discontinuous particles but with a simple particle as in symbolic logic:

1. Sarah take apple   ⊃   Mary give Sarah chocolate
2. Sarah take banana   ⊃   Mary no give Sarah chocolate

However, in adopting a single particle, we did not at the same time adopt the truth-functionally defined properties of the material conditional. The "horseshoe" or material conditional of propositional logic differs from the conditional relation of natural language in several ways, as Strawson (1952) has shown more clearly perhaps than anyone else. Although we have adopted the single-particle approach of logic, we have used the particle essentially as a substitute for natural language "if–then," as the many examples in this chapter show.

That strings as complex as those above could serve as a training program is a reflection on Sarah's notable progress. Her first training program was based on stringes of the form ⊖ __ ⊖ , where the known terms were physical items and the unknown was the simple predicate "same." From there she progressed to strings of the form, "cup name of ⊖," where at least one of the arguments was a word. Soon she reached a point where as with "red__apple," used to introduce "color of," both arguments were words. The present training sentences represent a still further advance. Not only did the strings consist exclusively of linguistic items, but the arguments were themselves complete sentences. Over the course of her training, therefore, arguments of the predicate advanced from nonlinguistic objects to objects and words, then to words alone, and finally to combinations of words or sentences. One factor, constant throughout her training, was quite likely the most significant factor in its success. Sarah was made thoroughly familiar with all known terms before they were combined to form training sentences. In the beginning, judging whether cups and spoons are same or different must be notably easier than making comparable judgments for pairs of sentences and this difference should be reflected in shorter latencies for the nonlinguistic objects. Yet as familiarity with the linguistic entities increases, we may expect the difference in latencies to decrease, even to the point where the former may take no more time than the judgments about cups and spoons have taken in the beginning. Suppose that ultimately the processing time for making, say, same–different judgments about complex linguistic items were no greater than it once was for simple objects. At that point the subject should be as capable of learning new predicates, instanced by complex linguistic items, as it was initially of learning predicates instanced by simple objects.

We began the language training by giving Sarah the question, "Sarah take apple ? Mary give Sarah chocolate" (What is the relation between Sarah's taking apple and Mary's giving chocolate?). She was given only one alternative, the conditional particle, with which she displaced the interrogative marker, forming the sentence, "Sarah take apple ⊃ Mary give Sarah chocolate." In addition, a piece of apple was made available to her and, when she ate it, a piece of chocolate.

Next, she was given the question "Sarah take banana ? Mary no give Sarah chocolate" (What is the relation between Sarah's taking banana and Mary's not giving Sarah chocolate?). Again, given only the conditional particle, she displaced the interrogative marker with it, forming the sentence "Sarah take banana ⊃ Mary no give Sarah chocolate." This time a piece of banana was made available to her (which she sometimes ate), but it was never followed by a piece of chocolate.

After five trials on each of the two questions, we shifted from the production to the comprehension mode and tested her understanding of the conditional particle by presenting her either of two pairs of sentences in a mixed order:

1. Sarah	Sarah	or	2. Sarah	Sarah
take	take		take	take
apple	banana		apple	banana
⊃	⊃		⊃	⊃
Mary	Mary		Mary	Mary
give	no		no	give
Sarah	give		give	Sarah
chocolate	Sarah		Sarah	chocolate
	chocolate		chocolate	

The first pair of sentences state that the choice of apple results in chocolate, but the choice of banana does not; in the second pair the conditions are reversed. Pieces of both banana and apple were set before her on each trial, and she was considered to have responded correctly whenever her choice of fruit led to her being given chocolate.

She made over 20 errors, accompanied by emotional outbursts, based on the persistent choice of apple. She then abandoned this approach, only to alternate between the two fruits for about 14 trials. Finally she took into account the instructions and consistently chose the fruit that led to the chocolate.

Although it took Sarah longer to learn the conditional relation than most of the other concepts, once she learned it she gave her customary performance on the transfer test. On the first of several transfer tests both a piece of apple and banana were placed before her and she was given the following instructions in the order stated:

	Sarah's responses
1. Sarah eat apple ⊃ Mary give candy Sarah	1. Ate apple
2. Sarah no eat apple ⊃ Mary give candy Sarah	2. Took banana
3. Sarah no eat banana ⊃ Mary give candy Sarah	3. Took apple
4. Sarah eat banana ⊃ Mary give candy Sarah	4. Ate banana
5. Sarah no eat banana ⊃ Mary give candy Sarah	5. Took apple

She made no errors and received chocolate on all five trials. The test is of special interest because of the manner in which she dealt with items for which there was no explicit instruction. Notice that on Trials 2, 3, and 5, whereas one alternative was prohibited, there was no instruction whatever regarding the other alternative. For example, on Trial 2 she was told not to eat the apple but nothing was said about the banana. Interestingly, on these trials she consistently took the alternative about which nothing was said. Would she have dealt with this situation in the same way had the unmentioned alternative been not a familiar item that had been correct on previous trials but a totally new item, never associated with the receipt of chocolate and quite different in its class properties from items that had this history? The choice of an unprohibited alternative (in a two-choice situation) may be a primitive form of responding, or merely an extrapolation from former training based on the use of alternatives that have been familiar and correct on some trials. We found the same mode of responding in psychotic children, where in a sense it was a good deal more surprising, for the children were otherwise seriously impaired. If was of further interest that whereas Sarah took the unprohibited items, she did not treat them the same way she did the explicitly correct items. She ate the latter as she was instructed to do but the former, about which she was told nothing, she merely took. At the end of the lesson, a nod from the trainer confirmed her prerogative, and she then ate the items she had been more or less holding in reserve.

The next transfer test was based on the following five instructions in the order stated:

Sentence	Alternatives
1. Sarah give red card Mary ⊃ Mary give candy Sarah	1. Red card/green card
2. Sarah give candy Mary ⊃ Mary give candy Sarah	2. Candy/red card
3. Sarah give apple Mary ⊃ Mary give candy Sarah	3. Apple/banana
4. Sarah give banana Mary ⊃ Mary give candy Sarah	4. Apple/banana
5. Sarah give apple Mary ⊃ Mary give candy Sarah	5. Apple/banana

Sarah made no errors in five trials. The test was perhaps less difficult than might appear. The consequent (Mary give candy Sarah) was invariant and the antecedents involved only two alternatives. However, the antecedents were sentences different from those used in training. Indeed, they were not only new to this test situation but new altogether. For example, "Sarah give red card Mary" and "Sarah give candy Mary" were sentences that Sarah had never previously seen. Even in its simplicity, therefore the test proved that Sarah could comprehend the conditional particle when it was applied to sentences that had no history as atomic sentences but were encountered for the first time as part of the molecular sentence.

Two trainers were present in the next session, part of the attempt to require Sarah to process sentences that distinguished specifically who gave to whom. In addition, strawberry and canteloupe, which Sarah knew and liked but which had no names, were introduced into the lesson as "red fruit" and "yellow fruit," respectively. She was given 40 trials, five replications of the following eight sentences in a mixed order:

Sentence	Alternatives
1. Mary give cracker Debby ⊃ Sarah eat yellow fruit	1. Yellow/red fruit
2. Mary give cracker Debby ⊃ Sarah eat red fruit	2. Yellow/red fruit
3. Debby give cracker Mary ⊃ Sarah eat red fruit	3. Yellow/red fruit
4. Debby give cracker Mary ⊃ Sarah eat yellow fruit	4. Yellow/red fruit
5. Debby give cracker Mary ⊃ Sarah insert green card	5. Green card/red card
6. Debby give cracker Mary ⊃ Sarah insert red card	6. Green card/red card
7. Mary give cracker Debby ⊃ Sarah insert red card	7. Green card/red card
8. Mary give cracker Debby ⊃ Sarah insert green card	8. Green card/red card

She made seven errors in 40 trials, or 83% correct. This test was followed by a similar one based on the following 11 trials:

Sentence	Alternatives
1. Debby give apple Mary ⊃ Sarah insert cracker dish	1. Cracker/chocolate
2. Mary give banana Debby ⊃ Sarah insert chocolate dish	2. Cracker/chocolate
3. Debby give banana Mary ⊃ Sarah insert cracker dish	3. Cracker/chocolate
4. Mary give banana Debby ⊃ Sarah insert chocolate dish	4. Cracker/chocolate
5. Debby give apple Mary ⊃ Sarah insert cracker dish	5. Cracker/chocolate
6. Mary give banana Debby ⊃ Sarah insert chocolate dish	6. Cracker/chocolate
7. Debby give apple Mary ⊃ Sarah insert cracker dish	7. Cracker/chocolate
8. Mary give banana Debby ⊃ Sarah insert chocolate dish	8. Cracker/chocolate
9. Debby give apple Mary ⊃ Sarah insert chocolate dish	9. Cracker/chocolate
10. Mary give apple Debby ⊃ Sarah insert cracker dish	10. Cracker/chocolate
11. Debby give banana Mary ⊃ Sarah insert chocolate dish	11. Cracker/chocolate

She made one error on 11 trials.

Both tests have been intended to require Sarah to discriminate who has given what to whom but a moment's reflection reveal that they do not succeed in their aim. The trainers invariably carried out the action called for in the antecedent. It would have been better if they had not and instead had complied only sometimes, for when the antecedent of a conditional instruction is always true, one can ignore the antecedent and carry out the instruction simply by paying attention to the consequent. In addition, the consequent was itself a simple atomic sentence, for example, "Sarah insert cracker dish," or "Sarah eat yellow fruit," of a kind which we already knew Sarah could comprehend. Therefore, although the two tests resulted in an impressive number of words being placed on the board at the same time they were not necessarily as demanding as they may appear. We have no clear evidence, however, that Sarah actually simplified the tests for herself in keeping with the logical possibilities. Did she learn to ignore the antecedent, having observed over some number of trials that an antecedent which was invariably affirmed could be ignored? Regrettably we did not think at the time to give her other tests in which the trainer did not always comply with the antecedent. This would have forced attention to the antecedent, presumably increasing the difficulty of the test, and should have led to a lower performance level than tests in which the trainers always complied with the antecedent.

Even if the trainers had occasionally failed to carry out the antecedents, however, the tests would still have fallen short of their aim. They were intended to require Sarah to identify who gave to whom, for example, to behave in one way if Mary gave to Debby and a different way if Debby gave to Mary. As the test stood, however, it was necessary to identify only either the donor or the recipient· but not both. In a representative pair of contrasting antecedents, "Mary give apple Debby" versus "Debby give apple Mary," one antecedent could be distinguished from the other merely by deciding who gave or who received; it was not necessary to decide both.

An arrangement that would require identifying both the donor and the recipient depends on the use of six sentences and three trainers, as shown below:

1. Mary	2. Mary	3. Debby	4. Debby	5. John	6. John
give	give	give	give	give	give
X	X	X	X	X	X
Debby	John	Mary	John	Mary	Debby
⊃	⊃	⊃	⊃	⊃	⊃
Sarah	Sarah	Sarah	Sarah	Sarah	Sarah
take	take	take	take	take	take
red	green	green	red	red	green

In the antecedents, Mary, Debby, and John occur as a donor on some occasions and as a recipient on others. The consequents demand only one or the other of two simple actions—take the red or green card—but they are called for equally when Mary is a donor and when she is a recipient; and the same applies to Debby and John. Therefore, the only condition uniquely identifying which of the two acts to carry out is the donor–recipient relation. The writing board, laid out with the prescribed sentences, looked like a mystic tablet. The trainers summoned Sarah to the lesson. She needed only a glance at the board before springing to the other side of the cage, where she remained until the board was erased.

The following lesson, last in the transfer series, was a compromise between the desired information and the level of difficulty Sarah would entertain. On each of the eight trials she was given one of the following pairs of sentences:

1. Mary	2. Mary	3. Debby	4. Debby
give	give	give	give
green	red	red	green
Debby	Debby	Mary	Mary
⊃	⊃	⊃	⊃
Sarah	Sarah	Sarah	Sarah
eat	eat	eat	eat
candy	cracker	cracker	candy

5. Mary	6. Mary	7. Debby	8. Debby
give	give	give	give
red	green	green	red
Debby	Debby	Mary	Mary
⊃	⊃	⊃	⊃
Sarah	Sarah	Sarah	Sarah
eat	eat	eat	eat
cracker	candy	candy	cracker

This lesson accomplished most of the desiderata sought in the previous two lessons. First, because two antecedents were possible on each trial, it was necessary to observe the trainer's action and to read the sentences in order to find the antecedent to which the action conformed. Second, the instructions could not be carried out simply by memorizing which antecedent went with which consequent; there were four different antecedents and each of them went with both consequents. Sarah made only 2 errors in 8 trials (or 16 sentences), concluding the transfer tests. For all their shortcomings, the tests established two important points. She comprehended conditional sentences when the constituent atomic sentences were (1) different from those used in training and (2) not previously seen as atomic sentences but confronted for the first time in the context of the molecular sentence. Despite this evidence, we cannot yet claim a specific meaning for the conditional particle. The connectives represent a cluster of concepts, and to contend that the subject knows any one of them it is necessary to show that the subject can discriminate among them.

Perhaps the sheer complexity of the conditional relation was responsible for Sarah's difficulty in learning to mark the relation. Indeed, how shall we assess the complexity of a relation except through the subject's performance in learning it? This is a reasonable assumption provided the training is equally effective in all cases. As the training of "same–different" has already shown, however, this is a difficult if not impossible condition to satisfy and the present case only adds to the sense of the difficulty.

In the prelanguage phase we taught her that the choice of apple was always correct. This was a serious error, we may see in retrospect, for it gave her little reason to do other than consistently choose apple and so little reason to pay attention to the instructions. Regrettably, the training mistake was not even serendipitous. I should like to maintain that language can be taught only when the sentences used in training coincide with the prelanguage experience, which they do not in the present case, because apple has been consistently correct in the prelanguage phase and only sometimes correct in the language phase. But the present outcome is subject to an even simpler explanation—merely a failure in attention, a tendency to choose apple without even looking at the instructions.

Can errors of the above kind be avoided or are they recognizable only in hindsight? Because the training has a standard format, one way to answer the question is by determining whether or not the actual training adheres to the format. Standard training consists of two positive instances and two negative instances, followed by trials on which the subject is required to choose between alternatives. Fortunately, it does not require hindsight to observe that the present training has not conformed to the format.

Sarah should have received not one kind of positive trial but at least two. Chocolate should have been available not only by taking apple but also by taking at least one other fruit. This alone would have eliminated the condition most responsible for the difficulty in the present procedure. Because apple was always correct, Sarah learned to choose only it. However, if apple had been correct some of the time and, say, raisin other times, both responses would have been strengthened in the prelanguage phase, forcing her to attend to the instructions in order to know which fruit to choose. Our mistaken procedure built into Sarah a response bias that interfered with her learning in much the way that Elizabeth's "natural" bias interfered with her learning (see page 109).

CONJUNCTION: "AND"

Before we taught Sarah an explicit marker for "and," we invited her to engage in an implicit form of conjunction reduction on her own. In previous drills on simple sentence production, a piece of food had been placed before her along with a small set of words, her task being simply to request the food—for instance, to write "Mary give apple Sarah" when the food was apple and "Mary give banana Sarah" when it was banana, etc. After many such drills, we invited Sarah to behave conjunctively, by placing before her pieces of two different fruits and giving her the usual set of words, including names for both fruit. On the first eight trials, she responded in keeping with her previous training, writing "Give apple Sarah," and "Give banana Sarah," her usual individual sentences. On the ninth trial, however, she changed her approach and wrote, "Mary give Sarah apple orange," for the first time requesting both items in one sentence. On a subsequent lesson when given three items per trial, she requested all three of them, writing for example, "Give banana apple orange Sarah."

Actually a still earlier form of implicit conjunction-reduction occurred with names of actions rather than objects. In the early drill on sentence formation Sarah wrote "Wash apple," resulting in the apple being washed, handed back the words, wrote "Cut apple," resulting in the apple being cut, handed back the words again, and finally wrote, "Give apple," receiving the apple and closing the sequence. Early in training she was given only one action name at a time, one appropriate to the point in the sequence to which the action had progressed. Later, several verbs were made available to her at the same time, enabling her to write, "Wash apple, cut apple," or "Cut apple, give apple," etc. Sarah did not write pairs of sentences of this kind, but wrote instead "Cut give apple," and

"Wash give apple," although not always observing the correct order. If we overlook the errors in word order it is reasonable to conjecture that in producing strings in which two verbs preceded one object name, her intention was the equivalent of "Cut and give the apple," or "Wash and give the apple." Elizabeth produced similar constructions in the context of self-description (see page 89).

These results suggested that Sarah was capable of the perceptual judgments underlying the elimination of redundant elements, but they did not themselves introduce a marker for conjunction. To introduce a marker, the new particle was simply placed in Sarah's pile of available words, formerly acceptable sentences such as "Give apple banana" were rejected, and she was required to write instead "Give apple and banana." Subsequently, her use of the conjunction marker was tested by four lessons based on the following sentences:

1. "Cookie ? cracker ? pl breadstuff"
2. "Apple ? banana ? pl fruit"
3. "Blue ? green ? pl color"
4. "Big ? small ? pl size"

Her alternatives were: "and," "and," "is," "is." She was correct on 11 out of 20, 13 out of 20, 12 out of 20, and 20 out of 20 trials per total trials on the first through the fourth lesson, respectively. After four lessons she was not only consistently correct in writing, for example, "Apple and banana is pl fruit," but also transferred the use of "and" to new cases. Probably her initial difficulty in learning "and" came from the fact that we had violated our own rule against accepting forms that were later rejected. The constructions ". . . apple banana" ". . . orange apple," etc., accepted in the beginning, conflicted with the ". . . apple and banana," ". . . orange and apple," etc., that was subsequently required, delaying learning. However, it had been necessary to violate the rule to find out whether Sarah could invent conjunction without training or a model.

EXCLUSIVE "OR":
A OR B BUT NOT BOTH

Before we were able to finish the training of "or" and had a chance to contrast the several connectives, Sarah became untestable. Nonetheless, the disjunctive case is interesting to consider, although more for the nature of the training than for Sarah's accomplishment. The exclusive "or" (*A* or *B* but not both) was the first word we attempted to introduce by explicit definition rather than by the customary ostensive one. That is, we did not illustrate or exemplify the meaning of "or" by arranging a nonlinguistic state of affairs in which one of two alternatives but not both of them was operated on in a particular way; instead we attempted to introduce "or" in a strictly verbal way with the following sentence:

take		take		take
apple		banana		apple
$\supset$	and	$\supset$	same	or
no		no		banana
take		take		
banana		apple		

The distribution of the words on the board was intended to convey that "same" was the major predicate, with the two sentences on the left as one of the arguments, the one sentence on the right as the other argument. Because we had yet to introduce parentheses, we attempted to use space as a bracketing device, the range of the connective being proportional to the amount of space between it and the other elements.

Note the extension on "same" which the training sentences involve. "Same" was introduced originally as a relation between objects; now it was used as a relation between linguistic entities. This was only one of several such extensions on "same–different," another one being the case in which Sarah was given pairs of sentences and required to judge whether they were "same" or "different" (see Chapter 15).

In English paraphrase, the instructions state an equivalence between "if *A* then not *B* and if *B* then not *A*," on the one hand, and "*A* or *B* but not both," on the other. The two expressions are not strictly equivalent, however. To make them so would require reducing the right hand side to read simply, not *A* and *B*, or else, adding to the left side, *A* or *B*. As stated, there is one nonequivalent case, viz., the one in which the subject takes neither apple nor banana. Because both the apple and banana were desired objects, however, it seemed gratuitous to add "and you must take one or the other." The exclusive "or" makes sense only if the subject wants both alternatives, for it is only by merit of the subject's interest in both items that one gives the instruction allowing the subject to take one item or the other but not both. Nevertheless, the marker that we treated as the exclusive "or" really meant "not *A* and *B*," or more generally, "not both of the alternatives."

Before presenting the whole construction shown above, we first presented some introductory material that was intended to give Sarah a few hints and even pieces of the definition. The whole construction, presented out of hand, was likely to have driven her to the other side of the cage. First, we gave a lesson intended to further acquaint her with the fact that "same" could take not only cups and spoons as arguments but sentences as well. Her ability to use "same" in this forceful manner would be a key factor in the effectiveness of the explicit definition. In addition, the lesson was designed to call attention to the possibility of rearrangement and to the economy that could result from it. In the definition of "or," the argument on the right side was shorter than the one on the left. To a lesser extent, this was also the case in the lesson shown below:

apple		apple
is		and
fruit		banana
?	same	is
banana		pl
is		fruit
fruit		

The only word given to her in this deliberately errorless lesson was "and," which she substituted for the interrogative marker, producing a sentence for which the rough English equivalent is: "Apple is fruit and banana is fruit = apple and banana are fruit." There were no new words but, as noted earlier, there was a structural parallel between this precursor material and the target definition: (1) "Same" is the key predicate and (2) the argument on the right is a shortened version of the one on the left. We had no formal evidence that Sarah could be assisted by structural parallel, but we had none to the contrary either, so we gave her 20 trials in the hope that repetition might drive the structural parallel home. Next, we gave her two instructions, "Take apple ⊃ no take banana" (If you take apple do not take banana) and the reverse "Take banana ⊃ no take apple," ten of each in a mixed order, with pieces of apple and banana as alternatives. She was given specifically these sentences because, as shown in the diagram, it was the conjunction of these two sentences that would be used to explicitly define the new word "or." She was correct on 16 of 20 instructions, making only one error in the first five trials, further evidence of her grasp of the conditional particle.

As the last preliminary step we gave her the whole left argument of the target construction, viz.,

take		take
apple		banana
⊃	and	⊃
no		no
take		take
banana		apple

(If you take apple then do not take banana, and if you take banana then do not take apple; in other words, do not take both of them.) She was given ten compound sentences of this kind in mixed order, with pieces of apple and banana as alternatives, and was correct on seven of the ten. Then we gave her the full definition shown above in a more or less standard errorless format. That is, the only particle given her was "or," the new word, with which she displaced the interrogative marker, forming the target construction. We gave her 20 such trials.

The next lesson repeated the above material but added the possibility of error by giving both the words "or" and "and," thus requiring her to choose between them. She made no errors in 20 trials, a rare performance. Her accuracy notwithstanding, the lesson was not a serious test of her grasp of "or." The first such test came in the next lesson, which consisted of instructions of the following kind:

1. Sarah take apple and banana
2. Sarah take cookie or candy
3. Sarah take banana or cookie
4. Sarah take cookie and apple

Twenty trials were given based on various combinations of the four instructions. She was correct on 18 of 20 trials, the first performance that showed the apparent effectiveness of the explicit definition.

In the next lesson we made only a slight change—requiring that she choose from four alternatives rather than two—and discovered a shocking disagreement between what we were teaching and what she had learned. In the previous lesson when told, for example, to take apple or banana on one trial, apple and banana on another, the items before her were apple and banana. In this lesson, the alternatives were increased; they included the customary pieces of apple and banana, but also pieces of candy and cookie. When told to take X and Y or X or Y, therefore, she was required to take some items and to leave others behind. Slight as this change was it served to reveal that Sarah had not learned the exclusive "or."

Her performance on instructions involving "and" declined a bit, mainly through occasional incorrect choice of items, but it still remained close to the 80% level. The revelation came rather from her performance on instructions involving "or." When told in the presence of four items to take X or Y, she did not take one item as the instructions required but took two items most of the time and sometimes three. For example, on eight such trials, she took two of the four items on seven trials and three of the four on one trial.

Her performance on four alternatives suggested that to her "or" meant something like "Take half of what is there" or more simply, "Do not take all of what is there." Although quite incorrect, the rule was nonetheless compatible with her former training. Given two alternatives, she was judged correct whenever she took only one of them. Interestingly "and" did not seem to mean "Take all of what is there." Although four alternatives disrupted her performance on "or," it did not significantly affect her performance on "and." As already noted, she erred on "and" merely by the occasional incorrect choice of items but not by taking an incorrect number of items. When told to take A and B, she took only two items, as accurately when there were four alternatives as when there were only two. The training program used to teach "or" may have been at fault because of its consistent use of two alternatives. Nevertheless, if

Sarah had understood the explicit definition she could not have made the mistake she did.

Organisms may be primed to learn certain concepts. Two species may both be capable of learning to label the same concept, but the exemplars that teach it to one species may not teach it to the other. Because I know of no proved cases, I offer a hypothetical one instead. The hypothesis springs from existing data, however, and is simply an extrapolative conjecture on the data. The case concerns triangularity and monkeys and is one of many pioneering studies on conceptual learning in the rhesus macaque by Andrew and Harlow (1948). Monkeys first trained on a series of object choice problems in which the correct choice was always a triangular object were then tested for transfer on new cases. Although disappointing in the beginning, the ultimate transfer results suggested that the monkeys had learned the concept of triangularity. A test was then given in which neither of the two objects presented was a triangle but one was more pointed than the other; not surprisingly the monkeys chose the pointed objects. My point can be made by adding one further step to the experiment: offer a choice between triangular objects that are not especially pointed and nontriangular ones that are extremely pointed. It would seem possible that the monkeys would choose the hyperpointed nontriangle rather than the only mildly pointed triangle. That is, the monkey may abstract pointedness rather than triangularity. So may the child, of course, but if it did not and instead inferred triangularity on the basis of the same exemplars, this would support the possibility that species are primed for specific concepts.

The exemplars we used in attempting to teach Sarah "or" may prove to be generally "bad" in the sense that they may be ineffective with any species. However, if the same exemplars should teach the exclusive "or" to the child, this would illustrate the hypothesis that, whereas different species might be capable of labeling the same concept, they might be primed for different ones and so might require different exemplars. Some of the accomplishments of the chimpanzee suggest that it may no longer be sufficient to ask merely what they can and cannot learn. We may have to ask the more subtle question: What exemplars are needed to teach them the linguistic marker? Can they use exemplars that are sufficient for man or is a more structured input needed, one that carefully eliminates possible erroneous hypotheses?

Before taking too seriously a species-specific priming hypothesis, however, compare Sarah's failure in learning "or" with her evident success in learning the correct rule for pluralization (see page 227). She learned pluralization despite a training program that failed to eliminate a major erroneous alternative, viz., that the "pl" marker was to be used whenever there were two or more words to the left of the copula. Sarah did not use this incorrect feature but appeared to use the correct feature, the number of items referred to by the subject of the sentence.

Sarah's success in the case of "pl" and failure in the case of "or" may have less to do with a vague concept of priming than with the more down to earth matter of the social appropriateness of the exemplars. Suppose in teaching the exclusive "or" we had used a small cake that both the trainer and Sarah dearly wanted but that had to be shared by them, neither party to receive both pieces. In this situation "Take *A* or *B* but not both" seems likely to have been more subject to intuitive interpretation. Indeed, we might measure the excellence of a training program by the subject's ability to guess the meaning of the unknown particle. Training programs consist not only of the sentences introducing the new linguistic marker but also of the extralinguistic states of affairs mapped by the sentences. The sentences per se may be fine, completely in accord with the dicta of one unknown at a time, highly familiar items, and a sentence-producing operation consisting exclusively of one-to-one substitution. Yet if the extralinguistic situation mapped by the sentences is not socially plausible, the excellence of the training sentences may be wasted. The cognitive event to be associated with the new marker must be made available to the subject by that situation and by the subject's understanding of it.

CONCEPT OF CAUSALITY

Arbitrary relations, such as "If Sarah take apple, then Mary give Sarah chocolate," are but one of three distinguishable topics that can be expressed by the same conditional form. The other two are nonarbitrary and concern physical and psychological relations, respectively. "If the glass is dropped it will break" or "If the sponge is put in water it will soak up the water," etc., are ways of expressing physical relations or the dispositions of certain materials. Dispositional relations are not found only in the physical realm but occur also in the psychological domain. "If you hit Mary she will be angry with you" or "If you say 'hello' to Jane she will like you better," etc., are ways of expressing psychological relations or the dispositions of certain agents. That cases as semantically diverse as those involving physical, psychological, and arbitrary relations can all take the same grammatical form is no novelty, however. It recalls other cases, the genitive most prominently, where an even greater diversity of conceptual relations is each represented in the same way. Indeed, in the genitive the conceptual diversity is such that there is real difficulty in formulating a generic notion from which to derive all the many variants.

Causality is the underlying concept in the case of all the conditional sentences. The physical case is probably the simplest of the three, or at least the domain in which the causal inference is first made. Piaget (1954) has argued that the child first learns the concept of causality in the action of its own body. In acting on the world, as it is enabled to do by an ever increasing sensory–motor development, the child discovers invariances between its own action and changes that result from them. However, not only the inanimate world but in time the animate one also provides opportunities for discovering invariances between one's acts and the acts that follow. One of the earliest of these is the relation between the child's smile and the mother's smiling in return. Yet, even this elementary psychological relation may not be as simple as the elementary physical case. For example, all objects the child pushes off the edge of the bed drop to the floor, whereas the mother may not smile back if she is in a bad mood and, further, not all faces into which the child smiles smile back (I have watched a child smiling into the faces of strangers—as it rode about a super-market in a shopper's cart—weep when several faces have failed to smile back). Nevertheless, if psychological relations differ from elementary physical ones it is only in complexity, in the number of parameters that may need to be con-sidered; a causal inference is as likely to be made in the one case as in the other. Finally, the so-called arbitrary cases—for example, "If you touch red, then Mary will give you apple"—only appear arbitrary to the outside observer. Spanking a child when it touches forbidden objects may be said to carry out an arbitrary rule, in the sense that the rule is not observed in every part of the world, perhaps not even next door. Yet, from the child's point of view, there can be little difference between being spanked when touching the lamp and burned when touching the toaster. The child will, I believe, be as quick to make a causal inference in one case as the other.

We come now to the interesting question: Does the chimpanzee make causal inferences or are inferences of that kind limited to man? It may be thought that we have already answered the question affirmatively. Sarah learned the condi-tional marker and responded accurately to all the lexical substitutions made on the conditional sentences. If the relation between the antecedent and the consequent in the conditional sentence is equivalent to that of cause and effect—as we have argued above—then Sarah's language behavior already con-stitutes evidence for causal inference. This argument is sound, I believe, but attenuated in the present case by limitations in the language use. First, the conditional marker was not contrasted with the other connectives, leaving open the degree to which Sarah distinguished between "and," "or," and "if–then." Second, the conditional sentences were not applied to either physical or psycho-logical cases, which in a sense are the more revealing cases, but only to the so-called arbitrary case. If Sarah had produced such sentences as "If you take that orange, I'll bite you," "If you close the door, I can't see the workmen go by," "If you leave the tap on a little longer, I'll get a really cold drink," etc.—if her day had been filled with sentences of this kind, there could be no stronger evidence for causal inference. However, Sarah's use of the conditional was not broad enough to be more than suggestive.

To obtain further evidence, we devised some nonverbal tests that could also be applied to the other subjects. We presented the subject a visual representation of a simple action, which was incomplete in some respect, and required the animal to complete the representation by choosing the correct alternative. For example, we presented an intact apple and a severed apple and required the animal to choose from a set of alternatives—that included a bowl of water, a writing instrument of some kind, and a knife—the object it considered appropriate. If the animal chose the knife, placing it between the intact and severed apple and forming the sequence apple–knife–severed apple, we considered it to have answered correctly—in effect, to have chosen the appropriate instrument for bringing about the represented change in the object. In a second example, the animal was given a dry and a wet sponge and again required to choose from among alternatives that included a cutting instrument, a writing instrument, and a bowl of water. This time it was judged correct if the sequence it produced consisted of dry sponge–bowl of water–wet sponge.

We tested three different actions—cutting, wetting, and marking—each of which could be considered a prototypic or simple action on these grounds:

1. There is no delay between what is considered to be cause and effect, as there can be in more subtle cases.

2. The critical events are conspicuous instead of being embedded in a larger matrix and thus difficult to identify.

3. There is a simple proportionality between the magnitude of the cause and the effect rather than a disproportionate one as there can be in more complex cases.

All simple actions can be represented by a sequence of three elements—an object in an initial state, an implement that is the operator by which the object is changed from one state to another, and the object in its terminal state. The visual representation we have used has obviously been guided by the above analysis, but other formats are possible. For example, placing the instrument above the objects—rather than on a line with them—may be thought to carry out the intuition that the instrument is like the verb in the sentence and therefore should have the dominant position of a predicate, whereas the two states of the object, e.g., the wet and dry sponge, should be lower and off to the side, in positions suited to the arguments of the predicate. Even though there can be no one correct visual representation of action, some representations may be more intuitively compelling than others, and they may yield more systematic results than others.

On each trial, the subject was given two of the three elements that comprised the complete sequence and was required to select the third element from a set of three elements. The test sequence is readily seen to be an implicit form of interrogation, analogous to sentence completion. In fact, to make the interrogative character of the test explicit, we placed the interrogative marker in the position of the missing element and required the animal to deal with the visual sequence in exactly the same way it had been trained to deal with verbal questions, that is, to remove the interrogative marker and to replace it with the element(s) that completed the sequence. There were two different versions of the test, one requiring the subject to supply the missing instrument and the other requiring the subject to supply the missing terminal state of the object. A third version of the test differed from the other two in that the action was represented not by an instrument but by a word naming the action—by the plastic word for either "cut," "wash" or "draw."

In the first test, the three-element sequence given the subject consisted of an object, the interrogative marker, and another object, plus three alternatives—implements for cutting, wetting, and marking. The subject was required to complete the sequence by replacing the interrogative marker with the implement of its choice. Each action was tested four times, each time with different materials, making a total of 12 trials. The first test consisted of the following 12 trials given in a mixed order:

whole apple	?	two halves apple
whole cookie	?	two halves cookie
whole ball	?	two halves ball
whole sponge	?	two halves sponge
dry sponge	?	wet sponge
dry cloth	?	wet cloth
dry paper towel	?	wet paper towel
dry monkey chow	?	wet monkey chow
unmarked paper	?	marked paper
unmarked cup	?	marked cup
unmarked paper towel	?	marked paper towel
unmarked ball	?	marked ball

Twelve alternatives were used, four different knives, four different drawing instruments (pencils, crayons, etc.), and four different containers of water. The subject was given three alternatives on each trial, one each of the three different kinds of implements. In addition to the presentation of new combinations of objects and implements on each trial, it may be seen that some objects were associated with two acts, for example, sponge with both cut and wash, ball with both cut and mark, and paper towel with both cut and mark. Each test was scheduled for 12 trials, although occasional problems forced a reduction in the actual number of trials given.

In the second test, the plastic words "cut," "wash," and "draw" were substituted for the previous implements (a more accurate interpretation for "wash" would be wet or immerse in fluid, whereas that for "draw" would be scribble or mark, chimpanzee versions of the human referents). The sequences given were the same as in the previous test but now, instead of replacing the interrogative marker with an implement, the subject replaced it with a word, either "cut," "wash," or "draw."

In the third test, the missing item was no longer the operator but was instead the terminal state of the object. Three alternatives were given on each trial as before, designed according to the following paradigm: (1) correct object‾correct implement, (2) incorrect object‾correct implement, and (3) correct object‾incorrect implement (the most obviously incorrect alternative, incorrect object‾incorrect alternative, was omitted). For example, as shown in Figure 12.1, in the test sequence consisting of whole apple, knife, and ?, the alternatives offered

Causality

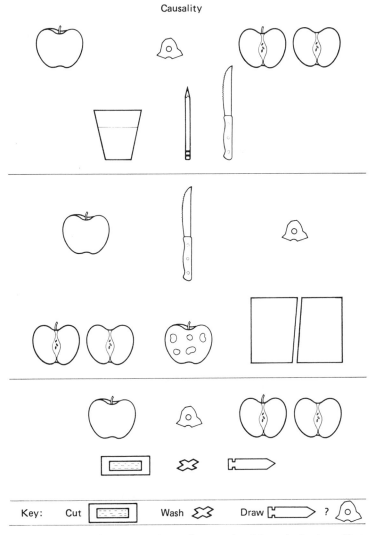

FIG. 12.1 Examples of three types of causality tests involving substitution of instrument, terminal state of object, and name of action.

were two halves of sponge, two halves of apple, and an apple punctured with holes. Analogously, in the test sequence consisting of dry sponge, container of water, and ?, the alternatives offered were a sponge wet with water, a paper towel wet with water, and a sponge wet with fruit juice.

The main results are summarized in Table 12.1, separately for the four animals. Only Sarah and Peony were tested on all three tests. Elizabeth was already sick (undiagnosed convulsions) by the time of the second test and her failure on the verbal test, after she had already passed the nonverbal form of the test, was more indicative of illness than failure. Walnut, in contrast, failed the first test conclusively. He has not been tested on the other versions because, despite special training, he has not yet passed even a reduced version of the first test.

All three female subjects passed the first test, which required selecting the appropriate implement or operator. Peony was given only nine trials because she was unwilling to pick up the container of water, apparently fearful of spilling it, and rather than risk upsetting her—and losing 25% of our population—we excused her from all such trials. On the verbal version of the test, the container of water was replaced by the word "wash," eliminating the problem, and she made no errors on "wash." Both Sarah and Peony passed the second test, requiring selection of the name of the appropriate action, and the third test, requiring selection of the appropriate terminal object. The errors made by the three female subjects on the three tests are summarized in Table 12.1; errors were somewhat fewer on cut than on the other actions, although the effect was not significant.

The three female subjects passed the first test—which was their original exposure to visual representations of causal sequences—without a model or special training and with only the usual number of errors on the first few trials. They were not taught the correct answers during the course of the testing, for although they were given differential feedback—approval and a bit of food for correct responses, disapproval and nothing for incorrect ones—they were never given the same trial twice. Each trial was essentially a transfer test for the preceding trials, for on each trial either a new object and implement was used or a new combination of object and implement.

Unlike the female subjects, whom there has been no need to teach, Walnut cannot be taught (thus far, at least). He did not respond correctly by himself as the other subjects did, nor did he benefit from the trainer modeling the answers. Once it was evident that Walnut did not understand the test, he was given special training. Basically this consisted of demonstrating one of two acts—marking was eliminated as too complex—and then promptly giving him a test on the act demonstrated. For example, after an apple had been cut virtually under his nose, Walnut was given the sequence Apple ? severed apple, with a bowl of water and the very knife used in cutting the apple as alternatives. Despite numerous trials

TABLE 12.1
Summary of Main Results for Causality Tests

Subject	Tests		
	I Visual operator	II Verbal	III Terminal object
Sarah	9/12	10/11	8/12
Peony	8/9	10/11	9/12
Elizabeth	9/12	5/12	–
Walnut	5/12	–	–

Summary of errors

Subject	Errors		
	Wet	Cut	Mark
I. Sarah	2		1
Peony		1	
Elizabeth	2		1
Total:	4	1	2
II. Sarah			1
Peony		1	
Elizabeth	4	2	1
Total:	4	3	2
III. Sarah			
Peony	1	1	2
Elizabeth	1		2
Total:	–	–	–
	2	1	4
TOTAL:	10	5	8

of this kind, in which the demonstration of an act was immediately conjoined with a question about the act, Walnut made no progress whatsoever. We have given up this approach and are now attempting to induce him to use objects in the playful way the other subjects do spontaneously. Walnut is markedly aberrant in this regard, for as a species the chimpanzee is highly manipulative, second only to man perhaps (although challenged by the *Cebus* monkey, the "poor man's chimp"; cf. Klüver, 1973; Premack & Bahwell, 1959). We cannot say why he does not manipulate objects in the normal chimpanzee manner.

Reared by a commercial animal trainer until almost 4 years old, he was doubtless punished in a way the other subjects were not. Yet it is years since he has last been struck and it seems that suppression from earlier punishment should have extinguished. His failure both on the tests and to engage in the acts that the tests concern may, of course, be coincidence or, as I suspect, a suggestion as to the kind of experience that is necessary to pass the tests.

These results can be defended as evidence for causal inference, first, by eliminating alternative explanations, and second by noting that there is a substantial disparity between the real actions of cutting, wetting, and marking and our visual representations of these actions, despite which the animals passed the tests. The main alternative to causal inference is that the animals have responded simply through previously established associations between the test elements. All of the animals had ample opportunity indeed to observe fruit being cut and, in the case of the female subjects, to use a knife approximately in this way themselves. Similarly, all three female subjects immersed sponges in water and marked or scribbled on paper with a variety of writing implements.

However, not all of the test objects had been associated with the test implements. For example, in the animal's experience cups and balls had not been marked or scribbled on, nor had balls and sponges been severed. Nevertheless the animals responded as accurately to the new object–implement combinations as to the old combinations. In addition, on five trials in each test, the correct choice required the animal to choose in opposition to previously established object–implement associations, yet on these occasions too the animals performed as accurately as on other trials. For example, despite frequent past associations between water and sponge and water and ball, all female subjects chose knife in both cases, the appropriate implement for converting an intact ball or sponge into a severed one. Likewise, paper towel was most frequently associated with writing implement, yet container of water was chosen and not pencil or crayon.

In choosing a knife when given an intact sponge and a severed one, the animal could not have been guided by previous object–implement associations. None of the implements was associated with an intact sponge, whereas water was the implement most frequently associated with an intact sponge. Yet the animals chose knife, an implement not associated with either an intact or a severed sponge. Choices of this kind indicate that the animals responded not on the basis of established object–implement associations but in terms of action schemas (Piaget, 1954), abstract internalized representations of the relation between a kind of implement and a kind of outcome or terminal state. This too is an association but not one between specific objects and implements. Instead, it is a relation the variables or arguments of which must be defined with sufficient abstractness so that one can identify indeterminately many new instances of the relation. Although the animals had not previously seen a severed ball or a marked cup, they were nonetheless able to identify them as the outcome or

terminal state of a particular operation and so to chose the appropriate implement as accurately as when the relation was instanced by old variables.

Object–implement associations can be further discounted as an explanatory
factor by comparing real action with the visual representations of action used in
the tests. They are far from identical. The remarkable extent to which you and I
tend to overlook this fact is itself a measure of the degree to which we have
internalized abstract representations of cutting, wetting, etc., and so can effort-
lessly use a host of representations to instance or reconstruct action. Real action,
of course, is a continuous sequence. An agent uses an instrument, producing a
continuous change in an object—an apple parting beneath the downward moving
knife, the sponge filling with water, the paper becoming covered with marks. It
is evident that the three-element sequences used in the test departed dramatically from real action. There was no agent; the instrument was not brought into
play but simply lay alongside the objects; both the intact and the operated-on
object were present at the same time, unlike real action in which the object in its
initial state turns gradually into the object in its terminal state. In brief, there
was no progressive change characteristic of real action, but only the two digital
highlights of the analog sequence. If these tests had failed one might then have
reasonably proposed that the animals could not identify or reconstruct real
action from such static or discrepant representations. It will be necessary to use,
say, motion pictures, realistic depictions from which perhaps the animal can
then recognize real action and supply the missing elements. Obviously, however,
this was not the case.

Moreover, the present representations need not constitute the most extreme
reduction that the chimpanzee can manage. The animal may succeed with still
weaker representations. If we can establish the representations that the animal
can and cannot use this must further our understanding of the perception and
reconstruction of reality; but it is as difficult to deal with this matter as it is
critical, and so far we have not studied it. Even the present results make clear,
however, that the chimpanzee can reconstruct action from weak representations;
it does not need more nearly veridical representations, such as motion pictures.

Because Sarah had been taught the conditional particle more than 3 years
before being given the nonverbal tests and was expert in its use, one might
conclude in a Whorfian manner (Whorf, 1956) that her competence in the
conditional sentence contributed to her success on these tests. However, we
neglected to teach Sarah to use "if–then" specifically in the context of physical
relations—e.g., "If you put a sponge in water it will absorb water"—and instead
used it only in so-called arbitrary cases—e.g., "If Sarah takes red (not green),
then Mary give Sarah chocolate." It is difficult to see how this use of the
conditional could contribute to an understanding of physical action. Furthermore, and more conclusively, neither Peony nor Elizabeth had been taught the
conditional particle nor any other connective, and yet Peony's performance was

indistinguishable from Sarah's, and Elizabeth, too, before she became sick, passed the first and therefore most critical test. If we equate causal inference in at least the physical domain with the action schema, then it is clear that language plays no essential role in the development of causal inference.

FUNCTIONAL KNOWLEDGE VERSUS CAUSAL INFERENCE

Suppose we say that the visual tests do not prove that the subject makes a causal analysis but only that, as one student put it, the chimps know "that scribbles go with pencils" or that water makes things wet or that knives cut. What is the difference, however, between knowing what an instrument does and making a causal inference? To answer this we must first decide what is involved in knowing what an instrument does.

Cutting, wetting, marking and other similar acts involve an assymetrical relation between two classes of items—in cutting, for example, those with a sharp edge on the one hand and those with a penetrable surface on the other. To be expert in these acts one must be able to recognize members of both classes. In addition, one must be able to recognize the endpoint, when an object is cut, wet, marked or the like, so that one knows when to stop applying the instrument. A subject who was paid for the rate at which it cut would show its expertise by choosing a sharp rather than dull blade, oranges rather than rocks, and by moving to the next orange as soon as the preceding one was cut. All of this information can be summarized by saying that a knowledge of cutting entails the assumption that if one applies an appropriate instrument to an appropriate object, a predictable outcome will result. I see little difference between this functional knowledge and causal inference except in the greater generality of the latter.

A theory of causality would seem to be a generalized version of the functional knowledge, having perhaps three main aspects. First, every cause has an effect and every effect a cause. An organism that held this theory could never experience a change, the cause of which escaped its attention, without supposing that in the preceding instant there was an event that further inspection would show qualified as a cause. A somewhat comparable view would be the assumption that the world can be divided into pairs of classes, each pair of which carried out the assymmetrical relation of cause and effect or instrument and object.

Second, the cause–effect relation is invariant. If a knife pressed into an apple on Monday causes the apple to split, on Tuesday the same knife pressed in a comparable way into a comparable apple must have the same effect. This is an example of our general assumption about the stability or orderliness of the world. We further believe in irreversibility for most cases. For example, we do not expect to see an egg unboil or a severed apple reverse the change and return to its intact state.

Third, if a knife is pressed into an apple, it is the apple acted upon that is cut and not some other object that is related to the apple. For example, we do not try to cut the fruit in a basket by removing one fruit from the basket and cutting it. One can, however, picture a world in which once a group of items was established by common features, locale or the like, the whole group could be affected simply by acting on one member of the group. We believe instead in what can be called specificity; it is only the item acted upon that changes and not other items, no matter how intimately they may be related to the item in question.[1]

These three beliefs are part of human causal analysis and are not directly evidenced by the visual tests. One might suppose they could not be evidenced except with the use of language. In a linguistically competent species there are two other kinds of evidence that can be used in addition to tests of the visual kind. Competence in the conditional sentence form is itself one of the least refutable forms of evidence for causal inference. We anticipate this form in the child. In the adult, a second form is also possible, for the inference presupposed by the child's linguistic competence is itself likely to become cognitively available, so that the adult talks about the inference. The adult may combine the two forms of evidence, using the conditional sentence form to discuss causal inference: "If Hume recognized that causal inference was not a logical but a perceptual inference, then he was as much a psychologist as a philosopher." These forms of evidence seem to go beyond the nonverbal evidence. Perhaps they do, however, only because we mistakenly equate the subject's awareness of the inference, which is at its maximum in the adult above, with the propriety of our inferring that the subject makes the inference. It is not awareness of the inference but the inference per se we are trying to establish at this point.

I leave open the question of whether there is a class of questions that can be answered only with verbal evidence, that is, only by communicating with the other one through language. My basic intuition is that there is no such class. The evidence that can be obtained with language has a uniquely high resolving power and some of the devices that account for this exceptional resolution can be specified but the difference seems to be one of degree; not to mention, of course, the extraordinary convenience that language affords compared to nonverbal procedures. Moreover, we do not obtain, and probably should not seek, conclusive evidence in any case, either with language or without it. Our best hope is a convergence, of several verbal tests, nonverbal tests, and of each with

---

[1] If an orange were chosen from a bowl of oranges and cut, the other oranges would be unaffected. However, if a person were chosen from a group of people and shot, the other people would not be unaffected. The specificity condition does not apply with equal force to all cases.

the other, so for this reason alone we are better off with the linguistically competent organism.[2]

Although there may be no questions that can be addressed only with language, there are, however, answers (that is, theories) that can be defended only with certain kinds of evidence. This evidence does not depend strictly on language, however, but on the ability of the organism to recognize representations of its own behavior and/or that of another. As we have already seen, moreover, there is an intimate relation between the two: language is not possible without the capacity. However, it is the capacity—and not specifically a linguistic elaboration of the capacity—that is needed in order to defend certain answers or theories.

[2] We are more accustomed to the opposite side of the argument, where evidence obtained with the use of language is deprecated as being "merely verbal." The deprecation comes from a context very different from the one we have been considering. In that context, language is used to ask the subject to state his attitude or belief about some issue (in effect, to describe his previous behavior and/or predict his future behavior), and an inconsistency is discovered between what the subject says and does, or between what he says on different occasions. For instance, a subject who is asked, "Do you think blacks cause crime?" answers "No" unequivocally, but later is found resisting the purchase of real estate in his neighborhood by blacks and extolling police procedures in the ghetto.

In asking the subject "Do you think blacks cause crime?" we, of course, presuppose the concept of cause. Only on that presupposition is it reasonable to accuse the subject of inconsistency between what he says and does, and to regard him as a liar. In the context which verbal evidence is extolled, however, all the basic concepts presupposed by the former context are themselves at issue. The difference is that between does the subject think X causes Y, and does the subject understand the notion of cause.

The relation between nonverbal evidence and the first question is far simpler than that between nonverbal evidence and the second question. We are confident that we know what nonverbal evidence to collect in order to determine whether or not the subject thinks X causes Y—and use verbal interrogation only as a shortcut. It would be inconvenient to trail each subject around, actually collecting the nonverbal evidence that could serve as a test basis.

In the second case, however, we are not at all clear about what nonverbal evidence to collect. What does a subject do if he makes causal inferences that he does not if he does not make causal inferences? That question is not nearly as easy to answer as "What does a subject do if he thinks blacks cause crime?"—and it is the difficulty of answering that question which creates the intense desire to be able to talk to the subject.

Verbal evidence is also commonly deprecated on the grounds that only with language is it possible to lie or behave deceitfully. In fact, you can lie or deceive quite nicely without language. For example, imagine the inconsistent subject from the example above to encounter a black evidently in flight from the police. He gives the black refuge, even serving as a lookout, finally when the coast is clear gesturing the black out of hiding. Later when the police arrive, he informs them of the black's presence, pointing out the direction in which he fled. Deceit depends not on language but on a capacity for second-order inference. The organism which believes that if it behaves in a certain way the other one must draw certain conclusions about why it has behaved that way is qualified for deceit or lying. The capacity for second-order inference may or may not be elaborated linguistically, but it is that capacity and not language per se on which lying depends.

For example, if a species did not have the representational capacity, it would not be possible to defend the view that the species made causal inferences. The only kind of tests that could be made in this case would be those that dealt with first-order events. For example, we could show, as Köhler (1951) did, the chimpanzee's impressive problem-solving ability. Evidence of this kind persuades many that the ape is thoughtful and almost certain to make causal inferences; but such evidence can always be accounted for without inferring causal inference, in terms of standard stimulus—response—reward formulas. This does not prove that the animal does not make causal inference, but the burden of proof is then on the other party. This says that the kind of inference one can defend for a species depends on the kind of tests one can make with the species, and this in turn depends on the capacity of the species.

13
Quantifiers and This/That

Our attempts to teach counting to the chimpanzees have enjoyed notably little success—so little that even the elementary stages of counting now loom as a far greater challenge than the elementary stages of language. Of course, this view is not incompatible with the development of the child—it displays a considerable grasp of language before showing any numerical skills. However, the view is contradicted by at least one reported success of teaching chimpanzees to count (Ferster, 1964). Unfortunately, this study is marred by the absence of a test requiring the animals to respond to magnitudes different from those used in training, and the number of magnitudes used in training were "small," easily within the chimpanzee's memorization capacity. Although it does not do simply to darken this reported success by placing it in the shadow of our failure, I cannot but remain skeptical until shown the results of a transfer test.[1]

[1] Counting is not the only method for assigning magnitudes to collections of items. In an analysis by Klahr and Wallace (1973), counting is one of three quantification operators, the other two being *subitizing* (Kaufmann, Lord, Reese, & Volkmann, 1949) and *estimating*. "Subitizing" is the name given to the assignment of magnitudes that cannot be the result of counting. The assignment is either by young children or animals who do not know how to count, or by adults who are not given enough time to count. The magnitude is always "small," the limit being five or six in the adult, no more than two or three in the young child. Subitizing is not a process understood as such, therefore, but simply the name given to the assignment of magnitudes to "small" collections of items by organisms that either cannot count or cannot in the time allowed them.

Once an organism becomes able to count it does not necessarily give up subitizing but may combine the two methods. For example, when asked to report the number of items in a display, adults take 40 msec for up to about five items, and 300 msec per item thereafter. Klahr and Wallace suggest that the first five items may be judged by subitizing, those beyond five by counting. If the adult is given sets larger than five, say, 200 or more, and given them in an interval of time too short for counting, the judgment may then be made by estimation, the third of the operators proposed by Klahr and Wallace, and according to

ONE-TO-ONE CORRESPONDENCE

Aletha Solter (1975) has worked out a training program to teach counting to very young children which begins by teaching one-to-one correspondence and progresses from there through several intermediate steps to the cardinality rule, which makes counting possible. In attempting to teach one-to-one correspondence to the chimps, we used Solter's approach. A small set of wooden cubes was the counters, and a set of blocks was one of several target sets that it was hoped the chimps could ultimately be taught to count. By the usual combination of modeling and passive guidance we attempted to teach Sarah, Peony and Elizabeth to put one counter on each block, in effect to carry out this rule: Leave no countee without a counter and do not put more than one counter on any countee. This simple rule can be given various interpretations, such as that of Orthodox Judaism: every man shall wear a hat but no man shall wear more than one at a time.

---

them the most complex and the last to form. In brief, subitizing is a precounting process for judging "small" magnitudes and estimating is a postcounting process for judging "large" magnitudes. Although Klahr and Wallace attempt to define estimation in terms of explicit steps, there is no evidence that estimation can be taught and still less that subitizing can be reduced to a set of steps and taught to organisms that do not subitize. Counting, which can be applied to all magnitudes of course, is so far the only quantification procedure that is understood well enough to be subject to even the possibility of being taught.

Animals make numerosity judgments that appear to be examples of subitizing. The best known are those reported by Koehler (1937) for ravens, parrots, jackdaws and other birds. In Koehler's tests, the bird was given a collection of corn or grain and at the start of each daily session taught to eat a specific number of them, at first only two, another day three, up to seven for the ravens and parrots, only about five for the pigeon. Later, the bird demonstrated its ability to "count" by stopping at the designated number when given other collections of grain, different from the original set in both number and geometrical arrangement.

There were two apparent boundary conditions. The criterion number was changed between but not within sessions, and the items enumerated were homogeneous, all grains, never for example a mixture of grain and pieces of apple. Although Koehler did not report that the birds could not manage collections of mixed items, it would be surprising if they could. Children, when three or four years old, successfully judge collections of up to four items, but only when the collections are homogeneous. If given collections of diverse items, they divide the items into two groups of like items and tend to ignore the smaller group (Gast, 1957).

We find the same limitations, albeit in a slightly different form, with the chimps. Given counters which they are to put into one-to-one correspondence with a small collection of items, they tend to skip the odd item. For instance, they put a counter on each of three items that are the same size, but none on a fourth item that is either smaller or larger than the other three. Gelman and Tucker (1975), however, have questioned the generality of these results. They have found children as young as $2\frac{1}{2}$ years to quantify over heterogeneous as well as homogeneous sets, and suggest that Gast may have trained his subjects exclusively on homogeneous sets. As far as the chimpanzees are concerned, Gelman and Tucker are correct, and their point is well taken.

Despite the apparent simplicity of one-to-one correspondence, the rule was not readily learned. A major difficulty was the lack of agreement between the subjects and the trainers as to what constituted the end of an episode. A subject might put a counter on each block but, if the trainer did not approve promptly, proceed to add a counter or two to some of the blocks for good measure or, as Elizabeth was fond of doing, put counters into perfect correspondence with the blocks, but then replicate the process, that is, take away a counter, replace it with a new one, and go on doing so, never violating the one-to-one rule but never quite consummating it either. It became necessary to introduce a formal period marker, which we did by giving the subject a bell that it was required to ring when it had completed an episode. Sarah adapted to the bell readily and went on to learn one-to-one correspondence with the training materials as well as to pass some of the many transfer tests that lay ahead.

In a sample of children, average age 3 years, 11 months, Solter (1975) found all children to learn one-to-one correspondence on the first session, typically after only one demonstration. In contrast, Sarah required many sessions, and the other subjects have never fully learned it. Even after reaching the point when they were likely to carry out one-to-one correspondence, they still "spoiled" the occasional trial by dribbling out an extra counter, removing a needed one, looking quizzically into the trainer's eyes, asking in effect, "Am I really done?" None of this difficulty was seen in the child.

One could dismiss the comparison by noting that children are generally more imitative (of human trainers) than are chimps, which is probably true. What I would add, however, is that if the tasks on which chimps imitate man were rank ordered, one-to-one correspondence would be low on the list. It is not salient for chimpanzees in the way it is for children. When the ape placed cubes in egg carton holes or alongside boxes, it appeared to be forming aesthetic configurations, not exemplifying a logical rule.

A comparable difference between the two species, even more striking in degree, was seen in yet another precursor of counting, viz., forming an ordered series. We tested for this capacity in three ways. First, we gave the chimpanzees a set of three items, such as three sticks, dolls or stones, that differed in length, width, thickness, weight or combinations thereof, and simply looked for any spontaneous tendency they might show to arrange the items in a monotonic order. Next, with the children we asked them either to put the dolls "in order," or to "line them up." Finally, with both species we placed the items in a monotonic order and invited them to do the same. The apes did not produce monotonic orders more often than would be expected by chance (most of their arrangements could not even be judged for monotonicity because the items were overlapped rather than being placed in parallel or end to end), and they were generally poor at imitating order when it was shown them.

In contrast, three to seven year old children readily produced monotonic order both imitatively and from instructions. Figure 13.1 illustrates what was most

Arrangement	Frequency	
	old	young
Ⅰ Ⅰ Ⅰ	1	0
 Ⅰ Ⅰ Ⅰ	13	4
 Ⅰ Ⅰ Ⅰ	1	8
 Ⅰ Ⅰ Ⅰ	1	2
 ☰	1	0
 ⅼ ⅼ ⅼ	1	1
 ☰	1	0
●—● ●—● ●—	1	0
 ●— ●— ●—	1	0
 ☰	0	1
 ⤳	0	1
 ☰	0	1

FIG. 13.1 The frequency with which younger and older children used different physical arrangements to place different-size dolls in a montonic order, in response to either instructions or a model.

notable about the children's performances. Every arrangement shown was produced at some time by one child or another, and most children produced more than one arrangement. We ran two groups of children, 12 who were 5 years, 2 months to 6 years, 9 months with an average age of 5 years, 1 month, and 14 who were 2 years, 7 months to 5 years, 1 month with an average age of 3 years, 8 months. Half of the children in each group were tested first on the imitation condition and then on the instructions and the other half were tested in the reverse order. Eleven of 12 children in the older group and 11 of 14 in the younger group produced monotonic orders when told either to "line them up" or "put them in order," with no significant effect of instruction. On the imitation test, all children in the older group and 10 of 14 in the younger group produced monotonic orders. Interestingly, on the imitation test significantly more children in the older group copied the trainer exactly: 10 of 12 in the older group compared to only 4 of 14 in the younger group ($p < .05$). On a second session give 48 hours later, somewhat more older children used the same arrangement as they had on the first session, 6 of 12 older children compared to only 3 of 14 younger children ($p < .10$). By even 3 years of age, therefore, the child has a concept of ordered series, one sufficiently abstract so that the concept can be realized by physically different arrangements. This is admittedly order for size not numerosity but it seems likely that the two are related. Perhaps the difference between the older and younger children can be understood in terms of metaknowledge; the older child may better know what it knows than the younger child or have a more acute access to its own behavior.

When items are used simply to form patterns, ordered series and one-to-one correspondence are not likely outcomes. Perhaps the difference between the species comes simply from the fact that the child is either less disposed than the ape to use items in this aesthetic fashion, or better able to suppress the disposition. Although the child may have greater suppressive powers, it seems in addition to have a clearer perception of the rule-exemplifying patterns; for the trained chimpanzee is by no means blind to the cultural distinction in question. As discussed in another context (page 82), it distinguishes between canonical and noncanonical ways of handling objects and, once school is announced, largely suppresses the latter. It is not sufficient to say that the ape draws this distinction with less surety than the child. In the case of size-orderable nonverbal items, the ape seems not to have a clear grasp of what constitute canonical operations. Ultimately, however, this comparison is confounded for the experience of the two groups is not comparable. Even in the course of a day the child is exposed to arrangements that either instance necessary conditions for monotonic order or are actual examples of such order. In almost any direction in which the child looks there are stacks of items—books, magazines, records, clothes, plates, towels—not to mention layered cakes and silverwear laid side by side. Some of the items are stacked according to size and are therefore actual cases of monotonic order. Although the child may or may not be affected by these cases, the fact that it has more opportunities of this kind than the laboratory chimpanzee confounds the comparison between the two. The chimpanzee's failure to seriate may be more experiental than species specific.

TRANSFORMATIONS THAT DO AND DO NOT
PRESERVE UNITARY STATUS

Whenever the individual blocks in the one-to-one correspondence tests were placed "too" close together, all three subjects made an interesting kind of "error." Peony especially was inclined to place one counter across the juncture of the two blocks rather than a separate counter on each block; Sarah and Elizabeth did this too although in lesser degree. Does Peony simply enjoy conquering the meticulous demands of laying counters across gaps or, as seems more likely, is it rather that once the separation between two items falls below a limit, the two items are no longer viewed as separate? The effect of *adjacency* was brought out still more sharply by our attempts to use the vertical axis as part of a transfer test. We put one block on top of another, rather naively assuming that the subject would put two counters on the top block; but more often they put only one. Did this mean that the chimps did not understand one-to-one correspondence or rather, as was suggested by their earlier treatment of horizontally adjacent items, two vertically superimposed blocks do not equal two items?

What initially were viewed as transfer tests for one-to-one correspondence came subsequently to be seen as transformations under which items did and did not preserve their unitary status. Although for the human subject simple physical adjacency is not likely to deprive most items of their unitary status, there are other operations which will have this effect even in the adult human. Consider, for example, that when given a peeled banana the human subject places one counter into correspondence with it, indicating the unitary status of the banana. On another occasion, when given just the peel of a banana, the same subject indicates the unitary status of the peel by placing one counter into correspondence with it. Now, when subsequently given an intact banana, how many counters does the subject place into correspondence with it? Does it put out one for the peel and one for the banana inside the peel, or with the banana inside its peel, is it not more likely to put out only one counter for both the banana and the peel?

The semantic primitive in this example is *containment,* instanced not only by natural cases such as bananas and their skin, but also by artificial ones such as beans and cans, powder and boxes, or paints and trays. For example, although a pile of beans and an empty can are seen as two items, once the beans are inside the can the combination is seen as one item and linguistic usage follows perception. When the can and the beans are separate, we talk about a can and beans. Once the beans are inside the can, however, we talk no longer of a can and beans but rather of a can of beans. Containment is a strong transformation that overcomes the unitary status of items in a way that simple adjacency does not. In containment, one plus one equals one. One could conceive of a device, different from ourselves, for which containment would be a weak transformation, one preserving the unitary status of the items. For such a device an intact banana would be two items, and so would a can of beans.

With young children we tried a different kind of transformation, one designed to unify originally separate items on the basis of a common semantic function. We considered that appropriate animation might turn a chain of wooden blocks, originally judged to be separate items, into an animal, vegetable, or shelter, after which the children would judge the chain to be one item. Suppose the experimenter pulled a chain of blocks toward a dish of water, raised the lead block from the table, and repeatedly dipped the "head" into the water, giving the chain of blocks a good drink. Would the children now place one counter into correspondence with the whole chain or still place counters into correspondence with individual blocks? Or suppose the chain of blocks was suspended from a tree and a toy animal stepped forward and greedily ate the blocks. Would the bunch of blocks receive one counter or as many as there were blocks? Solter tested this possibility with a similar animation of a 3-block chain with 10 3⁻4-year-old children. After moving the blocks about in an animal-like manner, she curled the chain up to sleep in a nest. The children watched attentively. But when given the counters, they put one on each block quite as they had before the animation. At 3⁻4 years of age, the children were younger than the age at which children are said to use functional classes (e.g., Bruner, 1968). Also, there was the possibility, suggested by some of the children's remarks, that in putting a counter on each block the child was enumerating the separate parts of the animal. To do the experiment properly, we may need to use not one kind of counter but several, each appropriate to a different level of organization. Little counters, say, for parts of the animal, medium size for the animal, still larger for a herd of animals, etc.

VERBAL QUANTIFIERS

Although the chimpanzees have not yet fully mastered one-to-one correspondence, let alone learned to count, there is nonetheless a form of quantification that Sarah has acquired readily. Peony and Elizabeth have not yet been tried. Sarah learned to use "all," "none," "one," and "several," and thus to specify in which of four degrees a collection of items possessed a given property. For virtually any "small" group of items she could say whether one, some, none, or all members of the group were round, square, red, large, etc. That is, once trained on the quantifiers she could apply them to any of the properties for which she had been taught a name.

ALL VERSUS NONE

"All" and "none" were the first quantifiers taught Sarah, followed by "one" and "several." Two sets of five crackers each were used in training: All crackers were round in one set and all square in the other. The set consisting of square elements was placed before her and she was given the question: "? crackers is pl square" (What or how many crackers are square?). The only word given her was "all," with which she displaced the interrogative marker, forming the sentence

"All crackers is pl square" (All crackers are square). Next, we placed the set of round crackers before her and gave her the same question, "? crackers is pl square," but this time the one word given her was "none." She displaced the interrogative marker, forming the sentence "None crackers is pl square" (None of the crackers is square). (Notice that in the case of all—none, we arbitrarily elected to pluralize both forms: "All is pl round" and "None is pl round.")

When the same questions were repeated with Sarah choosing between "all" and "none," she quit after only 8 trials, which was not uncommon, but she made 3 errors in the 8 trials, which was uncommon. On the next lesson she was given 20 more choice trials of the same kind and made 12 errors, with 6 on "none" and 6 on "all."

The lessons were modified by adding a third set of crackers, all of them triangular, and two further questions. The original and modified lessons are diagramed in Figure 13.2, the left portion of the figure showing the original form of the lesson, the right portion the revised form. To gain a sense of the task that confronted Sarah, cover all the material in each lesson except for one question and one set of crackers. Notice that in the original form of the lesson only one question was asked—"? crackers is pl square"—sometimes in the presence of crackers that were exclusively square, other times in the presence of those that were exclusively round (making the proper answer to the question "all" in the first case and "none" in the second). In the revised lesson, three different questions were asked instead of one, and each one was asked in the presence of three different sets of crackers. On the revised form of the training she made four errors in 15 trials, dividing her errors evenly over the possibilities. Her 74% correct was still below criterion but was an improvement over the preceeding lessons.

The original lesson in all—none was atypical and provided Sarah with less information than the standard lesson. Typically, Sarah was given two pieces of positive and negative information, respectively. In the case of color, for instance, she was told: "Red color of apple," "Yellow color of banana," "Red not color of banana," and "Yellow not color of apple." In effect, this is A, this is B, A is not B, and B is not A. In the first version of the present lesson, however, Sarah was given only half of the usual information. "All crackers are square" was associated with the square set and "None of the crackers is square" with the round set. In effect, this is A, and A is not B. If the lesson had followed the usual format, "All crackers are round" would have been associated with the round set and "None crackers is round" with the square set. The missing information was provided in the revised lesson in which three sentences were associated with each set. Two sets of crackers would have been sufficient to convey the standard amount of information but we added a third set for emphasis. In doing so, we may actually have provided too much information.

What is the optimal amount of information for teaching names for the various concepts? It is going to be some time before we really know, for we have

QUANTIFIER LESSONS

FIGURE 13.2

deferred systematic changes in training procedures of a kind that are needed to answer such questions. We have simply relied heavily on two positive and two negative instances of each concept, having changed training programs only when forced to do so by failure.

ONE VERSUS SEVERAL

A number of arrangements can be used to teach the distinction between "one" and "several." In the approach we used, each word was instanced by six different sets, each set consisting of five crackers of two different shapes. The sets used to teach "one" contained one cracker with a shape different from that of the other four crackers, whereas the sets used to teach "several" contained either two or three crackers of one shape, the remainder of a different shape. "Several" could therefore mean either two or three crackers of the same shape. For instance, "Several crackers are round" could be applied to the following four sets: two round and three square, two round and three triangular, three round and two square, and three round and two triangular.

Each of the 12 training sets was placed before Sarah one at a time and she was asked a question appropriate to it. For example, in the presence of the set containing only square crackers, she was asked the question, "? cracker is square," (What or how many crackers are square?). The only alterntive given here was "one," with which she replaced the interrogative marker to form the sentence "One cracker is square." On other occasions, a set containing two round and three square crackers was placed before her and she was asked the question "? cracker is pl square" (What or how many crackers are square?). Because the only alternative given her was "several," she formed the sentence "Several cracker is pl square."

Next she was presented with the same sets and questions but was given both "one" and "several" and so was required to choose between them. She made only one error on the first ten trials. The one¬several distinction may be simpler than the all¬none distinction, not merely because it was taught later but also because "several" and "one" correspond with the presence and absence, respectively, of the plural marker. We say "One is round" but "Several is pl round" (whereas in all¬none we say "All is pl round" and also "None is pl round").

Because her terminal performance on all¬none was substandard (74% correct), we gave her a review on this distinction, using ten questions from the revised lesson, with the same three sets shown in Figure 13.2.

She was correct on eight of the ten review trials. Then the sets from the all¬none and the one¬several exercises were combined for the first time and she

FIG. 13.2 Examples of material used to teach quantifiers: (a) original lesson; (b) modified lesson (after Premack, 1971).

was asked the same questions as before but with the requirement that she choose among all four alternatives—"all," "none," "one," "several." She was correct on eight of the first ten trials.

The transfer test presented a special problem. Notice that the sets used to instance the quantifiers have differed from one another solely in terms of shape, which is a narrower inductive base than we have had occasion to use with previous words. Moreover, the few shape words Sarah knew had all been used in training, leaving no new shape words for the transfer test. We were therefore left with a choice of either teaching her new shape words or conducting the transfer test with a class property other than the one used in training. The latter was decidedly the more interesting alternative, for it raised this question: Could she transfer the quantifiers not only to nontraining items but also to items that differed in properties other than shape?

CROSS-DIMENSIONAL TRANSFER

The properties used in the transfer test were color and, to a lesser extent, size. Sets differing in color were prepared in one case by dying pieces of apple red and green and in the other case by leaving the yellow and green peel on slices of ripe and unripe banana, respectively. Sets based on size were composed of pieces of bread of two different sizes. Ten of the 18 sets used in the training of the four quantifiers were duplicated, with either color or size values substituted for the original shape values. For example, color sets consisted of five red pieces of apple, four green and one red, two red and three green, four pieces of yellow banana and one green, etc. Seven of the sets were based on color and three on size. She was asked the same question as before, although now the questions were framed in terms of color and size rather than shape, and, as before, she was given all four quantifiers among which to choose.

For example, in the presence of a set consisting of three green and two red pieces of apple, she was asked, "? apple is pl green" (What or how many apples are green?). She answered correctly by replacing the interrogative marker with "several," forming the sentence "Several apple is pl green." Sarah was correct on nine of the first ten trials. Had she failed this test, we might then have sought to devise training procedures conducive to cross-dimensional transfer, but she succeeded, and on the basis of a training program that would seem to make a minimal contribution to cross-dimensional transfer. The power in this case must be attributed to the organism, not to the training program. Indeed, if an organism were deficient in matters of this kind, it would by no means be clear what one could do to overcome the deficiency, although it would be of the greatest interest to try.

QUANTIFIERS APPLIED TO IMPERATIVE SENTENCES

Could she use the quantifiers in sentences of a grammatical structure different from those used in training? All the training sentences had been descriptive or declarative: All (one, none, several) cracker (apple, banana) is (pl) round (square, red, big, etc.). Therefore, in the test, we used the quantifiers in sentences of an imperative form. A dish and a large number of both crackers and candies were arrayed before her, and she was given instructions of the following kind: "Sarah insert all (the) crackers (in the) dish." When she responded correctly, she was allowed to keep whatever she put into the dish. The routine was familiar to her, as was the use of the imperative sentence. The only new element was the application of quantifiers to imperative sentences.

She responded correctly to the first five instructions: (1) "Sarah insert all cracker dish"; (2) "Sarah insert several cracker dish"; (3) Sarah insert one candy dish"; (4) "Sarah insert all candy dish"; and (5) "Sarah insert several candy dish." On the next two instructions, when told to insert "none" cracker and "several" cracker, she obeyed insofar as the crackers were concerned but supplemented the instructions a little with candy, inserting one piece in the first case and all in the second. The trainer was nonplussed but decided to allow the performances to pass on the grounds that, first, the action on the candy was not specifically interdicted and second, the explicit part of the instructions dealing with crackers were, in fact, carried out. The trainer gave one more instruction, "Sarah insert one candy dish." At this point, Sarah took all the candy and the lesson was terminated. The first five instructions, and even the next two to some extent, point to this same conclusion: Sarah's grasp of the quantifiers was not limited by a syntactic factor; she understood them in sentences of a grammatical form different from those used in training.

SARAH'S REACTION TO "NONE" OR DENIAL

A test similar to the one above was given several months later to review and keep alive the quantifiers which had received little use in the interval. It was of interest on two scores: first, the sheer magnitude of the retention that Sarah showed and second, the behavior she displayed in meeting instructions that took the form of denial. Her versatility in dealing with denial is not merely a comical aspect of chimpanzees but an indicator of a high grade of complexity or intelligence.

The test consisted of 15 instructions to put specified amounts of cracker in a cup. On each trial five crackers were placed before her in the presence of the cup and the trainer wrote one of the following instructions on the board: "Sarah insert all (one, several, none) cracker."

She made only one error, on Trial 7, taking two crackers when told to take one. On the trials involving "none" she did not err in inserting an improper number of crackers but operated on the crackers and other materials in the lesson in ways not explicitedly covered by the instructions. When told "Sarah take none cracker" on Trials 4, 10, and 14, she responded as follows: On Trial 4 she ate one cracker, on Trial 10 she took the cup, and on Trial 14 she removed the word "none" from the board. In no case did she insert a cracker. Overall her interest in crackers was apparently only moderate. On one of five instructions involving the word "several" she took three crackers, but on the other four she took only two. Despite her modest appetite for crackers, her level of retention (94% correct) was impressive. Unfortunately, we cannot generalize from it to her ability to remember words in general, for we did not systematically remove parts of her lexicon and then test her on them after varying periods. In general, we took the opposite approach, that is, tried to keep her vocabulary alive by not allowing any word to lie fallow for a long period.

PREVERBAL ASSESSMENT OF QUANTIFIERS

A form of match-to-sample can be used to assess the subject's ability to learn the quantifiers. We tested Sarah in this manner, although not until after we had taught her the quantifiers, three years after, so that one might claim she passed the nonverbal tests as a result of having been first taught the quantifiers. This is not only highly unlikely but aside from the point, which is simply that with the quantifiers too it is possible to use nonverbal procedures to assess the conceptual structure that is presupposed by the quantifiers.

Because Sarah had already learned the quantifiers, we used a far more demanding preverbal test than we would have otherwise, in order to answer a further question. Specifically, the test demanded not only that Sarah quantify but that she do so over information that was not physically present and had therefore to be reconstructed from memory.

Consider the match to sample test in Figure 13.3. The striking thing about the test is that physically one alternative is no more like the sample than the other. The sample and alternatives all consist of the same three items—a hat, a dress, and a shoe. Nevertheless, the sample and one alternative share a simple property not shared by the sample and the other alternative. The three items in the sample all belong to Mary; similarly, the three items in the correct alternative all belong to Jane. In contrast, in the incorrect alternative the hat belongs to Sally, the dress to Ruby, and the shoe to Barbara. Thus the sample and correct alternative both instance *all*—all Mary's, and all Jane's—whereas the incorrect alternative instances one or some but not all. To be sure, although the incorrect alternative does not instance all on a criterion of ownership, it instances all

FIG. 13.3 Match-to-sample tests based on alienable possession. All items in the sample belong to Mary, all those in the correct alternative to Jane, whereas each item in the incorrect alternative has a different owner. The sample and correct alternative instance all, the incorrect alternative does not.

on other criteria, for example, manufactured goods, material, clothes. However, these criteria cannot be used to differentiate one alternative from the other.

This form of test is obviously more demanding than one in which the items to be quantified over are perceptually apprehendible. In a simple test, the sample could consist of, say, all blue items, the correct alternative of all red ones, and the incorrect alternative of items mixed in color. In this case too the sample and correct alternative both instance *all* (all blue, all red), but this fact is directly perceivable whereas if certain simple precautions are observed ownership can only be reconstructed from memory.

In testing Sarah we did not use clothes but fruit, a category more germane to her experience. However, the change in category in no way changed the logic of the test: possession or belonging remained the criterion over which it was necessary to quantify. In the example shown in Figure 13.4, one of many given Sarah, we again encounter three sets no two of which are uniquely alike physically. The sample and alternatives each consist of components of fruit—a stem, a peel and a wedge of fruit. In the sample, all three items come from apple;

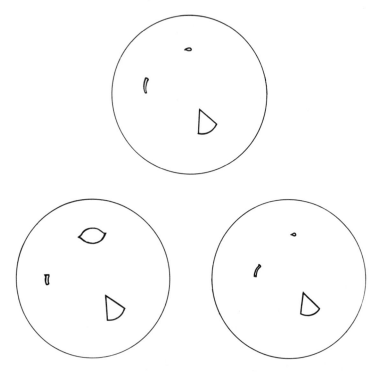

FIG. 13.4 Match-to-sample tests based on inalienable possession. All items in the sample come from apple, all those in the correct alternative come from peach, whereas each item in the incorrect alternative comes from a different fruit. The sample and correct alternative instance all, the incorrect alternative does not.

similarly in the correct alternative, all three come from peach. In contrast, in the incorrect alternative the stem comes from lemon, the peel from cherry, and the wedge from banana.

The difference between the fruit tests and the tests based on clothing is exactly the difference between alienable and inalienable possession. The relation between clothes and one who wears the clothes is a case of alienable possession; it presupposes that the subject understand ownership, or at least associate the items of clothing with specific users. The fruit and its parts exemplify inalienable possession, a bond stronger than that of ownership or association. This distinction depends upon theories about animacy and the biological integrity of an object, and we had no direct evidence that the chimpanzees held such theories, though they did appear to recognize ownership and to distinguish between the food bowls and toys that we called Sarah's, Elizabeth's, Peony's, etc. In any event, we substituted fruit for clothes not because we doubted the ape's sense of ownership, but because evidence from other tests (described in Chapter 15) showed that Sarah and the others could reliably identify the source of fruit components.

Before actually testing Sarah, we primed her with an extensive series that was intended to advise her of the topic on which we proposed to test her. One does not lead a human subject into the laboratory and, without preamble, try to test him on one of the infinitely many issues on which testing is possible. Similarly, having decided one day that we would test Sarah on her ability to quantify, specifically over part¬whole relations, it seemed advisable to inform her of that decision. I cannot prove at this time that the pretests we used are ideal or even necessary, but I think it could be shown that some form of priming—verbal or nonverbal—delimiting the alternatives from which the subject is to choose is, if not necessary, then highly facilitating; and for the human subject no less than the ape (see Restle, 1975).

To prime Sarah we used material like that to be used in the test proper, fruit and parts of fruit. Moreover, in the priming procedure samples consisted of whole fruit, unlike the test proper where they consisted of parts of fruit. In a representative priming case we gave Sarah a sample consisting of an intact apple, along with alternatives each consisting of the same three kind of items—a wedge, a seed and a cardboard outline of the shape of the fruits in question. In the correct alternative, all three came from apple, whereas in the incorrect, two came from apple and a third from banana. Although the part¬whole relation underlay the whole series, it was only implicit in the tests proper. The relation was therefore made explicit in the priming phase by using alternatives and samples that consisted of parts and wholes respectively.

In both the priming and the tests proper, training was restricted to one pair of fruit and she was given differential feedback, that is, told when correct and incorrect. Once she reached criterion on the training pair, she was given transfer tests—new fruit and no differential feedback (all of her choices were accepted and praised). The possible use of olfactory cues was eliminated by storing all fruit components in the same container. After one day's storage everything smelled like lemon; after three or four days there was a general fruit odor no longer ascribable to individual fruits, and after about two weeks the parts were dry and virtually odorless. Moreover, after inspecting the fruit in the priming phase, Sarah made her choices on a visual basis, no longer even picking up the parts, let alone tasting or smelling them. The whole series, including priming cases, consisted of 14 different tests, carried out over a period of about three months, interleaved with her other training.

Her overall success is well represented by her performance on the last three tests in the series. On the first of these tests, the sample consisted of wedge, stem and peel of apple (all); the correct alternative of color, shape and peel of banana (all); the incorrect alternative of color of orange, shape of grape, and peel of cherry (some). (Notice that by now the tests have reached the point where the kind of items in the sample are not even the same as those in the alternatives.) In seven trials she made only one error and was therefore given a transfer test involving fruit different from those used in training as well as sets consisting of new combinations of fruit parts. She made 2 errors in 12 trials.

In the next test, the sample consisted of wedge of orange, stem of grape and peel of cherry; the correct alternative of color of grape, shape of cherry and peel of orange; the incorrect alternative of color, shape and peel of apple. Thus, *some* was now the matching feature as *all* had been in the previous test. Following 16 training trials on which she made four errors, she was given two transfer tests involving both new fruit and new combinations of parts. On the first test, she made 1 error in 8 trials, and on the second, none in 10.

On the last test of the series trials of the kind used in both preceding tests were combined, so that *all* was correct on some trials and *some* on others. She was tested on the transfer condition directly, without introductory training trials. Five different fruits were used—apple, banana, orange, grape, and cherry—and five different components—peel, stem, wedge, color, and shape—and the combinations were changed from one trial to the next. She made only one error in ten trials.

These nonverbal tests established that Sarah could distinguish between conditions exemplifying all and some, hardly a surprise given that she had already acquired "all" and "some" and used them appropriately in transfer tests. Nevertheless the results for the nonverbal series contributed substantively, further defining the conditions under which the chimpanzee can process information. Most species below the ape apparently cannot make full-fledged same–different judgments even for objects let alone features of objects. The ape, in contrast, can make such judgment not only for features such as color and shape but also for *all* and *some*, features that apply not to individual items but to sets of items. Moreover, the features that can be coded as "all" or "some" can be either physically present or not. That is, *all* can be instanced by three red items, or by three parts of the same fruit, and in the latter case the source of the parts cannot be judged from visual inspection alone but must be reconstructed from memory. The subject must first tag the components in some fashion as, say, apple and then quantify over the tags. In brief, the results show that the chimpanzee can make same–different judgments over items the identity of which must be coded from memory.

All of the fruit used in the tests were items for which Sarah had been taught names. Unfortunately, we do not have comparable tests on items for which Sarah had not been taught names, and therefore although we may guess that the names facilitated her performance, we cannot prove it.

FREE VARIABLES AS PRECURSORS OF "THIS/THAT"

The use of pronouns and demonstrative adjectives makes two demands not made by previous words. The meaning of "I" and "you," for example, changes depending on who is the speaker; that is the main feature that comes to mind in thinking of these words. However, these words also differ from others in the simpler fact that they do not have a fixed referent. For example, if I say "X is red and large—take X" and on another occasion "X is yellow and small—put X in the basket," the term X functions as a pronoun in one sense but not in another. Like the pronoun, X has no fixed referent. It refers to a large red thing on one occasion, a small yellow thing on another, etc. This much is exactly analogous to a pronoun, but X differs from and is simpler than the pronoun in that its definition does not vary with the speaker. If I say to you "X is red and large, take X," and you hesitate, asking "Did you say take X," and I confirm "Yes, take X," the shift in the speaker is not accompanied by a shift in the meaning of X. For the duration of the speech episode, X is that alternative of those present which best fulfills the condition of being red and large.

Whether or not natural language has words equivalent to X as used in the example above, there is nothing to prevent our introducing such words into the chimpanzee language. The purpose of teaching Sarah such words was to learn whether or not she could use words that could be made to refer to one thing in one speech episode, and to another thing in a different speech episode. Since she had no difficulty, as this section is to show, we have taken the next step. We taught her words that could not only change referent as occasion demanded but also change with changes in the speaker. Specifically, we taught her the demonstrative adjectives "this/that," which are analogous to the pronouns in being defined relative to the speaker. "This" refers to the object closer to the speaker, "that" to the object farther from the speaker.

X/Y: PRECURSORS OF "THIS/THAT"

We taught Sarah two free variables X and Y, instead of just one, for another and separate purpose. In this period, Sarah had finally acquired the ability to say the same thing in two different ways, that is, to form synonymous constructions. Her previous competence of this kind was limited to the equivalence between "no-same" and "different," on the one hand, and "no different" and "same," on the other. With the introduction of the copula, however, the possibilities for synonomous constructions were extended to examples of this kind: "Cherry is red" and "Red color of cherry," "Apple is big" and "Big size of apple," etc. Every property she could formally ascribe to an object with a predicate adjective she could now also ascribe with a copular form. As already noted, the predicate adjective form is awkward when used to ascribe multiple properties to the same object, for example, "Red color of, large size of, round shape of watermelon," whereas the copular form handles multiple properties easily, for example, "Watermelon is large, red, round." In the present exercise we introduced X as a free variable to be used in sentences of the predicate adjective form, Y as a free variable to be used in sentences of the copular form.

The basic exercise consisted of showing Sarah eight objects, identifying one of them, and then instructing her to take it. The objects were generated by factorially combining three dimensions, each in two degrees. Each block of wood was either round or square, yellow or green, and large or small. To identify an object required stating all three of its features, and this could be done in either of the two sentence forms. On some occasions the trainer wrote "Y is round, yellow, small" in the presence of the eight objects, and then added the instruction "Sarah take Y." On other occasions the trainer wrote "Yellow color of X, small size of X, round shape of X" and then added "Sarah take X." In addition to the objectives already noted, the exercise also tested Sarah's ability to use a conjunction of three properties as the basis for identifying an object.

She was adapted to the full form of the exercise by starting with simpler cases. First, only two alternatives were used and objects were identified on the basis of only one property; then three alternatives were used and objects were identified on the basis of two properties; and finally, eight alternatives were used requiring three identifying properties. Only one lesson was devoted to these preliminary forms, however, for Sarah made only one error in ten trials (taking the large yellow circle rather than the small yellow one) and was reported by the trainers to "like the test," meaning in large part that she chose without hesitation and was not disruptive.

Over the course of four lessons she was given 51 trials, on each of which an object was identified in terms of three features and she was required to select it from eight alternatives. Descriptions took either the copular form, for example, "X is green, triangular, small," or the predicate adjective form, for example, "Green color of Y, triangular shape of Y, small size of Y." In both cases, the descriptions were left on the board to avoid memory problems, and she was told "Take X" or "Take Y" as was appropriate. Three different sets of objects were used involving the following contrasts: yellow versus green, orange versus brown, big versus small, round versus square, square versus triangular, and round versus triangular. On any trial only one of the eight objects conformed to all three properties in the description, three conformed to two, three conformed to one, and one conformed to none.

Sarah made seven errors in 31 trials on the copular form and six errors in 20 trials on the predicate adjective form. Copular statements involved only five words and predicate adjective statements nine words, perhaps accounting for the apparently better performance on the copular sentences (although the difference is not significant). All of her errors involved the choice of an object differing from the correct one by only one feature and were evenly distributed over size (where she tended to take the larger object), color, and form. Interestingly, the trainer did not describe the objects with a fixed adjective order in either the copular or the predicate adjective form, an interesting failure of (the trainer's) natural language to carry over into the plastic system. We do not know whether Sarah has a preferred adjective order, like or unlike that found in most natural languages, or whether her comprehension may be benefitted by such an order (Bever, 1970; Slobin, 1970). The results showed, first, that she could use a conjunction of three properties to identify an object and, second, that she could use words the referents of which were not fixed but varied over trials.

"THIS/THAT"

Can the chimpanzee learn words the meanings of which change with changes in the speaker? We answered that question in the affirmative by teaching Sarah "this" and "that," both as pronominal forms, for example, "Sarah insert this" vs "Sarah insert that," and as demonstrative adjectives, for example, "Give Sarah this candy" versus "Give Sarah that candy."

The training was standard in all respects except for the important fact that it was carried out concurrently in both comprehension and production. By using both modes Sarah played the role of speaker and listener at each stage and in this way was exposed to the critical fact that the meaning of "this" and "that" changed depending on whether she was the speaker or the one spoken to. Specifically, when she was the speaker, "this" referred to the object closer to her (and farther from the trainer or listener). Conversely, when she was the listener, "this" referred to the object farther from her (and closer to the trainer or listener). Therefore, "Give this cookie" referred to different cookies depending on who made the statement—and we made this difference consequential by using cookies of strikingly different size.

With the trainer and Sarah seated on opposite sides of the table, the errorless training began in the comprehension mode. Only one object was placed on the table, either closer to Sarah or to the trainer, along with a dish placed in the middle of the table. The trainer wrote "Sarah insert this" when the object was close to her and farther from Sarah, or "Sarah insert that" when the opposite condition prevailed. The dish in the center of the table served as the recepticle in both cases. The objects used—paper clips, plastic barrel, wooden block, etc.— were changed from trial to trial, as was the exact position of the object on the table. Five instructions were given of each kind.

The errorless training was then continued in the production mode. An object was placed near Sarah and across from the trainer on some trials, across from Sarah and near the trainer on other trials. Sarah was given the words "Sarah," "give," and either "this" or "that." When the object was near her she wrote

"Give Sarah this" and when it was across from her and near the trainer "Give Sarah that." She was given three errorless trials of each kind. In brief, the errorless training could be said to have introduced "this" as the name of the item closer to the speaker, "that" as the name of the item closer to the listener.

In the choice test on the comprehension mode Sarah was given the same instructions "Sarah insert this" or "Sarah insert that," but now two like objects were present, one in front of her and the other in front of the trainer. Because the objects on the table were alike, the only cue as to the meaning of "this" and "that" was the position of the object relative to Sarah and/or the trainer. She made nine errors in 40 trials over the course of three lessons, with only one error on the first five trials of the first session.

On the first test in the production mode a preferred and a nonpreferred object were placed on the table, the goodie closer to Sarah on some trials, across from her and closer to the trainer on other trials. She was given both the words "this" and "that" along with the words "give" and "Sarah." In order to obtain the preferred item she had to write "Give Sarah this" when the item was closer to her and "Give Sarah that" when it was farther from her. The test was based on the well-warranted assumption that Sarah preferred candy to a 2 × 4 card and to the extent that she knew the meaning of "this-that" would use them in such a way as to get the candy. She made 11 errors in 40 trials over the course of four lessons, again with only one error on the first five trials of the first session.

Although the choice trials were already to some extent a transfer test, some of the objects used being new, a more formal transfer test was made examining her ability to employ "this/that" in new settings. We used the comprehension mode to check the possibility that, because the position of the table had been constant throughout training, Sarah had defined "this/that" not as intended but relative to some dominant aspect of the environment. For example, the layout of the room was such that "this" could have been defined as closer to the mesh wall, "that" as the object more nearly under the light. Although this did not seem likely, we tested it by moving the table to different positions in the cage. In each new position we instructed either "Sarah insert this" or "Sarah insert that." She made three errors on 21 trials, with none in the first five trials, effectively ruling out that "this/that" was defined relative to fixed environmental cues.

In the production mode we turned to the use of "this/that" as modifiers or demonstrative adjectives. Two cookies were placed on the table, one notably larger than the other, with the larger one closer to Sarah on some trials and closer to the trainer on other trials. She was given the words "give," "Sarah," "cookie," "this," and "that" and without further training was required to write either "Give Sarah this cookie" or "Give Sarah that cookie" depending on the location of the desired cookie. The trials were repeated using large and small portions of candy and the words "give," "Sarah," "candy," "this," "that." She made three errors in 15 trials, with none on the first five trials.

14
Synonymy

Sarah was taught to deal with equivalent sentences in three ways, each one more demanding than the other. First, she was given pairs of sentences and required to make same–different judgments about them. Next she was given only one test sentence and a set of alternative sentences and was required to choose the sentence that matched the meaning but not the structure of the test sentence. Finally, she was given only one sentence along with a set of words and required to produce from scratch a sentence equivalent in meaning but different in structure from the test sentence (see Figure 14.1).

Sarah could be required to produce sentences matching the meaning but not the structure of a test sentence because we controlled the words that were available to the subject. We eliminated those words that would make possible repeating the meaning of a sentence simply by producing another sentence exactly like the test one and at the same time made available other words that permitted duplicating meaning without duplicating structure.

This procedure has a considerable advantage for subjects whose basic intelligence may be obscured by an overly powerful tendency to imitate. In fact, we have found children with exactly this problem—children whose meaningful responses were masked by a tendency to repeat not only what was said to them but also what was shown to them. Echolalic children not only repeated speech that was addressed to them but also, in a visual test, chose the same objects as those chosen by the experimenter. For example, when the experimenter chose the body of a doll from a set of alternatives, the echolalic child also chose the body of a doll from the same alternatives. In marked contrast, the nonecholalic child chose the head of the doll, thus *completing* the doll rather than repeating the experimenter's choice. This predilection to duplicate by the echolalic child and to complete by the nonecholalic one was not restricted to dismembered figures. It was found in an extensive range of materials including objects that

Synonymous sentences

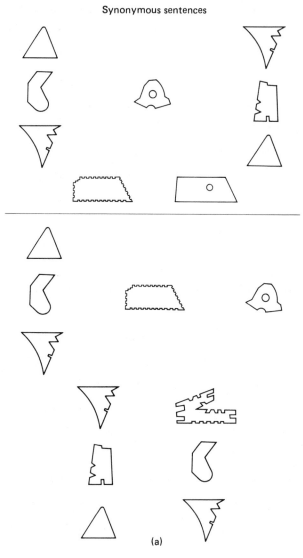

(a)

FIG. 14.1(a)

were not parts of one object but merely frequently associated with one another, such as cup and saucer, or hammer and nail. For instance, the experimenter choice of hammer led the echolalic child to choose another hammer and the nonecholalic child to choose a nail. Interestingly, however, when imitation was precluded—by removing from the set of alternatives that item which made imitation possible—the echolalic child then responded like a normal

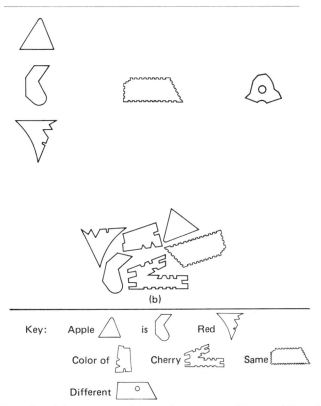

FIG. 14.1   Examples of three steps used to teach synonymy: (a) same–different judgment on a pair of sentences; choice of a semantically matching sentence; (b) construction of a semantically matching sentence.

one, completing rather than duplicating the object that the experimenter had chosen (Premack & Premack, 1974).

In the first step, Sarah was given five errorless trials on sentences of this kind: "Apple is round ? round shape of apple" (What is the relation between apple is round and round shape of apple?), "Apple is red ? red color of apple" (What is the relation between apple is red and red color of apple?), and on the negative cases "Apple is red ? round shape of apple," etc. She was given only one word on each trial, either "same" or "different" as was appropriate, with which she displaced the interrogative marker and formed the desired sentence, e.g., "Apple is red same red color of apple." The objective of the five errorless trials was simply to acquaint Sarah with the propriety of applying "same–different" to the relation between sentences. Previously her use of these words was confined to objects, such as cups and spoons. Perhaps Sarah could have made the extrapolation herself, without the errorless trials, although few of them were given in any case.

Following the five errorless trials she was asked the same questions, but with the requirement that she choose between "same" and "different." She made five errors in 20 trials, with one on the first five and three on "different." She was then given a transfer test in which the training material was retained and new material was added to it. The positive version of the new sentences consisted of "Caramel is brown same brown color of caramel" and "Caramel is square same square shape of caramel." These sentences were also paired to form the negative cases, "Caramel is brown different square shape of caramel," etc. She made two errors in 14 trials and promptly corrected both of them herself; this gave a rate of 86% correct, an improvement over her first test (75%) on this kind of material. A further transfer test was given by interpolating questions on the sentences "Nut is small ? small size of nut," and "Nut is brown ? brown color of nut." In addition, questions were asked about sentences of this kind: "Nut is brown ? caramel is brown" and "Caramel is small ? nut is small." She made only one error in ten such questions, with none on the first five. These procedures established that Sarah could make same–different judgments on sentences, and this made possible the next step.

Next, she was given only one sentence and was required to choose from a pair of sentences the one synonymous with the test sentence. Her training began with five errorless trials on the following sentences: "? same brown color of chocolate" (What is equivalent to "brown is the color of chocolate"?). On each trial she was given one complete sentence, either "Apple is red" or "Chocolate is brown," whichever was appropriate to the question. She displaced the interrogative marker with the sentence forming, for example, "Chocolate is brown same brown color of chocolate." Following the errorless trials, she was given eight trials on the same questions, but with both sentences available, and was required to choose between them. She made one error, none on the first five. The above procedure was then repeated with new sentences—"Triangular shape of cracker same cracker is triangular" and "Cracker is square same square shape of cracker." Five errorless trials were given on these sentences, followed by nine choice trials, on which she made one error and none on the first five.

The material from these lessons was then combined, so that she received four kinds of questions in the lesson and on each trial was required to choose, from four alternative sentences, the one that was equivalent to the test sentence. She made two errors in 11 trials, with one on the first five. We skipped the transfer test and went directly to the last step, which was to teach her not merely to select the synonymous sentence from a set of existing sentences but to produce such sentences from scratch. We therefore returned to the same questions asked her earlier, but now offered words as alternatives rather than already formed sentences. She was given five essentially errorless trials on "Apple is red same ?" (To what is "apple is red" equivalent?) and "Chocolate is brown same ?" (To what is "chocolate is brown" equivalent?). On each trial the three words needed to form the equivalent sentence were the only alternatives given her, so she was required only to arrange them in the sentential order. Because she made no errors on these trials, she was then given choice trials on the same questions. On each trial she was given six words, for example, "is," "brown," "color of," "red," "chocolate," and "apple," three of them needed to form the correct sentence, synonymous with the test sentence, and three incorrect, suitable for forming a nonsynonymous sentence. She was therefore required both to select the correct words and to arrange them sententially. She made one error in 14 trials, with none on the first five.

She was then given two transfer tests, first, one in which the other pairs of sentences—"Caramel is square" plus its synonym and "Caramel is brown" plus its synonym—used earlier in training were added to those already present and, second, a test in which new sentences were introduced.

On the first transfer test she was required to produce from scratch sentences equivalent to the following: "Apple is red," "Red color of apple," "Brown color of chocolate," "Chocolate is brown," "Caramel is square," "Caramel is brown," "Square shape of caramel," and "Brown color of caramel." On each trial she was given six words drawn from the set "red," "brown," "apple," "chocolate," "caramel," "color of," "is," and "square," the only restriction being that the three needed to form the correct sentence were always included. She made two errors in 17 trials, with none on the first five, or about 88% correct.

On the last transfer test of this series, sentences not used in any of the previous training steps were introduced. These included "Banana is yellow," "Grape is green," "Apple is big," and "Cherry is red." Two kinds of questions were given in a mixed order, one requiring that she make same—different judgments (Stage 1), and the other requiring that she answer with a sentence produced from scratch (Stage 3). An example of the former is: "Cherry is red ? apple is red" (What is the relation between cherry is red and apple is red?), for which the alternatives were "same" and "different." An example of the latter was "Grape is green ?" (What is equivalent to "grape is green"?), for which a representative set of alternatives was "green," "shape of," "color of," "grape," "brown," and "nut," She made 3 errors in 16 trials, 2 on same—different judgments and one on sentence production.

The sentences between which she was asked to judge were physical entities, of course, but to answer correctly her judgment could not be based on the physical identity between the two sentences. For example, "Apple is red" and "Red color of apple" are not physically alike, yet she called them "same." In fact, they are less alike physically than, for example, "Apple is red" and "Apple is round," a pair of sentences that she called "different."

We can also eliminate the possibility that the judgment was based simply on the number of overlapping words in the two sentences. Consider, again, "Apple is red" and "Red color of apple," on the one hand, and "Apple is round" and "Apple is red," on the other. Each pair of sentences shared two words, yet one pair was called "same" the other "different." Overlap in word order can also be eliminated as a basis for judgment. "Apple is red" and "Cherry is red," for example, were judged "different" although they differed in only one word and not at all in word order. In contrast, "Apple is red" and "Red color of apple" also differ only in one word but differ substantially in word order, "apple" and "red" being reversed in the two sentences. Nonethless, she called them "same." Her judgment was therefore based not on the physical makeup of the sentences but on their meaning or internal representation.

A more disturbing possibility is that she assigned essentially no meaning either to "is" or to the relational predicates "color of," etc., and instead read sentences containing these predicates simply on the basis of their associations between the noun and the adjective. That is, "Apple is red" and "Red color of apple" were read as "apple⁻red" and "red⁻apple," respectively, and these two forms were not differentiated. Moreover, since "is" was not used to distinguish tense, for example, is versus was, "is" was in many respects a dummy or expendable word. But the hypothesis is easily disconfirmed in the case of the predicate adjectives. When asked, for example, "? red color of apple" (Is red the color of apple?) and "? red shape of apple" (Is red the shape of apple?) she answered "Yes" in the first case and "No" in the second—showing that she did not ignore the predicate and read such sentences as simply "red⁻apple." Moreover, when asked to state the relation between a property and an object and given the alternatives "name of," "color of," "size of," and "shape of," she selected the correct predicate at her usual level of accuracy. There is ample reason, therefore, to discount the view that in Sarah's reading predicate⁻adjective sentences degenerated into mere noun⁻adjective associations.

Synonyms could have been used to increase the structural difference between equivalent sentences but we had few of them to use. Those we did have were accidents resulting from a turnover in trainers along with occasional lapses in communication. For instance, peach had two names, one given during the peach season of 1969, another given a year later. In a lesson on this point, Sarah had no difficulty calling these physically unrelated words "same" while at the same time calling "apple" and "peach$_1$," "orange" and "peach$_2$," and "orange" and "apple" "different," although the last three pairs were if anything physically more alike than the first pair.

A more important case we overlooked were synonymous sentences that differed not in word constituency but in word order. Many sentences employ exactly the same words with only slight variation in their order, presumably as a means of shifting the emphasis from one element to another. Even within Sarah's limited competence it would have been possible to make a study of her reaction to such forms. For example, but one of indeterminantly many families of synonymous sentences that could have been but unfortunately were not studied with Sarah was: "Big red apple is on table," "On table is big red apple," "Apple on table is big and red," etc. That they all mean the same thing can be proved by converting each of them into a yes–no question. The subject should give the same answer to each of them. Moreover, any change in size, color, or location of the apple leading to a change in the answer given to any one of the questions should bring about an identical change in the answer given to the rest of them.

That even a system as limited as Sarah's can accept so many versions of the same sentence—in the face of the confusion that such prolixity can generate—is justified presumably on the grounds that each version focuses on a slightly different aspect of the situation. One answers the question "What is on the table?"; another, "Where is the apple?"; and still another, "Which apple is on the table?" If this emphasis interpretation is correct, Sarah may have been less willing to say "same" to sentences of this kind than to those on which she has been tested. It is not clear that sentences with the form "Apple is red" and "Red color of apple" are associated with any systematic contrast—and in this sense they may have been ideal for the test.

Another interesting case we overlooked was the equivalence between sentences that were both false. For example, "Banana is blue ? blue color of banana" or "Apple is square ? square shape of apple," and the like. Although each sentence in the pair is false, each pair is nonetheless synonymous. We overlooked this case and restricted the examples of "same" to the special case in which the two sentences were not only equivalent but also true.

VISUAL VERSUS VERBAL EQUIVALENCE

Sarah was capable of producing a sentence equivalent to a given one and also of judging pairs of sentences to be same or different. Because the sentences she judged to be "same" were physically different, she must have had a method for converting one sentence form into the other or for converting both into some more elemental form. What are some possible forms and what is the process by which Sarah may convert the two sentences into a common form?

An ostensibly simple theory is decoding to a visual representation. On this view, one reduces, say, "Apple is red" to a visual representation and does the same with "Red color of apple." If the two images are the same the sentences are judged "same." This is an intuitively appealing view but notice some of the trouble it creates. For such sentences as "Apple is red" and "Cherry is red," sentences that Sarah labeled "different," the theory is ideal. In one case the image is of a cherry and in the other of an apple. Sentences the visual representations of which differ in that degree should be called "different" and in fact they are. However, consider the sentences "Apple is red" and "Apple is round," sentences that she has labeled "different." What are the differences between the visual representations in this case?

Trabasso, Rollins, and Shaughnessy (1971) and Clark and Chase (1972) have pointed out further difficulties that specifically negative sentences pose for a visual theory. We did not, unfortunately, test Sarah on any such cases, although her competence in the negative would have made it possible to have done so.

Consider, for example, "Apple is not square ? cherry is not square" (What is the relation between "apple is not square" and "cherry is not square"?).

The major alternative to the visual representation is a verbal one, which could have either of two forms: both sentences are reduced to a common elemental form, or one of the two is assumed to be in an elemental form and the other sentence is reduced to it. The present data cannot decide between these alternatives.

Is the form of the chimps' verbal representation necessarily different from the human form simply because the physical basis of the language was visual rather than auditory? This suggestion misunderstands a structural model. Presumably Sarah's words are no more stored as little pictures than human words are stored as little sounds. The form of the long-term storage of the lexicon must be independent of modality; there must be rules by which the organism can get from the long-term storage to a representation in any of the modalities in which the language happens to be realized. It is probably also a mistake to contrast visual and verbal storage in terms of the pictorial quality of the one. The difference must have to do more with the structural organization or logic of the two systems. Languages can be represented in predicate form because they are linear; visual representations are not linear, however, and their grammars must differ accordingly.

STATING THE BASIS OF EQUIVALENCE

Ultimately it is important to get beyond both the judgment and production of equivalence to the point where the subject can state the basis on which it considers two sentences to be the same. It is one thing to judge sentences to be "same," quite another to state the grounds on which one judges them to be the same. In this section we consider methods that may be used to achieve this fuller objective. Although there was no opportunity to try them with Sarah, we discuss them to get a sense of the distance that stands between the organism which can produce equivalence and the one which can state the basis of the equivalence. How vast is the distance? Can we state training programs that can bridge the distance? Are the programs merely suggestive or so well defined that their effectiveness is virtually unquestionable?

USE OF "SAME" AS A MODIFIER

A major step toward achieving the fuller objective can be made simply by teaching the subject to use "same" as a modifier. Instead of asking, say, "Apple is red ? cherry is red" (What is the relation between "apple is red" and "cherry is red"?) and receiving the answer "different," we could ask instead in what sense

"Apple is red" and "Cherry is red" are the same and receive the answer "same color." Two main kinds of sentences could be used to introduce "same" as a modifier. In one approach we could use questions of this kind: "Apple and cherry is pl same ?" offering "color of" as the alternative. It would be hoped that in this context, as in an earlier one, "Red is a color," the subject would learn to read "color of" as "color." Then the errorless substitution of "color" would produce the desired sentence "Apple and cherry is pl same color."

The second possible training sentence could be of the form: "Apple and cherry is pl ? color" with "same" given as the errorless training alternative. Then substitution would produce "Apple and cherry is pl same color" (Apple and cherry are the same color). This may be the better training sentence because it puts the emphasis squarely on the use of "same" and "different" as modifiers. The earlier alternative, in which the predicates are the substituted terms, may be more appropriately used in a test of transfer. The same procedure could be applied, of course, to the other property classes, so that the subject could also be taught to say "Cherry and ball is pl same shape," "Nut and cherry is pl same size," etc.

Given the successful introduction of "same" and "different" as modifiers, the next step would be to introduce questions the answers of which constituted a statement of the respect in which the two objects were the same. Sentences that would have the desired effect are of this form: "? apple and cherry is pl same" or "? apple and cherry is pl different," or, in English translation, In what respect (or how or even why) are apple and cherry the same, are apple and cherry different?

In fact, we do not have an interrogative form that is specific to *how* or *what manner*-type questions, any more than we have one specific to *how many*-type questions. This presents a problem that arose earlier in teaching the quantifiers. We used such questions as "? cracker is pl square" (How many crackers are square?) in teaching the quantifiers, and although we did not encounter any problems, it was only because of special precautions; in fact, all such questions are ambiguous. "Cracker is pl square" (Crackers are square) is after all a complete construction, so that once a "?" is appended to it there are grounds for treating it as a *yes-no* question and not as a *how many* question. We sidestepped this problem in teaching the quantifiers simply by removing "yes" and "no" as alternatives. But this obviously avoids, rather than solves, the problem. Fortunately, the solution to the problem is quite simple. All ambiguity of the above kind can be eliminated merely by giving the interrogative marker a special tag whenever it stands for "how many"—that is, when the proper substitute for the "?" is a quantifier—"why," "how," or any other interrogative sense for which the appropriate answer is not "yes" or "no." That is, whenever an interrogative particle is appended to a complete construction and the intention is not a *yes-no* question, the interrogative particle must be marked—either inflected or accompanied by a special particle—to distinguish the construction from a *yes-no* question.

LABELING KINDS OF EQUIVALENCE

Another approach to sameness-difference judgments is to separate the several kinds of sameness and teach the subject an individual word for each. "Same" has been used to apply to objects, with which it was first taught, and also to sentences. However, "same-different" could be restricted to objects and a new word, "synonymous," introduced for specifically sentences. Natural language has special terms for the most important or common cases of "same X," where X is the criterion on which sameness is judged. Meaning and number are apparently uniquely important dimensions, for equivalence judged to hold on these criteria has the special words "synonymous" and "equal," respectively.

Several other concepts could be introduced in this context that would add appreciably to the subject's ability to state the basis for a judgment of equivalence. As a preliminary, the conjunction transformation could be made explicit in a way that it was not. "Same" could be used for this purpose as follows:

1. "Apple is red and cherry is red *same* apple and cherry is pl red"
2. "Mary give Sarah banana and Mary give Sarah apple *same* Mary give Sarah apple and banana"
3. "Sarah cut apple and Sarah take apple *same* Sarah cut and take apple"

These transformations could be taught in few or many steps depending on the subject's skill.

"Implies" might also be introduced in this context. For example, "Apple and cherry is pl red *implies* apple and cherry is pl same color." Transfer tests could be made by using the other predicates, for example, "Nut and caramel is pl small implies nut and caramel is pl same size," etc. "Implies" would also afford a strong case for examining Sarah's grasp of asymmetry. *Yes-no* questions could be applied revealingly to this predicate, for example, "? size of nut and caramel is pl same implies nut and caramel is pl small," to which Sarah should answer "No."

One last form that might be taught in this context is the genitive phrase. Given, say, "Apple and cherry is pl fruit," which Sarah already had, and adding "Apple and cherry is pl same color," which was to be taught in this context, these two sentences could then be combined with the use of "same" as follows: "Apple and cherry is pl fruit and apple and cherry is same color implies apple and cherry is pl fruit *of* same color," where "of same color" is the new phrase. Sentences of this form can be elaborated, for example, "Apple and cherry is pl fruit of same color, size, shape, taste." They are formed by deletion and recombination, as are all conjunctions, and are distinctive only in the addition of the genitive particle. Notice, incidentally, how well the use of plastic symbols, as opposed to transient gestures or sounds, serves to demonstrate the exact nature of the transformations that produce the target sentence. We have not had an opportunity to try these powerful extensions on the use of "same" with Sarah and look forward to doing so with the new subjects. The sentences seem formidable in their length and complexity, and so they may prove. However, unfamiliarity may be mainly responsible for the impression of formidability. Naturally we will build up to the larger sentences exactly as before, step by step, introducing each new particle one at a time. All I have been interested in demonstrating in this section is that these powerful extensions can be derived from well-defined training programs.

15
Words and Memory

A common expression speaks of the "power of words"—but this refers, of course, to human words. Can we talk about chimpanzee words in a similar vein, or are the pieces of plastic a lesser device that only appear to be like words but differ from them in critical respects? To answer this question we must first decide what is meant by "power of the word." I suspect that what the phrase celebrates is the extraordinary extent to which the word can be substituted for its referent. This substitution is made possible by the subject's ability to use the word as an information retrieval device. The phrase therefore implies that, in the human case, the name of an object can be virtually as informative as the object itself, which is to say, the word can be used to retrieve a remarkably complete representation of its referent.

We touched on this topic earlier in requiring Sarah to identify the features of apple from the word "apple" alone. In this chapter, however, we greatly extend this kind of test, examining a number of words, including names of both objects and properties. In brief, we have obtained measures of the subject's visual and verbal memory for the same set of objects, making it possible to compare the information the subject can retrieve about the objects from visual cues, on the one hand, and from the name of the object, on the other. This is the comparison we need in order to decide whether it is sensible to speak of the "power of words" in the case of the chimpanzee.

Of all the prerequisites for language none is more vital, or more easily overlooked, than memory. Yet language is possible in the first place only because of memory. It is not objects, actions, or properties as such that are associated with words but the representations of these items that the subject has stored in memory (see Kintsch, 1970; Martin, 1972, for extended discussion of Höffding's problem: the fact that associations are between memory representations—not objects directly). If the stored representation of an item is complete, then, barring some form of "leakage," the information associated with the name of the item should be commensurately complete.

A representation might be incomplete for either of two reasons. First, a young organism or an inexperienced old one might know little about the item in question. Children know far less about the world than do adults and when asked about the world reveal their ignorance by the inaccuracy of their answers. Do lions have stripes? Do buffaloes have horns? Do chimpanzees have tails? Two to 3-year-old children answer these questions incorrectly (D. Premack, unpublished data, 1974), either because the words are not yet associated with the intended referents or because their stored representations of the animals in question is incomplete and the information they can retrieve with the words "lion," "buffalo," etc. is therefore incomplete. But normal children only need adequate experience in order to form well-defined representations.

Second, despite extensive experience with the items in question, certain species may never form well-defined representations. That is, an organism may see an item clearly or accurately and yet be unable to form an accurate representation of what it has seen. We do not yet know whether, in fact, species differ in their representational capacity. If they do, however, this sets a limit on the effectiveness of the language they can acquire. For the name of an item cannot be more informative than the representation of the item with which the name is associated.

To assess the subject's memory of objects, on the one hand, and the information it had associated with names of the objects, on the other, we used fruit and the names taught for the fruit. We did not choose fruit simply because chimpanzees are frugivorous. Fruit is a good example of the kind of item that is interwoven into the fabric of a species' life without ever becoming the object of formal inquiry. Even as we experience food, clothing, vehicles, dishwear, and the like every day of our lives and yet never study them, so the chimpanzees experience fruit. That such items still remain in our lives is amazing, for school has come to touch nearly everything in our lives. That is, in contemporary Western society ever more of what was once learned on a simple observational basis is being transferred to explicit instruction. Nevertheless, despite this obsession with pedagogy, we still do not study most of the items that compose the material basis of our lives—diet, clothing, vehicles, etc. It is apparently an unexamined assumption that daily experience is a sufficient pedagogy for acquiring all the knowledge one needs about such items. A side interest of the present study is to shed some light on this assumption. How complete is the representation that organisms store in memory about objects they experience daily, but always casually and never as the object of formal instruction?

To test the subject's memory for fruit we decomposed the fruit into a number of pieces, gave them one piece, and then asked them to identify the other pieces belonging to the same fruit. The logic of this measurement is based on the assumption that if the subject knows a great deal about an object, it should need only a small sample to identify the object from which the sample has been taken. For instance, if given only a stem or a seed or a taste, the knowledgeable subject should be able to identify the fruit from which the component is taken.

In addition, this kind of procedure makes it possible to differentiate between what a subject can perceive about an object and what it can reconstruct from memory. For instance, when the subject is required to match redness to an apple, both the sample and correct alternative can instance the matching criterion, giving a measure of perception. If, however, the sample remains red but the apple is now painted white, the sample and correct alternative no longer instance the matching criterion. Instead, they match on the basis of information that is associated with but not directly represented by the correct alternative, and the subject must reconstruct the missing information from memory.

Tests that require reconstructing information from memory do not depend specifically on distorted alternatives, however; they can be done equally well with normal alternatives. For instance, the relation between the taste of a fruit and any of its visual properties is such a case, as are the relations between many of its features, many of its components, and many of the combinations of features and components. The relation between stem and peel, stem and seed, seed and peel, etc.; color and shape, shape and size, etc.; and color and stem, shape and seed, etc., are all cases of this kind. Items in these pairs do not share common features but are related simply through being attributes of the same object. That is, there are no principles from which to infer that apple is red (or banana is not red), or that apple tastes as it does; the relation must be reconstructed from memory.

Reconstruction of missing information could also take place by inference, as in Figure 15.1. In this case the samples consist of two hypothetical fruits into which a knife enters more deeply in one case than in the other. The alternatives consist of saggital sections of the fruit, revealing a larger pit in one case than in the other. A subject with a knowledge of everyday physics and a capacity for the appropriate perceptual transformations should be able to match the deeply entered fruit to the small pit and vice versa. We have collected too little information on this case to do more than mention it for the sake of completeness. Although inferential problem solving is of unusual interest, reconstruction from memory is the more general case, for not all associations can be reconstructed inferentially. Many items are simply associated because of one vicissitude or another; their relation does not instance any principle.

We divided the fruit into four canonical components and two features. The components were half wedge, stem, peel, and seed. The features were color and shape, the former represented by a 2 X 4 painted card and the latter by a two-dimensional uncolored paper outline that did not preserve size, being larger than some fruit, smaller than others. To the otherwise visual aspects we added taste as the one intermodal possibility. Six of eight fruits were used in each test.

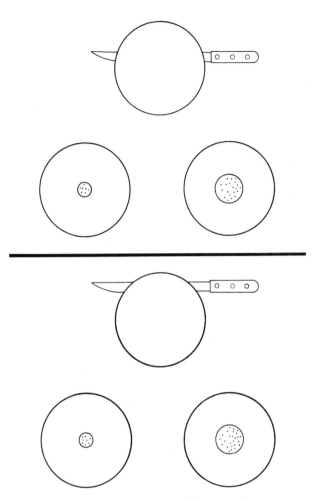

FIG. 15.1   Example of reconstruction by inference rather than memory.

Every test included banana, orange, lemon, and apple plus a variable two from the seasonal subset of peach, pear, grape, and cherry (see Figure 15.2).

Each test was divided into a training and a transfer phase. In the training phase, one pair of fruits was used consistently to teach the subject the criterion. For example, in the case of seed and whole fruit, most of the subjects were given either apple or orange seed as the sample and intact apple and orange as alternatives. On these trials, they were told when they were correct and incorrect and given a preferred tidbit when correct. Subjects varied greatly in the number of training trials they received. Sometimes as few as five trials without error established that the subject was using the intended matching criterion and the

Memory tests on fruit

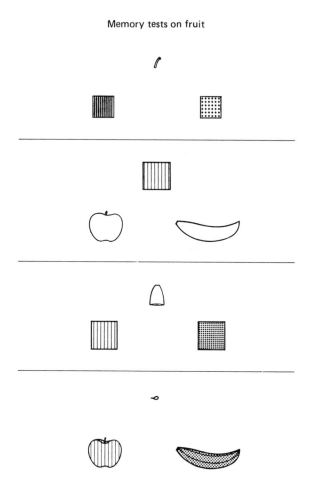

FIG. 15.2 Examples of memory tests on fruit using attributes of fruit in match-to-sample format. The cases shown are stem of apple, peel of apple and of orange; red cardboard square, white cardboard shape of apple and of banana; peeled wedge of banana, red cardboard square, and yellow cardboard square; seed of apple, real intact apple, and banana.

transfer tests were begun immediately. On other occasions, even after five training sessions with an average of 15 trials per session, the subject still had not passed the training session, and then no transfer tests were given.

   In the transfer tests the subjects were given new pairs of fruit, as well as pairs made up by combining old fruits with new ones, and they were told "correct" on every trial. The transition from rewarding only correct responses in training to rewarding all responses during testing was less abrupt than may appear. Subjects were generally not advanced to the transfer phase until they performed successfully during training; therefore, the actual transition was typically from reward for most trials to reward for all trials.

Each subject received from 23 to 26 different test conditions in the same order, with the partial exception of Walnut, who lagged somewhat behind and was exempted from certain tests. Approximately 70 sessions, distributed over a period of about 5 months, were required to complete the nonverbal series. Two weeks after completion of the nonverbal series, the three female subjects were given the verbal form of the tests, and 3 weeks later they were retested on some part of the nonverbal series. In the verbal form of the test, the plastic words were substituted for the previous nonlinguistic alternatives and a part of the test series was repeated. Walnut had not been taught names for most of the fruit until after he finished the nonverbal series, so in his case the verbal tests were delayed. Two months after he had learned names for all the fruits he too was tested on the verbal series and then 3 weeks later, he was retested on part of the nonverbal series.

RESULTS FOR THE NONVERBAL SERIES

The individual results for the 23–26 test conditions are shown in Table 15.1 in terms of scores on the training and transfer sessions given for each condition. Scores for the training sessions generally precede those for transfer, although occasionally the two kinds of sessions were intermixed. Subjects were tested somewhat differently in keeping with their performance. For instance, Peony, the least attentive subject, was often given more transfer sessions per condition than any other subject, simply to assure that a failure was genuine. Because the general performance of all four subjects was high, the most economical summary can be given by considering the conditions the subjects failed.

In Table 15.1 we see that Walnut failed 9 conditions, Elizabeth 6, Peony 4, and Sarah none. In some cases the subjects not only failed the transfer tests but also did not even learn the original discrimination. Walnut had 3 such failures, Elizabeth 2, and Peony 1. For instance, despite repeated differential reinforcement, Walnut failed to learn to associate the taste of apple and banana with their respective shapes; not surprisingly, he failed the transfer test requiring that he associate the taste of each of six fruits with their respective shapes. Taste to stem and seed to shape were the two other conditions for which Walnut failed to learn even the original discriminations. Elizabeth failed to learn the discrimination in the case of seed to peel, seed to wedge, and seed to color and Peony failed in the case of stem to seed. Sarah had no such failures; indeed, she not only performed correctly on all the training pairs but passed all the transfer tests.

An analysis of variance made on each subject's score on the last transfer session given for each test condition showed that differences among subjects

TABLE 15.1
Results for Nonverbal Memory Tests[a]

Conditions		Sarah		Peony		Elizabeth		Walnut	
Sample	Alter-natives	Train	Transfer	Train	Transfer	Train	Transfer	Train	Transfer
Shape	Wedge	NT	3/15	NT	1/15	5/15 A/B	0/10	2/10 A/B	4/15 2/11
Taste	Whole fruit	2/10 A/B	3/15	3/11 A/B	1/15	1/10 A/B	2/15	1/6 A/G 0/5 A/G	5/12 2/15
Taste	Color	4/12 A/B 0/5 A/B	2/15	4/12 A/B 1/6 A/B	2/16	1/7 A/B 1/10 A/B	4/7 2/15	4/15 O/B	2/10
Taste	Shape	7/20 G/P 5/18 G/P 2/10 G/P	1/15	4/12 A/B	6/15 4/14 3/15	3/12 A/B	5/15* 7/18 6/15	7/15 A/B 7/15 A/B 4/13 A/B	* 4/10 5/8
Peel	Whole fruit	0/5 L/G	5/11 3/15	0/6 L/G	3/14	4/14 L/G	2/14	1/8 L/G	2/12
Peel	Color	11/20 O/C 8/20 O/C 0/5 O/C	0/12	0/5 O/C	3/15	1/6 C/O	1/15	0/5 C/O	2/12
Peel	Shape	6/15 B/P 1/6 B/P	3/12	0/5 B/P	* 7/15 7/20 8/15 7/13	0/5 B/P	2/15	4/15 B/P	2/10

Taste	Peel	10/15 A/G 5/15 A/G	0/10	1/6 A/G	3/15	3/11 A/G	5/15 1/12	8/21 A/G 1/7 A/G	* 4/15 6/16
Seed	Whole fruit	5/15 O/G 3/10 O/G	1/11	7/15 A/O 0/5 A/O	3/15	2/10 A/O	3/15	9/15 O/G 8/20 O/G 9/15 O/G 3/12 O/G	2/12
Taste	Seed	5/15 A/G	2/10	0/5 O/Pc	3/15	4/15 O/Pc	5/15 3/15	4/10 O/G 2/10 O/G	* 7/15 6/12
Seed	Peel	2/10 O/P	3/11	1/7 A/Pc	2/15	7/15 A/Pc 11/20 A/Pc 11/15 A/G	* NT	4/13 O/P	5/12* 4/15
Shape	Color	0/5 C/L	3/12 1/10	0/5 C/L	3/15	2/10 C/L	3/15	11/20 C/L 3/10 C/L	2/12
Seed	Shape	3/11 A/P	3/12 1/10	8/15 A/Pc 8/15 A/Pc 0/5 A/G	* 7/15 7/18	5/20 A/Pc 3/12 A/Pc	* 6/15 5/12	20/35 A/G	NT*
Seed	Wedge	0/5 A/O	3/12 4/20	14/15 A/O 0/5 P/G	2/10	12/15 A/O 9/20 P/G 10/20 P/G 9/15 P/G	* NT	9/20 A/O 0/5 A/O	6/15 9/15

(continued)

301

TABLE 15.1 (continued)

Sample	Alternatives	Sarah Train	Sarah Transfer	Peony Train	Peony Transfer	Elizabeth Train	Elizabeth Transfer	Walnut Train	Walnut Transfer
Seed	Color	8/20 A/O 7/15 A/O 2/10 A/O	3/12 1/11	1/7 A/O	5/5 8/16 5/15 1/10	8/15 A/O 5/15 A/O 8/15 A/O	* NT		
Stem	Whole fruit	6/6 C/G	1/12	4/10 C/G 1/7 C/G	2/10	8/15 C/G 4/15 C/G	3/15	8/25 C/G 0/5 C/G	2/12
Stem	Color	3/10 A/P	7/20 3/15	8/15 O/B 1/7 O/B	2/10	0/5 O/B	0/10	10/20 O/B 1/6 O/B	* 6/15 6/15
Stem	Shape	3/10 A/P	7/20 3/15	8/15 A/P 3/12 A/P	* 7/15 11/20	2/7 A/P	1/10	1/6 A/P	8/15* 6/12
Taste	Stem	1/8 C/P	2/12	0/5 C/P	5/8 3/15	7/15 C/P 3/10 C/P	3/15	9/15 C/P 12/20 C/P 12/22 C/P	* NT
Stem	Peel	3/12 O/B	0/10	0/5 O/B	3/15	0/5 O/B	1/10	3/10 O/B	3/12
Stem	Wedge	7/10 A/G 2/10 A/G	1/10	2/10 A/G	2/12	0/5 A/G	2/11	6/15 A/G 4/15 A/G	2/12
Stem	Seed	9/20 O/P 9/20 O/P 2/10 O/P	2/10	7/15 O/P 9/15 O/P 8/15 O/P 10/20 O/P	* NT	4/15 P/O	6/15 6/15 4/20		

[a]A = apple, B = banana, C = cherry, G = grape, L = lemon, O = orange, P = pear, Pc = peach, NT = no test, * = failure.

TABLE 15.2
Summary of Transfer Results for Nonverbal Memory Tests

| | Alternatives | | | | | | | |
Sample	Whole fruit	Color	Peel	Seed	Shape	Stem	Wedge	Total
Taste	87	84	80	73	72	68	–	77.3
Stem	84	79	83	66	63	–	85	76.7
Seed	84	66	64	–	50	–	60	64.8
Peel	82	89	–	–	72	–	–	81
Shape	–	81	–	–	–	–	86	83.5
			75.67	69.5	64.25	68		
Total:	84.25	79.8	78.35	67.15	73.88	72.35	72.5	

were significant ($p < .01$), as were differences among conditions ($p < .01$). Scheffe's tests showed that Sarah differed significantly from all other subjects, and Walnut likewise, but that Elizabeth and Peony did not differ significantly from each other. Among test conditions, only two differed significantly from every other condition, whole fruit and seed, the strongest and weakest conditions, respectively. Both color and peel differed significantly from seed and stem but not from other conditions; and taste differed significantly from seed. Differences among the other conditions did not reach the .05 level.

Table 15.2 shows the percentage correct (on the last transfer session) for each test condition averaged over all four subjects; conditions presented as samples are listed on the vertical and those presented as alternatives on the horizontal (for conditions that occurred as both sample and alternative, the final score is an average of both).

A rank order of the effectiveness of the different components and features is shown in Table 15.3. Not surprisingly, whole fruit was the strongest condition. Not only does whole fruit offer the most information but in four of six cases the

TABLE 15.3
Rank Order of Effectiveness of Whole Fruits and Their
Attributes Averaged over Subjects

Whole fruit	84.25
Color	79.8
Peel	78.35
Taste	77.3
Shape	73.9
Wedge	72.5
Stem	72.35
Seed	67.15

sample and correct alternative can be matched on a perceptual basis; only in the cases of taste to whole fruit and seed to whole fruit is memory required. Color was the next strongest condition, impressively so because in only two or six cases was perceptual matching possible. In the other four cases—color to taste, color to stem, color to seed, and color to shape—matching could be done only on the basis of memory. Both Sarah (who succeeded on all conditions) and Peony performed as well with color as with the whole fruit, despite the fact that more tests depended on memory with color than with the whole fruit.

Seed was the weakest condition. Only Sarah could match seed to every other condition. All other subjects failed at least two cases involving seed, and Walnut failed every condition in which seed occurred either as sample or as alternative. Walnut's fingers were so large that he could not pick up most seeds, which would make it difficult for him to inspect them in the course of eating, although there was no doubt that he could see them and in the test he was required only to touch or push them. All six cases involving seed depended on matching from memory. However, all six cases involving taste also depended on matching from memory, and yet taste was one of the stronger conditions, significantly stronger than seed. Notice that the associations between taste and whole fruit and taste and other visual attributes are intermodal; the success of all four subjects in forming these associations belies the proposal that intermodal associations are found only in man (Geschwind, 1965).

Some conditions were more strongly associated than others. For example, the association between stem and peel (83% correct) was significantly stronger than that between either stem and seed (66% correct) or seed and peel (64% correct; $p < .05$). This may be explicable in terms of the physical composition of fruit, stem and peel being physical neighbors, unlike the other pairs. Also, taste and color (84% correct) were more strongly associated than taste and shape (72% correct; $p < .05$), perhaps because color is often a clue to ripeness and thus to taste. Taste and color may simply be more strongly linked than taste and shape, however, in which case there should be a strong taste—color linkage even in foods where ripeness is not a factor.

The individual differences on the present tests are like those we have found on all other tests given these same subjects, including general language training, reconstruction of disassembled figures (Premack, 1975a), and precursors to counting (see Chapter 13). Sarah is approximately 12 years old compared to ages of approximately 6—8 years for the other subjects; certainly we expect a 12-year-old child to do better than children comparably younger than itself. However, her performance on the present tests was remarkable by any standards. How many human subjects of any age could do as well? Unfortunately, however, because Sarah identified every attribute of the six fruits from every other attribute, the tests failed in their primary objective, which was to provide relative measures of the differential informativeness of the several conditions. Latency measures may have revealed differences not disclosed by accuracy. In her language performance, difficulty more often affected her processing time than her accuracy.

VERBAL TESTS

After the nonverbal series were finished, the pieces of plastic that served as names of the fruit were introduced as alternatives in four of the conditions: taste, color, shape, and seed. On these tests the subject was given, say, a taste of the fruit and required to choose not the actual fruit or an attribute of it but its name. Similarly, the subject was shown a color, shape, or seed and required to choose between two names rather than between two fruits or parts of fruits. Unlike the nonverbal tests, many of which could be done on a perceptual basis, all of the verbal tests could be done only from memory because none of the fruit names were even remotely iconic.

Sarah, Elizabeth, and Peony were given the verbal series about 2 weeks after the nonverbal series, following a brief review on the fruit names, some of which had not been used in the language training for several months. Walnut was tested on the verbal series about 6 weeks later, after first being taught the names of the fruits in the usual manner.

The results for the verbal series, which are summarized in Table 15.4, can hardly have been more clear-cut. Every subject passed every condition. When given either the shape, the color, the taste, or the seed of any of the six fruits, therefore, each subject successfully identified the name of the fruit. In so doing they succeeded on a total of 12 tests that they had failed when given the corresponding nonverbal version of the test. For example, Elizabeth had been unable to identify the shape of a fruit from its taste but was able to identify the name of a fruit from its taste. Likewise, she was unable to identify either the shape, the wedge, or the color of a fruit from its seed but was able to identify the name of a fruit from its seed. Peony, whose nonverbal performance was somewhat better than Elizabeth's, was unable to identify the shape of a fruit from its seed but was able to identify the name of a fruit from its seed.

With names as alternatives, Walnut passed seven of the eight tests he had failed on the nonverbal series. He had been unable to identify shape, peel, or stem from the taste of a fruit but succeeded when names were substituted for the three attributes. Similarly, he had been unable to identify the peel, color, wedge, or shape of a fruit from its seed but succeeded when names were substituted for the attributes. Because Sarah had not failed any nonverbal condition she could not have done better on the verbal series. She could have done worse, however, although she did not. She passed all verbal tests even as she had all the nonverbal ones.

The massive improvement could not be attributed to an order or practice effect. When retested on cases they had failed in the original nonverbal series, only Peony improved, passing two tests she had failed earlier; other subjects

TABLE 15.4
Results for Verbal Memory Tests[a]

Sample	Sarah		Peony		Elizabeth		Walnut	
	Train	Transfer	Train	Transfer	Train	Transfer	Train	Transfer
Shape	2/10 B/P	2/16	1/10 B/P	3/15	0/5 B/P	1/15	3/15 B/P	2/12
Taste	0/5 A/O	3/15	7/10 A/O 7/15 A/O 1/10 A/O	3/15	3/15 A/O	1/15	2/10 A/O	1/12
Color	1/10 G/B	3/15	8/20 G/B 1/10 G/B	0/15	1/10 G/B	0/10	14/40·B/G	1/12
Seed	0/5 P/G	4/15 2/15			4/20 P/G	1/10	10/30 G/P	8/20 2/15

[a] A = apple, B = banana, G = grape, O = orange, P = pear.

repeated their original failures. Retesting was limited to a few appropriate cases even as the verbal series was limited to only four conditions; it was impractical to repeat the entire 5-month-long nonverbal series and not essential to do so when only one subject showed any improvement on the cases tested.

PAINTED FRUIT

A special set of tests was done using painted plastic fruit. Plastic apple, banana, orange, grape, cherry, and lemon—all familiar to the subjects from other tests—were painted white. Both a nonverbal and a verbal form of the test was done, with colored cards as samples in the first case and names of colors as samples in the second case. In contrast to the first verbal tests, where the words substituted were "apple," "banana," or names of objects, in the present tests the words substituted for the colored cards were "red," "yellow," or names of properties. Names of colors were achromatic pieces of plastic—either white, black, or gray—and so were no more iconic than names of the fruits. The alternatives in both cases were the painted fruit. The matching could not be done on a perceptual basis in either the nonverbal or the verbal form of the tests. For instance, to match a white apple to red, whether red was a colored card or the word "red," the subject would have to know or have stored in memory the fact that apple is red. In addition, the subject had to be able to recognize the fruit in their color-distorted form. When shown, say, a white lemon, one could conclude either that (1) this is a lemon painted white, or (2) this white fruitlike item is a new fruit with which I am unfamiliar. Only the first conclusion would make matching possible.

The results for these tests, which are summarized in Table 15.5, were entirely comparable to those for the other verbal tests. Walnut had not yet been taught the names of properties and so was exempted, but for the three females, all of whom had been taught color names, names of the colors could be substituted for the colored cards without loss of accuracy. There is only one way in which a subject could match, say, a white cherry to the grey piece of plastic meaning red. That is by both knowing that cherry is red and by having associated with the word "red" some actual representation of the color. The association of a representation of the color with the name of the color should come as no surprise, however. In principle it is not different from the association of a representation of a fruit with the name of a fruit. That is, the results for the color names and for the object names are confirming of one another.

WORDS AS INFORMATION RETRIEVAL DEVICES

The word is a remarkable information retrieval device—in the chimpanzee as in man: that is the main result of the study. For Sarah, ceiling effects obscured possible differences in the informativeness of the various conditions; for her we

TABLE 15.5
Nonverbal and Verbal Results on Painted Fruit Tests[a]

	Conditions	Sarah		Peony		Elizabeth		Walnut	
Sample	Alternatives	Train	Transfer	Train	Transfer	Train	Transfer	Train	Transfer
Color	Painted fruit	NT	3/16	NT	2/16	NT	8/16 5/20	6/16 A/B 0/5 A/B	5/12 1/7
Wedge	Painted fruit	9/15 C/L 9/5 C/L	2/12	6/16 C/L 6/15 C/L	0/10	6/10 C/L 2/10 C/L	1/5 1/10	1/7 C/L	2/12
Peel	Painted fruit	5/15 O/G 3/11 O/G	1/10	0/5 O/G	2/7 0/6	8/20 O/G 2/10 O/G	2/8	0/5 O/G	2/10
Name of color	Painted fruit	1/10 C/G	4/15 2/15	3/15 C/G	1/10	0/5 C/G	1/13	–	–

[a]A = apple, B = banana, C = cherry, G = grape, L = lemon, O = orange, NT = no test.

can say only that the name was at least as strong as any other cue. For the other subjects, however, no ceiling effects obscured the fact that names were more informative than any condition other than the whole fruit itself. For example, with seed as the sample, Elizabeth could not identify color, shape, or wedge of the fruit to which the seed belonged. Peony could not identify the shape, and Walnut could not identify any attribute. With seed as sample, there were only two conditions for which all three subjects succeeded: when the alternatives consisted of whole fruit and when they consisted of names. The information available when names were alternatives was therefore comparable to that when whole fruits were alternatives and was greater than that for all other conditions.

Why is the word so effective a retrieval cue? The answer must lie in its use. Words were used to request fruits, to describe actions applied to fruits, and to answer questions about them. Attributes of the fruit were never used in these ways. No animal put aside a stem, peel, or seed and then used it as a kind of self-initiated icon to request the whole fruit or an edible part of it. Although from a physical point of view the attributes were far more intimately associated with the fruit than were the pieces of plastic, the attributes were never used as linguistic devices, never used as symbols of fruit and never used to represent them in sentences about fruit. For most subjects, the attributes did not have the retrieval power of the word. Most subjects could reconstruct more about the fruit from the arbitrary piece of plastic that stood for fruit than it could from an actual part of the fruit. These results are highly compatible with Tulving and Thomson's (1973) encoding specificity principle that a retrieval cue is successful only if it has been specifically encoded previously with the item to be remembered. The present training procedure guarantees that such specific encoding is the case for the word.

DISCRIMINABILITY

An alternate explanation of these results is that the words were simply more discriminable than the attributes of the fruit. In one sense this must have been true, for words differed multidimensionally, whereas the features, color and shape, differed only in the dimension in question. Moreover, there were a total of 6 cases in which Walnut (3 cases), Elizabeth (2), and Peony (1) failed to learn even the original training problem, suggesting that the failure was indeed owed to indiscriminability of the attribute pairs. In contrast, there were a total of 13 cases in which Walnut (6), Elizabeth (4), and Peony (3) learned the training problems—thus demonstrating that the pairs of attributes were discriminable—and nonetheless failed to pass the transfer tests despite repeated opportunities. Differences in reaction time may be explained in terms of discriminability, but differences in percent correct cannot be explained in these terms. The transfer results indicate instead that, even though the attributes were discriminable, the subjects could not use some of them to retrieve a sufficient representation of the referents to pass the transfer tests.

A further reason for discounting discriminability comes from a special set of tests given only to Elizabeth and Peony. In these tests, attributes on which the subjects had failed were combined, producing alternatives that consisted not of one cue but of several. For instance, because Elizabeth failed to associate seed with either shape, color, or wedge, she was given tests in which seed was the sample and each alternative consisted of the shape + color + wedge of a particular fruit. Likewise, Peony, who failed to associate stem with either seed or shape, was given tests in which stem was the sample and each alternative consisted of both seed and shape of a particular fruit. (Attributes in each compound alternative were placed in physical contact on a doily to increase their union.) Although shape + color + wedge (or seed + shape) must be more discriminable than any of the individual cues alone, neither subject showed any improvement on these special tests. Apparently if none of N cues has any retrieval capacity, the combination of these cues will have no more retrieval capacity than the individual cues. This is an acceptable conclusion, although it becomes troublesome once the combination of individual cues approaches the intact fruit. Why should a subject succeed with the intact fruit and fail with a conjunction of the individual attributes of the fruit? There are at least two answers: (1) the conjunction may not be exhaustive and/or (2) concatenating attributes on a doily is not equivalent to the organization the attributes have in the intact fruit.

MATCHING INTERNAL EVENTS

In matching names of colors to painted fruit the chimpanzees gave further evidence of their ability to make use of internal events. In one sense, the tests involving painted fruit merely provided information like that produced by the other tests in the series. They showed that the three female subjects had associated representations of the colors with names of the colors, even as the other tests showed they had associated representations of the objects with names of the objects. But the painted fruit tests imposed an additional requirement. In matching the name of a fruit to a piece of the fruit, it is necessary to compare the internal representation that is associated with the name of the fruit to an actual piece of fruit, and so to compare an internal event with an external one. However, when the subjects matched the word "red" to the white apple there were no external instances of red. Both the representation of red associated with the white apple and with the word "red" were necessarily internal. Chimpanzees are evidently able to compare not only an external and an internal event but also two internal events and to base a decision on the outcome of such comparisons (see Figure 15.3).

Perceptual and memory tests on fruit

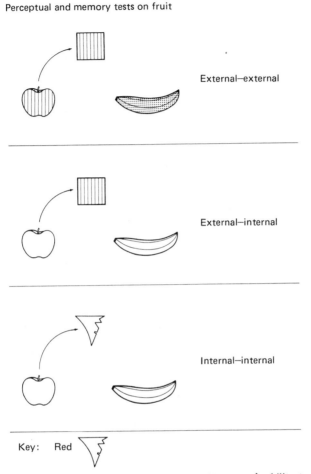

External–external

External–internal

Internal–internal

Key: Red

FIG. 15.3 Examples of match-to-sample tests showing chimpanzee's ability to match two external representations of red (apple and red card), an internal with an external representation (white apple and red card), and two internal representations (the word "red" and a white apple).

The slow learning of first words that all four subjects showed (see Chapter 3) can be explained by considering that words are not associated with what a subject perceives about an item, but only with the representation of the item which the subject has stored in memory. This hypothesis requires assuming that the subjects know relatively little about the fruits in the early period. Yet preference tests indicated that the subjects were able to discriminate each fruit from the other. However, it does not follow from this fact that the representations of the fruit the subjects had stored at an early stage were equally discriminable. We must distinguish between the information a subject can glean by the visual inspection of an item and the information it can reconstruct from memory. These need not be the same. Moreover, the information contained in the stored representations may be sufficiently less than that available by direct inspection that "perceived fruit" is highly discriminable and "remembered fruit" is not. Then, if words were associated with the stored representations, they could not be discriminated either and would not become so until the representations were themselves discriminable.

Adults must store in memory a substantial part of the ambient world, probably all but eliminating the disparity between what they perceive and what they know or can reconstruct from memory. In the young or inexperienced organism, however, the disparity between perceived or perceivable information and stored information may be substantial. If so—and if words are associated with stored representations—this may retard the early learning of words, especially for physically similar objects, such as fruit. Unfortunately, the present results do not provide direct tests of this hypothesis, for they have been made after the subjects already know names for the fruit. The tests provide independent measures of the information associated with representations of the fruit, on the one hand, and of the names associated with the fruit, on the other, but not until after the subjects have had extensive experience with the fruit and, in three of four cases, have already learned names of the fruit.

Both the fruit and the color names were substituted for their referents without loss of accuracy, showing that a major consequence of giving an arbitrary object various linguistic prerogatives is to transfer to the object some or all of the information contained in the associated referent. Under what circumstances does this transfer of information take place? Perhaps it occurs only after the piece of plastic has been used in a wordlike way, say, to request or describe the referent some number of times. Certainly that would be the most tenable hypothesis if the only way to produce names was by repeatedly associating them with their referents in one linguistic context or another. However, we already know that this procedure can be short circuited. Names can be generated far more directly by instructions of the form "X is the name of Y," where X is a so far unused piece of plastic and Y a so far unnamed object. Following instruction of this kind, Sarah used X in all the ways she used names introduced in the more standard way. This suggests that the effect of such instructions as "X is the name of Y" is to transfer to X some or all of the information the subject has stored in memory about Y. This fact clarifies some of the power of language, and at the same time suggests the kind of intelligence a species must have in order to acquire it.

To qualify for language a species must have at least two capacities. First, the species must be capable of storing a rich representation of Y. If not, the information transferred to X would be weak and the name would be a poor substitute for the referent. That is, if the mnemonic capacity of the species were limited, then information associated with names would be commensurately limited; and names could not then be substituted for their referents in match-to-sample tests without loss of accuracy as, in fact, we saw they could be in the chimpanzee. Second, instructions of the form "X is the name of Y" must have the force of transferring to X some— ideally all—of the information that the subject has stored about Y. These are not the only capacities a species must have in order to qualify for language, but they are two that seem to be basic.

From previous tests we know that Sarah is capable of displacement, of comprehending statements about "things that are not there" (see Chapter 10). When given the instruction "Brown color of chocolate" as a means of intro- ducing "brown" and subsequently told "Take brown," she performed correctly, chosing the brown disk from the four that were offered. If this accomplishment has seemed a trifle unbelievable at the time, the present results make the accomplishment more subject to explanation.

The chimpanzee can comprehend statements about "things that are not there" because it can both store adequate representations of items and use words to retrieve the information it has stored about them. In substituting, say, the word "apple" without loss of accuracy for an actual apple in all of the matching tests, it gave direct proof of this ability. Displacement is not a uniquely linguistic phenomenon but the consequence of a certain quality of memory.

When a subject learns to discriminate one item from another, what determines the features to which it attends? It is a common view that one's choice of features is determined by practical advantage. For example, if a young child had coded the physical stimulus of its mother in terms of a few olfactory and visual features, it could be upset on encountering another female who shared these features: in approaching her it could be handled in unexpected ways. According to the standard view, the child would increase the features it associated with the stimulus *mother* in a degree sufficient to protect it against similar confusions. Practical advantages of this kind probably are a sufficient condition for in- creasing the coding or stored representation of an item; but they are apparently not a necessary condition.

Sarah could associate every attribute of the fruit with every other attribute; for Peony color was as effective as the whole fruit. There is no evident way to explain, as a practical advantage to either subject, the peculiar efficacy of color for Peony, nor even less Sarah's remarkably complete representation of the fruit. Sarah was never required to discriminate one fruit from the other on the basis of its seed, stem, shape, or the like. The contingencies did not demand representa- tions nearly so complete; her knowledge of the fruit went far beyond that for which the world provided practical advantage.

In another common answer to the question of how one codes an object, the growth of knowledge is made a by product of the growth of language. For example, the child who calls a horse "bow wow" and is corrected for this overextension is said to add to its coding of dog those additional features that permit it to avoid this mistake. This explanation is a variant of the first one, differing from it not in deemphasizing practical advantage but only in making language the context in which the practical advantage is felt. The condition it describes is probably a sufficient one, too, but it cannot be a necessary one.

First, animals without language appear to have internal representations comparable to those of children with language. For example, Walnut's knowledge of fruit, which was tested before he had been taught names of fruit, proved to be equal or superior to that of 2- and 3-year-old children who did know names of the fruit and to whom we subsequently gave the same tests. Clearly not all knowledge is acquired in the course of acquiring language. Second, neither of the practical advantage-type hypotheses explain why all of the chimpanzees associate names of the fruit with specifically taste of the fruit. They were never given a taste of a fruit and then required to request more of it by using its name. On the contrary, the circumstances in which they requested fruit with words were typically ones in which they could see the fruit. Nevertheless, names and tastes were at least as strongly associated as were names and visual attributes. In summary, the growth of knowledge cannot be exhaustively explained in terms of practical advantage either in the subject's prelanguage or in its language-associated experience.

16
Syntax

We perceive much of the world in terms of an action paradigm. One or more agents are seen to act on an object (physical case), another agent (social case), or both, changing either its (his or her) state, its location, or both. Action is a cornerstone of human experience—so much so that to claim someone has a knowledge of the world amounts to claiming that the individual can (1) divide the temporal sequences into appropriate segments and (2) accurately predict the conditional probabilities among the segments. On a practical level, individuals with a knowledge of the world apply suitable operators on appropriate occasions—for example, heat to raw meat, mortar to bricks, water to flour—as well as, in the social case, smile, frown, attack, speak, etc., on appropriate occasions. It is difficult to overestimate the degree to which knowledge of the everyday (macrophysics) world can be represented as knowledge of the causal sequences into which we parse the world.

Although we describe action as a linear sequence in which the agent of the action, the action, and the object or patient of the action are temporally conjunctive items, there is in fact no linear sequence of this kind in action. The agent, the action, and the object or patient—the elements into which we analyze action or causal sequence—all occur or participate simultaneously. You have only to look at any act through your eyes rather than your syntax to see that this is so. It is only the syntax of English that deceives us into supposing that the elements of action not only occur successively but also in a particular succession, that is, agent, action, object. In fact, even in the simplest act there is no cue from the act itself as to whether an agent–action–object order is more iso-morphic with the act than, say, an action–agent–object order, or still another order. The languages of the world reflect this fact. They differ in their base form. In some languages the base form is "John cut apple," in others "John apple cut," and in still others "Apple John cut," although apparently the latter is less frequent than the other two (Greenberg, 1966).

It may be said that syntax arises from the fact that, on the one hand, action is a cornerstone of human experience and, on the other, the elements into which we analyze action are not temporally disjoint. If the perceptually analyzed elements of action were conjunctive, if they occurred in a temporal sequence, words could simply be mapped onto the sequence. There might still be a need for syntax on other grounds, but it would not seem to be a need that arose so early in the interface between perception and language. However, because the perceptual content of action is not a sequence of items, it is not possible to talk about actions—to describe them, request them, ask questions about them—by the simplest possible mapping, a one-to-one correspondence between words and perceptual elements. It is necessary to adopt a more complex form of mapping. The analyzed content of action is mapped not onto words standing in simple correspondence to the items in the action but onto a structure that has an organization of its own.

The structure, of course, is the sentence. The organization of the sentence, its subject–predicate form, is not totally independent of the world; in fact, it seems highly reminiscent of the actor–object relation, which cannot be a surprise as the human sentence has not been designed for a hypothetical world. Nevertheless, the sentence does not simply borrow its organization from the visual scene. It is defined by internal criteria more or less independent of any visual scene. Once the subject has acquired syntax, it can organize the information in any visual scene in terms of the intrinsic organization of the sentence.

Contrast this natural use of language with a hypothetical one in which language is used simply to reconstruct objects with good internal organization. For example, Sarah was capable of reconstructing objects, such as faces, from their disassembled parts (Premack, 1975a). She put the eyes, nose, and mouth in their appropriate places. No doubt if she had been taught names for the parts, she could have deployed them as she did the parts, i.e., put the word "eye" where she put the actual eye, "nose" where she put the nose, etc. Notice that with this use of language there would be no need for syntax. Instead, the words could be put into one-to-one correspondence with locations in the face. The betweeness relations among the words, instead of being determined by a syntax, would be determined exhaustively by the betweeness relations among the parts of the face.

When the child's two-word utterances observe a fixed word order, the child has both analyzed action and developed a grammar. Psycholinguists (Bloom, 1970; Bowerman, 1973; Braine, in press; Brown, 1973; Schlesinger, 1974; Slobin, 1970, 1973) classify the child's first two-word utterances into about eight categories, for example, actor–action, action–object, actor–object, attribute–object, essentially the categories one anticipates in a species in which action is a dominant paradigm. The child's grammar is simple, consisting of one rule; the elements in each of the two-term relations, for example, actor and action, are mapped specifically onto word order. Perhaps the child's rule is even as simple as: In each of the eight relations, say first the name of the more salient item. Is word order the only property children use? It is not known whether children attempt to map onto other properties, such as amplitude, nasality, etc., for example, expressing possession by saying the agent more loudly—MOMMY purse (purse MOMMY)—before abandoning these properties to settle on word order. In one respect, word order is the most sensible property—it is the only obligatory property, the one that must be expressed in order to speak at all.

Chimpanzees can be taught word order, but only with explicit training, and they therefore differ from children, who acquire it on the basis of observational learning. One may attempt to augment the difference between the two species by noting that the forms that children produce—for example, "All-gone TV," "Daddy home"—are not even found in adult speech. However, word order as a general strategy is exemplified by adult speech, even in inflected languages and perhaps especially so in mother—child discourse. Moreover, there is the suggestion that children adopt from adult speech not only a general word-order strategy but also specific word-order patterns. For instance, children raised by adults whose base form is VSO (e.g., Samoan) are reported to use an action—actor form, whereas those raised by adults for whom the base form is SVO, use an actor—action form (Bowerman, 1973). But this is not to question the radical difference in the readiness with which children and chimpanzees acquire word order.

The difference between the two species could be attributed to any of at least three factors or their combinations. First, the ape may make a less incisive analysis of action than the child; the perceptual elements of action and the relations among these elements would then be less salient, less cognitively available for mapping. Second, words in the ape may not have the information retrieval power they have in the child, in which case it would be more difficult to match the appropriate word to its referent. Third, the predilection to map the language system unto the perceptual one may be stronger in the child than in the ape. Although it is difficult to evaluate the third or motivational factor, it is possible to minimize the contribution of the first two factors. Words, as we have seen, have an appreciable information retrieval power in the ape; and as we have also seen, apes are capable of perceiving or organizing information in terms of action schema. The ape's capacity for syntax therefore seems out of proportion with its greater ability to make causal analysis and to use words in a humanlike way. Is this a genuine disparity and, if so, what does it imply? Even if the disparity is borne out by further research, it need not support a nativist position. The ape's relative incapacity for syntax may reflect the absence of an inherited syntactic competence or simply a weaker theory-constructing capacity in general. Finding the evidence that can decide between these alternatives is not likely to be easy.

COMPARISON WITH CHILDREN

In teaching Sarah we have made no attempt to simulate the natural case, yet if we compare Sarah's record with that of the Stage I child, we find only two forms that Sarah has not been taught, the genitive and the stative. Omission of the genitive had untoward consequences for the training of other words, primarily the copula. However, the genitive is not itself an intrinsically difficult form. Washoe's data includes the alienable form of the genitive (Gardner & Gardner, 1971).

The stative, which deals with intransitive verbs referring to sensory or perceptual states, such as seeing or hearing, rather than with actions, such as giving and cutting, was also a neglected form. Obviously Sarah participates in such states, i.e., sees, hears, smells, touches. Is she capable of distinguishing between when she is and is not seeing, is and is not hearing, and can she distinguish between seeing and hearing, etc.? Because the answers to all these questions can only be affirmative, there should be no difficulty in teaching her words to label the several states. Indeed, using, say, "see" and "touch" as exemplars, it should be possible to teach her "feel" as a class word for reception in general or active state in any modality. I will not describe the training programs here, although I have written them out and they are entirely straightforward.

GENERATING NEW SENTENCES

The normal child enters Stage II, advancing toward adult language, by combining the strings of Stage I. For example, the actor–action and action–object phrases of Stage I are combined to form the actor–action–object strings of Stage II. The child no longer says "Mommy wash" or "Wash dolly" but combines them to form "Mommy wash dolly." Likewise "Wash dolly" and "Red dolly," or "Dolly there" may be combined to form "Wash red dolly," "Wash dolly there," "Wash red dolly there," or "Mommy wash red dolly," etc. Sentences of Stage II consist basically of combined strings of Stage I, but more than simple combining is involved. The child does not say, "Mommy wash wash doll," but rather "Mommy wash doll," not only combining phrases but also deleting redundant elements. Furthermore, the child does not say "Wash dolly Mommy wash," although it might say "Wash dolly Mommy" (as an equivalence for "Mommy wash doll"), and likewise "Red doll wash Mommy" (as an equivalence for "Mommy wash red doll"). In the transition from Stages I to II combining already formed elements may be the basic operation, but the combining involves deletion, as well as decisions about which phrases to join and the order in which to join them, for example, whether to concatenate the existing strings A and B as AB or BA.

The progression from simple to complex forms specifically through combining previously formed units is probably not unique to language development but may be the general format for much if not all cognitive development. Kellogg's (1955) description of the child's development of representational drawing takes this same form. The child first develops the ability to produce some number of basic elements, such as lines, dots, and wiggles. These are combined in Stage II to form crosses and the like. Then the Stage II elements are combined to form, say, crosses inside circles in Stage III, which too are combined, etc. In Kellogg's account of the data, four such stages carry the child from scribbles to representational drawing, each stage characterized primarily by the combining of the elements of the previous stage.

As in language, so in drawing, more than simple combination is involved. The number of lower stage elements that can be combined in each higher stage is extremely large, increasing geometrically from stage to stage; but in the thousands of children's drawings that Kellogg has examined only a relatively small number of the possible combinations are actually found. Moreover, where simple combining would lead to redundant elements, such as two lines side by side— analogous to "Mommy wash wash doll"—only one line appears in the child's drawing even as only one instance of "wash" appears in its sentence.

We did not teach Sarah to produce, say, "Mary give apple Sarah," by first teaching her the phrases "Mary give," "give apple," and "apple Sarah" and then providing the opportunity for her to combine them into the desired "Mary give apple Sarah." With a 1- to 2-year-old child, whose attention span is limited and in whom the semantic relations are only in the formative stage, there may be no better alternative than to proceed by teaching phrases, units shorter than the target ones. However, Sarah was 5–6 years old, presumably in full possession of all the intended semantic relations and with a short-term memory that made four-word strings a ready possibility. With such an organism there was no reason to adopt a training procedure simulating the acquisition process dictated by the limitations of a younger organism. (Some of the early results for Peony and Elizabeth, in contrast, who were only about 3 years old when training began, suggest that it may have been sensible to have adopted the child's acquisition process with them. After advancing to four-word strings, they refused to continue producing them. They may have done better if prepared for the four-word string by first being made competent in the phrases the selective combination of which constituted the target sentences.)

Because Sarah was not taught phrases, we cannot examine her ability to form new sentences specifically by combining existing phrases, as we can with the child. However, there are at least five different cases sifted through her record in which Sarah comprehended (and in a few cases produced) sentences formed by a process more demanding than that of combining phrases.

ATTRIBUTION

Consider action‑attribute‑object or actor‑action‑attribute‑object forms, for example, "Take red dish" or "Sarah take red dish." A child would not produce sentences of this kind before it had first produced both "Sarah take" and "red dish." In the child, both the attributive "red dish" and actor‑action "Sarah take" forms have separate developmental histories. Both phrases would occur on numerous occasions before the child combined them to produce the actor‑action‑attribute‑object—"Sarah take red dish"—form. Sarah, in contrast, arrived at the complete attributive form in a different and in many respects more demanding way.

She was first taught sentences of the form "Sarah take X," where X was the name of an object. Next, she was taught sentences in which X was the name of a property, for example, "Sarah take red." Finally, she was given sentences of the target form, for example, "Sarah take red dish." In taking the red dish, instead of either the green dish or the red/green pail, she demonstrated comprehension of the attributive form. Her accomplishment went beyond that of the child, for although she had been taught "Sarah take dish" and "Sarah take red," she had never been taught "red dish." Unlike the sentences the child produces at Stage II, Sarah comprehended a sentence involving a unit that had no history of independent occurrence.

One might ascribe Sarah's success to the fact that earlier she was taught the attributional case in being trained to distinguish, say, "jam‑bread" from "honey‑bread" and the like. But training of this kind is not a necessary condition. Neither Peony nor Elizabeth were trained on the spread‑receptacle, that is, "jam‑bread" form, yet they both responded correctly to such attributive forms as "Peony (Elizabeth) take big apple," etc. In brief, after mastering the actor‑action‑object form (where "object" was both object and attribute used as object), all three subjects responded correctly to the actor‑action‑attribute‑object form. They did so without being taught the encoding of attribution per se.

FROM DEMONSTRATIVE PRONOUN TO DEMONSTRATIVE ADJECTIVE

Sarah showed a similar form of sentence productivity with "this/that." Her training was restricted to the pronominal use of "this/that," for example, "Sarah take this" versus ". . . that" (comprehension) or "give Sarah this," versus ". . . that" (production). Despite this restriction, when required to produce "Give Sarah this cookie" versus ". . . that cookie," she made only 3 errors in 15 trials, with none on the first five trials. She wrote the incorrect "Give Sarah cookie this" almost as often as the correct "...this cookie," but there was no reason why her word order should have been correct. Sentences of that kind had never been modeled for her. Her own production of the demonstrative adjective form on that occasion was her first experience with the form.

CONJUNCTION

Both Sarah and the other female chimps use conjunction, which, along with nominalization and relativization, is a major recursive form. Sarah, as we saw earlier, used two simple forms of conjunction. In the beginning she requested separate fruits with separate sentences, say, "Mary give Sarah apple" and "Mary give Sarah banana," but subsequently requested the separate fruits with a single sentence "Mary give Sarah apple banana." She showed a similar form of contraction with verbs. At first she wrote, say, "Wash apple" and "Give apple," requesting each of two acts with a separate sentence; but later she wrote "Wash give apple," requesting the same two acts with a single sentence. Comparable behavior was seen in both Peony and Elizabeth. In describing either the trainer's behavior or their own, they too contracted verbs, writing, say, "Elizabeth apple wash cut" (self-description) or "Amy apple cut insert" (description of the trainer). Their use of conjunction was impressive, in part because of its several forms and the different contexts in which it occurred, but more important because it was invented by them. No aspect of conjunction was taught Sarah or the other subjects. The stringing together of object names in one case and action names in the other was their contribution. Perhaps the present physical medium potentiates conjunction reduction. In being cumbersome, it may put a premium on economical expression.

NOMINATIVE VERSUS ACCUSATIVE PHRASES

Sarah comprehended "name of" when it was used as part of an accusative phrase although, in all of her previous experience, it was confined to the nominative phrase. She had been trained to produce "X name of Y" statements (where X was the name of the object Y), yet she subsequently carried out instructions of the form "Sarah insert name of cracker in cup" versus "...insert cracker in cup," where "name of" occurred as part of the accusative phrase. She was equally successful in transferring the quantifiers from the nominative phrase in which they were taught her to the accusative phrase in which they were later presented. For example, she had been trained to produce sentences of the form "Some cracker is round," "All cracker is pl square," etc., and later performed correctly when instructed "Sarah take some cracker," etc. Thus although both "name of" and the quantifiers were learned originally as parts of nominative phrases, she comprehended them when she later experienced them as parts of accusative phrases.

Although all five cases are simple and do not begin to involve the complexity of adult recursive forms, in each case a new sentence form has been either comprehended or produced without explicit training on the form, in some cases despite the fact that a portion of the sentence can be shown to have had no prior history as an independent phrase. Several of the cases involve using words that have been acquired in one grammatical case (for example, nominative) in a new case (for example, accusative), which is a part of what is involved in sentence productivity. All five cases go beyond lexical substitution in which new words are merely substituted in old forms, for in all cases the forms have themselves been new. It seems premature to conclude, as do Fodor *et al.* (1974) and Brown (1973), that the chimpanzee is limited to lexical substitution and cannot comprehend structural novelty.

LANGUAGE-PRODUCING OPERATIONS

Innovative capacity can be examined not only at the level of the sentence per se but also at the level of those operations that are considered to produce the sentence. In looking at syntactic models (e.g., Chomsky, 1965), we find concatenation, deletion, rearrangement, addition—exactly the operations one expects to find in the construction and modification of linear sequences. To produce even a simple sentence one must be able to concatenate items; to produce structural novelty, one must in addition be able to delete, rearrange, and in some cases add items. These are inferred operations, of course, thought to go on in the head, yet it seems sensible to study them or their counterparts in the overt behavior of the subject; if a subject cannot concatenate, delete, etc., external items, how likely is it to be able to do the same in its head (if a subject cannot add on paper, what is the likelihood it can do mental arithmetic?)?

Sarah was not taught any of the linguistic operations, for virtually all of her training was confined to one operation—one-to-one correspondence—which was perhaps the logically simplest training procedure. When each new word is taught by arranging it so that its introduction at a marked location in a string of known words has the effect of completing the sentence, three primary sources of difficulty are eliminated:

1. Only one new word is presented, so the subject cannot err in choice of words.

2. The blank location in the (potential) sentence is marked (with the interrogative marker) so the subject cannot err as to where in the sentence to put the word.

3. The completing operation always consists of addition, rather than addition plus the possibility of deletion and/or rearrangement.

If one-to-one substitution is the simplest language-teaching procedure, then by systematically imposing complications upon it we can test the limits of the language-acquisition capacities of different species:

1. We can leap from one-to-one to many-to-one substitution and examine the subject's ability to negotiate the leap.

2. Incorrect elements can be inserted in incomplete sentences and completion of the sentence made to depend not only on addition of new elements but on deletion of existing ones.

3. Correct words can be incorrectly ordered and sentence production made to depend on rearrangement.

Although Sarah's training was largely restricted to one-to-one substitution, other of the linguistic operations occurred in the broader use of the language. Some of them were introduced by Sarah, others were demanded by the lessons, but none of them was in any sense taught Sarah. For example, in the course of her early sentence production, Sarah relied heavily on rearrangement. Instead of copying the trainer's production order, although it was repeatedly modeled for her, she produced sentences by systematic rearrangement. The rearrangement was neither taught her, nor even modeled for her, but was her own invention.

Many-to-one substitution was another operation Sarah used, different from the one-to-one substitution she was taught. It was used first in teaching her that "different" could be formed by negating "same," and "same" by negating "different." Later it was used in training the plural particle "pl." Although the negative instance of a word was typically formed by appending the negative particle to it, it was not sensible to append "no" to "pl." This being so, it was not possible to use the usual positive and negative alternatives in a choice test as the way to assess learning. We gave her instead sentences with two adjacent interrogative markers, along with three words from which to choose. After only five trials of this kind, we removed one of the question marks while still requiring the substitution of two words. For instance, although "apple banana ? ? fruit," the two-question marker form used in the beginning, required the substitution of "is" and "pl" in that order, the subsequent one-marker form, for example, "apple banana ? color," required substitution of "is-not" and "pl" (in that order) and so was a genuine case of many-to-one substitution. A third case involved questions concerning the color of more than one object. The lesson exposed her for the first time to cantaloupe and strawberry, which were referred to as "yellow fruit" and "red fruit," respectively, because neither were yet named. [For instance, she was given the instruction "Insert red fruit (in) dish" and correctly put the strawberry (not the cantaloupe) in the dish (not the pail).] The lesson dealt mainly with her ability to apply modifiers to class words (as opposed to proper nouns) and she was asked questions of the following kind: "?

color of cantaloupe strawberry" (What are the colors of the pieces of cantaloupe and strawberry?). She answered correctly "Yellow red color of cantaloupe strawberry," picking the two color words from a set of eight words and substituting the two words in the proper order for the one interrogative marker.

Deletion, another sentence-producing operation, was used both on an explicit and implicit basis. Implicit deletion first occurred in Sarah's untutored inclusion of two or more words of the same grammatical class in the same sentence. She put two verbs in the sentence, applying both to the same noun or object, for example, "Wash give apple." Later, she put two and sometimes three nouns in the same sentence, all of them as objects of one verb, for example, "Mary give Sarah apple banana orange." The complex forms involving double verbs and objects did not occur until after she had first produced equivalent outcomes by using multiple simpler sentences; for example, she did not write "Wash give apple" until she had written "Wash apple" and "Give apple" many times before. The deletion in these cases was implicit, the compound forms serving to eliminate redundant elements that would have appeared had she used the customary two or more sentences to achieve the same effect. That is, each compound form could be seen as a functional replacement for the multiple sentences that had preceded it, and the compound form was invented by Sarah.

Later, in giving her questions of the following kind: "Red yellow ? color," "Red ? pl color," and so forth, we made a more explicit test of her ability to use deletion. The first sentence was properly completed simply by substituting "is" for the interrogative marker; but the second sentence required not only the introduction of "is" but also the deletion of "pl." That is, because "red," the subject of the second sentence, is obviously singular, the verb should not be accompanied by a plural marker. Sarah failed to delete the plural marker in sentences of the second kind. She was given only four such sentences in a set of nine, the others consisting of sentences with a plural subject. Her relevant alternatives on all the trials in this lesson were two "pl" markers and two "is" particles.

Her failure is ambiguous. It could not be interpreted to mean that she was incapable of discriminating singular from plural subjects: she had already passed more demanding tests on that topic. For instance, she had used a pluralized verb when the subject was, say, "red, yellow" or "apple, banana"—two words that referred to two objects—but a singular form of the verb when the subject was, say, "red apple," two words both referring to the same object (page 328). Most likely her failure to delete reflects her undue observance of the well-taught rule: Do not alter the incomplete sentences given you except by adding to them. If so, she was improperly prepared for the test. Sarah should have been taught in some other context that overt deletion was a legitimate operation before being required to carry out deletion in this context.

HIERARCHICAL ORGANIZATION

Consider the sentence in the chimp language, "Sarah insert banana pail apple dish." Translated into English this is the instruction to put the banana into the pail and the apple in the dish. To carry out that simple instruction, however, or instructions of that general kind requires a knowledge of the internal organization of the sentence, an organization that can be shown by using parentheses to indicate the dependencies among the words. For example, "Sarah { insert [(banana pail) (apple dish)] }" shows that "banana" and "pail" go together, likewise "apple" and "dish"; that "insert" applies not only to "banana‒pail" but also to "apple‒dish"; and finally that it is Sarah who is to carry out the entire action.

This example carries us beyond word order to a second contribution of syntax—hierarchical organization of the sentence. How essential is that factor? What would be lost if, for example, the strings of words in the language were sensitive to order but were not organized hierarchically? We can answer that question by comparing the subject's behavior to the above sentence under conditions in which its understanding is based on either of three levels of organization: (1) word knowledge or gross semantic rule, (2) refined semantic rule, or (3) hierarchical.

Several years ago, in working with psychotic children, R. Metz and I devised some tests of language comprehension to determine whether the severely impaired speech production that characterized these children was owed to performance factors or to something deeper. Some of the children failed all of the comprehension tests, while at the same time performing adequately on nonlanguage tests. They had what we ended up calling "word knowledge" but, so far as our tests could determine, little else. Response to the sentence in question at the level of word knowledge would amount to the following.

Understanding of the word "Sarah" would result in Sarah's carrying out whatever action was carried out rather than waiting for, say, Mary to act, as she would on the occasion of sentences that began with "Mary." Second, an understanding of the word "insert" would assure action of one kind—putting one thing into another—as opposed to cutting, taking, giving, etc., the other verbs or operators that she knows. Third, the objects acted on would be confined to those named. With no more than word knowledge, however, there would be great latitude in what was inserted into what. The dish could go into the pail as readily as the banana went into the dish. The specific pairing of banana with pail and apple with dish that would alone constitute evidence of an understanding of the sentence would not be guaranteed by knowledge limited to individual words.

A higher level of organization could be provided by semantic covariation rules. They could limit the possible outcomes, bringing them closer to the desired one, but would still fall short. Actually, what we have called word knowledge can be formulated as a coarse semantic covariation rule; the second level of organization then amounts to the addition of a second semantic rule, refining the first rule. For example, the first case could be analyzed in a manner already suggested above, as a rule in which the verb was the predicate and the agents and objects were the arguments taken by the predicate. This could be diagrammed as

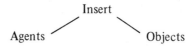

emphasizing the focal role of the verb and the secondary role of that which instanced the verb—inserters, on the one hand, and objects of insertion, on the other.

The addition of a second semantic rule could differentiate the object class, separating the containers (dish, pail) from that which got contained (apple, banana, etc.). This better defined situation could be diagrammed as

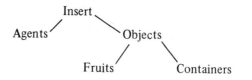

The increased definition of semantic space would further delimit the subject's behavior; for example, it would keep the dish out of the pail, but it would no more assure the exact outcome indicative of an understanding of the hierarchically organized sentence than would the first organization. Indeed, no combination of semantic rules could assure that outcome because, so to speak, pails and dishes would accept one kind of fruit as readily as the other.

Training procedure for compound sentence. Proving competence in syntax is ticklish because highly inferential hypotheses are always more difficult to test than those which lie closer to the surface of the data. The problem is aggravated by a factor that the reader may guess by recalling his or her own childhood. Grammar was not Sarah's favorite subject—there was a limit to the number of tests she would accept on this topic and that limit could not always be stretched to include all the control sentences one might desire.

We taught Sarah the compound sentence in three steps, all in the comprehension mode. First, she was trained on the four atomic sentences from which the target or compound sentence could be derived. These included:

1. Sarah banana pail insert
2. Sarah apple pail insert
3. Sarah banana dish insert
4. Sarah apple dish insert

She was given two errorless instructions on each of the four sentences. The trainer wrote a sentence on the board and then placed before Sarah the object and the container specified in the sentence. This was followed by six lessons in which two containers and two objects were placed before her, and she was required to select the correct object and insert it in the correct container. The containers were always a dish and a pail and the objects consisted of all possible pairs of chocolate, apple, cracker, and banana. The instructions were given to her one at a time in a mixed order. She was correct on 58 of 85 trials, or just below 70% and well above chance which, with four alternatives (two containers and two objects) was 25%.

In the second step, the same sentences were presented in pairs, side by side, one parallel to the other, simply to accustom her to carrying out the two acts of insertion that were required by the target sentence. The first pair, given in an errorless manner, was followed by the pairs "Sarah apple dish insert," "Sarah apple pail insert," "Sarah nut dish insert," and "Sarah nut pail insert," which were not errorless and required that she choose both the object and the container. She was given two additional lessons, with all possible pairs of sentences, and was correct 22 times in 30 trials (15 pairs), or about 77% correct. She started both lessons by processing the sentence on the left first but then shifted to starting with the right hand sentence. She forsook this strategy, too, before the lessons were over, so that she ended up processing one sentence first as often as the other.

The pairs of sentences that had been presented side by side were then written one immediately above the other as shown below. In the course of the next four lessons the two vertically joined atomic sentences were converted into one compound sentence. The procedure generated sentences of the kind shown below:

1	2	3
Sarah	Sarah	Sarah
banana	banana	banana
pail	pail	pail
insert	insert	cracker
Sarah	cracker	dish
cracker	dish	insert
dish	insert	
insert		

Neither putting one sentence above the other nor the stepwise deletion of the two redundant elements disrupted her performance. (The redundant words were deleted in two steps to be on the safe side; there was no actual evidence that they could not have been deleted in one step.) On the vertically joined individual sentences, she made one error in 12 instructions (6 pairs). The redundant "Sarah" was removed in the next lesson, forming sentences of the second type shown above, and she was given five of them, or ten instructions. She was incorrect on both parts of the second instruction but was correct on all other instructions.

In the next lesson, the second redundant element was removed, forming the target sentence of which she was given the following eight:

1. Sarah chocolate dish, cracker pail insert
2. Sarah cracker dish, cracker pail insert
3. Sarah chocolate dish, cracker pail insert
4. Sarah chocolate pail, cracker dish insert
5. Sarah cracker pail, chocolate dish insert
6. Sarah cracker pail, chocolate dish insert
7. Sarah chocolate pail, cracker dish insert
8. Sarah chocolate dish, chocolate pail insert

She was incorrect on the second part of the second instruction and on both parts of the third instruction but corrected herself in that case before the trainer could intervene and made no other mistakes.

On both sentence Types 1 (no deletion) and 2 (deletion of redundant proper name), she started with the top of the sentence as often as with the bottom. With the true compound sentence, however, she showed a consistent tendency to carry out the second clause or bottom part of the instruction first, perhaps because the verb was now found only in that part of the sentence. For example, on the first and second sessions with the compound sentence she processed the second clause first on seven of eight and five of seven instructions, respectively ($p < .05$).

Three kinds of transfer tests were then given, the first using new object names and the second a new verb, whereas in the third modifiers were added producing "red dish," "yellow dish," etc., instead of just "dish" or "pail."

A still more basic change was incorporated in these tests; some clauses now specified two objects and so contrasted with clauses that specified only one, for example, "Sarah insert apple cracker dish cracker pail." Such an instruction required that she put both apple and cracker in the dish but only cracker in the pail.

On the first transfer test, "peanut" and "orange" were added to the object names used in training, and she was given 11 compound sentences (or 22 instructions); she made only two errors, with none of them on the new words "peanut" and "orange." Next the lessons were expanded by sentences in which sometimes both clauses specified one object and other times one specified one and the other specified two. For example, "Sarah insert chocolate dish cracker pail" versus "Sarah insert chocolate dish chocolate cracker pail." This complication did not reduce either her accuracy or, in gross qualitative terms at least, the speed of her performance. On two such lessons she was correct on 15 of 19 trials and on 14 of 17, respectively, or about 87% correct.

"Take" was then substituted for "insert" and now the familiar dish and pail were given to her but already equipped with both of the objects in question; she was required to remove a specified object from the appropriate container rather than to put them in the container. She made two errors in 13 such instructions.

Later, she was given a more difficult test in which two pairs of containers were placed before her, one pair consisting of an empty pail and an empty dish, and an identical pair in which the pail and dish each held a piece of banana and apple. Additional apple and banana were placed midway between the two pairs of containers, and the position of the containers was changed over the course of the test. She was instructed to take a specified object from a specified location on some trials, and to insert a specified object in a specified location on other trials. She made only one error in nine trials, with none on the first five. The test was more difficult than the preceeding tests because, first, the instructions to insert or to take were combined in the same session, and second, there were no situational cues as to when to carry out either act. Interestingly, when carrying out instructions to insert, she did not choose items that were already in containers, although their use was not proscribed, but chose items that were not yet in any container.

In the last test on this series, the considerable complexity already at hand was added to by modifying the containers, generating nine-word sentences of the following kind: "Sarah cracker candy yellow dish cracker blue dish insert." The instructions were simplified perhaps by the limited variation in each factor, two colors and two containers throughout the session and two objects per trial, yet they were presented in all possible combinations. On two such lessons she was correct on 10 of 12 and 9 of 11 trials per total trials, respectively, or about 82% correct. In English paraphrase, these instructions told her to separate the foods that were before her, to put one or more into one container and one or more into another. Containers were sometimes distinguished as to type—pail or dish— and were then referred to by one word, but other times they differed in color only and were then referred to by modifier plus the type word. Finally, the instructions sometimes told her to take objects already in the containers and at other times to put them into the containers.

Did syntax play any role or were the compound sentences processed on an exclusively semantic basis? She may have used a rule that says, in effect: Apply the container word to the object word above. This would work for the individual sentences but not when one sentence was written above the other; then the bottommost container word would apply to two object words, one directly and one indirectly above it. In the compound sentences used in training (see page 327) the rule would lead her to apply dish correctly but pail incorrectly, for pail would apply to both apple and banana, both of which were above it. There was no evidence for an error of this kind.

This error could be overcome if the rule were expanded to read: Apply the container word to the fruit word immediately above it. But this modification would fail in the case of sentences of this kind: "Sarah insert apple dish apple banana pail," where apple would go into dish but would fail to make it into the pail. That is, the effect of "immediately" would be to confine pail to banana. She was tested on sentences of this kind and performed at the same level as on the other instructions in this series.

What then was the rule she used in processing such sentences? The functional effect of the rules, although not necessarily the rules themselves, can be described by grouping the words in the sentence by parentheses and brackets as shown above. The bracketing emphasizes the following features of her performance.

She recognized that the word "Sarah" applied to the whole sentence and not just to the first clause; that is, she did not confine her behavior to the first clause but carried out the whole instruction. By the same token, she must have recognized that the word "insert" applied across the sentence, to all appropriate items mentioned in the sentence, and not just to the second clause. Additionally, she divided the fruit and container words appropriately, using a container word as a break and grouping together all fruit words that occurred above any container word.

REDUCED LANGUAGE

Variants of human language can be produced only by reducing human language, for we have no system other than language with which to represent possible distinctions not found in language. David McNeil (1974) recently proposed a specific reduction on human language not as a hypothetical but as a language actually realized in the protocol of Washoe, a female chimpanzee trained in American Sign Language by Beatrice and R. A. Gardner (1971). According to McNeil, Sarah has learned a humanlike language only because of strict training; if the ape is left more nearly to its own resources, as Washoe has been, it induces a language different from the human one. In working through Washoe's spontaneous constructions, McNeil finds a simple rule: the addressee or party being addressed always precedes the addressor or speaker. For instance, in "Roger Washoe tickle," presumably a request for Roger to tickle Washoe, "Roger" the addressee, precedes "Washoe" the addressor. Likewise in "Give you Washoe banana," "You give Washoe banana," "You banana give Washoe," etc., the addressee "you" (pronouns are ikons in ASL, consisting merely of pointing to the party in question, and so have none of the complexity of pronouns in natural language) consistently precedes "Washoe," the addressor. The addressee–addressor rule, according to McNeil, is the only rule instanced by Washoe's protocol. Actions and objects are marked, e.g., "banana," "tickled," "give," but they are not bound by grammar and are essentially in free variation. McNeil argues that such a grammar makes good sense for the chimpanzee because it is preoccupied with social relations and not with objects and actions.

Of the several difficulties that confront McNeil's proposal, one seems insuperable. There is no Washoe protocol from which McNeil or anyone else can induce a grammar, for the Gardners have not recorded the word order of Washoe's production (Gardner & Gardner, 1971). To whom then shall McNeil's rule be attributed? The rule is an embarrassment in a sense for the record on which it is based is not a literal record of Washoe's signs but an attempt to preserve their sense or meaning. As such, the "protocol" reflects dispositions of the recording organisms no less than of the organism recorded; if the rule is valid, it must reflect regularities in the response of Washoe's recorders no less than of Washoe. But is is also possible to question the rule itself. For example, in arriving at it, McNeil has translated "Roger," which is almost certainly the name of Fouts, one of Washoe's main trainers, as "thank you"; if translated as Fouts, or the name of an agent, the rule breaks down.

Despite its difficulties, McNeil's hypothesis is an intriguing response to the Washoe data. Moreover, the interesting problems in McNeil's proposal do not come from difficulties in the protocol. Ignore the fact that there is apparently no Washoe protocol from which to induce a would-be chimp syntax and consider instead his proposal on the face of it.

First, it is interesting to see how narrow the difference between man and chimp would become on this proposal.

1. Both species have "rich" conceptual structures. They distinguish between agent, object, action, etc. Indeed, it is the chimp's ability to make these distinctions that makes impressive its failure to use these distinctions as the basis of its syntax. Were a species conceptually incapable of distinguishing one trainer from another, one action from another, one psychological state from another, it would be of no interest that it was either unable to adopt human syntax or had a different one of its own.

2. Both species symbolize, that is, use one thing to represent another, and do so with regard to all possible kinds of things. Unlike the *Cebus* monkey, which we have tentatively found capable of acquiring names for objects but—so far at least—not for properties, the chimpanzee can symbolize over the whole human conceptual domain.

3. Both species have a syntax (independent of semantics or general cognition) and their basic logical structure is the same, chimp syntax differing only in detail from that of man. Like man, the chimp abstracts from extremely complex

situations a relatively few features and devises a system based on those features. In the human case, the basic features are agents, actions, and objects and the system answers the question: Who is doing what to whom, where and when? In the chimp, however, the features abstracted are simply agents and the question answered is: Who is addressing whom? Nevertheless, both systems use word order to answer the questions with which they are respectively concerned. In human syntax, therefore, agents may precede action and objects, whereas in chimp syntax addressee precedes addressor.

Because McNeil (1970) rejects the view that language can be derived from general cognition but insists instead on an innate language-specific competence, his conclusion follows with good logic from his overall position: Any species, chimpanzee or otherwise, in which language is demonstrable must also have an innate, unique language-specific competence. If two language-competent species differ, they do so in the kind of syntax they have. McNeil ends, therefore, not by denying syntax to the chimpanzee but by shrinking the distance between man and chimpanzee to a difference in kind or complexity of syntax.

Does it make sense that a species should have a lexicon including names for agents, actions, objects, and properties, on the one hand, and a syntax that includes rules for only agents, on the other? If, as McNeil suggests, the chimpanzee does not operate on the material world but only on the social one, then I should expect to see that preoccupation revealed in its lexicon as well as its syntax. I do not see the sense in making the lexicon strikingly richer than the syntax. The result is the anomalous one in which the syntax is simply not germane to most of the distinctions the species draws, that is, to most of the words that it utters. If the chimpanzee were generally indifferent to the material world, I should suggest it would not mark objects, actions, properties—things of no interest to it—or would learn to do so only with great difficulty. More likely its lexicon would instead consist only of names of agents and so would be in perfect accord with its syntax, which too consisted of a rule concerned only with agents.[1]

---

[1] Moreover, granting the species a lexicon richer than its syntax makes it possible for the species to produce sentences that are conceptually independent of its syntax. For example, if McNeil's account were accurate, Washoe might produce strings that did not merely violate McNeil's rule but could not even be judged by it. "Daddy home," "I want to play," "I like apple," etc., have nothing to do with addressor–addressee relations and so do not fall under the governance of the syntax; yet they may occur nonetheless simply because the lexicon is less restricted than the syntax. This problem could be averted either by disallowing strings with contents independent of the syntactic topic—in effect, by not allowing the creature to talk about anything except addressor–addressee relations—or else by allowing such strings but requiring that if they occur their word order be random. These problems could not arise in the first place, however, if the lexical reduction were commensurate with the syntactic one. Then the subject could not talk about anything that it could not talk about in an orderly way.

On the other hand, it may be reasonable for a species to have a strong lexicon and a weak syntax, such that a large part of every sentence it utters is independent of grammatical constraint. One might even argue that in the evolution of language such a condition represented an intermediate stage. Lexicon preceded syntax; growing at a more rapid rate, it applied pressure for syntactic rules to develop and encompass ever more of the lexical categories. Perhaps contemporary human language, in which syntactic rules encompass all lexical categories, is merely a stage and earlier systems have not had this character or have had it in lesser degree. Whether this speculation is credited or not, some down to earth evidence remains that speaks against McNeil's syntax. Nothing in Sarah's data protocol or that of Peony and Elizabeth points to a propensity for the agent class as opposed to the other classes. In fact, agent names were learned less rapidly than those of objects and actions, and not because the training method for this class was in any way troubled. Chimps and trainers wore their names around their necks like medallions, offering an admirably direct contact between word and referent. From a lexical point of view, therefore, there was no support for the contention that agents, or agent relations, had unique salience for chimpanzees.

There was equally little support from a syntactic point of view. Sentences concerning nonsocial, strictly physical relations, such as "Red on green" or "All cracker is pl square" were learned without difficulty, certainly as readily as any that dealt with social relations. For an animal for which physical relations are said to be irrelevant the chimp does a remarkably good job in mastering the predicate relations "Red color of apple," "Square shape of cracker," etc. Of course, it need hardly be pointed out that it is less than correct to assume that the chimp does not operate on the material world. The animal busies itself with the physical universe from morning to night and, when the required materials are at hand, sorts the physical world in all possible ways. It is true that the chimp has remarkable social skills but not at the expense of those dealing with the physical world.

In mapping the transaction of giving, we have assumed that Sarah can make extensive, if not unlimited, substitutions on the transaction—a trait that may have emerged at the pongid level of complexity and gone on to reach its fullest expression with man. Therefore we have taught her names for donors, recipients, and the objects transferred, the three points at which giving is subject to change. Moreover, because agents need not give but can also wash, cut, insert, etc., she has also been taught names for these other actions. In so proceeding, perhaps we imposed on Sarah a human analysis of giving. But what is the alternative? Can we divide the give transaction in a way other than we have?

The order in which the transaction has been mapped—object, donor, operator; or donor, recipient, etc.—is not something we have yet tested. Also, it may make a difference how many members of one class are established before a new class is introduced; this too remains to be tested. The effect of the order of the mapping can readily be converted into an experimental question, as can the number of entries that should be established in one class before proceeding to another, for we have no difficulty in proposing alternative orders or numbers.

However, the effect of alternative partitionings, of dividing the transaction one way rather than another, does not seem to go over into an experimental question, for we are apparently incapable of proposing significantly different partitionings. We see the transaction one way and one way only. All partitionings that we may propose as alternative to donor, recipient, object, etc., turn out to be trivial variations on this one, proposals either to omit a class or to slice an existing class more finely. Our freedom in this matter appears to consist in our choice of situations to map. Instead of starting with giving, for example, we might have begun with body care, leading into the operator "wash" and names for parts of the body. Once having chosen a transaction, however, we are not free in how to partition it.

Although the attempt to picture languages different from the human one is more frustrating than illuminating, before we leave this topic consider one variant that departs more radically than those we have so far considered. In treating donor, recipient, object, and action as major sources of variation, we relegated to a secondary status such matters as quantity or quality of the object given, as well as speed, force, or other intensive properties of the action. For instance, in such sentences as "Mary gave Sarah a big apple," or ". . . gave the apple quickly," we treated the modifiers, such as "big" and "quickly," as secondary sources of variation in comparison to the four primary ones, and although ultimately we mapped at least some of them, we did not do so until later.

This judgment could be turned around, so that modifiers were made primary and the normal objects of modification, secondary. Although it would not be easy to rationalize the circumstance that would favor this emphasis, perhaps a species that showed little variation in either kind of act of kind of object acted on would find this emphasis compatible. When asked by a voice from on high, "What is going on down there?" a species that did little except, say, exchange apples, would reply in terms of sentences linking speed, force, and manner to color, size, weight, temperature, etc. From this information one would know that, for example, "fast" and "forceful" were linked to "yellow" and "sweet," "slow yet forceful" to "small and cold," "slow and delicate" to "red and shiny."

Examples of this alien language are provided in Table 16.1, where we compare four versions of the "same" sentence: first, sentences with no modifiers whatever, which is essentially what Sarah has been taught in the beginning; second, modifiers added to normal English sentences; third, the inverse of the first, modifiers now replacing the items they normally modify; and fourth, only modifier pairs, the fully alien language. A human being given the information in the alien language would be thoroughly provoked; he would seek to get behind it, to the agents, actions, and objects that in his view were its causes. If he knew

TABLE 16.1
Examples of Alien Languages

No modifiers	English + modifiers	Modifiers replace modified	Alien language
He gave her an apple	He quickly gave her a red apple	He quickied her a red	Quick–red
Sarah gave Mary a cracker	Sarah hesitantly gave Mary a cracker	Sarah slowed Mary a square	Slow–square
John gave Mary a cantaloupe	John proudly presented Mary a big cantaloupe	John proudlied Mary a round	Proud–round

the circumstances to which the information applied, he would combine his knowledge of general laws and local correlations to attempt to determine what acts carried out on what objects resulted in a linkage between, say, forceful and sweet. But the information provided by this alien language would be deeply frustrating for man. It does not answer the questions of interest to him; it focuses on secondary events from which he can only dimly infer the events that are primary for him.

17
Mechanisms of Intelligence: Preconditions for Language

Language is so deeply enmeshed in intelligence that a discussion of the psychological prerequisites for language is at the same time a discussion of some of the mechanisms of intelligence. In this concluding chapter I review the following mechanisms: causal inference, intentionality, representational capacity, memory, and second-order relations—in each case, attempting to decide, often on the basis of meager evidence, in which species the mechanisms are likely to be found.

CAUSAL INFERENCE

In acquiring language one acquires labels for existing concepts; this proposal can be tested with admirable directness in many cases. Can the subject discriminate between conditions that exemplify same and different?, all and none?, red and black?, etc. If so, according to the proposal, it should be possible to teach the subject names for same—different, the quantifiers, and the like. Not all concepts are as simple as those in the examples, however, and some of them must be approached differently. For instance, in the case of if—then or the conditional relation, we observe that the conditional sentence is a way of expressing a causal relation. "If you drop that, it will break." "If you smile at Mary, she will smile back." "If you touch that, you'll get burned." These sentences and the infinitely many possible like them express a causal relation between the antecedent and the consequent. Only a species that made a causal analysis of its experience would use sentences of this form productively. Hence, in the case of the conditional relation, we designed the test to answer the question, Does the subject make a causal analysis of its experience? To answer this question we used a simple visual test.

The subject was given an intact object, a blank space, and the same object in a changed or terminal state, along with various alternatives, and was encouraged to complete the sequence by placing one of the alternatives in the blank space. For example, the subject was given such items as an intact apple and a cut apple; a dry sponge and a wet sponge; a clear piece of paper and one with writing on it. In these cases, the three alternatives given the subject consisted of a knife, a bowl of water, and a writing instrument.

Three of the four chimpanzees tested in this way required no more than general adaptation to the test format before responding correctly. Their ability to place the knife between the intact and severed apple, the water between the dry and wet sponge, and the pencil between the unmarked and pencil-marked paper showed that they correctly identified the instrument or operator needed to change each object from its initial to its terminal state. Simple as this outcome is it can be given a stronger interpretation than may first meet the eye. The visual sequences are infinitely ambiguous: each can be coded in indefinitely many ways, such as red–blank–red, one–blank–two, round–blank–flat, large–blank–small. Not only the test items but also the three alternatives are subject to indeterminately many codings. Knife, for instance, need not be read as knife (instrument that cuts) but can be coded as sharp, metal, long, shiny, etc., and the same holds for the other alternatives. The subjects evidently did not code the sequences or alternatives in these ways, for they consistently chose alternatives compatible with only one coding, viz.: How do you change the object from the intact to the terminal stage? With what instrument do you produce the change? Because the subjects read the sequences in a specific and consistent way—finding the same question in each of the sequences—I infer that they have a schema, a structure that assigns an interpretation to an otherwise infinitely ambiguous sequence.

The ape's ability to respond in this fashion was by no means limited to familiar object–implement pairs. They performed equally well not only on pairs they had never experienced, but also on pairs that were anomalous, such as apples that had been written on, sponges that had been cut, and writing paper that had been dunked in water. Choices of this kind indicate that they had not merely associated implements with objects, but had formed broader associations involving implements and outcomes. How different is knowledge of this kind from causal analysis? To say that an individual knows what a knife does is tantamount to saying: it knows that if an item of a certain kind is applied appropriately it will produce an outcome of a certain kind. I see little difference between this functional knowledge and causal inference except for the greater generality of the latter.

Perhaps, however, the chimpanzee's ability to respond in this fashion indicates merely that it has learned the content of certain sequences, that is, what comes after what. The fact that it can respond to new sequences need not counter this argument, but may indicate only that it has defined the elements in the sequence abstractly, which is what we would expect with the chimpanzee in any case. Yet how likely is it that the chimpanzee has learned only the content of the sequences, without learning how they are brought about? Consider the two main ways in which the sequences could be brought about. In the first, an agent applies an instrument to an object, producing the change in question. In the second, an agent may be present as an observer but play no role otherwise. In the case of cutting, for example, once an apple comes within a threshold distance of a knife, it throws itself upon the knife (or alternatively, the knife upon attaining a threshold distance, applies itself to the apple). My point is that the chimpanzee can discriminate between these two theories of action as well as we can, can eliminate the latter as readily as we can, and indeed, in all likelihood has never so much as contemplated the fanciful or second theory.

It is desirable, of course, to have direct proof of this claim, and while it should be possible to get such proof, the best I can do at this time is provide indirect evidence. Two kinds of data suggest that the chimpanzee has a concept of both agency and animacy (that is decidedly more compatible with the first theory of action than with the second). At an early stage of training, when first being taught word order, Sarah wrote 409 3- or 4-word sentences requesting that one of several fruits be given her. Although she made 76 errors of word order (and many more errors of word choice) in doing so, only three times did she begin a sentence with the name of an object, mistakenly putting the object in the agent's role, as in, for example, "Orange give Sarah apple." The infrequency of this kind of error is compatible with the view that she divides the world as we do, assigning different functions to objects and agents. It is also compatible with the classification or sorting data from Peony and Elizabeth, showing that they could separate animate from inanimate, putting teeth, feathers, hair, etc., in one place, and rocks, metal, glass, etc., in another.

It is noteworthy, also, that the visual sequences were by no means iconic representations of the actions tested. Cutting, wetting, and marking are analogue processes in which an agent brings about a continuous change in an object. In cutting, for example, an agent applies a knife to an apple, exerting pressure until the apple divides. The test items did not portray the gradual division of the apple, but presented only the digital highlights of the analogue process, and did not present the agent at all. Nevertheless, the chimpanzees evidently recognized the test sequences as representations of the actions. If the tests had failed, we might then have considered using motion pictures or other iconic forms of representation; but the animals succeeded despite the abstract form of the representation. Thus, chimpanzees not only have a schema for cause–effect relations but one that can be activated by noniconic representations.

Because the present tests dealt only with the physical domain, they leave open whether or not the chimpanzee can recognize cause–effect relations in the psychological or social domain. The lack of appropriate stimuli has prevented us from making such tests, yet it is easy enough to describe the form such tests would take. For example, in one such test, frame one would show Elizabeth begging food from Peony, frame two would be blank and would be filled in by the subject, and frame three would show Elizabeth and Peony playing, engaging in mutual grooming, or hugging one another. The alternatives given the subject would include Peony ignoring Elizabeth's request, Peony sharing with Elizabeth, Elizabeth stealing Peony's food, and the like. Of these alternatives, only Peony sharing with Elizabeth would be compatible with the harmonious outcome shown in frame three, and the chimpanzee's appropriate choice in this and comparable tests would indicate that it can recognize representations of social as well as of physical actions. Notice, incidentally, that the test is designed so that selection of the missing frame cannot be based simply on a knowledge of physical action. If in frame three both animals were shown to be eating, one could conclude on physical grounds alone that Peony must have shared with Elizabeth. But since in frame three neither animal is shown eating, the content of the second frame can only be inferred from the social character of the behavior in the third frame.

Let us assume for the sake of discussion that the chimpanzees can pass the social tests as they have passed the physical ones—which does not seem too risky an assumption. If the chimpanzees can recognize representations of both physical and social actions, perhaps they can take the next step and recognize higher order structures that are composed of physical and social actions. Physical and social acts are the building blocks of stories, novels, tales, and the like. Indeed, all narrative prose is formed by appropriately combining physical and social acts. If a species can recognize the basic elements of which stories are formed, perhaps it can also recognize stories themselves.

Finally, however, both the actual and hypothetical evidence show only that the chimpanzee can recognize representations of action. How well the chimpanzee would deal with a natural situation, one more demanding than dunking a sponge in water or applying a knife to an apple, is not shown. Some of this is shown by Köhler's (1951) data, of course, and more recently there are field observations (e.g., Teleki, 1974b) for situations more complex than those Köhler contrived, such as those involved in hunting and the extraction of termites from their mounds. Moreover, some of these observations provide the rare opportunity to compare three species all attacking the same problem, for in Africa, it is not only the chimpanzee that eats termites, but the baboon and man as well (Teleki, 1974b).

Each species has developed its own technology for separating the termite from its mound or nest, in a way that nicely reflects its intelligence. None of the three species has been so crude as to simply crush the mound. This would be undesirable on several grounds. The exterior shell of the mound is thick and hard; breaking the mound would mix earth and termites in a fashion that all three species would find unsavory; and finally, it would destroy an otherwise nearly permanent resource. When the separation is carried out nondestructively, the same mounds are harvested perennially.

The chimpanzee, as is now well known, separates the termite from its nest by a fishing technique. The ape selects an appropriate straw, sometimes from as much as 100 yards from the nest, finds the "hidden" orifices near the surface of the mound, inserts the straw, jiggles it while waiting patiently in the manner of all fishermen, and then withdraws the straw in a characteristic motion. Observers (e.g., Teleki, 1974b) who have trailed the chimpanzee, attempting to duplicate its skills, have reported numerous difficulties, all testifying to the subtleties of the technology. Their difficulties concern the straw, the distinctive jiggling motion, and especially inserting the straw into the mound. Where the apes locate concealed orifices on the surface of the mound and deftly open them with their fingernail, the human observer was often reduced to chopping holes.

One finds in the chimpanzee's technology evidence of at least three aspects of its intelligence: planning, memory, and inference:

1. In selecting the straw at a distance from the mound the chimpanzee appears to be able to plan. If planning is correctly said to depend on the ability to hold in mind a representation of one's objective, then there is no question but that the chimpanzee should be able to plan. Its ability to generate and use—in highly determinate ways—internal representations has been amply demonstrated in the present research.

2. The individual chimpanzee is said to collect from over 25 different mounds. Its ability to remember the locations of the mounds, and the orifices concealed in each of them, testifies to the ape's long-term memory. Our own evidence confirms this capacity most dramatically in the animal's ability to identify the "anatomy" of various fruits.

3. I have not been in a position to interrogate the field chimpanzee, but if I were, I would ask it whether or not it knows what goes on in a termite mound. Can it infer what happens between the time when it inserts an empty straw into the mound and withdraws it full of termites? Fishing is after all a cognitively special activity, a kind of black-box technology in which input is related to output by a hidden middle. We could use the visual causality tests described earlier to interrogate the chimpanzee, and find out whether or not it knows the content of the hidden middle. The three pictures would consist of a chimp fishing, a blank frame, and a chimp holding a laden straw, about to eat the termites. The chimp's task would be the usual one of selecting the missing picture. The alternatives could include: (1) termites with their feet or antenna caught in cracks in the straw; (2) termites caught while using the straw essentially as a bridge to cross little streams inside the mound; (3) termites either attacking the straw or trapped by their own curiosity, and carried out even while exploring the straw, etc. Let us assume that the third alternative is the correct one. Whether it is or not, if the chimpanzee chose it consistently, this would

demonstrate that it could identify the fishing situation as one that induced curiosity, and could picture another species responding to the situation in the same way it would. But perhaps this exceeds pongid intelligence.

Baboons have been observed to observe chimpanzees fishing and to eat the termites the apes leave behind, but no baboon has otherwise benefited from its observations. Baboon technology is vastly simpler. When rainy weather brings the termites out of the mound and into the air, the baboons catch them in flight.

Man neither fishes for the termites nor waits for rainy weather to enable him to catch them in flight. Instead he taps on the mound with a stick, or makes a distinctive sound with his mouth. This sound sufficiently resembles the sound of rain so that the termites think it is raining outside, and they emerge from the mound, where they are either eaten on the spot, or collected and carried away for later eating. Unlike the baboon which is at the mercy of the weather, man creates his own weather, the sound of it at least.

If the reader has not detected my anthropomorphism, let me then call his attention to it. How do I know what the termite thinks? Certainly it is possible to give a simpler account of termite behavior, without referring to its putative thought, by treating the sound of rain either as a CS for leaving the mound or as a signal for rain. Anyone who has taken introductory psychology or who has been otherwise warned against anthropomorphism could give such an account. But I suggest that, all such warnings notwithstanding, anthropomorphism is probably the basis of the human technology. To be able to put yourself in the position of the other one requires a well-developed self concept, one that may be exclusive to human intelligence. Anthropomorphism may be a methodological sin of which only the human species could be guilty.

Needless to say, I cannot prove this interpretation any more than the interpretation of any observation can be proved nonexperimentally. People may make the sound of rain, rather than pouring water on the mound, simply because water is less available.[1] Yet, quite apart from the matter of availability, water or

---

[1] Urination would solve the problem of availability, yet there are no reports of its use in the accounts I have seen. Freud (1964) once remarked that civilization began when the job of fire caretaking was transferred from man to woman, for then it was no longer convenient to extinguish the fire in the manner in which it had been. We can all be grateful to Freud for having published this remark; it is always encouraging to know that bad ideas are not one's exclusive province and that they need not kill off better ones. On the more sensible side, Freud's comment raises the question of how technologies began. Premack (1976) has speculated that all the technologies of a species, such as the chimpanzee's nest building and more recently hunting, were originally "invented" by gifted individuals—as is known to be the case with the Japanese Macaques, where two recent and striking innovations in food technology are both attributable to the same female. She "invented" washing when a young animal and the more subtle separating of grain from sand by winnowing when a juvenile. Putting together Freud's conjecture with the suggestion contained in the Japanese data leads to an obvious conclusion: urination has not been used in human technology because the technology was not invented by a male.

wetness and not sound should be more likely to be used causally by someone who has made his analysis as an outside observer. Standing outside in the rain, the observer will note a correlation between wetness (the salient feature of rain to an observer in that position) and the emergence of the termites. To an observer inside the mound, however, or to one who has put himself there mentally, the salient feature of rain cannot be wetness but can only be the sound of rain. The correlation the inside observer will note is that between the sound of rain and the emergence of the termites, and such an observer may be more likely therefore to use sound as the causal event. This is the sort of mystery for which the laboratory was invented.

INTENTIONALITY

Communication, which we are only now beginning to study (though see Premack, 1973b, for research plan), is of interest in part because it provides a setting in which to glimpse intentionality, and intentionality of interest in turn because it gives evidence of a concept of self. Indeed, communication and causal analysis can be brought together by the concept of self, both giving evidence of the concept but in different ways. Consider several examples, all of them hypothetical though some are in progress at this time.

Suppose Sarah asked a trainer a question, and the trainer answered but then stood in front of the board, blocking Sarah's view of the answer. Any attempts Sarah made to recover the answer would be accepted as evidence of intentionality. This would be so even if her attempts were no more than bodily efforts to remove the trainer from the board, though more so, of course, if she were to express her predicament linguistically, writing, say, "Move, please . . . I can't see the board" (notice, incidentally, that when both parties write on the same board as in our customary arrangement, there would be no linguistic way to unblock a blocked board; one could only remove the trainer bodily. After having done so, of course, the subject could return to verbal behavior, explaining or justifying her action, even expressing her regrets). Comparable evidence could be provided by the converse case. If a trainer asked Sarah a question, and then utterly neglected her answer, Sarah could give evidence of intentionality by calling the trainer's attention to this lapse, either by gently turning the trainer's head toward the board, or more impressively by an appropriate linguistic rebuke. Both cases would testify to Sarah's intentionality, showing that Sarah had "spoken"—in one case by asking and in the other by answering—with her listener in mind.

A second type of example goes further, for in addition to showing intentional communication, it invites the subject to dissemble, that is, give false information, and to do so with both false negatives and false positives. Lying has been linked exclusively to language—mistakenly, for the relation upon which lying depends can be realized without language. Prevarication, which we might adopt as the general term covering both verbal and nonverbal forms, occurs whenever a sender who has information that could increase his listener's chances of success, sends instead information that—provided that the listener used it in the normal fashion—would either reduce or at the least not increase his listener's chances of success.

The test situation we are now using to study dissembling involves communication between three-year-old, non-language-trained chimpanzees, and a trainer; later experiments will use two chimpanzees, but it is simpler to start with only one. The experiment starts when a trainer, carrying a young animal in her arms, shows it where she has hidden an item in the room, and then turns the animal over to another trainer who was outside the room and not watching. The animal is brought back to the room by the uninformed trainer—only to find itself placed on one side of a mesh divider, with the trainer and hidden object on the other side. The trainer does not, in fact, know where the item is hidden and he is to find it, not, however, by searching, but by reading the chimp's behavior. The animal's bodily orientation alone may give away the location of the hidden item, although if it does not the trainer is free to help his cause in any way he can. For instance, he can move from one possible hiding spot to another, glancing back at the chimp each time, and perhaps uttering food calls as he goes. Doubtless, in one way or another, the trainer will succeed in eliciting tell tale signs from the chimp, and whether they are intentional or not, so long as the trainer can read them, the chimp will benefit. For in the cooperative mode, whenever the trainer finds the hidden item, the chimp will be given a reward greater than the hidden one.

The competitive version of the game is played the same way except that the trainer's success spells misfortune for the animal. Should the trainer find the hidden item the chimp gets nothing. This should encourage the animal to dissemble, either by withholding information (false negative) or by making the same general kind of positive signs it made earlier in the cooperative mode only by making them on incorrect occasions, when the trainer is far from rather than near the hidden item (false positive). In a final version of the game, the animal will be allowed to choose between the two modes, to see if perhaps there are not chimpanzees that prefer dissembling to truth telling.

Abundant anecdotes from both laboratory and field hint that this work will not fail of its objective. The point of the work is not necessarily to show anything unsuspected about chimpanzee behavior, but to amplify and delineate what is suspected. Even in species that can dissemble, the practice is likely to have a developmental course—one reason for using young animals—and its appearance may coincide with that of other aspects of the self concept, such as, for example, anthropomorphic explanation.

Perhaps one could go further. After the chimp had "fooled" the trainer for a time, the trainer could adjust his strategy to the animal's deceit. Although there is no simple counterstrategy for false negatives, false positives could be countered by choosing the location opposite to the one indicated, and would be most effective when the alternatives were few, indeed perfect when there were only two. The question of interest is whether or not the chimpanzee could recognize and adjust to the trainer's strategy. As Grice (in preparation) has noted, in normal conversation truth is assumed on both sides (and I think this can be extended to nonverbal communication). The listener assumes he is being told the truth, and the speaker assumes that the listener takes him as telling the truth. Successful dissembling depends on the listener continuing to make this assumption even when, in fact, the assumption is false. The ability of a sender to adjust to a receiver (who changed his assumption so that he was no longer fooled) by changing his assumption and no longer dissembling, would give additional evidence of his ability to make inferences about the other one. Conversely, if the chimpanzee were largely unable to make adjustments of this kind, as compared to children or adults, this would suggest limitations on the depth of either its self concept or inferential processing.

REPRESENTATIONAL CAPACITY

The representational capacity of the chimpanzee is such that the experimenter can, for example, place a red card on a green one and ask the chimpanzee "? red on green" (Is red on green?). Similarly, the chimpanzee can be asked not the *yes–no* form, but the *wh-* form, of the question, "? on green" (What is on green?). In correctly answering such questions, the chimpanzee shows that it can recognize the relation between an item, red on green, and a representation of the item, "red on green." Furthermore, in answering similar questions in the *absence* of the red and green cards—tests that we have carried out more recently—the chimpanzee shows that it can also recognize the relation between its knowledge of an item and a representation of its knowledge.

This representational capacity can be appreciated by contrasting it with the probable parallel incapacity of the bee. The bee has a code—a correlation between items inside and outside of its body—but not necessarily a language in the sense that a language is a code that can be used in specific ways. The most critical of these ways depends on the capacity in question, on being able to recognize representations of one's self—body, behavior, and knowledge.

Suppose a forager bee were allowed to gather information about the direction and distance of a food source from its hive. The bee can encode this information in its dance (and a second bee decode the dance), but if it were shown a dance could it judge whether or not the dance accurately represented the direction and distance of the food source? That is, could the bee recognize the dance as a representation of its own knowledge? It is precisely this kind of judgment that the chimpanzee can make and it is the capacity for this judgment, more than any other perhaps, that qualifies the chimpanzee for language. When shown one or another condition, such as an apple in a pail, a red card on a green one, even an act of one kind or another carried out by some trainer, the chimpanzee can be asked to judge the agreement between the condition it has observed and a representation of the condition. The chimpanzee can be interrogated, as the bee presumably cannot, and as a consequence it can make what amount to true–false judgments, which to my knowledge the bee cannot.

MAP READING

The representational capacity involved in language is of a nonspatial kind. A second kind of representational capacity is spatial and is involved, for example, in the reading of maps. There are two reasons, in addition to the chimpanzee's nonspatial representational capacity, to suppose that it may be able to read maps. First, the chimpanzee can negotiate the two formal transformations involved in a map, dimension and size. For instance, the ape can match pictures to objects and vice versa (Davenport & Rogers, 1970; Hayes & Nissen, 1971), as well as match objects reduced in size. Furthermore, since the pictures used in these studies were not the same size as the objects they represented, the chimpanzee can evidently negotiate the transformations even when they are applied together, as they are in a map.

Second, when chimpanzees were shown the location of a number of items hidden in a one-acre compound, they subsequently retrieved the items in a direct way, rather than searching circuitously as they did when hunting similar items the locations of which were not known to them (Menzel, 1973). Tinklepaugh (1932) reported similar data for chimpanzees and, to a lesser extent, even monkeys. Performance of this kind led Menzel to infer that the chimpanzee had stored a "cognitive map." Although the use of Tolman's expression here is a metaphor, and one does not know the form in which the information is stored in the ape's head, a maplike representation must be included among the possibilities (cf. Shepard, 1975, for elegant defense of this form of storage in man). For these several reasons, Menzel and I are now testing the chimpanzee's ability to learn to use maps.

In human infants, sucking and visual orientation can be reinforced with still and motion pictures (cf. Salapetek, 1975). Yet we cannot conclude from this that the infant recognizes the relation between the pictures and the items they represent. Suppose the infant were given a number of pictures from the same class, such as smiling faces or people (in keeping with the pigeon experiments) until it habituated, whereupon it was shown another picture that either did or did not belong to the class. If the infant showed greater recovery from habituation for the picture that did not belong to the class, this would show that it could distinguish between members and nonmembers of the class. But it would not show that the infant recognized the relation between the class of pictures and the class of objects it represented.

What evidence shall we use to decide whether or not an individual recognizes the relation between an item and a picture of the item? This question can be directed not only at the infant but with potentially greater results at the pigeon, for it is only speculation that the infant can respond differentially to a class of pictures, whereas it has already been shown that the pigeon can discriminate pictures of man from nonman. What has not been established, however, is whether or not the pigeon can recognize the relation between a picture and the item pictured.

The proof that an organism recognizes the relation between a picture and the item pictured (while appreciating the essential difference between them) can be given by two kinds of evidence, one more conclusive than the other. In the conclusive case the picture is used as a communication device. Hays and Nissen (1971) report several examples of this kind in their home-reared chimpanzee, Vickie. Vickie commonly requested a ride by presenting them a picture of a car. Likewise, she requested a drink by presenting a human friend a picture of a glass of iced tea while at the same time pulling the friend along with her toward the refrigerator. In both cases Vickie responded in different ways to the picture and the item pictured: she did not attempt to drink the one picture nor to sit on the other. The high resolving power of this kind of evidence comes from this difference. When pictures are used communicatively there is no difficulty in defending the claim that the subject can tell the difference between the picture and item pictured

In the second and more equivocal kind of evidence the subject does not use the picture communicatively, but responds to the picture more or less in the same way it responds to the item pictured. Recently, when shown a videotape of a TV program on wild orangutans, Sarah provided an example of this second kind. She watched with uninterrupted attention for almost 30 minutes. When a young male was captured in a net, Sarah hooted and threw pieces of paper at the screen, seemingly aimed at the animal's captors. The trainer, watching with Sarah, reached up and touched the image of the captured animal on the screen; Sarah shuddered and turned a wildly startled face to the trainer.

The difficulty with this kind of evidence is that it does not eliminate the possibility that the subject has confused the picture with the item pictured. Notice, however, that we do not contemplate this alternative when interpreting comparable evidence in man. People commonly touch their lips to pictures, stroke tenderly clothing, and otherwise respond amorously to momentoes of their loved ones. From this we do not conclude that they have confused their loved ones with the representations of them. Similarly, the fact that we may sob while reading a book or attending a movie does not lead us to conclude that we have confused the referent and the representation. On the contrary, we view the depth of our participation not as indicative of confusion but as a measure of the artistry of the representation. I suggest that, in addition, we view the depth of the participation as a measure of the intelligence of the species. Only a highly intelligent species could hoot while observing the filmed capture of a conspecific, aim missiles at the captors, and yet *not* either flee the scene or attempt still stronger retaliation. The outward signs of participation are, I suspect, indicative of an internal participation that may include recalled scenes of aggression, real or metaphorical, in which the subject has either participated or observed in others. This kind of participation is indicative of intelligence, in part because it demands an inhibitory system that allows the subject to experience the affective equivalent of actual capture without at the same time engaging in the skeletal behavior that would normally accompany capture.

Because the chimpanzee provides both kinds of evidence, the communicative as well as the dramatic use of pictures, we are not obliged to interpret the second use as being based on confusion, any more than we are in the case of man. If, however, a species gave only the second kind of evidence, we would have no alternative but to consider the possibility that the species did not know the essential difference between the picture and the item pictured.

The evidence we have presently for the pigeon (and infant) does not tell us whether these organisms can recognize the relation between the picture and the item pictured. We need to be shown, in addition, that procedures affecting the infant's or pigeon's response to a class of pictures will transfer to the items represented by the pictures. For instance, birds taught to peck at pictures of people should be more inclined to peck at actual people than birds taught to peck at nonpeople. Yet, as we have already seen, this kind of evidence is inconclusive by itself. We need also to be shown that the subject can distinguish between occasions on which it is and is not appropriate to respond in the same way to items and representations of items.

In the chimpanzee, in contrast to the birds and infants, both kinds of evidence are available—not only in the pictorial or iconic case but also in the linguistic case, which 'is not surprising since the difference between the iconic and noniconic cases is far less consequential than traditional discussions imply (see Premack, 1975a). For instance, Sarah and the other subjects chose the same alternatives in match-to-sample tests when the sample was a blue triangle (meaning apple) as when the sample was an actual apple—which is a necessary but not a sufficient condition for the representational claim. In addition, the chimpanzees showed that, even as there were functions for which they were prepared to exchange apple and "apple," there were other functions for which they would not accept the exchange. After a certain point in training, the apes did not apply pieces of apple or other fruit to the board or, conversely, put the word apple or other words into their mouths. They neither wrote with nonlinguistic items nor made any attempt to eat the linguistic ones. Furthermore, when told to put the cracker in the pail on one occasion, and the name of the cracker on another, Sarah responded appropriately.

Notice how these tests profit from the present language system. With a vocal language or one based on sign, it would be a struggle to find acts that could be applied equally to words and to referents, very likely a futile struggle. Yet only if there were acts that could be applied equally to both words and their referents would the fact that the subjects did not apply them equally provide the desired evidence.

One could go on to describe still stronger evidence. The subject's ability to write an essay on representation could allay any further doubts one might entertain on the basis of the evidence described. Yet I think the twofold evidence described above is both necessary and sufficient for the claim, though I am always in favor of allaying residual doubts.

MULTIPLE INTERNAL REPRESENTATION AND THE USE OF MAPS AND LANGUAGE

Why is it that the chimpanzee can recognize representations of various items including its own knowledge whereas other species presumably cannot? It cannot be because nonprimates do not have knowledge of any kind. One of the most demonstrable forms of knowledge is that of spatial relations and not only primates but rats (Olton & Samuelson, 1976) and even insects can be shown to have information of this kind. For instance, the homing of insects (Van Iersel & van den Assam, 1969) shows that these species have a maplike knowledge of their home terrain, and the inference is supported as well in their case as in the case of the ape. Although it is not possible to say for any species how the information is actually stored in the head, the simplest assumption in all cases is that of either an image or a cognitive map.

Since not only primates but even insects have a knowledge of spatial relations, the question can be repeated in a more explicit form: Why is a cognitive map not itself a sufficient condition for the use of an actual map? Perhaps I am mistaken in assuming that nonprimates could not be taught to use maps, but if I am not then we must explain why a species could have a maplike representation of its home terrain in its head and yet not recognize the relation between its cognitive map and an actual map.

Perhaps either the quality or abstractness of the image or cognitive map must attain a certain level before representations of it could be recognizable. But that seems an unprofitable line of inquiry for neither the measurement of quality nor the definition of abstractness is simple. A more interesting—and ultimately testable—hypothesis is that the ability of a species to use either maps or language depends in the first place on the species having at least two different forms of representation or information storage.[2] If the species can store information not

---

[2] This attractive idea arose in a lunchtime conversation with my colleague Randy Gallistel, and is more his than mine.

only in a pictorial form, to which insects may conceivably be restricted, but also in a propositional form, which is demonstrably the case for at least man and chimpanzees, then it seems certain that on occasion the same information will be stored in both forms. Cases of this kind would provide the opportunity for species to recognize (not the right word but I cannot find a more suitable one) the equivalence between the two internal representations. And experience of this kind may help a subject recognize the relation between an item and a representation of the item as, in principle, that relation is not different from the one between two equivalent internal representations.

A certain kind of information may naturally lend itself to an image or maplike form, and another kind to a propositional form (and these extremes may never be represented in both ways), but other kinds may be intermediate with respect to form and may be represented in both forms either more or less automatically or on different occasions. For instance, the kind of information Tinklepaugh (1932) used in his memory tests with apes and monkeys could be fairly easily modulated so as to potentiate an image form of storage on one occasion, a propositional form on another, and possibly both forms on yet another occasion.

Tinklepaugh tested the apes by arranging 16 pairs of containers in a circle (diameter 20 ft), baited one container of each pair while the ape observed from the center of the circle, and then after varying delays released the ape to find the baited containers. The 16 containers consisted of painted and unpainted wood boxes, tin cans and cups, and one pair of cigar boxes that were as dissimilar as possible. Tinklepaugh did not change the order of the containers from trial to trial, but the original order was not systematic and the baiting was essentially random.

For Tinklepaugh's arrangement and baiting system, an image seems the most revealing form of storage. The circular arrangement he used would make the coordinate system on which maps are based less suitable; half of the pairs of containers would have the same value on the abscissa and the other half the same value on the ordinate, which must reduce their identifiability (if the containers had been arranged on a line this would not be the case, and then a map and an image would be equally suitable). A propositional form of storage would also seem unsuited. It could be used, as it always can be, but the lack of systematic relations between the type of container and the baiting system would deny the propositional format those advantages this form of storage can have once the information is patterned or systematic.

For example, if for all tin containers the left member of each pair was baited, whereas for all wood containers the right member of each pair was baited, this information could obviously be stored economically in a propositional format. Moreover, the propositional format would not seem to involve any predicates not included in the conceptual structure of the chimpanzee. Sarah was successfully taught the quantifiers, the use of modifiers comparable to wood and tin in "wood and tin containers" and though not taught "right–left," taught to label other distinctions, for example, "top–bottom," of seemingly comparable difficulty.

In principle, it would seem possible to titrate the subject's form of storage—image, map, or propositional—by modulating several parameters: the pattern or lack of pattern in the information, the shape of the geometrical arrangement, and whether or not the experimenter changed the position of the containers after baiting them (such changes should have no effect on the subject's performance if it used a propositional format, but should seriously impair it if it used either an image or a map). At intermediate values of these parameters, subjects who are capable of more than one form of storage may be inclined to use both forms, thereby setting up an equivalence between two different internal representations, which, I suggest, is the kind of experience that may be helpful in leading a subject to recognize the relation between an item and an external representation of the item. Although at the moment I do not see how to test this hypothesis with a satisfying degree of directness, indirect or circumstantial tests have already suggested themselves, and it may be hoped that they will suggest more direct tests.

MNEMONIC CAPACITY

Of all the prerequisites for language none is more vital, or more easily overlooked, than memory, yet language is possible in the first place only because of memory. It is not objects, actions, or properties as such that are associated with words, but rather the representations of these items which the subject has stored in memory. If the stored representation of an item is complete, then, barring some form of "leakage," the information associated with the name of the item should be commensurately complete.

A representation might be incomplete for either of two reasons. First, a young organism or an inexperienced old one might know little about the item in question. Children know far less about the world than do adults, and when asked about the world, reveal their ignorance by the inaccuracy of their answers. However, normal children only need adequate experience in order to form well-defined representations. Second, despite extensive experience with the items in question, certain species may never form well-defined representations. An organism may see an item clearly, and yet be unable to form an accurate representation of what it has seen. We do not yet know whether, in fact, species differ in the quality or power of the information they can store. But if they do this would set a limit on the effectiveness of the language they could acquire. For the name of an item cannot be more informative than the stored representation of the item with which the name is associated.

A common expression speaks of the "power of word," although this refers, of course, to human words. Can we talk about chimpanzee words in a similar vein, or are the pieces of plastic and manual signs that chimps have been taught lesser devices that only appear to be like words but differ from them in critical respects? To answer this question we must first decide what is meant by "power of the word." I suspect that what the phrase celebrates is the extraordinary extent to which the word can be substituted for its referent. This substitution is made possible by the subject's ability to use the word as an information retrieval device. Thus, the phrase implies that, in the human case, the name of an object can be virtually as informative as the object itself.

To assess the chimpanzee's memory of objects on the one hand and the information it had associated with names of the objects on the other, we used fruit and the names for the fruit. We dissected the fruit into a number of pieces, gave the apes one piece of the fruit and then asked them to identify other pieces that belonged to the same fruit. The logic of this measurement is based on the assumption that if one knows a great deal about an object, one should need only a small sample to identify the object from which the sample was taken. For instance, if given only a stem or a seed or a taste, the knowledgeable subject should be able to identify the fruit from which the component was taken.

Consider the difference between what a subject can perceive about an object and what it can reconstruct from memory. When the subject is required to match redness to an apple, both the sample and correct alternative instance the matching criterion, giving a measure of perception. If, however, the sample remains red but the apple is now painted white, the sample and correct alternative will no longer instance the matching criterion. Instead, they will match on the basis of information associated with but not directly represented by the correct alternative, and the subject must reconstruct the missing information from memory. However, tests that require reconstructing information from memory do not depend specifically on distorted alternatives. The relation between stem and peel, stem and seed, seed and peel, etc.; color and shape, shape and size, etc.; and color and stem, shape and seed, etc., are all cases of this kind. Items in these pairs do not share common features but are related simply through being attributes of the same object.

In making the present tests, fruit were divided into four canonical components and two features, viz., wedge, stem, peel, and seed; plus color and shape. Taste was added as the one nonvisual attribute. Eight fruit were dissected in this manner—banana, orange, apple, lemon, peach, pear, grape, and cherry. The subject was given one or another of the components or features as a sample, along with two other components or features as alternatives, and was required to select the alternative that came from the same fruit as the sample. For instance, the subject was given an apple seed as the sample and two stems as alternatives, one apple the other lemon, and required in this case to choose the apple stem.

After completing the test series of approximately 24 individual tests with each of the four subjects, it was possible to rank the components and features according to their informativeness. Not surprisingly, the whole fruit was the most informative cue. Color and peel were next, followed closely by taste, after which there was essentially a tie between shape, wedge, and stem, and lastly there was seed, the least informative cue of all. Sarah, in an impressive fashion, was able to use all cues correctly; but the other three subjects whose results differed were most able to identify the source of the attribute of a fruit from its color or peel, and least able from its seed.

In the next test series, actual parts of the fruit were no longer given as alternatives. They were still given as samples but now the alternatives were plastic words that named the fruits. The results of these tests were unusually clearcut. When the informativeness of the plastic words was compared with that of the actual parts of the fruit, the words were found to be more informative than any part except the whole fruit itself. In brief, words could be substituted for their referents in match-to-sample tests without loss of accuracy. In another test series, we used names of colors rather than of objects and obtained identical results. For instance, the word red could be substituted for an actual instance of red in the matching tests without loss of accuracy. In the ape, too, the word substituted vigorously for its referent. For these reasons it seems proper to speak of the "power of the word" for the chimpanzee and not only for man.

The ability of fruit and color names to substitute for their referents without loss of accuracy shows that a major consequence of giving arbitrary objects, such as pieces of plastic, linguistic prerogatives is to transfer to the arbitrary object some or all of the information contained in the associated referent. Under what circumstances does this transfer of information take place? Perhaps it occurs only after the piece of plastic has been used in a wordlike way, to request or describe the referent a certain number of times. That would be the only tenable hypothesis if the only way to produce names was by associating them with their referents in one linguistic context or another. However, we already know that this procedure can be short-circuited. Names can be generated more directly by instructions of the form "X is the name of Y," where X is thus far an unused piece of plastic and Y thus far an unnamed object. Following instruction of this kind, Sarah used X in all the ways she used names introduced in the more standard way. Thus, the effect of such instructions as "X is the name of Y" must be to transfer to X some or all of the information the subject has stored in memory about Y. This fact clarifies some of the power of language, and at the same time suggests the kind of intelligence a species must have in order to acquire it.

To qualify for language a species must be capable of storing a rich representation of Y; if not, the information transferred to X would be weak and the name would be a poor substitute for the referent. That is, if the mnemonic capacity of the species were limited, then information associated with names would be commensurately limited; and names could not then be substituted for their referents in match-to-sample tests without loss of accuracy as, in fact, they can be in the chimpanzee. In addition, instructions of the form "X is the name of Y" must have the force of transferring to X some—ideally all—of the information that the subject has stored about Y. These are not the only capacities a species must have in order to qualify for language, but they are two that seem to be basic.

Sarah was capable of displacement, of comprehending statements about "things that are not there." When given the instruction "brown color of chocolate" as a means of introducing "brown" and subsequently told "take brown," she performed correctly, chosing the brown disk from the four that were offered. The chimpanzee's ability to comprehend statements about "things that are not there" derives from its demonstrated ability to store adequate representations of items and to use words to retrieve the information it has stored. In substituting, say, the word apple without loss of accuracy for an actual apple in all of the matching tests, it gave direct proof of this ability. Displacement is not a uniquely linguistic phenomenon but the consequence of a certain quality of memory.

SECOND-ORDER RELATIONS

Even the simplest sentence contains both relational and absolute terms. Consider such sentences as "Daddy home," "Mommy purse," "Bill hit Mary," and "Mommy take flower." In the last two cases, the relational terms—"hit" and "take"—are explicit, whereas in the first two strings the relations are not explicitly marked, and strings of this kind are interpreted as sentences by inferring the relations. In the first case, we may infer a locative type relation between daddy and home, for example, "Daddy is home," and in the second, convert the two-word string into a sentence by interpreting the string as a genitive relation, for example, "Mommy's purse." These examples suggest that a sentence could be defined, in the weakest possible sense, as a string of words in which there is an implicit or explicit dependence among the words of a kind that can be represented by the relation between a predicate and its arguments. The point of this definition is to stress that a sentence is inconceivable without a relational term, either explicit or implicit. A species that could not learn a relational term and thus could not fulfill even this weak condition could not possibly fulfill the inordinately stronger conditions imposed by adult sentence structures.

Second, it is not sufficient that the species be capable of responding to relations; to acquire language it must be able to respond to relations between relations. This can be seen even in such simple predicates as "same–different," which are nonetheless representative of more complex predicates such as "name of," "color of," "if–then," and the like. For instance, when pigeons are given two red particles on some trials, a red and a grey particle on other trials, and are required to peck on the left when given the former and on the right when given the latter, they ultimately learn to do so, that is, to respond differentially to $A–A$ and $A–B$. However, when given $B–B$, or comparable cases instanced by new elements, for example, $C–C$, $C–A$, etc., they respond at chance. Correct responding requires that the subject be able to observe not only that the relation between, say, red and red is same, as that between, say, grey and grey is likewise same, but also that the relation between red and red is the same as that between grey and grey. Calling the first relation same$_1$ and the second one same$_2$, the subject must recognize that same$_1$ is the same as same$_2$—a recognition involving a second-order relation, or the ability to respond to a relation between relations. Identical requirements apply to all other language predicates. For instance, to use "name of" productively, the subject must recognize that the relation between, say, "apple" and apple ("apple" name of apple) is the same as that between, say, "banana" and banana, that is, that name of$_1$ is the same as name of$_2$.

If the subject belonged to a species that lacked a capacity for acquiring second-order relations, each time a predicate occurred with a new argument, the subject would have to be retaught the predicate. The tendency to diminish this phenomenon by calling it (nothing but) generalization does not evade the fact that, even if we view the phenomenon in this light, it is evidently not a kind of generalization that is open to all species.

The evidence for second-order relations in nonprimates is slight. The pigeon fails to show transfer on match to sample but shows transfer on differential responding to $A–A$ versus $A–B$ provided the training and transfer dimensions are the same (Honig, 1965). At face value, this says the bird can recognize but not produce conditions that exemplify same–different—which is an assymetry not found in the chimpanzee data for same–different or any other concept. (After sufficient training, every word taught the chimpanzee in either production or comprehension transferred to the other mode.) It is also possible, however, that even the positive pigeon data prove nothing beyond stimulus generalization—which by itself is not a sufficient basis for inferring a capacity for same–different judgments.[3] That the rat may be capable of acquiring second-order relations in

[3] Consider a bird trained to peck left when given pairs of like colors, right when given pairs of unlike colors. The bird could have learned either peck left and right when given like and unlike pairs of colors respectively; or peck left when given yellow–yellow, red–red, green–green, etc., and right when given yellow–red, green–yellow, red–green, etc. The usual way of distinguishing between these alternatives, a transfer test involving new colors and new combinations of old colors, will not work, for even if the bird responds appropriately, we cannot conclude that it responded on the basis of same–different. From the facts of

the case of brightness is indicated in an ingenious study by Lawrence and DeRivera (1954), a study that in view of its importance seriously needs to be replicated. There is some evidence available for the dog for the case of same–different judgments (Premack, 1971), a finding that needs to be amplified as well as repeated; and recent more substantial evidence for this same capacity in the dolphin (Herman & Gordon, 1974). Although we can say that a capacity to learn second-order relations is a necessary condition for language, we cannot yet say in which species the capacity is found. Neither can we say whether if a species evidences the capacity for one predicate, it will do so for all other predicates. Although in man capacities tend to be general, this is apparently less so in other species. Conceivably, the rat could learn second-order relations for the case of brightness but not for other distinctions.

This survey did not lead to the discovery of qualitative differences between man and other species. Those who find satisfaction in this failure will insist that this is the simple truth of the matter: There is both mental and anatomical continuity from one species to another; all differences are quantitative. It is also possible, however, that the inability to find more radical differences reveals not the genuine lack of such differences but simple ignorance. I do not think the latter view can be dismissed at this time, and in this sense I may be in closer accord with the humanist than the biologist. In one sense, however, I am surely not in accord with the humanist. Even on those occasions when my intuitions outbid my logic, and "I" insist that man is unique, I cannot accept the arrogance that believes it knows of what the uniqueness consists.

---

stimulus generalization alone, it is possible to predict that the bird will tend to respond to, say, orange–orange in the same way it was trained to respond to yellow–yellow, and to, say, orange–red in the same way it was trained to respond to yellow–red. To distinguish between the two alternatives, the stimuli substituted for the training stimuli must not be such that it is possible to predict transfer from stimulus generalization alone. This can be arranged in at least two ways. If the bird transferred to like and unlike pairs of shapes after being trained on like and unlike pairs of colors, this would be evidence for same–different. But this test is too strong, for it proves not only same–different but also the transfer of this judgment from one stimulus domain to another. A sufficient test could be made simply by training with stimuli whose similarity relations cannot be predicted from stimulus generalization. For instance, if a bird trained on like and unlike pairs of circles and rectangles survived the substitution of squares and triangles, this would be evidence for same–different.

References

Andrew, G., & Harlow, H. F. Performance of Macaque monkeys on a test of generalized triangularity. *Comparative Psychology Monographs,* 1948, **19**, 1–20.

Aries, P. *Centuries of childhood.* New York: Knopf, 1962.

Azrin, N., & Holz, W. C. Punishment. In W. K. Honig, (Ed.), *Operant behavior: Areas of research and application.* New York: Appleton-Century-Crofts, 1966.

Berlin, B., & Kay, P. *Basic color terms: Their universality and evolution.* Berkeley: University of California Press, 1969.

Berlin, B., Breedlove, D. E., & Raven, P. H. General principles of classification and nomenclature in folk biology. *American Anthropologist,* 1973, **75**, 214–242.

Bever, T. Cognitive basis for linguistic structures. In J. R. Hayes (Ed.), *Cognition and development of language.* New York: Wiley, 1970.

Bloom, L. *Language development: Form and function in emerging grammars.* Cambridge, Massachusetts: M.I.T. Press, 1970.

Bloom, L. Talking, understanding, and thinking. In R. L. Schiefelbusch & L. L. Lloyd (Eds.), *Language perspectives.* Baltimore: University Park Press, 1974.

Bloomfield, L. *Language.* New York: Holt, 1933.

Bousfield, W. A. The occurrence of clustering in the recall of randomly arranged associates. *Jounal of General Psychology,* 1953, **49**, 229–240.

Bowerman, M. F. *Early Syntactic Development: A Cross-linguistic study with special reference to Finnish.* Cambridge, England: Cambridge University Press, 1973.

Braine, M. D. S. Children's first word combinations. *Monograph of the Society for Research in Child Development,* in press.

Bransford, J. D., & Johnson, M. K. Contextual prerequisites for understanding: Some investigation of comprehension and recall. *Journal of Verbal Learning & Verbal Behavior,* 1972, **11**, 717–726.

Brown, R. A. *A first language: The early stages.* Cambridge, Massachusetts: Harvard University Press, 1973.

Brown, R. A., & Hanlon, C. Derivational complexity and order of acquisition of child speech. In J. R. Hayes (Ed.), *Cognition and the development of language.* New York: Wiley, 1970.

Bruner, J. S. *Processes of cognitive growth: Infancy. Heinz Warner Lectures.* Worcester, Massachusetts: Clark University Press, 1968.

Carlyle, F., Jacobson, M., & Yoshioka, J. G. Development of an infant chimpanzee during her first year. *Comparative Psychological Monographs,* 1932, 9 (1) (Serial No. 41).

Carrier, J. K., Jr. Application of functional analysis and non-speech response mode to teaching language. Report 7, Kansas Center for Research in Mental Retardation and Human Development, Parsons, 1973.

Caudill, W. A. *Japanese American acculturation and personality.* Chicago: University of Chicago Press, 1950.

Chomsky, N. *Aspects of the theory of syntax.* Cambridge, Massachusetts: M.I.T. Press, 1965.

Clark, E. Non-linguistic strategies and the acquisition of word meanings. *Cognition: International Journal of Cognitive Psychology,* 1973, 2, 161–182.

Clark, E. Some aspects of conceptual basis for first language acquisition. In R. L. Schiefelbusch & L. L. Lloyd (Eds.), *Language perspectives–Acquisition, retardation and intervention.* Baltimore: University Park Press, 1974.

Clark, H. H., & Chase, W. G. On the process of comparing sentences against pictures. *Cognitive Psychology,* 1972, 3, 472–517.

Cofer, C. N. Constructive processes in memory. *American Scientist,* 1973, 61, 537–543.

Cumming, W. W., & Berryman, R. The complex discriminated operant: Studies of matching-to-sample and related problems. In D. I. Mostofsky (Ed.), *Stimulus generalization.* Stanford, California: Stanford University Press, 1965.

Davenport, R. K., & Rogers, C. M. Intermodal equivalence of stimuli in apes. *Science,* 1970, 168, 279–280.

Deich, R. F., & Hodges, P. M. Learning from Sarah. *Human Behavior,* 1975 (May), 40–42.

De Villiers, J., & Naughton, J. M. Teaching a symbol language to autistic children. *Journal of Consulting and Clinical Psychology,* 1974, 42, 111–117.

DeVore, I., & Konners, M. Infancy in hunter-gatherer life. In N. F. White (Ed.), *Ethology and psychiatry.* Toronto: University of Toronto Press, 1974.

Dobzhansky, T. Evolution and environment. In S. Tax (Ed.), *Evolution after Darwin,* I. Chicago: Chicago University Press, 1960.

Donaldson, M., & Wales, R. J. On the acquisition of some relational terms. In J. R. Hayes (Ed.), *Cognition and the development of language.* New York: Wiley, 1970.

Dulany, D. E., Jr. The place of hypotheses and intentions: An analysis of verbal control in verbal conditioning. In C. W. Erikson (Ed.), *Behavior and awareness.* Durham, North Carolina: Duke University Press, 1962.

Eimas, P. D. Speech perception in early infancy. In L. B. Cohen & P. Salapatek (Eds.), *Infant perception.* New York: Academic Press, in press.

Estes, W. K. Reinforcement in human learning. In J. Tapp (Ed.), *Reinforcement and behavior.* New York: Academic Press, 1969.

Feigl, H. The scientific outlook: Naturalism and humanism. In H. Feigl & M. Brodbeck (Eds.), *Readings in the philosophy of science.* New York: Appleton-Century-Crofts, 1953.

Ferster, C. B. Arithmetic behavior in chimpanzees. *Scientific American,* 1964, 210(5), 98–106.

Fodor, J., Bever, T., & Garrett, M. *The psychology of language.* New York: McGraw-Hill, 1974.

Fouts, R. The use of guidance in teaching sign language to a chimpanzee. *Journal of Comparative Psychology,* 1972, 80, 515–522.

Freud, S. Civilization and Its Discontents. In the *Standard edition of the complete Psychological works of Sigmund Freud.* Vol. XXI. London: Hogarth Press, 1964. Pp. 64–145.

Gallup, G. Chimpanzees: self-recognition. *Science,* 1970, 167, 86–87.

Gardner, B. T., & Gardner, R. A. Two-way communication with an infant chimpanzee. In A. Schrier & F. Stollnitz (Eds.), *Behavior in nonhuman primates.* New York: Academic Press, 1971.

Gardner, W. R., & Hake, H. W. The amount of information in absolute judgments. *Psychological Review,* 1951, 58, 446–459.

Gast, H. Der Umgang mit Zahlen und Zahlgebilden in der frühen Kindheit. *Zeitschrift für Psychologie,* 1957, **161,** 1–90.

Gelman, R., & Tucker, M. F. Further investigations of the young child's conception of number. *Child Development,* 1975, **46,** 167–175.

Geschwind, N. Disconnexion syndromes in animal and man. Part I. *Brain,* 1965, **88,** 237–294.

Guess, D. A functional analysis of receptive language and productive speech: Acquisition of the plural morpheme. *Journal of Applied Behavioral Analysis,* 1969, **2,** 55–64.

Guess, D., & Baer, D. An analysis of individual differences in generalization between receptive and productive language in retarded children. *Journal of Applied Behavioral Analysis,* 1973, **6,** 311–329.

Greenberg, J. H. *Language universals.* The Hauge: Mouton, 1966.

Grice, H. P. Logic and conversation, in preparation.

Harlow, H. F. Analysis of discrimination learning by monkeys. *Journal of Experimental Psychology,* 1950, **40,** 26–39.

Harlow, H. F. Learning set and error factor theory. In S. Koch (Ed.), *Psychology: A study of a science.* New York: McGraw-Hill, 1958.

Hayes, K. J., & Nissen, C. H. Higher mental functions of a home-raised chimpanzee. In A. M. Schrier & F. Stollnitz (Eds.), *Behavior of nonhuman primates,* Vol. 4. New York: Academic Press, 1971.

Herman, L. M., & Gordon, J. A. Auditory delayed matching in the bottlenose dolphin. *Journal of Experimental Analysis of Behavior,* 1974, **21,** 19–26.

Herrnstein, R. J., & Loveland, D. H. Complex visual concept in the pigeon. *Science,* 1964, **146,** 549–551.

Hewes, G. W. Lateral dominance, culture, and writing systems. *Human Biology,* 1949, **21,** 233–245.

Hockett, C. F. Animal "languages" and human language. In J. N. Spuhler (Ed.), *The evolution of man's capacity for culture.* Detroit: Wayne State University Press, 1959.

Honig, W. K. Discrimination, generalization and transfer on the basis of stimulus differences. In D. I. Mostofsky (Ed.), *Stimulus generalization.* Stanford, California: Stanford University Press, 1965.

Hughes, J. Acquisition of a nonvocal 'language' by aphasic children. *Cognition,* 1975, **3,** 41–55.

Hume, D. An enquiry concerning human understanding. In *Great books of the western world.* Vol. 35. Chicago: Benton, 1952.

Jakobson, R., Fant, C. G. M., & Halle, M. *Preliminaries to speech analysis.* Cambridge, Massachusetts: MIT Press, 1952.

Kaufman, E. K., Lord, M. W., Reese, T. W., & Volkmann, J. The discrimination of visual number. *American Journal of Psychology,* 1949, **62,** 498–525.

Kellogg, R. *What children scribble and why.* San Francisco: Author, 1955.

Kintsch, W. *Learning, memory, and conceptual processes.* New York: Wiley, 1970.

Klahr, D., & Wallace, J. G. The role of quantification operators in the development of conservation of quality. *Cognitive Psychology,* 1973, **4,** 301–327.

Klima, E., & Bellugi, U. Syntactic regularities in the speech of children. In J. Lyons & R. Wales (Eds.), *Psycholinguistic papers.* Edinburgh: Edinburgh University Press, 1966.

Klüver, H. Re-examination of implement-using behavior in a *Cebus* monkey after an interval of three years. *Acta Psychologica,* 1973, **2**(3).

Koehler, O. Können tauben "Zählen?" *Zeitschrift für Tierpsychologie,* 1937, **1,** 39–48.

Köhler, W. *Mentality of apes.* New York: The Humanities Press, 1951.

Kohts, N. *Infant ape and human child.* Moscow: Scientific Memoirs of the Museum Darwinium in Moscow, 1935.

Konner, M. Aspects of the developmental ethology of a foraging people. In N. G. Blurton Jones (Ed.), *Ethological studies of child behavior*. Cambridge, England: Cambridge University Press, 1972.

Lawrence, D. H., & DeRivera, J. Evidence for relational transposition. *Journal of Comparative and Physiological Psychology*, 1954, 47, 465–471.

Lenneberg, E. H. *Biological foundations of language*. New York: Wiley, 1967.

Levine, M. Hypothesis theory and non-learning despite ideal S–R reinforcement contingencies. *Psychological Review*, 1971, 78, 130–140.

Lubow, R. E. High-order concept formation in the pigeon. *Journal of Experimental Analysis of Behavior*, 1974, 21, 475–483.

Malott, R. W., Malott, K., Svinicki, J. G., Kladder, F., & Ponicki, E. An analysis of matching and non-matching behavior using a single key, free operant procedure. *Psychological Record*, 1971, 21, 545–564.

Martin, E. Stimulus encoding in learning and transfer. In A. W. Melton & E. Martin (Eds.), *Coding processes in human memory*. Washington, D.C.: Winston, 1972.

McClure, M. Chimpanzees' same–different judgments in the combined match-to-sample and oddity-learning paradigm. Unpublished doctoral dissertation, University of California, Santa Barbara, 1975.

McNeil, D. *The acquisition of language: The study of developmental psycholinguistics*. New York: Harper & Row, 1970.

McNeil, D. Sentence structure in chimpanzee communication. In K. J. Connolly & J. S. Bruner (Eds.), *The growth of competence*, New York: Academic Press, 1974.

Menzel, E. W., Jr. Communication of object locations in a group of young chimpanzees. In D. Hamburg & J. Goodall (Eds.), *Behavior of great apes*. New York: Holt, Rinehart & Winston, in press.

Menzel, E. W., Jr. Chimpanzee spatial memory organization. *Science*, 1973, 182, 943–945.

Miller, G. A. The magical number seven, plus or minus two: Some limits on our capacity for processing information. *Psychological Review*, 1956, 63, 81–97.

Morris, C. *Signs, languages and behavior*. Englewood Cliffs, New Jersey: Prentice-Hall, 1946.

Morse, P. A. The discrimination of speech and nonspeech stimuli in early infancy. *Journal of Experimental Child Psychology*, 1972, 14, 477–492.

Munn, N. *Walbiri Iconography*, Ithaca, New York: Cornell University Press, 1974.

Münsterberg, H. *On the witness stand: Essays on psychology and crime*, New York: Clark Boardman, 1925.

Olton, D. S., & Samuelson, R. J. Remembrance of places passed: spatial memory in rats. *Journal of Experimental Psychology: An. Behav. Proc.*, 1976, 2, 97–116.

Piaget, J. *The construction of reality in the child*. New York: Norton, 1954.

Premack, A. J. *Why chimps can read*. New York: Harper, 1976.

Premack, D. A functional analysis of language, *Journal of the Experimental Analysis of Behavior*, 1970, 14, 107–125.

Premack, D. Language in chimpanzee? *Science*, 1971, 172, 808–822.

Premack, D. Cognitive principles? In F. J. McGuigan & D. B. Lumsden (Eds.), *Contemporary approaches to conditioning and learning*. Washington, D.C.: Winston, 1973.   (a)

Premack, D. Concordant preferences as a precondition for affective but not symbolic communication (or how to do experimental anthropology). *Cognition*, 1973, 1, 251–264.   (b)

Premack, D. Putting a face together. *Science*, 1975, 188, 228–236.   (a)

Premack, D. Symbols inside and outside of language. In J. Kavanaugh & J. E. Cutting (Eds.), *The role of speech in language*. Cambridge, Massachusetts: M.I.T. Press, 1975.   (b)

Premack, D., & Anglin, B. On the possibilities of self-control in man and animals. *Journal of Abnormal Psychology*, 1973, 81(2), 137–151.

Premack, D., & Bahwell, R. Operant-level lever pressing by a monkey as a function of intertest interval. *Journal of Experimental Analysis Behavior*, 1959, 2, 127–131.

Premack, D., & Premack, A. J. Teaching visual language to apes and language deficient persons. In R. L. Schiefelbusch & L. L. Lloyd (Eds.), *Language perspectives.* Baltimore: University Park Press, 1974.

Premack, D., & Schwartz, A. Preparations for discussing behaviorism with chimpanzee. In F. L. Smith & G. A. Miller (Eds.), *The genesis of language.* Cambridge, Massachusetts: M.I.T. Press, 1966.

Restle, F. The selection of strategies in cue learning. *Psychological Review,* 1962, **69,** 320–343.

Restle, F. *Learning: Animal behavior and human cognition.* New York: McGraw-Hill, 1975.

Rosch, E. Classification of real-world objects: origins and representations in cognition. *Bulletin de psychologie,* in press.

Rumbaugh, D. M., & von Glasersfeld, E. C. A Computer-controlled language training system for investigating the language skills of young apes. *Behavioral Research Methods and Instruments,* 1973, **5,** 385–392.

Salapetek, P. Pattern perception in early infancy. In L. B. Cohen & P Salapetek (Eds.), *Infant perception: From sensation to cognition,* Vol. 1. New York: Academic Press, 1975.

Sapir, E. Study in phonetic symbolism. *Journal of Experimental Psychology,* 1929, **12,** 225–239.

Schlesinger, I. M., & Meadow, K. P. *Sound and sign.* Berkeley: University of California Press, 1972.

Schlesinger, I. M. Relational concepts underlying language. In R. L. Schiefelbusch & L. L. Lloyd (Eds.), *Language perspectives.* Baltimore: University Park Press, 1974.

Shepard, R. N. Form, formation, and transformation of internal representations. In R. Solso (Ed.), *Information processing and cognition: The Loyola Symposium.* Hillsdale, New Jersey: Lawrence Erlbaum Assoc., 1975.

Siegel, R. K., & Honig, W. K. Pigeon concept formation: Successive and simultaneous acquisition. *Journal of Experimental Analysis of Behavior,* 1970, **13,** 385–390.

Skinner, B. F. *Behavior of organisms.* New York: Appleton-Century-Crofts, 1938.

Simpson, G. G. *This View of Life.* New York: Harcourt Brace, 1964.

Skinner, B. F. *Verbal behavior.* New York: Appleton-Century-Crofts, 1957.

Slobin, D. I. Cognitive prerequisites for the development of grammar. In D. I. Slobin & C. Ferguson (Eds.), *Studies of child language development.* New York: Holt,· Rinehart & Winston, 1973.

Slobin, D. Universals of grammatical development in children. In G. d'Arcais, & W. Levelt (Eds.), *Advances in psycholinguistics.* Amsterdam: North-Holland Publ., 1970.

Solter, A. Teaching counting to nursery school children. Unpublished doctoral dissertation, University of California, Santa Barbara, 1975.

Strawson, P. F. *Introduction to logical theory.* London: Methuen, 1952.

Teleki, G. The omnivorous chimpanzee. In S. H. Katz (Ed.), *Biological anthropology.* San Francisco: Freeman, 1974. (a)

Teleki, G. Chimpanzee subsistence technology: Materials and skills. *Journal of Human Evolution,* 1974, **3,** 575–594.

Tinklepaugh, O. L. Multiple delayed reactions with chimpanzees and monkeys. *Journal of Comparative Psychology,* 1932, **13,** 207–243.

Trabasso, T., Rollins, H., & Shaughnessy, E. Storage and Verification stages in processing concepts. *Cognitive Psychology,* 1971, **3,** 239–289.

Tulving, E. Subjection organization in free recall of "unrelated words." *Psychological Review,* 1962, **69,** 344–354.

Tulving, E., & Thomson, D. M. Encoding specificity and retrieval processes in episodic memory. *Psychological Review,* 1973, **80,** 352–373.

Turner, T. S. Social structure and political organization of the Northern Cayapo (Kayopo). Unpublished doctoral dissertation, Harvard University Library, Cambridge, 1965.

Underwood, B. J., & Schultz, R. W. *Meaningfulness and verbal learning.* New York: Lippincott, 1960.

van Iersel, J. J. A., & van den Assam, J. Aspects of orientation in the diggerwasp *Bembix rostrata. Animal Behaviour Supplement,* 1969, 1, 145–162.

Van Lawick-Goodall, J. The behavior of free-living chimpanzees in the Gombe Stream Reserve. *Animal Behavior Monographs,* 1968, 1, 161–311.

Velettri-Glass, A., Gazzaniga, M., & Premack, D. Artificial language training in global aphasics. *Neuropsychologia,* 1973, 11, 95–103.

Whorf, B. L. *Language, thought and reality; Selected writings.* J. B. Carroll (Ed.). Cambridge, Massachusetts: M.I.T. Press, 1956.

Wier, R. *Language in the crib.* The Hague: Mouton, 1962.

Wright, S. Method of path coefficient. *Annals of Mathematical Statistics,* 1934, 5, 161–215.

Yin, R. K. Looking at upside-down faces. *Journal of Experimental Psychology,* 1969, 81, 141–145.

Zentall, T., & Hogan, D. Abstract concepts learning in the pigeon. *Journal of Experimental Psychology,* 1974, 102, 393–398.

Author Index

A

Andrew, G., 248, *356*
Anglin, B., 129, *359*
Aries, P., 4, *356*
Azrin, N., 23, *356*

B

Baer, D., 112, *358*
Bahwell, R., 255, *359*
Bellugi, U., 154, *358*
Berlin, B., 214, *356*
Berryman, R., 175, *357*
Bever, T., 15, 281, 322, *356, 357*
Bloom, L., 112, 316, *356*
Bloomfield, L., 44, *356*
Bousfield, W.A., 219, *356*
Bowerman, M.F., 316, 317, *356*
Braine, M.D.S., 316, *356*
Bransford, J.D., 129, *356*
Breedlove, D.E., 214, *356*
Brown, R.A., 3, 18, 31, 34, 129, 316, 322, *356*
Bruner, J.S., 268, *356*

C

Carlyle, F., 28, *357*
Carrier, J.K., Jr., 1, 11, 39, *357*
Caudill, W.A., 3, *357*

C (continued)

Chase, W.G., 289, *357*
Chomsky, N., 4, 322, *357*
Clark, E., 92, 93, *357*
Clark, H.H., 289, *357*
Cofer, C.N., 219, *357*
Cumming, W.W., 175, *357*

D

Davenport, R.K., 39, 345, *357*
Deich, R.F., 1, *357*
DeRivera, J., 355, *359*
De Villiers, J., 1, 148, *357*
DeVore, I., 3, *357*
Dobzhansky, T., 19, *357*
Donaldson, M., 152, *357*
Dulany, D.E., Jr., 4, *357*

E

Eimas, P.D., 42, *357*
Estes, W.K., 4, *357*

F

Fant, C.G.M., 46, *358*
Feigl, H., 4, *357*
Ferster, C.B., 262, *357*
Fodor, J., 15, 322, *357*
Fouts, R., 68, *357*
Freud, S., 343, *357*

Subject Index